Lecture Notes in Computer Science 1575

Edited by G. Goos, J. Hartmanis and J. van Leeuwen

Springer

Berlin
Heidelberg
New York
Barcelona
Hong Kong
London
Milan
Paris
Singapore
Tokyo

Stefan Jähnichen (Ed.)

Compiler Construction

8th International Conference, CC'99
Held as Part of the Joint European Conferences
on Theory and Practice of Software, ETAPS'99
Amsterdam, The Netherlands, March 22-28, 1999
Proceedings

 Springer

Series Editors

Gerhard Goos, Karlsruhe University, Germany
Juris Hartmanis, Cornell University, NY, USA
Jan van Leeuwen, Utrecht University, The Netherlands

Volume Editor

Stefan Jähnichen
Technische Universität Berlin, Fachbereich 13 - Informatik
Sekretariat SWT FR 5-6
Franklinstr. 28-29, D-10587 Berlin, Germany
E-mail: jaehn@cs.tu-berlin.de

Cataloging-in-Publication data applied for

Die Deutsche Bibliothek - CIP-Einheitsaufnahme

Compiler construction : 8th international conference ; proceedings /
CC '99, held as part of the Joint European Conferences on Theory
and Practice of Software, ETAPS '99, Amsterdam, The Netherlands,
March 22 - 28, 1999. Stefan Jähnichen (ed.). - Berlin ; Heidelberg ;
New York ; Barcelona ; Hong Kong ; London ; Milan ; Paris ;
Singapore ; Tokyo : Springer, 1999
  (Lecture notes in computer science ; Vol. 1575)
  ISBN 3-540-65717-7

CR Subject Classification (1998): D.3.4, D.3.1, F.4.2, D.2.6, I.2.2

ISSN 0302-9743
ISBN 3-540-65717-7 Springer-Verlag Berlin Heidelberg New York

© Springer-Verlag Berlin Heidelberg 1999
Printed in Germany

Typesetting: Camera-ready by author
SPIN 10703066   06/3142 – 5 4 3 2 1 0   Printed on acid-free paper

Foreword

ETAPS'99 is the second instance of the European Joint Conferences on Theory and Practice of Software. ETAPS is an annual federated conference that was established in 1998 by combining a number of existing and new conferences. This year it comprises five conferences (FOSSACS, FASE, ESOP, CC, TACAS), four satellite workshops (CMCS, AS, WAGA, CoFI), seven invited lectures, two invited tutorials, and six contributed tutorials.

The events that comprise ETAPS address various aspects of the system development process, including specification, design, implementation, analysis and improvement. The languages, methodologies and tools which support these activities are all well within its scope. Different blends of theory and practice are represented, with an inclination towards theory with a practical motivation on one hand and soundly-based practice on the other. Many of the issues involved in software design apply to systems in general, including hardware systems, and the emphasis on software is not intended to be exclusive.

ETAPS is a loose confederation in which each event retains its own identity, with a separate programme committee and independent proceedings. Its format is open-ended, allowing it to grow and evolve as time goes by. Contributed talks and system demonstrations are in synchronized parallel sessions, with invited lectures in plenary sessions. Two of the invited lectures are reserved for "unifying" talks on topics of interest to the whole range of ETAPS attendees. As an experiment, ETAPS'99 also includes two invited tutorials on topics of special interest. The aim of cramming all this activity into a single one-week meeting is to create a strong magnet for academic and industrial researchers working on topics within its scope, giving them the opportunity to learn about research in related areas, and thereby to foster new and existing links between work in areas that have hitherto been addressed in separate meetings.

ETAPS'99 has been organized by Jan Bergstra of CWI and the University of Amsterdam together with Frans Snijders of CWI. Overall planning for ETAPS'99 was the responsibility of the ETAPS Steering Committee, whose current membership is:

André Arnold (Bordeaux), Egidio Astesiano (Genoa), Jan Bergstra (Amsterdam), Ed Brinksma (Enschede), Rance Cleaveland (Stony Brook), Pierpaolo Degano (Pisa), Hartmut Ehrig (Berlin), José Fiadeiro (Lisbon), Jean-Pierre Finance (Nancy), Marie-Claude Gaudel (Paris), Susanne Graf (Grenoble), Stefan Jähnichen (Berlin), Paul Klint (Amsterdam), Kai Koskimies (Tampere), Tom Maibaum (London), Ugo Montanari (Pisa), Hanne Riis Nielson (Aarhus), Fernando Orejas (Barcelona), Don Sannella (Edinburgh), Gert Smolka (Saarbrücken), Doaitse Swierstra (Utrecht), Wolfgang Thomas (Aachen), Jerzy Tiuryn (Warsaw), David Watt (Glasgow)

ETAPS'98 has received generous sponsorship from:

- KPN Research
- Philips Research
- The EU programme "Training and Mobility of Researchers"
- CWI
- The University of Amsterdam
- The European Association for Programming Languages and Systems
- The European Association for Theoretical Computer Science

I would like to express my sincere gratitude to all of these people and organizations, the programme committee members of the ETAPS conferences, the organizers of the satellite events, the speakers themselves, and finally Springer-Verlag for agreeing to publish the ETAPS proceedings.

Edinburgh, January 1999   Donald Sannella
                                            ETAPS Steering Committee Chairman

Preface

The present proceedings of the 1999 Compiler Construction Conference are, quite apart from the highly topical nature of the subjects addressed, remarkable for two reasons. First, I feel they illustrate very well the fact that this is still one of the most interesting research areas in computer science, and that it is possible to push the boundaries of knowledge here even further, thanks in large part to the growing theoretical penetration of the subject-matter. Second, both the quantity and quality of the contributions are a clear indication that the Compiler Compiler Conference has become firmly established not only as a part of ETAPS, but in its own right and with its own "regular" and highly motivated group of participants.

The number of papers submitted has remained roughly the same compared with previous years, as has the number of papers selected for presentation. Although, to begin with, I had – in my capacity as Program Committee Chair – favored a physical meeting of PC members and had practically called for such a meeting in my letter of invitation, I soon decided to first wait and see how the selection process and electronic discussion went – with the result that we were, ultimately, able to dispense with the meeting.

This proved possible thanks not only to the use of an electronic conference system, provided courtesy of Vladimiro Sassone, but also and in particular to Jochen Burghardt's willingness to assist me in the PC work and to take full charge of technical support for the installation and use of the relevant software. And I think all PC members will join me in saying he did a great job and is owed our thanks for ensuring that the submission, selection and publication procedures went so smoothly.

I am also indebted, though, to my colleagues in the Program Committee for their willingness to cooperate so closely in these procedures and to offer their technical expertise in the refereeing and discussion process, thus making a major contribution to the successful production of the present volume. My thanks also go to Don Sanella, who was in charge of the ETAPS organization, for his many practical suggestions on how to improve procedures and for his strict but necessary demands that deadlines be met.

Last but not least, I wish to thank all those who submitted papers for the conference. Even if your paper was not accepted this time, I would like to express my appreciation for the time and effort you invested and hope to be able to welcome you to the conference in Amsterdam all the same.

Finally, a last word of thanks to the team at Springer-Verlag for their excellent work and cooperation in preparing the present volume. I hope you will all enjoy reading it!

Berlin, January 1999   Stefan Jähnichen
                                           CC Program Committee Chairman

Program Committee

Rudolf Eigenmann (USA),
Guang R. Gao (USA),
Francois Irigoin (France),
Stefan Jähnichen (Chair, Germany),
Thomas Johnsson (Sweden),
Derrick Kourie (South Africa),
Olivier Michel (France),
Jerzy Nawrocki (Poland),

Lawrence Rauchwerger (USA),
Yves Robert (France),
Mooly Sagiv (Israel),
Martin Simons (Germany),
Chau-Wen Tseng (USA),
David A. Watt (Scotland),
Reinhard Wilhelm (Germany),
Hans Zima (Austria)

Referees

V. Adve	C. Dubois	M. Langenbach	S. Rubin
G. Agrawal	C. Eisenbeis	E. Laure	H. Saito
M. Aiguier	A. Engelbrecht	D. Lavery	D. Sehr
N. Aizikowitz	T. Fahringer	Y. Lee	H. Seidl
J. Amaral	C. Ferdinand	A. Marquez	G. Silber
R. Amir	A. Fraboulet	L. Marshall	V. Sipkova
J. Bechennec	T. Geiger	E. Mehofer	A. Stoutchinin
B. Blount	J. Giavitto	J. Merlin	B. Su
W. Blume	M. Gupta	A. Mignotte	X. Tang
R. Bodik	M. Hall	P. Moreau	S. Thesing
P. Brezany	P. Havlak	J. O'Donnell	D. Xinmin Tian
J. Burghardt	R. Heckmann	Y. Paek	P. Tu
F. Cappello	J. Hoeflinger	I. Park	T. Vijaykumar
M. Chakarvarty	G. Huard	W. Pfannenstiel	M. Voss
S. Chatterjee	D. Kaestner	A. Pierantonio	J. Wang
W. Complak	R. Kennell	S. Pinter	B. Watson
Q. Cutts	S. Wook Kim	J. Prins	B. Wender
A. Czajka	J. Knoop	C. Probst	A. Wojciechowski
F. Delaplace	U. Kremer	F. Rastello	A. Zaks
J. Delosme	P. W. Kutter	N. Ros	C. Zhang
S. Diehl	A. Lallouet	J. Ross	W. Zhao

Table of Contents

Compiler Generation

Data Structure Free Compilation 1
João Saraiva, Doaitse Swierstra

Debugging Eli-Generated Compilers with Noosa 17
Anthony M. Sloane

Faster Generalized LR Parsing 32
John Aycock, Nigel Horspool

Interprocedural Analysis

Interprocedural Path Profiling 47
David Melski, Thomas Reps

Experimental Comparison of *call string* and *functional* Approaches
to Interprocedural Analysis 63
Florian Martin

Link-Time Improvement of Scheme Programs 76
Saumya Debray, Robert Muth, Scott Watterson

Code Optimization

Expansion-Based Removal of Semantic Partial Redundancies 91
Jens Knoop, Oliver Rüthing, Bernhard Steffen

Register Pressure Sensitive Redundancy Elimination 107
Rajiv Gupta, Rastislav Bodík

Code Optimization by Integer Linear Programming 122
Daniel Kaestner, Marc Langenbach

Evaluation of Algorithms for Local Register Allocation 137
Vincenzo Liberatore, Martin Farach-Colton, Ulrich Kremer

Parallelization Techniques

Efficient State-Diagram Construction Methods for Software Pipelining ... 153
Chihong Zhang, Ramaswamy Govindarajan, Sean Ryan, Guang R. Gao

A Comparison of Compiler Tiling Algorithms 168
Gabriel Rivera, Chau-Wen Tseng

Implementation Issues of Loop-Level Speculative
Run-Time Parallelization 183
Lawrence Rauchwerger, Devang Patel

Compiler Systems

Compilation and Memory Management for ASF+SDF 198
Mark van den Brand, Paul Klint, Pieter Olivier

The Design of the PROMIS Compiler 214
*Hideki Saito, Nicholas Stavrakos, Steven Carroll,
Constantine Polychronopoulos, Alex Nicolau*

Program Transformation

Floating Point to Fixed Point Conversion of C Code 229
Andrea Cilio, Henk Corporaal

Optimizing Object-Oriented Languages Through
Architectural Transformations 244
Tom Tourwé, Wolfgang De Meuter

Cache Specific Optimization

Virtual Cache Line: A New Technique to Improve
Cache Exploitation for Recursive Data Structures 259
Shai Rubin, David Bernstein, Michael Rodeh

Extending Modulo Scheduling with Memory Reference Merging 274
Benoît Dupont de Dinechin

Tool Demonstrations

*TRAP*ping Modelica with Python 288
Thilo Ernst

A Programmable ANSI C Code Transformation Engine 292
Maarten Boekhold, Ireneusz Karkowski, Henk Corporaal, Andrea Cilio

Tool Support for Language Design and Prototyping with Montages 296
Matthias Anlauff, Philipp W. Kutter, Alfonso Pierantonio

Author Index 301

Data Structure Free Compilation

João Saraiva[1,2] and Doaitse Swierstra[1]

{saraiva,swierstra}@cs.uu.nl

[1] Department of Computer Science,
University of Utrecht, The Netherlands

[2] Department of Computer Science,
University of Minho, Braga, Portugal

Abstract. This paper presents a technique to construct compilers expressed in a strict, purely functional setting. The compilers do not rely on any explicit data structures, like trees, stacks or queues, to efficiently perform the compilation task. They are constructed as a set of functions which are directly called by the parser. An abstract syntax tree is neither constructed nor traversed. Such deforestated compilers are automatically derived from an attribute grammar specification. Furthermore this technique can be used to efficiently implement any multiple traversal algorithm.

1 Introduction

Traditionally, compilers are organized in two main phases: the *parsing phase* and the *attribute evaluation phase*, with an abstract syntax tree as the intermediate data structure. The *parser constructs* the *abstract syntax tree* and the *attribute evaluator decorates* that tree, *i.e.*, it computes *attribute* values associated to the nodes of the tree. In most implementations the attribute evaluator walks up and down in the tree, while in the mean time decorating it with attribute values. The abstract syntax tree guides the evaluator and stores attributes that are needed on different traversals of the compiler.

This paper presents a new technique for constructing compilers as a set of strict, side-effect free functions. Furthermore the compilers are completely *deforestated*, *i.e.*, no explicit intermediate data structure (*e.g.*, abstract syntax tree) has to be defined, constructed, nor traversed. The parser directly calls attribute evaluation functions, the so-called *visit-functions*. Moreover all the attributes are handled in a canonical way: they just show up as arguments and results of visit-functions.

Because our attribute evaluators are independent of any particular data structure definition, they are more generic than classical attribute evaluators. They are highly reusable and new semantics can easily be added to the attribute evaluators, even when separate analysis of compiler components is considered. For example, new productions can be incorporated to an existent compiler without changing its attribute evaluator. The visit-functions which implement the new productions are simply added to the compiler.

Although it is possible to apply these techniques in hand-written compilers, it is much easier to generate them from an *Attribute Grammar* [Knu68].

Our techniques were developed in the context of the incremental evaluation of (Higher-order) attribute grammars: efficient incremental behaviour is achieved by memoization of visit-function calls [PSV92].

In Section 2 we briefly introduce attribute grammars, present a simple attribute grammar and describe attribute evaluators based on the visit-sequence paradigm. In Section 3 λ-attribute evaluators are introduced. Section 4 deals with parse-time attribute evaluation. Section 5 discusses other applications of our techniques and section 6 briefly discusses the current implementation. Section 7 contains the conclusions.

2 Attribute Grammars

The compilers considered in this paper are specified through an Attribute Grammar (AG) [Knu68] which belong to the class of Ordered Attribute Grammars [Kas80]. These AGs have proven to be a suitable formalism for describing programming languages and their associated tools, like compilers, language based editors, etc. From an AG a *parser* and an *Attribute Evaluator* (AE) can automatically be derived.

This section introduces an attribute grammar which acts as the running example throughout this paper. Using it, we present the concept of *visit-sequences* [Kas80] which are the basis of our techniques.

2.1 The Block Language Example

This section presents a analyser for an extremely small language, called BLOCK, which deals with the *scope* of variables in a *block structured language*. An example BLOCK program is:

> blk *main* : (**use** y;
>   blk (**dcl** w; **use** y; **use** w);
>   **dcl** x; **dcl** x; **dcl** y; **use** w;
>);

This language does not require that declarations of identifiers occur before their first use. Furthermore an identifier from a global scope is visible in a local scope only if is not hidden by an a declarations with a same identifier in a more local scope. In a block an identifier may be declared at most once. The above program contains two errors: at the outer level the variable x has been declared twice and the use of the variable w has no binding occurrence at all.

Because we allow a *use-before-declare* discipline, a conventional implementation of the required analysis naturally leads to a program that traverses each block twice: once for processing the declarations of identifiers and constructing an environment and once for processing the uses of identifiers using the computed environment to check for the use of non-declared names. The uniqueness of names is checked in the first traversal: for each newly encountered declaration it is checked whether that identifier has already been declared in this block. In that case an error message is computed. Since we need to distinguish between identifiers declared at different levels, we introduce an inherited attribute *lev* indicating the nesting level of a block. The environment is a list of bindings of the form (*name, lev*).

In order to make the problem more interesting, and to demonstrate our techniques, we require that the error messages produced in both traversals are to be merged in order to generate a list of errors which follows the sequential structure of the program.

Figure 1 presents the attribute grammar defining the BLOCK language. We use a *standard* AG notation: Productions are labelled with a name for future references. Within the attribution rules of a production, different occurrences of the same symbol are denoted by distinct subscripts. Inherited (synthesized) attributes are denoted with the down (up) arrow $\downarrow$ ($\uparrow$). As usual in AGs we distinguish two classes of terminals: the *literal symbols* (*e.g.*, ' : ', 'decl', etc) which do not play a role in the attribution rules and the *pseudo terminal symbols* (*e.g.*, name), which are non-terminal symbols for which the productions are implicit (traditionally provided by an external lexical analyser). Pseudo terminal symbols are syntactically referenced in the AG, *i.e.*, they are used directly as values in the attribution rules. The attribution rules are written as HASKELL-like expressions. The semantic functions *mustbein* and *mustnotbein* define usual symbol table lookup operations.

root *Prog*
Prog < $\uparrow$ *errors* >
Prog → ROOTP (*Its*)
      Its.lev   = 0
      Its.dcli   = []
      Its.env   = *Its.dclo*
      Prog.errors = *Its.errors*

Its   < $\downarrow$ *lev*, $\downarrow$ *dcli*, $\downarrow$ *env*, $\uparrow$ *dclo*, $\uparrow$ *errors* >
Its → NILITS ()
      Its.dclo   = *Its.dcli*
      Its.errors = []
  | CONSITS (*It* ' ; ' *Its*)
      It.lev   = *Its₁.lev*
      Its₂.lev   = *Its₁.lev*
      It.dcli   = *Its₁.dcli*
      Its₂.dcli = *It.dclo*
      It.env   = *Its₁.env*
      Its₂.env   = *Its₁.env*
      Its₁.errors = *It.errors*++*Its₂.errors*

It   < $\downarrow$ *lev*, $\downarrow$ *dcli*, $\downarrow$ *env*, $\uparrow$ *dclo*, $\uparrow$ *errors* >
It → USE ('use' name)
      It.dclo   = *It.dcli*
      It.errors = name 'mustbein' *It.env*
  | DECL ('dcl' name)
      It.dclo   = (name, *It.lev*) : *It.dcli*
      It.errors = (name, *It.lev*) 'mustnotbein' *It.dcli*
  | BLOCK ('blk' ' (' *Its* ')')
      Its.lev   = *It.lev* + 1
      Its.dcli = *It.env*
      Its.env = *Its.dclo*
      It.dclo = *It.dcli*
      It.error = *Its.errors*

Fig. 1. The Block Attribute Grammar.

2.2 Structured Visit-Sequences

The attribute evaluators considered in this paper are based on the visit-sequence paradigm [Kas80].

A visit-sequence describes, for a node in the tree, the sequence of states the node will go through when the abstract syntax tree is decorated. The essential property is that this sequence depends solely on the production at the node, and not on the context in which it occurs, hence we denote $vis(p)$ to denote the visit-sequence associated to production p. In a visit-sequence evaluator, the number of visits to a non-terminal is fixed, and independent of the production. We denote the number of visits of non-terminal X by $v(X)$. Each visit i to a node labelled with a production for a non-terminal X has a fixed *interface*. This interface consists of a set of inherited attributes of X that are available to visit i and another set of synthesized attributes that are guaranteed to be computed by visit i. We denote these two sets by $A_{inh}(X, i)$ and $A_{syn}(X, i)$, respectively.

Visit-sequences are the outcome of attribute evaluation scheduling algorithms. They can be directly used to guide the decoration of a classical attribute evaluator [Kas91]. Visit-sequences, however, are the *input* of our generating process. It is then convenient to use a more structured representation of the visit-sequences. Thus, they are divided into *visit-sub-sequences* $vss(p, i)$, containing the instructions to be performed on visit i to the production p.

In order to simplify the presentation of our algorithm, visit-sub-sequences are annotated with *define* and *usage* attribute directives. Every visit-sub-sequence $vss(p, i)$ is annotated with the *interface* of visit i to X: $\text{inh}(\alpha)$ and $\text{syn}(\beta)$, where α (β) is the list of the elements of $A_{inh}(X, i)$ ($A_{syn}(X, i)$). Every instruction $\text{eval}(a)$ is annotated with the directive $\text{uses}(bs)$ which specifies the attribute occurrences used to evaluate a, *i.e.*, the occurrences that a depends on. The instruction $\text{visit}(c, i)$ causes child c of production p to be visited for the ith time. We denote child c of p by p_c and the father (*i.e.* the left-hand side symbol of p) by p_0. The visit uses the attribute occurrences of $A_{inh}(p_c, i)$ as arguments and returns the attribute occurrences of $A_{syn}(p_c, i)$. Thus $\text{visit}(c, i)$ is annotated with $\text{inp}(is)$ and $\text{out}(os)$ where is (os) is the list of the elements of $A_{inh}(p_c, i)$ ($A_{syn}(p_c, i)$).

Figure 2 presents the structured and annotated visit-sub-sequences[1] for the productions ROOTP and BLOCK.

---

[1] The visit-sequences were obtained using the *Chained Scheduling Algorithm* [Pen94]. Chained scheduling is a variant of *Kastens' Ordered Scheduling Algorithm* [Kas80]. It was designed with the aim at minimizing the number of attributes that must be passed between traversals and, in this way, improving the behaviour of functional attribute evaluators. Chained scheduling chooses the attribute evaluation order such that every attribute is computed as early as possible. The visit-sequences of figure 2 are similar to the ones produced by Kastens' algorithm. The only exception is the schedule of the instructions $\text{eval}(Its.lev)$. Kastens' algorithm schedules this instruction to the second visit-sub-sequence of production BLOCK. In that case, the occurrence $It.lev$ must be retained for the second sub-sequence. A detailed analysis of both scheduling algorithms can be found in [Pen94] (chapter 5).

```
                                    plan BLOCK
                                    begin 1 inh(It.lev, It.dcli)
plan ROOTP                            eval    ( Its.lev )
begin 1 inh() ,                               uses(It.lev),
  eval    (Its.lev)                   eval    (It.dclo)
          uses(),                             uses(It.dcli)
  eval    (Its.dcli)                  end 1   syn(It.dclo)
          uses(),                     begin 2 inh(It.env)
  visit   (Its, 1)                    eval    (Its.dcli)
          inp(Its.lev, Its.dcli)              uses(It.env),
          out(Its.dclo),             visit   (Its, 1)
  eval    (Its.env)                           inp(Its.dcli, Its.lev )
          uses(Its.dclo),                     out(Its.dclo),
  visit   (Its, 2)                    eval    (Its.env)
          inp(Its.env)                        uses(Its.dclo),
          out(Its.errors),           visit   (Its, 2)
  eval    (Prog.errors)                       inp(Its.env)
          uses(Its.errors)                    out(Its.errors),
end 1     syn(Prog.errors)            eval    (It.errors)
                                              uses(Its.errors)
                                      end 2   syn(It.errors)
```

Fig. 2. Structured Visit-Sequences: the attribute occurrence $\boxed{Its.lev}$ is defined in the first traversal of BLOCK and is used in the next one.

3 Deriving λ-Attribute Evaluators

This section shows how to derive *purely functional and strict* attribute evaluators, starting from an available set of visit-sequences. The derived attribute evaluators are presented in HASKELL. We use HASKELL because it is a compact, well-defined and executable representation for our λ-attribute evaluators. We start by describing our techniques informally and by analysing a simple example. After that, we present the formal derivation of λ-attribute evaluators and we derive the evaluator for the BLOCK language.

The λ-attribute evaluators consist of a set of *partial parameterized visit-functions*, each performing the computations of one traversal of the evaluator. Those functions return, as one of their results, the visit-functions for the next traversal. Performing the visit corresponds to *totally parameterising* the visit-functions and, once again returning the function for the next traversal. The main idea is that for each visit-sub-sequence we construct a function that, besides mapping inherited to synthesized attributes, also returns the function that represents the next visit. Any state information needed in future visits is passed on by partially parameterising a more general function. The only exception is the final visit-function which returns synthesized attributes.

Consider the following simplified visit-sub-sequences for production $X \rightarrow$ PROD $(Y\ Z)$ (the annotations inp and out of the visit instructions are omitted since they are not relevant for this example):

```
plan PROD
begin 1 inh(X.inh₁)
   visit (Y, 1)
   eval  ···                        begin 2 inh(X.inh₂)
       uses(X.inh₁, ···),              visit (Z, 1)
   visit (Y, 2)                        eval  (X.syn₂)
   eval  (X.syn₁)                          uses(X.inh₁, ···)
       uses(···),                   end 2  syn(X.syn₂)
end 1  syn(X.syn₁)
```

Observe that, the inherited attribute $X.inh_1$ must be explicitly passed from the first visit of X (where it is defined) to the second one (where it is used). The non-terminal Y is visited twice in the first visit to X. These two visit-sub-sequences above are implemented by the following two visit-functions:

$\lambda_{Prod^1}\ \lambda_{Y^1}\ \lambda_{Z^1}\ \boxed{inh_1} = ((\lambda_{Prod^2}\ \boxed{inh_1}\ \lambda_{Z^1}), syn_1)$
where $(\boxed{\lambda_{Y^2}}, \ldots) = \lambda_{Y^1}\ \ldots$
       $(\ldots) = \boxed{\lambda_{Y^2}}\ \ldots$
       $syn_1 = \cdots$

$\lambda_{Prod^2}\ \boxed{inh_1}\ \lambda_{Z^1}\ inh_2 = (syn_2)$
where $(\ldots) = \lambda_{Z^1}\ \ldots$
       $syn_2 = f(\boxed{inh_1}, \ldots)$

$\boxed{inh_1}$ defined in λ_{Prod^1}
      used in λ_{Prod^2}

$\boxed{\lambda_{Y^2}}$ partial parameterized in the first traversal and totally parameterized in the second one.

The visit-functions λ_{Y^1} and λ_{Z^1} define the computations of the first traversal of non-terminal symbols Y and Z. The attribute occurrence $X.x$ is passed from the first to the second traversal as a hidden result of λ_{Prod^1} in the form of an extra argument to λ_{Prod^2}. Note that **no** reference to visits for non-terminal symbol Y is included in λ_{Prod^2} since all the visits to Y occur in the first visit to P. Observe also that the function λ_{Z^1} is directly passed to the second visit to X, where the first visit to Z is performed.

The λ-attribute evaluators can be automatically derived from the visit-sub-sequences, by performing an *attribute lifetime analysis*: for each attribute occurrence it is known in which visit it is *defined* and in which visit(s) it is *used*. Thus, let us introduce two predicates def and use. The predicate $\text{def}(p, a, v)$ denotes whether attribute a of production p is defined in visit v. Likewise, $\text{use}(p, a, v)$ denotes whether attribute a of production p is used in visit v:

$$\text{def}(p, a, v) = \text{eval}(a) \in vss(p, v) \lor \text{inh}(\ldots, a, \ldots) \in vss(p, v)$$
$$\lor \text{out}(\ldots, a, \ldots) \in vss(p, v)$$
$$\text{use}(p, a, v) = \text{uses}(\ldots, a, \ldots) \in vss(p, v) \lor \text{syn}(\ldots, a, \ldots) \in vss(p, v)$$
$$\lor \text{inp}(\ldots, a, \ldots) \in vss(p, v)$$

Pseudo terminal symbols may also be used as normal attribute occurrences within the attribute equations of the AG (like the symbol name of the BLOCK AG). Consequently, we need to perform a lifetime analysis of those symbols too. Thus, we extend the above predicates to work on terminal symbols too. The terminal symbols, denoted by Σ, are not defined in the attribute equations, but at parse-time. So, we assign visit number 0 to the parser. The predicate def is extended as follows:

$$\text{def}(p, a, 0) = a \in \Sigma$$

An attribute or pseudo terminal symbol of a production p is *alive* at visit i, if it is defined in a previous visit and it is used in visit i or later. For each production p and for each of its visits i, with $1 \leq i \leq \text{v}(p_0)$, we define the set $alive(p, i)$ which contains the *live* occurrences on visit i. It is defined as follows:

$$alive(p, i) = \{ a \mid \text{def}(p, a, k) \wedge \text{use}(p, a, j) \wedge k < i \leq j \}$$

Let us concentrate now on the analysis of the visits to the non-terminal symbols of the grammar. Let $alive\_visits(p, c, v)$ denote the list of visits to child c of production p, which have to be performed in visit-sub-sequence v to p or in later ones. This list is defined as follows:

$$alive\_visits(p, c, v) = [\text{ visit}(c, i) \mid \text{visit}(c, i) \in vss(p, j) , v \leq j \leq \text{v}(p_0)]$$

Consider the visit-sub-sequences of production PROD. For the first sub-sequence we have the following visits: $alive\_visits(\text{PROD}, 1, 1) = [\text{visit}(p_1, 1), \text{visit}(p_1, 2)]$ and $alive\_visits(\text{PROD}, 2, 1) = [\text{visit}(p_2, 1)]$. That is, in the first visit to PROD or later ones the non-terminal symbol Y is visited twice and the symbol Z is visited once. Note that according to the visit-sub-sequences the single visit to Z is performed in the second visit of PROD. Consider now the visit-function λ_{Prod^1}. Observe that its arguments contain the reference to the first traversal of Y only (argument λ_{Y^1}). The function for the second traversal is obtained as a result of λ_{Y^1}. Observe also that the reference to the visit to Z is passed on to the second traversal of PROD, where it is called. That is, the arguments of the visit-function contain a reference to the earliest visit (function) which has to be performed for all *alive* non-terminal symbols.

In order to derive our visit-functions we need references (the visits-functions) to the earliest visit-function: all following references are returned by evaluating the previous ones. Thus, we define the function $inspect(p, v)$ which takes the head of the list returned by nt_vis (*i.e.*, the following visit), for all non-terminal symbols of production p. This is a partial function, since the list returned by nt_vis may be empty. This occurs when no further visits to a non-terminal symbol are performed. This function is defined as follows:

$$inspect(p, v) = \{ hd\ alive\_visits(p, c, v) : alive\_visits(p, c, v) \neq [] \wedge p_c \in N \}$$

where hd is the usual operation that returns the head of a list and N denotes the set of non-terminal symbols.

We describe now the derivation of the λ-attribute evaluator. For each production p and for each traversal i of non-terminal symbol p_0 a visit-function λ_{p^i} is derived. The arguments of this visit-function are:

1. The attribute occurrences which are alive at visit i, $alive(p, i)$,
2. The deforestated visit-functions derived for the right-hand side symbols of p which are inspected in traversal i or later, $inspect(p, i)$, and
3. The inherited attributes of traversal i, $i.e.$, $A_{inh}(p_0, i)$.

The result is a tuple of which the first element is the partial parameterized function for the next traversal and the other elements are the synthesized attributes, $i.e.$, $A_{syn}(p_0, i)$. Thus, the visit-functions have the following signature:

$$\lambda_{p^i} :: <type\_pp\_args(p, i)> \; \mathcal{T}(inh\_1) \to \cdots \to \mathcal{T}(inh\_k) \to$$
$$(\mathcal{T}(\lambda_{p^{i+1}}), \mathcal{T}(syn\_1), \ldots, \mathcal{T}(syn\_l))$$

with $\{inh\_1, \ldots, inh\_k\} = A_{inh}(p_0, i)$, $\{syn\_1, \ldots, syn\_l\} = A_{syn}(p_0, i)$. $\mathcal{T}(a)$ should be interpreted as the derived type for element a. The fragment $<type\_pp\_args(p, i)>$ denotes the type of the elements in $alive(p, i)$ and in $inspect(p, i)$. This fragment is defined as follows:

$$<type\_pp\_args(p, i)> = \mathcal{T}(a_1) \to \cdots \to \mathcal{T}(a_m) \to \mathcal{T}(\lambda_{vt_1}) \to \mathcal{T}(\lambda_{vt_n}) \to$$

for all a_i such that $a_i \in alive(p, i)$ and for all vt_i such that $vt_i \in inspect(p, i)$.

The visit-function which performs the last traversal of a non-terminal does not return any partial parameterized visit-function. Its signature is:

$$\lambda_{p^n} :: <type\_pp\_args(p, i)> \; \mathcal{T}(inh\_1) \to \cdots \to \mathcal{T}(inh\_k) \to$$
$$(\mathcal{T}(syn\_1), \ldots, \mathcal{T}(syn\_l))$$

Let us now derive the code of the visit-function λ_{p^i}. It looks as follows:

```
λ_{p^i}  <par_par(p, i)>  <inherited(i)> =
         ((λ_{p^{i+1}}  <par_par(p, i + 1)>), <synthesized(i)>)
    where <body(i)>
```

and the visit-functions which performs the last traversal is:

```
λ_{p^n}  <par_par(p, n)>  <inherited(i)> = (<synthesized(i)>)
    where <body(n)>
```

where the code fragments defining the inherited and synthesized attributes look as follows:

$$<inherited(i)> \quad = inh\_1 \; inh\_2 \ldots inh\_k$$
$$<synthesized(i)> = syn\_1, syn\_2, \ldots, inh\_l$$

The code fragment $<par\_par(p, j)>$ denotes the *partial parameterisation* of the next visit-function.

$$<par\_par(p,j)> = a_1 \ldots a_m \; \lambda_{vt_1} \ldots \lambda_{vt_n}$$

The body $<body(i)>$ of each visit-function λ_{p^i} is generated according to the instructions of the visit-sub-sequence $vss(p,i)$. Every attribute equation of the form

$$\texttt{eval } (p_q.a)$$
$$\texttt{uses}(attroccs)$$

defining an attribute occurrence $p_q.a = f\,(attroccs)$ of production p, generates an equation

$$(a_q) = f\,(attroccs)$$

Attribute $p_r.a$ occurring in $attroccs$ is replaced by a_r. Local attribute occurrences of productions are copied literally to the body of the respective visit-functions.

Every instruction $\texttt{visit}(c,i)$ defining the visit i to non-terminal occurrence p_c introduces a call. Two cases have to be distinguished:

If $i < v(p_c)$ then the call returns the partial parameterized function for the next traversal. The following equation is generated:

$$(\lambda_{p_c^{i+1}}, syn\_1_c, \ldots, syn\_j_c) = \lambda_{p_c^i} \; inh\_1_c \ldots inh\_l_c$$

If $i = v(p_c)$ then only the synthesized attributes are computed by the function call.

$$(syn\_1_c, \ldots, syn\_j_c) = \lambda_{p_c^i} \; inh\_1_c \ldots inh\_l_c$$

with $\{inh\_1, \ldots, inh\_j\} = A_{inh}(p_c, i)$ and $\{syn\_1, \ldots, syn\_l\} = A_{syn}(p_c, i)$.

Let us return to the BLOCK AG and derive the visit-function for the most intricate production: the production BLOCK. First we compute the set $alive$ and the visit-trees for each visit to that production.

$$
\begin{aligned}
alive(\text{BLOCK}, 1) &= \{\,\} \\
alive(\text{BLOCK}, 2) &= \{\, lev_2 \,\} \\
inspect(\text{BLOCK}, 1) &= \{\, Its^1 \,\} \\
inspect(\text{BLOCK}, 2) &= \{\, Its^1 \,\}
\end{aligned}
$$

As expected, the attribute occurrence $It.lev$ must be passed from the first to the second traversal. The two visit-functions derived for this production are:

$\lambda_{Block^1} \; <par\_par(\text{BLOCK}, 1)> \; lev_1 \; dcli_1 = ((\lambda_{Block^2} \; <par\_par(\text{BLOCK}, 2)>, dclo_1)$
$\texttt{where } <body(1)>$

λ_{Block^2} $<par\_par(\text{BLOCK}, 2)>$ $env_1 = (errors_1)$
where $<body(2)>$

where the fragments $<par\_par>$ are:

$$<par\_par(\text{BLOCK}, 1)> = \lambda_{Its^1}$$
$$<par\_par(\text{BLOCK}, 2)> = lev_2\ \lambda_{Its^1}$$

The body of the visit-functions is trivially derived from the corresponding visit-sub-sequences (see figure 2): we present only the body of the visit-function for the second traversal to the production BLOCK.

$$<body(2)> = \quad \begin{aligned} dcli_2 &= env_1 \\ (\lambda_{Its^2}, dclo_2) &= \lambda_{Its^1}\ dcli_2\ lev_2 \\ errors_2 &= \lambda_{Its^2}\ dclo_2 \\ errors_1 &= errors_2 \end{aligned}$$

The complete λ-attribute evaluator derived from the BLOCK attribute grammar is presented in figure 3 (some copy rules were trivially removed from the AE code).

$\lambda_{RootP^1}\ \lambda_{Its^1} = errors_2$
where $lev_2 = 1$
  $dcli_2 = [\,]$
  $(\lambda_{Its^2}, dclo_2) = \lambda_{Its^1}\ dcli_2\ lev_2$
  $errors_2 = \lambda_{Its^2}\ dclo_2$

$\lambda_{ConsIts^1}\ \lambda_{It^1}\ \lambda_{Its^1_2}\ dcli\ lev =$
  $((\lambda_{ConsIts^2}\ \lambda_{It^2}\ \lambda_{Its^2_2}), dclo_3)$
where $(\lambda_{It^2}, dclo_2) = \lambda_{It^1}\ dcli\ lev$
  $(\lambda_{Its^2_2}, dclo_3) = \lambda_{Its^1_2}\ dclo_2\ lev$

$\lambda_{NilIts^1}\ dcli\ lev = ((\lambda_{NilIts^2}), dcli)$
$\lambda_{ConsIts^2}\ \lambda_{It^2}\ \lambda_{Its^2_2}\ env = errors$
where $errors_2 = \lambda_{It^2}\ env$
  $errors_3 = \lambda_{Its^2_2}\ env$
  $errors = errors_2 \mathbin{+\!+} errors_3$

$\lambda_{NilIts^2}\ env = [\,]$

$\lambda_{Block^1}\ \lambda_{Its^1}\ dcli\ lev =$
  $((\lambda_{Block^2}\ lev_2\ \lambda_{Its^1}), dcli)$
where $lev_2 = lev + 1$

λ_{Decl^1} **name** $dcli\ lev = ((\lambda_{Decl^2}\ errors), dclo)$
where $dclo = (name, lev) : dcli$
  $\cdot\ errors = (name, lev)\ `mustnotbein`\ dcli$

λ_{Use^1} **name** $dcli\ lev = ((\lambda_{Use^2}\ name), dcli)$

$\lambda_{Block^2}\ lev_2\ \lambda_{Its^1}\ env = errors_2$
where $(\lambda_{Its^2}, dclo_2) = \lambda_{Its^1}\ env\ lev_2$
  $errors_2 = \lambda_{Its^2}\ dclo_2$

$\lambda_{Decl^2}\ errors\ env = errors$

λ_{Use^2} **name** $env = errors$
where $errors = name\ `mustbein`\ env$

Fig. 3. The complete λ-attribute evaluator for the BLOCK Language.

As a result of our techniques all visit-functions have become combinators, *i.e.*, they do not refer to global variables. The type of the λ-attribute evaluator is the type of the visit-function of the root symbol:

$$\lambda_{RootP^1} :: ([a] \rightarrow Int \rightarrow ([a] \rightarrow b, [a])) \rightarrow b$$

This evaluator returns the attribute errors (type b) and it has one function as argument: the visit-function which performs the first visit to the non-terminal symbol *Its*. This function has the initial environment (type $[a]$) and the level (type Int) as arguments and it returns a pair: the function for the second visit to *Its* (with type $[a] \rightarrow b$) and the total environment.

As a result of generating HASKELL code we inherit many useful properties of this language. The λ-attribute evaluator of figure 3, for example, is completely polymorphic. In this evaluator nothing is defined about the type of the identifiers of the language. The identifiers are provided by an external lexical analyser. They can be a sequence of characters, a single character or even a numeral. The AE can be reused in all those cases, provided that the semantic functions *mustbein* and *mustnotbein* are defined on that type too.

This approach has the following properties:

- The λ-attribute evaluators have the tendency to be more polymorphic.
- The evaluators are *data type independent* and, thus, new semantics can be easily added: for example, new productions can be incorporated to a compiler without having to change the evaluator. This property will be explained in section 4.
- Attribute instances needed in different traversals of the evaluator are passed between traversals as results/arguments of partial parameterized visit-functions. No additional data structure is required to handle them, like trees [Kas91,PSV92,SKS97] or stacks and queues [AS91].
- The resulting evaluators are higher-order attribute evaluators. The arguments of the evaluators visit-functions are other AE visit-functions.
- The visit-functions find *all the values* they need in their arguments.
- No pattern matching is needed to detect the production applied at the node the evaluator is visiting.
- The visit-functions are strict in all their arguments, as a result of the order computed by the AG ordered scheduling algorithm.
- Efficient memory usage: data not needed is no longer referenced. References to grammar symbols and attribute instances can efficiently be discarded as soon as they have played their semantic role.
- The code of the attribute evaluator is shorter because no data structures are defined.

4 Parse-Time Attribute Evaluation

Traditional attribute grammar systems construct an abstract syntax tree during the parsing of the source text. This tree is used later to guide the attribute evaluator. For some classes of attribute grammars the construction of the abstract syntax tree may be avoided and the attribute evaluation may be performed in conjunction with the parsing (L-attributed grammars). In this case, it is the parser which guides the attribute evaluation. Such a model has several advantages, namely speed and space requirements. Methods exist which make one-pass attribute evaluation during parsing possible [ASU86].

Parse-time attribute evaluation is achieved as a by-product of our AG implementation: the parser directly calls the visit-functions which perform the first traversal of the λ-attribute evaluator.

Consider again the production BLOCK. The classic fragment of the parser derived from the AG which defines this production and constructs the corresponding tree node looks as follows[2]:

$$It : \texttt{blk '(' } Its \texttt{ ')'}$$
$$\{ \text{ BLOCK } \$3 \ \}$$

The type of the parser derived from this specification is a function from a string (*i.e.*, the source text) to the type of the term defined by the production.

$$parser\_It :: [Char] \rightarrow It$$

where It is a declared data type.

Using our techniques the parser derived from the AG generates a call to the attribute evaluator visit-functions which perform its first traversal. Our parser looks as follows:

$$It : \texttt{blk '(' } Its \texttt{ ')'}$$
$$\{ \ \lambda_{Block^1} \ \$3 \ \}$$

The deforestated visit-functions are partially parameterized with the arguments available at parse-time. Those arguments are the other visit-functions which are partially parameterized when parsing the grammar symbols of right-hand side of the production. No explicit abstract syntax tree is constructed.

Consider the visit-function λ_{NilIts^1} which returns the visit-function λ_{NilIts^2}. The function λ_{NilIts^2} is a constant function: it does not depends on its arguments. That is, it does not use the inherited attribute *env* and always returns an empty list (*i.e.*, it evaluates the synthesized attribute *errors*). As result, λ_{NilIts^2} can be computed at parse-time.

Generally, every visit-function, derived from a visit-sub-sequence i which does not have inherited attributes (annotation inh) or which does not use its inherited attributes, can be evaluated in visit $i - 1$. It has all the arguments it needs available on the previous visit. Observe that the visit-functions derived for productions applied to non-terminal symbols which only have synthesized attributes can be evaluated at parse-time. This is particularly important when implementing processors that produce code as the the input is being processed, *i.e.*, for implementing online algorithms.

---

[2] We use HAPPY [Mar97] notation, an Yacc equivalent for Haskell.

Suppose that we want to extend the BLOCK language with named blocks. That is, the BLOCK AG is extended with the following production:

$$It \rightarrow \text{NAMEDBLK ('blk' name ':' '(' } Its \text{ ')')}$$

In traditional AG implementations, the attribute evaluator would have to be modified, since the type of the abstract syntax tree changes. Our implementation, however, is independent of the abstract tree data type. The attribute evaluator of figure 3 can be reused, without any modification, to implement the AG extension. The only part of the compiler that has to be modified is the parser: the new production must be included, obviously. Furthermore the visit-functions $\lambda_{NamedBlk^i}$ which implement the different visits to the production have to be added to the compiler as a separate module. The new parser fragment looks as follows:

$$It : \text{blk name ':' '(' } Its \text{ ')'}$$
$$\{ \lambda_{NamedBlk^1} \ \$2 \ \$5 \ \}$$

The signature of the visit-functions $\lambda_{NamedBlk^i}$ must follow the partitions of the non-terminal symbol It (*i.e.*, the symbol on the left-hand side of the production).

This property of our AG implementation is particularly important when designing language processors, in a component based style: AG components and the respective evaluators can be easily reused and updated, even when separate analysis and compilation of such components is considered [Sar].

5   Applications

This section describes how our techniques are used in the context of *Higher-Order Attribute Grammars, Incremental Attribute Evaluation, Composition of Attribute Grammars* and *Lazy Attribute Evaluation*.

Higher-Order Attribute Grammars (HAG) [VSK89]: the techniques described in this paper were developed in the context of the (incremental) evaluation of HAGs. HAGs are an important extension to the classical AG formalism: attribute grammars are augmented with *higher-order attributes*. Higher-order attributes are attributes whose value is a tree with which we associate attributes again. Attributes of these so-called *higher-order trees*, may be higher-order attributes again. Higher-order attribute grammars have two main characteristics: first, when a computation can not easily be expressed in terms of the inductive structure of a tree, a better suited structure can be computed first, and secondly, every computation (*i.e.*, inductive semantic function) can be modeled through attribute evaluation. Typical examples of the use of higher-order attributes are mapping a concrete syntax tree into an abstract one and modelling symbol table lookups.

A higher-order attribute grammar may have several higher-order attributes (*i.e.*, higher-order trees). Thus, an attribute evaluator for HAG may contain a possibly large number of higher-order trees. As a result the efficiency of the attribute evaluator may be affected by the construction and destruction of those trees. The technique described in this paper can be used to implement higher-order attribute grammars [Sar]. The higher-order attributes are represented by their initial visit-functions.

Incremental Attribute Evaluation: one of the key features of our AG implementation is that the attribute evaluators are constructed as a set of strict functions. Consequently, an incremental attribute evaluator can be obtained through standard function caching techniques [PSV92]. The incremental behaviour is achieved by storing in a cache calls to the attribute evaluator functions and by reusing their results when such functions are later applied to the same arguments. This is the most efficient and elegant approach for the incremental evaluation of HAGs [Pen94,CP96]. Previous techniques, however, rely on additional data structures, *e.g.*, a *binding tree*, to handle attribute instances needed in different traversals of the evaluator [Pen94]. A large number of calls to tree constructor functions may have to be cached since the number of binding trees is quadratic in the number of traversals. Such an approach, albeit optimal in the number of reevaluations, can result in a substantial decrease of performance of the incremental evaluator due to the fast growth, and consequent overhead, of the cache [SKS96]. Using λ-attribute evaluators no constructor functions exist (*i.e.*, abstract tree nor binding tree constructor functions) and thus no constructor functions have to be cached! The calls to the visit-functions are the only calls actually cached. The incremental evaluators have less cache overhead [Sar].

Composition of Attribute Grammars: consider a compiler organized as follows: it has two AGs of the form $ag_1 :: T_1 \rightarrow T_2$ and $ag_2 :: T_2 \rightarrow T_3$. That is, it has two AGs which are *glued* by the intermediate tree T_2. Using traditional AG techniques the tree T_2 would have to be constructed. Using our techniques the attribute evaluator of ag_1 directly calls the deforestated visit-functions of the ag_2 attribute evaluator, like in a *normal* multiple traversal AE. As result, no intermediate tree is constructed. This strategy holds even when separate analysis (compilation) of both AGs is considered. In [Sar] this composition of attribute grammar components is presented.

Lazy Attribute Evaluation: attribute grammars can be easily and elegantly implemented in a programming language with lazy semantics [KS87,Joh87,SA98]. The techniques described here are orthogonal to the lazy mapping of attribute grammars. See [Sar] for the formal derivation of deforestated and lazily implementation of attribute grammars.

6 Implementation

The techniques described in this paper have been implemented in the LRC system [KS98], a purely functional attribute grammar system. The LRC processes Higher-Order Attribute Grammars, written in a super-set of SSL, the *synthesizer specification language* [RT89], and produces purely functional attribute evaluators.

We have developed a new back-end to the LRC in order to generate HASKELL based attribute evaluators. A (coloured) LaTeX version of such attribute evaluators is also generated by the LRC system. Actually the HASKELL code presented in this paper (including the AE of figure 3) was automatically produced by LRC from a SSL specification. The deforestation of HAGs and the lazy implementation of attribute grammars, discussed in section 5, have also been implemented.

Several small and medium size λ-attribute evaluators have been translated into C in order to use the caching mechanism of the LRC system and to achieve incremental evaluation. The automatic generation of λ-attribute evaluators in the C language is currently being incorporated to LRC.

7 Conclusions

This paper introduced a new technique for compiler construction. The compilers are constructed as a set of strict and purely functional visit-functions. All explicit data structure definition, construction and traversals have been removed. As a result of our technique the λ-attribute evaluators are totally generic and can easily be reused and updated across different applications. Because constructor funtions are never used, and all case statements have been "compiled way", one might in general expect better performance, since the flow of information is now clearly represented in the structure of the paremeters and results of the visit-functions. Thus, many compiler optimization techniques become enabled. Furthermore parse-time attribute evaluation is achieved as a by-product: the parser directly calls the visit-functions.

A simple language was analysed and the respective compiler was automatically derived from an attribute grammar. A mapping from attribute grammars into strict and purely functional attribute evaluator was defined. This mapping has been implemented in the LRC system.

The technique described in this paper is not restricted to the context of compiler construction only. It can be used to efficiently implement any algorithm which performs multiple traversals over a recursive data structure. It was used, for example, to implement a pretty printing combinator library [SAS98], which is a four traversal algorithm and that would have been extremely complicated to construct by hand.

References

[AS91] Rieks Akker and Erik Sluiman. Storage Allocation for Attribute Evaluators using Stacks and Queues. In H. Alblas and B. Melichar, editors, *International Summer School on Attribute Grammars, Applications and Systems*, volume 545 of *LNCS*, pages 140–150. Springer-Verlag, 1991.

[ASU86] Alfred V. Aho, Ravi Sethi, and Jeffrey D. Ullman. *Compilers: Principles, Techniques and Tools*. Addison Wesley, 1986.

[CP96]   Alan Carle and Lori Pollock. On the optimality of change propagation for incremental evaluation of hierarchical attribute grammars. *ACM Transactions on Programming Languages and Systems*, 18(1):16–29, January 1996.

[Joh87]   Thomas Johnsson. Attribute grammars as a functional programming paradigm. In G. Kahn, editor, *Functional Programming Languages and Computer Architecture*, volume 274 of *LNCS*, pages 154–173. Springer-Verlag, September 1987.

[Kas80]   Uwe Kastens. Ordered attribute grammars. *Acta Informatica*, 13:229–256, 1980.

[Kas91]   Uwe Kastens. Implementation of Visit-Oriented Attribute Evaluators. In H. Alblas and B. Melichar, editors, *International Summer School on Attribute Grammars, Applications and Systems*, volume 545 of *LNCS*, pages 114–139. Springer-Verlag, 1991.

[Knu68]   Donald E. Knuth. Semantics of context-free languages. *Mathematical Systems Theory*, 2(2):127–145, June 1968.

[KS87]   Matthijs Kuiper and Doaitse Swierstra. Using attribute grammars to derive efficient functional programs. In *Computing Science in the Netherlands CSN'87*, November 1987.

[KS98]   Matthijs Kuiper and João Saraiva. Lrc - A Generator for Incremental Language-Oriented Tools. In Kay Koskimies, editor, *7th International Conference on Compiler Construction*, volume 1383 of *LNCS*, pages 298–301. Springer-Verlag, April 1998.

[Mar97]   Simon Marlow. *Happy User Guide*. Glasgow University, December 1997.

[Pen94]   Maarten Pennings. *Generating Incremental Evaluators*. PhD thesis, Department of Computer Science, Utrecht University, The Netherlands, November 1994. ftp://ftp.cs.ruu.nl/pub/RUU/CS/phdtheses/Pennings/.

[PSV92]   Maarten Pennings, Doaitse Swierstra, and Harald Vogt. Using cached functions and constructors for incremental attribute evaluation. In M. Bruynooghe and M. Wirsing, editors, *Programming Language Implementation and Logic Programming*, volume 631 of *LNCS*, pages 130–144. Springer-Verlag, 1992.

[RT89]   T. Reps and T. Teitelbaum. *The Synthesizer Generator*. Springer, 1989.

[SA98]   S. Doaitse Swierstra and Pablo Azero. Attribute Grammars in a Functional Style. In *Systems Implementation 2000*, Berlin, 1998. Chapman & Hall.

[Sar]   João Saraiva. *Purely Functional Implementation of Attribute Grammars*. PhD thesis, Department of Computer Science, Utrecht University, The Netherlands. (In preparation).

[SAS98]   Doaitse Swierstra, Pablo Azero, and João Saraiva. Designing and Implementing Combinator Languages. In *Third International Summer School on Advanced Functional Programming, Braga, Portugal*, 1998.

[SKS96]   João Saraiva, Matthijs Kuiper, and Doaitse Swierstra. Effective Function Cache Management for Incremental Attribute Evaluation. Technical report UU-CS-1996-50, Department of Computer Science, Utrecht University, November 1996.

[SKS97]   João Saraiva, Matthijs Kuiper, and Doaitse Swierstra. Specializing Trees for Efficient Functional Decoration. In Michael Leuschel, editor, *ILPS97 Workshop on Specialization of Declarative Programs and its Applications*, pages 63–72, October 1997. (Also available as Technical Report CW 255, Department of Computer Science, Katholieke Universiteit Leuven , Belgium).

[VSK89]   Harald Vogt, Doaitse Swierstra, and Matthijs Kuiper. Higher order attribute grammars. In *ACM SIGPLAN '89 Conference on Programming Language Design and Implementation*, volume 24, pages 131–145. ACM, July 1989.

Debugging Eli-Generated Compilers With Noosa

Anthony M. Sloane

Department of Computing, Macquarie University
Sydney, NSW 2109 Australia
asloane@mpce.mq.edu.au

Abstract. Source-level tools are not adequate for debugging generated compilers because they operate at the level of the generated implementation. It is inappropriate to expect compiler writers to be familiar with the implementation techniques used by the generation system. A higher-level approach presents debugging in terms of an abstract model of the implementation. For example, finite-state machines might be shown while debugging a scanner. This approach is inappropriate for developers who are not compiler experts and even for experts may present more information than is desirable.

An even higher-level approach is used by the Noosa graphical debugger for the Eli compiler generation system. The compiler writer is required to understand a simple execution model that involves concepts that they already have to understand to write Eli specifications. Noosa allows high-level data examination in terms of the input to the compiler and the abstract trees upon which attribution is performed. An event system allows fine-tuned control of program execution. The result is a debugging system that enables developers to diagnose bugs without having to have any knowledge of the underlying mechanisms used by their compiler.

1 Introduction

A variety of methods have been developed for automatically producing compilers from specifications. Using these techniques, a compiler writer can write a high-level specification of compiler functionality and a generation system will produce an implementation that conforms to that specification. Compiler generation has been successful mainly due to the existence of a range of specification notations covering important sub-problems, and the development of efficient methods for implementing these notations (for example, see [4, 9, 12, 14, 19]).

The major advantage of generation systems is that they enable a compiler writer to concentrate on the important issues while the responsibility for producing a correct implementation rests with the system. A generation system that is functioning correctly is no guarantee of a correct compiler, however, because the specification may have bugs.

Compiler generation systems typically provide very little in the way of debugging facilities. Source-level debuggers such as Dbx [8] or GDB [16] can be applied to generated compiler implementations, but this approach is largely unsatisfactory because it requires compiler writers to have specific knowledge about the implementation methods used by the generator. Requiring such knowledge defeats the main purpose of a generation system.

This paper describes the Noosa debugger for programs generated by the Eli compiler generation system. Eli generates compilers using a collection of specification notations including regular expressions for token description, context-free grammars for concrete and abstract syntax, and attribute grammars for semantic analysis and later phases.

Noosa presents a graphical view of the execution of a generated compiler in terms of the input being processed by it. The compiler writer can examine how their regular expressions and grammar productions were used to structure the input. Access is also provided to major compiler data structures such as the abstract trees upon which attribution takes place, environment structures and the definition table. Attribute values of any tree node can be examined in a flexible browsing system that is easily extended to new data types. The developer also has access to an abstract event stream produced by the running compiler. User-specified event handlers can be written in the Tcl language. This facility enables the specification of complex debugging operations such as semantic breakpoints and correlation of information from disparate sources.

The goal of Noosa is to provide debugging facilities that operate at the specification level, hiding the implementation details as much as possible. The aim is to achieve a level of implementation-hiding similar to source-level debuggers operating on programs compiled to machine language. In those debuggers the developer is able to interact with their program's execution in terms with which they are familiar. For example, data can be accessed via variable names and the control state is presented in terms of a stack of active routines and the statement about to be executed. Knowledge of all of these aspects can be expected of any programmer familiar with the source language.

Noosa does not present details of the implementation of compiler components. According to this philosophy, if the specification of the compiler includes regular expressions to describe token types then it is appropriate to present information in terms of tokens, where they were located in the input, and the regular expressions that matched them. Detail about the functioning of the finite-state machine that implements the scanner is not suitable because it relies on knowledge that the compiler writer may not have. This approach contrasts with other debuggers for generated components that present a large amount of internal detail.

Noosa can also work in combination with source-level tools. Eli allows arbitrary C code to be included in the generated compiler to implement abstract data types or to code a part of the functionality that is hard to specify. To accommodate debugging of this code, Noosa can be used in conjunction with a source-level debugger. Thus specification-level and source-level debugging can be undertaken at the same time.

Section 2 considers the execution model that should form the basis of a debugger for generated compilers and describes the model used by Noosa. Section 3 describes the basic elements of the Noosa design with reference to the execution model. Section 4 illustrates the Noosa style of debugging by describing typical compiler bugs and how Noosa would be used to diagnose them.

2   Execution Model

The functionality of a debugger is grounded in the facilities it provides for controlling execution of the program and the methods by which the program's state can be examined. For example, in most source-level debuggers breakpoints allow execution to be stopped when specific points in the code are reached. When execution is stopped, the values of program variables can be printed. Some debuggers have more advanced features such as conditional and data-dependent breakpoints or graphical displays of data structures, but the basic features are common to all source-level debuggers.

The kind of execution control and data access provided by a debugger depends intimately on an *execution model* that the debugger shares with its user. An execution model is a description of the structure of a program execution in terms of elementary actions and data items. An understanding of the program code and the execution model used by a debugger is necessary for the user to be able to operate debugger facilities and understand the output from debugging operations. For example, to use breakpoints in a debugger for an imperative language a user must understand the basic units of execution (e.g., statements) and the way execution proceeds (e.g., step-wise execution of statements plus routine calls). The state displayed by the debugger might also rely on the execution model (e.g., a stack of currently active routine calls).

Different debuggers for the same language can have different execution models that reflect the outcomes of design decisions about the kind of debugging that is to be permitted. For example, some source-level debuggers provide facilities for debugging at the machine level such as instruction stepping or the ability to examine the contents of registers. Other debuggers might omit such features on the grounds that machine level details are not relevant for a user of a high-level language. In general, the execution model to be used by a debugger depends on the view of execution that the debugger is trying to present.

In the compiler generation domain there are choices of execution model. If a source-level debugger is used to debug a generated compiler, the execution model is one appropriate to the implementation language. Even if the compiler writer is familiar with that language, they will in general not be experts in the generated code. Thus the use of an implementation language execution model is inappropriate.

At a higher level of abstraction lies a class of execution models based on the methods used to implement compiler components. For example, a generated scanner might use a finite-state machine implementation. An execution model for a debugger operating at this level might include concepts such as finite-machine states, input characters, and legal state transitions. Execution could be presented in terms of the actual transitions performed during scanning, perhaps with a visual representation of the machine.

Some compiler tools offer tracing facilities at this level. For example, parsers generated by YACC [7] and derivatives like Bison [3], can produce a trace of the parsing process. The trace consists of events such as getting a token, shifting a symbol, reducing via a rule, and changing parser state.

More user-friendly alternatives at this level exist in the form of debuggers that present the same kind of information as a trace, but in a graphical, browsable form. For example, Visual Parse++ from SandStone Technology Inc. [6] presents the developer with an extremely detailed view of the operation of generated parsers. Information presented includes depictions of the parse stack, lookahead tokens and three-dimensional views of parse trees . The recently released ParseView debugger bundled with the latest version of the ANTLR tool [13] seems to offer similar features.

The design of Noosa follows a higher-level approach. The execution model used by Noosa does not include anything to do with the implementation of generated components. Of course, compiler writers may well need to know something about component implementations in order to use Eli. For example, writing an Eli grammar may require some knowledge of the LALR parsing method since both of Eli's parser generators use that method and the system will reject non-LALR(1) grammars. Similarly, using Eli's attribute grammar notations may require some knowledge of allowable patterns of attribute dependences and the methods used by generated evaluators. The philosophy behind Noosa is that knowledge of this kind is not needed during debugging.

Some anecdotal support for this position was obtained recently when Noosa was used by final year students in an introductory compiler unit at Macquarie University. The students were able to use Noosa to debug Eli specifications containing regular expressions and context-free grammars. In this unit the students are acquainted with the compilation phases and their purposes, but the implementation techniques used by the tools are only covered in outline form. Thus there is some evidence that such knowledge is not necessary for debugging.

Justification for the Noosa position as a goal can also be obtained from a recognition that the widespread availability of compiler generation systems has resulted in many non-compiler experts attempting to develop compilers (or compiler-like programs). For these users it is important that the debugging system not rely on knowledge that they do not have.

It should be noted that the more advanced features in the debuggers mentioned above are presumably at least partly inspired by the more complex specification notations and implementation methods used in those systems compared to Eli. For example, the ANTLR parsers use multiple symbol lookahead and more advanced debugger support may well be necessary for the user to understand what is happening. Whether this situation is an argument for more complex debuggers or less complex specification notations and implementation methods is unclear. In any event, Noosa operates within the environment provided by the Eli notations and methods.

Figure 1 shows the execution model used by Noosa expressed in pseudocode. An Eli-generated program under the control of Noosa will scan the input attempting to locate tokens and trying to group those tokens into syntactic phrases. When a complete phrase is recognised an abstract tree fragment will be built to represent it and its components. Once the complete input has been recognised the tree is then decorated with attribute values. Usually a side-effect of one or more attribute evaluations will be to produce the compiler output. (To simplify the discussion we ignore the fact that attribution can occur during tree construction and that attribution can produce further trees which are in turn attributed. Both of these aspects are also supported by Noosa.)

```
while there is more input do
    get the next token
    if a complete syntactic phrase has been recognised then
        build an abstract tree fragment for the new phrase
while there are more tree attributes to evaluate do
    perform an attribute evaluation
```

Fig. 1. Noosa's execution model.

The concepts in the Noosa execution model are ones with which an Eli user can be expected to be familiar. The form of tokens is specified by the user using regular expressions or literals in the context-free grammar. The context-free grammar also specifies the valid phrases. The user's attribute grammar describes the abstract tree structure and the attribute computations that must be evaluated. These specification notations and their underlying concepts must be understood before a compiler can be specified using Eli.

3 Noosa

Noosa's design is based on the execution model presented in the previous section. The input and the abstract tree play a central role in the user interface appropriate to their prominence in the model. Other data items can be accessed via a flexible browsing system designed to be easy to use and extensible to new data types. An event mechanism is used to allow both the debugger and the user to determine which actions are performed by the compiler being debugged and when they occur.

The rest of this section describes the main elements of the Noosa design. The discussion of features is structured according to the relevant elements of the execution model. Some mundane features such as menu invocations, searching in text windows, saving the context of text windows, file editing, on-line help, etc. are omitted. Example screenshots are taken from a debugging session for an Eli-generated C processor.

3.1 Input

The starting point of a compilation is the input that is to be analysed and translated. Thus the main user interface of Noosa features the input (Figure 2).

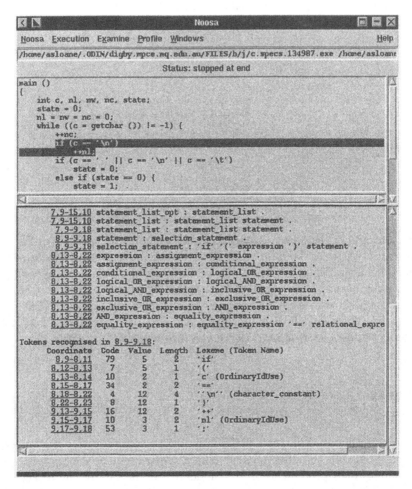

Fig. 2. Main Noosa window. The upper text window shows the compiler input (a C word counting program). The lower text window is a transcript of debugging output showing the phrase structure at the equality operator in the highlighted if statement and the tokens in that if statement.

Noosa correctly accounts for input processing that obtains text from multiple sources. For example, if the language has an "include" facility and the compiler expands includes during parsing, the input text window will show the complete input seen by the compiler. This removes any need for the user to guess what the compiler is working with or pre-process the input specially before debugging. The user can ask Noosa for the original source of any part of the input.

3.2 Phrases and Tokens

Syntactic phrases and lexical tokens play a central role in the user's understanding of their compiler. Noosa enables the user to determine which phrases and tokens are recognised by the compiler. Each one is associated with a region of the input text. Thus Noosa's "Phrase" and "Token" commands are invoked relative to coordinates in the input text.

To see the phrases recognised at a particular location in the input the user selects the location with the mouse and invokes "Phrase." This action produces a list of the concrete grammar productions that have been recognised whose coordinate ranges overlap the indicated location. For example, the transcript (bottom text window) in Figure 2 shows productions involved in recognising the equality operator in the highlighted if statement. The productions are listed in order from the axiom of the grammar (not shown) to the most specific. The coordinate range beside each instance indicates the input recognised by that instance.

The coordinate display for phrases is an instance of a "browsable value" (indicated by the underline). Browsable values can be clicked to obtain behaviour dependent on the kind of value. Clicking on a coordinate or coordinate ranges causes the indicated input to be highlighted in the input text window. Thus it is easy to see the input corresponding to a particular recognised production instance.

The "Token" command operates in a similar fashion to "Phrase." To see the tokens scanned in a particular region the user selects the region in the input text window with the mouse and invokes "Token." The transcript lists the relevant tokens (if any). For example, the transcript in Figure 2 shows the tokens from the highlighted if statement. The coordinate range of each token is shown along with the token code, intrinsic value[1], length and lexeme. Tokens which are non-literals and hence specified using regular expressions are also labelled with the regular expression name from the user's specification.

3.3 Abstract Tree

Once the input has been processed, focus switches to the abstract tree constructed during parsing. Noosa has two basic forms of tree display shown in Figure 3. The displays show the region of the tree around the while condition on line six of the input. Each node consists of the non-terminal it represents and the (user-specified) name of the abstract production applied at the node. Nodes are numbered for identification.

---

[1] The intrinsic value distinguishes different instances of general token classes. For example, the intrinsic value of an integer token might be the numeric value of the integer. For identifiers it might be the index of the identifier string in a global string table.

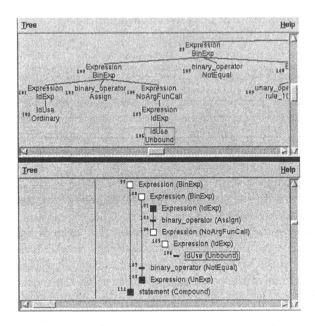

Fig. 3. Abstract tree displays: "complete" tree above and "expandable" tree below. Both windows are focussed on the node representing the `getchar` token in the word counting program.

The upper version of the tree shows every node in a "traditional" tree style. The lower version lays out nodes in an indented style which takes up less space and allows subtrees to be selectively hidden. Siblings are connected by vertical lines. Internal nodes are indicated by squares: white if the node's children are visible, black otherwise. Leaves are indicated by small black rectangles. In both displays the node corresponding to the `getchar` identifier occurrence is highlighted (indicated by the outline around the node).

Clicking on a node in a tree display causes the coordinate range of the node and the abstract production applied at the node to be displayed in the transcript. The coordinate range is also highlighted in the input window. Thus it is easy to relate tree nodes to the input text. Browsing in the opposite direction is also supported. Clicking on a location in the input window and invoking the "Node" command in a tree window causes that tree display to focus on the node farthest from the root whose coordinate range contains the selected location. This mechanism is commonly used to quickly focus attention on relevant parts of the tree.

3.4 Attributes

Each node in the abstract tree has a set of attributes associated with it. The user's attribute grammar specifies how the values of these attributes are to be calculated. Eli takes care of traversing the tree and calculating the attributes in an order consistent with the dependences between them.

Using a tree display the user can express an interest in the value of one or more attribute values. The right mouse button on a node brings up a menu of attributes and their types. Each attribute has a setting with options "Show", "Show, stop" and "Ignore" (default). Selecting "Show" or "Show, stop" causes Noosa to display the value of the attribute in the transcript when it is next calculated. If "Show, stop" is selected, the execution of the compiler will also stop when the attribute is evaluated. The state of the compiler can be examined and a "Continue" command used to resume execution.

Figure 4 shows the transcript window after the user has selected "Show" for all of the attributes of the identifier node representing the occurrence of nl in the statement ++nl;. The Key attribute is a definition table key which the compiler is using to represent the variable entity. The FunctionId attribute is a Boolean value which is one if and only if this identifier represents a function.

```
Node:118.Key = DefTableKey:134933788
Node:118.FunctionId = int:0

DefTableKey:134933788
  Type = DefTableKey:134923820
  IsExtern = int:0
  Index = int:3
  SynCode = int:10
  Symbol = int:4

DefTableKey:134923820
  OilType = tOilType:unknown
  PointedToBy = DefTableKey:134934472
  FunctionReturning = DefTableKey:134933980
  isComplete = int:1
```

Fig. 4. Attribute value display and browsing. Attribute values are displayed with their node number, name and type. Structured values such as definition table keys can be browsed. Here the first key represents a variable. It has been browsed to reveal the properties of the variable, including the key representing its type. The properties of the type have also been displayed.

In the attribute display some values will be browsable. The node number can be clicked to cause the tree display to focus on that node. This feature is used to switch attention quickly between nodes of interest. Also, the Key attribute value is browsable. Since it is a definition table key clicking on it causes the values of its properties to be displayed (middle part of Figure 4). In this case it has four integer properties and a key property that represents the type of the variable. In turn, clicking on that key brings up the properties of the type (bottom part of the figure). Browsing in this way makes it easy to examine the relationships between definition table keys which form the major representational mechanism for information such as the compiler's type system.

Incidentally, the "unknown" value for the OilType property in Figure 4 indicates that Noosa doesn't currently know how to display values of this type. The Eli library module exporting this type can be easily augmented with routines for Noosa to use to obtain a textual representation. It is also straight-forward to make values of new types browsable. This strategy keeps the knowledge of data types with the modules that define them and allows the user to extend the debugging system to support their own types.

3.5 Messages

Often bugs involve the compiler detecting errors when it should not. For example, erroneous regular expressions or context-free grammar productions will usually result in lexical or syntax errors during testing. In Eli each error message is associated with a particular input coordinate. To aid in tracking down this kind of error Noosa displays compiler messages and their coordinates in the transcript. Clicking on the coordinate takes the user directly to the site of the error from which tokens or phrases can be examined as described above. Similarly, a semantic error message can be easily traced back to the relevant tree nodes using the "Node" command.

3.6 Events

The capabilities discussed so far have been concerned with data viewing, with one exception. The "Show, stop" command enables execution to be stopped when a particular attribute is evaluated. Noosa also provides a more general event mechanism that allows complex control of the execution. Noosa's use of events is similar to the way they are used in algorithm animation and monitoring systems [1, 2, 15, 17, 18]. Abstract event systems have also been used in other debuggers [5, 10].

As the compiler executes, it generates a stream of abstract events. Each event represents an action in the execution model. For example, there is an event type to indicate that a token has been scanned. Other events represent the recognition of a concrete production, the construction of the abstract tree, and the evaluation of an attribute. Each event has parameters that distinguish the event instances. For example, a token event had parameters that describe the type of token, source coordinate, lexeme, and so on. Care is taken to ensure that event types and their parameters refer only to user-level concepts.

Noosa uses the event stream to implement the facilities described previously. The stream is also available to the user for more specific control. Event handlers can be specified via the window shown in Figure 5. The left list shows the event types and the right list the parameters of the currently selected event type. In the middle are the names of user-specified handlers.

User-specified event handlers are written in the Tcl language [11]. Tcl is a full-featured, imperative scripting language. Thus an event handler can perform arbitrary actions including querying event parameters, storing data for use by other handlers, and displaying information in the Noosa transcript window.

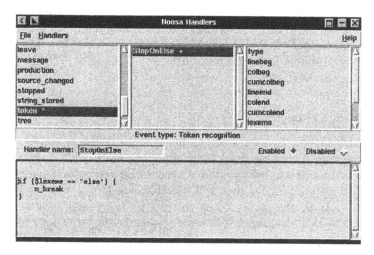

Fig. 5. Event handler window. The user is writing a handler for token events so that the compiler will stop each time an **else** token is scanned. Calling the **n_break** procedure achieves this effect.

Space limitations prevent presentation of a complex example, but as a simple illustration, the lower text window of Figure 5 shows a handler for token events which will stop execution each time an **else** keyword is recognised. The handler employs a conventional conditional statement checking the value of the lexeme parameter of the event (available via a Tcl variable). The **n_break** procedure is the published interface to Noosa's execution control mechanism.

4 Debugging Situations

To illustrate the use of Noosa's features, this section briefly considers a variety of typical debugging situations. The situations chosen are intended to be representative of the sorts of bugs that are encountered by Eli users, but are not meant to be exhaustive. In all cases it is assumed that the compiler input is correct; all bugs reside in the user-supplied specifications.

4.1 Lexical Bugs

A lexical error occurs when the lexical analyser is not able to assign a token type to some portion of the input. In the Eli context this means that an error exists in either the concrete grammar literals or the regular expressions describing the non-literal tokens. Eli-generated compilers report lexical errors by pointing to the characters that cannot be scanned.

To diagnose a lexical error with Noosa the user would first browse the error message coordinate to go to the problematic input location. Errors in literals are usually obvious at this point. Otherwise, the "Token" command would be used to examine the token stream around the error location. Usually the erroneous input should belong to one of the tokens surrounding the error and an insufficiently general regular expression is to blame. Less commonly, a non-literal token specification has simply been omitted. Both of these cases are readily diagnosed from the token stream.

4.2 Syntactic Bugs

Syntactic bugs arise in two ways. First, the concrete grammar may not describe the right language. Often focussing in on the problem area will make the reason obvious. Sometimes more information is needed. Eli-generated parsers incorporate error recovery strategies that will possibly insert or delete symbols in an attempt to continue the parse. When this occurs the parser generates a message noting the location from which parsing was continued. Thus the user can easily determine the extent of the problem. In an error situation the "Phrase" command will show the productions that were recognised as part of the error recovery. This information may show that a portion of the input was recognised using a production other than the intended one (leading to the syntax error later). The ability to match production instances to input coordinates is extremely useful in this type of situation.

Alternatively, a syntax error may be reported when the grammar is correct but the scanner is returning the wrong type of token for some portion of the input. For example, a real number may be scanned as three tokens: an integer, a period, and another integer. This may occur because the regular expression for a real number literal erroneously requires an exponent. The "Token" command can be used to diagnose this kind of problem.

4.3 Semantic Bugs

In Eli-generated compilers semantic processing is largely specified using an attribute grammar. Semantic bugs arise if the value of an attribute is incorrectly computed. Thus localising these sorts of errors is a matter of observing the value of attributes. Noosa's attribute value display capabilities are suitable for this purpose.

A semantic bug may be exhibited by an error message or the absence of an error message. For example, a bug in the compiler's handling of type rules may result in an error message for a correctly-typed construct or a missing message for an incorrectly-typed one. In either case the user needs to localise the problem to the portion of the tree that represents the concerned construct. If a message was produced, the coordinate provides access to the appropriate area of the input. If a message is missing, presumably the user knows which part of the input should have produced it. Once the relevant input location is known, the "Node" command can be used to focus attention on the appropriate part of the tree.

Attribute values of tree nodes around the error can be examined to diagnose the problem. This may require multiple executions to focus in on an attribute whose value is incorrect. (Note that attribute storage may be reused, so the value of an attribute computed earlier in the execution might not still exist to be examined at the current execution point.) Usually when this has been done, the user will have narrowed the problem down to a particular computation that is producing the wrong value and the cause of the bug has been located.

Sometimes a semantic bug results from attribute computations being performed in the wrong order. For example, the definition of an applied identifier occurrence might be looked up before relevant defining occurrences have been processed. This kind of error is often due to missing dependencies between attribute computations. It is usually sufficient to display the values of the attributes and to hand verify whether the order is satisfied by the order in which the values are printed. Once this kind of problem has been diagnosed, a fix must be devised in the form of additional dependencies. Noosa does not assist with static dependence analysis because its emphasis is on dynamic information. A similar design decision arises for imperative language debuggers when facilities such as static call graph display are considered.

Complex bugs can be diagnosed with the use of special-purpose event handlers. Since Noosa event handlers are Tcl code they can perform arbitrary computations. In particular, they can store information in global variables for access by other handlers and display information in Noosa's transcript.

For example, Eli's name analysis modules represent scopes as environments holding mappings from identifier names to definition table keys. Suppose that the user wishes to know the tree nodes corresponding to scopes that have at least one identifier defined in them. This can be achieved by three cooperating handlers: 1) one on "an attribute of type Environment has been evaluated" events to record the nodes which have environment attributes, 2) one on "a mapping has been added to an environment" events to increment a per-environment count, and 3) one on the "finalisation" event to print the list of nodes when execution is complete. (For the purposes of this example, it is assumed that only nodes representing scopes have environment attributes.)

Handlers can be saved in files and loaded into other Noosa sessions. Thus high-level debugging functionality can be reused and shared between users.

4.4 Source-level Bugs

An Eli-generated compiler may have user-supplied code to implement functionality not present in the Eli libraries. For example, abstract data type (ADT) implementations can be provided. Values of user-defined data types can be used in attribute computations.

Problems in user-supplied code can be diagnosed using a source-level debugger. While a debugger can be used independently of Noosa, a cooperative strategy is an advantage because it allows source-level behaviour to be examined in concert with high-level behaviour. For example, attributes of tree nodes may have types which are defined by a user-supplied module. It is useful to be able to examine the values of the attributes in their tree context while debugging the module.

Noosa allows source-level debugging to interoperate with specification-level debugging. In this case the source-level debugger runs as a child process of Noosa and the compiler is a child of that process. The event stream implementation "bypasses" the intermediate process so that Noosa is largely unaffected by the presence of the other debugger. The only complication from the user perspective is a need to be aware of which debugger has control at a given moment. For example, while the compiler is stopped at a source-level breakpoint Noosa has no access to the process, and vice versa. In practice this potential confusion is easily handled.

5 Conclusion

Noosa provides debugging functionality that operates at the level of the user's Eli specifications. Thus the execution of a generated compiler can be understood without knowledge of its internals. The focus is on the main compiler data items: the input and the abstract tree. A text-based browsing facility makes display of other data convenient and extensible. An abstract event stream enables the user to formulate sophisticated queries about the execution. While Noosa is targetted to Eli and its notations, the same general approach should be applicable to other compiler generation systems and specification methods.

Future work will concentrate on extending Noosa to incorporate specification views. This development will aid in the use of Noosa for execution-based specification understanding. Also, it will enable additional debugging capabilities to be triggered from the specifications rather than via the tree. For example, the user might express interest in the value of an attribute in a particular rule context by clicking on an attribute occurrence in that context. Other work is investigating debugging facilities based on the use of program slicing techniques at both the specification-level and on compiler intermediate forms.

Acknowledgements

Much of the functionality and style of Noosa has been influenced by past and current members of the Eli project. In particular, Bill Waite, Bob Gray, Uwe Kastens, Basim Kadhim and Matthias Jung have all contributed valuable suggestions, insights, comments and, in most cases, code to enable Eli and Noosa to interoperate. Thanks to them all. Noosa was implemented by the author with assistance from Tony Vanderlinden and Marianne Brown. The referees also made useful suggestions that improved the presentation of this paper.

References

1. Marc H. Brown. *Algorithm Animation*. The MIT Press, Boston, MA, 1988.
2. Marc H. Brown. Zeus: a system for algorithm animation and multi-view editing. Research Report No.75, Digital Equipment Corporation Systems Research Center, February 1992.

3. Charles Donnelly and Richard Stallman. *Bison—the YACC-compatible parser generator*. Free Software Foundation, 1.25 edition, November 1995.

4. Robert W. Gray, Vincent P. Heuring, Steven P. Levi, Anthony M. Sloane, and William M. Waite. Eli: A complete, flexible compiler construction system. *Commun. ACM*, 35(2):121–131, February 1992.

5. David R. Hanson. Event associations in SNOBOL4 for program debugging. *Softw. Pract. Exper.*, 8:115–129, 1978.

6. SandStone Technology Inc. Visual parse++. http://www.sand-stone.com.

7. S. C. Johnson. YACC – Yet another compiler-compiler. Computer Science Tech. Rep. 32, Bell Telephone Laboratories, Murray Hill, N.J., 1975.

8. Mark A. Linton. The evolution of Dbx. In *USENIX Summer Conference*, pages 211–220, June 1990.

9. Hanspeter Mössenbock. A generator for production quality compilers. In D. Hammer, editor, *Proceedings of Third International Workshop on Compiler Compilers*, number 477 in Lecture Notes in Computer Science, pages 42–55. Springer-Verlag, October 1990.

10. Ronald A. Olsson, Richard H. Crawford, W. Wilson Ho, and Christopher E. Wee. Sequential debugging at a high level of abstraction. *IEEE Software*, 8(3):27–36, May 1991.

11. John Ousterhout. *Tcl and the Tk toolkit*. Addison-Wesley, 1994.

12. T. J. Parr, H. G. Dietz, and W. E. Cohen. PCCTS reference manual. *SIGPLAN Not.*, 27(2):88–165, February 1992.

13. T. J. Parr and R. W. Quong. ANTLR: A predicated-LL(k) parser generator. *Softw. Pract. Exper.*, 25(7):789–810, July 1995.

14. Friedrich Wilhelm Schröer. *The GENTLE Compiler Construction System*. R. Oldenburg, 1997.

15. Rok Sosic. Design and implementation of Dynascope. *Computing Systems*, 8(2):107–134, Spring 1995.

16. Richard M. Stallman and Roland H. Pesch. *Debugging with GDB 4.17—The GNU source-level debugger*. Free Software Foundation, 1998.

17. John T. Stasko. A practical animation language for software development. In *International Conference on Computer Languages*, pages 1–10, 1990.

18. John T. Stasko. Tango: a framework and system for algorithm animation. *Computer*, 23(9):27–39, September 1990.

19. P. D. Terry. *Compilers and compiler generators: an introduction with C++*. International Thomson Computer Press, 1997.

Faster Generalized LR Parsing

John Aycock and Nigel Horspool

Department of Computer Science,
University of Victoria,
Victoria, B. C., Canada V8W 3P6
{aycock,nigelh}@csc.uvic.ca

Abstract. Tomita devised a method of generalized LR (GLR) parsing to parse ambiguous grammars efficiently. A GLR parser uses linear-time LR parsing techniques as long as possible, falling back on more expensive general techniques when necessary.

Much research has addressed speeding up LR parsers. However, we argue that this previous work is not transferable to GLR parsers. Instead, we speed up LR parsers by building larger pushdown automata, trading space for time. A variant of the GLR algorithm then incorporates our faster LR parsers.

Our timings show that our new method for GLR parsing can parse highly ambiguous grammars significantly faster than a standard GLR parser.

1 Introduction

Generalized LR (GLR) parsing was developed by Tomita to parse natural languages efficiently [21]. Tomita observed that grammars for natural languages were mostly LR, with occasional ambiguities; the same can be said of C++ declaration syntax. Grammars for Graham-Glanville code generation are highly ambiguous.

Not surprisingly, parsers which deal strictly with unambiguous grammars can operate much faster than parsers for ambiguous grammars. This is crucial when one considers that the speed of input recognition is often highly visible to users. As a result, most artificial languages have unambiguous grammars by design, and much research has targeted speeding up parsers for unambiguous grammars. However, applications such as natural language understanding are rarely able to choose a convenient grammar, so there is still a need for fast parsers for ambiguous grammars.

Our work begins to address this problem. In this paper, we present an alternative method for constructing pushdown automata for use in LR parsing. We then show how these pushdown automata can be used to drive a GLR parser, giving a substantial speed increase.

2 LR and GLR Parsing

Space limitations prevent us from providing definitions for all notations and conventions used in this paper. Unless stated otherwise, we are using conventions similar to those used in compiler texts, such as [1].

Recall that a LR parser operates by "shifting" its input onto a stack, and "reducing" the stack when a handle is recognized on top of the stack. A handle is the right-hand side of a grammar rule, but *only* when reduction to the rule's left-hand side would correspond to a rightmost derivation step of the input [1].

Formally, if $A \to \alpha$ is a grammar rule and $S \overset{*}{\underset{rm}{\Rightarrow}} \beta A w \underset{rm}{\Rightarrow} \beta \alpha w$, then α is a handle at β. Under these circumstances, any prefix of $\beta\alpha$ is called a viable prefix. We use the term "viable string" to refer to $\beta\alpha$ in its entirety. (α and β symbolize strings of terminal and nonterminal symbols.)

Most current LR parsers are table-driven. They employ an automaton to find handles; this automaton's transitions and the parser actions are encoded into tables. A short generic algorithm is then sufficient to drive the LR parser.

GLR parsing builds on LR parsing. As we mentioned, Tomita observed that a number of ambiguous grammars were mostly LR. With that in mind, Tomita's algorithm behaves as a normal LR parser until it reaches a LR parser state where there is a conflict — the LR parser has a set of conflicting actions it could perform, and is unable to choose between them. A Tomita parser is not able to choose the correct action either, and instead simulates nondeterminism by doing a breadth-first search over all the possibilities [6].

Conceptually, one can think of the Tomita parser reaching a conflict, and starting up a new parser running in parallel for every possible action; each new parser "process" would have a copy of the original stack. A parser process that finds what seems to be erroneous input may assume that the action it took from the conflict point was the wrong one, and can terminate.

This cycle of a parser process starting others yields a wholly impractical algorithm. The time spent making copies of parser stacks could be enormous, not to mention the potentially exponential growth of the number of processes [23]. To address this, Tomita made two important optimizations:

1. A new process need not have a copy of its parent's stack. N processes can *share* a common prefix of a stack. From an implementation perspective, elements of the stack can all contain pointers to point to the previous element of the stack. Then, multiple stack elements can point to a common prefix.
2. There are a finite number of automaton states the parser can be in. Several processes may be in the same state, albeit they may have different stack contents. A set of processes that are in the same state can merge their stacks together, leaving one resulting process. This places an upper bound on the number of parsing processes that can exist.

    In a LR parser, its current state is the topmost state on the stack. So to merge N stacks, one would remove the top node from each — they must all have the same state number s — and create one node with state s that points to the remainder of the N stacks.

34

The result of these optimizations is called a graph-structured stack. (A slight misnomer, since the stacks actually form a directed acyclic graph.) The graph-structured stack in Fig. 1, for instance, corresponds to four processes and five conceptual stacks (the stack tops are the leaf nodes on the left-hand side).

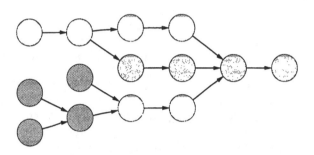

Fig. 1. A graph-structured stack

3 Faster LR Parsing

Much attention has been devoted to speeding up LR parsers, and the majority of this research pertains to implementation techniques. The argument is that interpreted, table-driven programs are inherently slower than hardcoded, directly-executable programs; given that, the best way to speed up a table-driven LR parser is to convert it into a directly-executable form that needs no tables.

[16, 8, 17, 3] all start with a LR parser's handle-finding automaton and translate it directly into source code — this source code can then be compiled[1] to create an executable LR parser. Basically, each state of the automaton is directly translated into source form using boilerplate code. This process tends to produce inefficient code, so these papers expend effort optimizing the source code output.

Several other papers [18, 19, 13, 14, 7] have taken a slightly different approach, introducing a technique called recursive ascent parsing. Here, a LR parser is implemented with a set of mutually recursive functions, one for each state[2] in a table-driven LR parser's handle-finding automaton.

Unfortunately, all of the above work is of limited use when applied to a GLR parser. LR parsers produce a *single* derivation for an input string. In terms of implementation, a LR parser only needs to keep track of a single set of information: the current parser state — what the parser is doing right now, and what it's done in the past. In a table-driven LR parser, this information is kept on an explicit stack; in a directly-executable LR parser, the information exists through a combination of the CPU's execution stack and program counter.

---

[1] Or assembled, as is the case in [16].
[2] Two functions per state are reputed to be required in [14].

In contrast, a GLR parser produces *all* derivations for an input string. This means that a GLR parser may need to keep track of multiple parser states concurrently. To construct a directly-executable GLR parser, one would need to maintain multiple CPU stacks and program counters. Certainly this is possible, but the overhead in doing so and switching between them frequently would be prohibitive, at least on a uniprocessor architecture.

Once direct execution of GLR parsers is ruled out, the obvious approach is to speed up table-driven LR (and thereby GLR) parsers. Looking at the LR parsing algorithm and its operation, one source of improvement would be to reduce the reliance on the stack. Fewer stack operations would mean less overhead, resulting in a faster parser.

The ideal situation, of course, is to have no stack at all! This would mean using finite automata to parse context-free languages, which is theoretically impossible [15]. Instead, we approximate the ideal situation. Our LR parsing method is an analogue to the GLR algorithm: it uses efficient finite automata as long as possible, falling back on the stack when necessary.

3.1 Limit Points

Our first step is to modify the grammar. When using a LR parser, the usual heuristic is to prefer left recursion in the grammar when possible; left recursion yields a shallow stack, because a handle is accumulated atop the stack and is reduced away immediately.

Non-left recursion may be ill-advised in regular LR parsers, but it is anathema to our method. For reasons discussed in the next section, we set "limit points" in the grammar where non-left recursion appears. A limit point is set by replacing a nonterminal A in the right-hand side of a grammar rule — a nonterminal causing recursion — with the terminal symbol $\perp_A$.

Figure 2 shows a simplified grammar for arithmetic expressions and the limit point that is set in it. The rules of the resulting grammar are numbered for later reference.

The process of finding limit points is admittedly not always straightforward. In general, there can be many places that limit points can be placed to break a cycle of recursion in a grammar. We will eventually be resorting to use of the stack when we reach a limit point during parsing, so it is important to try and find a solution which minimizes the number of limit points, both statically and dynamically.

For large grammars, it becomes difficult to select appropriate limit points by hand. The problem of finding limit points automatically can be modelled using the feedback arc set (FAS) problem [20]. Unfortunately, the FAS decision problem is NP-complete [9], and the corresponding optimization problem — finding the minimal FAS — is NP-hard [5]. There are, however, heuristic algorithms for the problem. We have used the algorithm from [4] due to its relative simplicity.

The number of limit points obtained for various programming language grammars is shown in Table 1. It is important to remember that these results were computed using a heuristic algorithm, and that the actual number of limit points

$$S' \rightarrow E\ \$$$
$$E \rightarrow E + F$$
$$E \rightarrow F$$
$$F \rightarrow (\ E\ )$$
$$F \rightarrow n$$

$\Rightarrow$

$$0\quad S' \rightarrow E\ \$$$
$$1\quad E \rightarrow E + F$$
$$2\quad E \rightarrow F$$
$$3\quad F \rightarrow (\ \bot_E\ )$$
$$4\quad F \rightarrow n$$

Fig. 2. Expression grammar and limit points

required may be lower. For example, starting with the computed limit points, hand experimentation revealed that no more than twelve limit points are needed for the Modula-2 grammar.

Table 1. Limit points derived heuristically

Ada	42
ANSI C	38
Java	23
Modula-2	23

3.2 Finite Automata

What we want to construct is a finite automaton which recognizes a viable string and remembers it. In other words, when a final automaton state is reached, the exact viable string is known. Simply recognizing a viable string with a finite automaton is unremarkable — standard LR parsers do this. The key point is being able to *remember* the viable string that was seen.

This means that the entire set of viable strings for a grammar must be enumerated, and a unique path must exist in our finite automata for each one. Unfortunately, while viable prefixes can be described by regular languages [11], most nontrivial grammars have an infinite number of viable prefixes, making enumeration of viable strings challenging.

This is where the limit points in the grammar come in. By choosing appropriate limit points, the set of viable strings for a grammar can be made finite and enumerable. Since viable strings can be generated by finding all paths through a LR parser's handle-finding automaton, this is the same as saying that the LR parser's automaton must have no cycles.

Once we have a finite set of viable strings, we build a finite automaton in three steps:

1. Construct a trie [12] from the viable strings, omitting any ϵ transitions. The trie structure ensures that each viable string has a unique path.

2. Add "reduction transitions," which indicate reduction by a particular grammar rule. Take all viable strings $\beta\alpha$, where α is a handle of the rule $A \to \alpha$. Let s be the start state; q_0 is the state at the end of the path $\beta\alpha$ starting with s; q_1 is the end state of the path βA, also starting with s. Assuming the rule $A \to \alpha$ is numbered k, add a transition from q_0 to q_1 labelled *reduce k*. As a special case, the final automaton state is the state at the end of the path $S\$$.

3. Delete transitions labelled with a nonterminal symbol, since these can never be read from an input string.

For example, the expression grammar in Fig. 2 has the set of viable strings $\{E\$, E+F, E+n, E+(\perp_E), F, n, (\perp_E)\}$. Its finite automaton is shown in Fig. 3. (We use a shaded circle to indicate the start state.)

3.3 Pushdown Automata

At this point, we have a finite automaton which only recognizes a subset of the original language. To remedy this, we add a stack and create a pushdown automaton.

How can a stack be incorporated? Intuitively, the $\perp$ transitions in the finite automaton are the natural places to push information onto a stack. When a $\perp$ transition appears, essentially the finite automaton is stating that it no longer has a sufficient number of states to remember any more. By pushing information at those points, a pushdown automaton is able to remember that which the finite automaton cannot.

To construct a pushdown automaton for a grammar G, we first build a finite automaton for G, FA_G, as described in the last section. Then, while there are $\perp$ transitions in FA_G, we perform the following steps:

1. Choose a transition $\perp_A$.
2. Create a new grammar $G_\perp$ from G. Initially, all rules in G are placed in $G_\perp$. Then set the start symbol for $G_\perp$ to be A, and remove all rules from $G_\perp$ that are unreachable from this new start symbol. Augment $G_\perp$ with the rule $A' \to A$ *pop*.
3. Construct a finite automaton for $G_\perp$ using the method in the last section; call it $\text{FA}_\perp$. $\text{FA}_\perp$ will act as a "subroutine" for FA_G in the sense that when FA_G reaches the $\perp_A$ transition, it will push a "return state" onto a stack, then go to $\text{FA}_\perp$'s start state. When $\text{FA}_\perp$ reaches a *pop* transition, it goes to a state which is popped off the stack.
4. Say that the transition on $\perp_A$ in FA_G was made from state q_0 to state q_1. Delete that transition from FA_G, replace it with a transition from q_0 to the start state of $\text{FA}_\perp$, and label the new transition *push q_1*.
5. Merge $\text{FA}_\perp$ into FA_G. Since these construction steps continue while there are $\perp$ symbols in FA_G, this means that all $\perp$ symbols in $\text{FA}_\perp$ eventually get replaced.

38

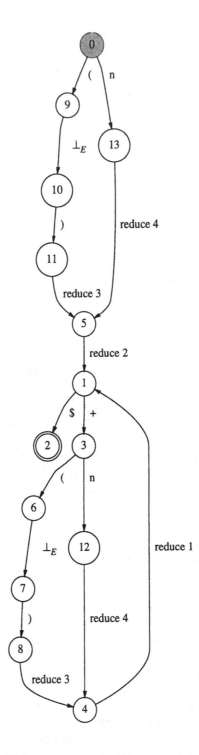

Fig. 3. Finite automaton for the expression grammar

The result of the above steps is a pushdown automaton for G; the pushdown automaton for our running example is shown in Fig. 4. As all the $FA_\perp$ "subroutines" are built independently of any left context seen by their "caller," they can be re-used in other contexts. So the maximum number of $FA_\perp$ that will be created for G is bounded by the number of limit points.

Figure 5 shows how the input string $((n + n))$ is recognized by the pushdown automaton in Fig. 4. This example demonstrates that our pushdown automaton requires much fewer stack operations than a conventional LR parser.

4 Faster GLR Parsing

4.1 Algorithm

To use a pushdown automata from the last section as the engine for a GLR parser, we have devised a modified algorithm which is based on the work of Tomita [21–23].

Our algorithm uses two major types of structures: one for processes, the other for stack nodes.

1. Processes. Each process structure has a automaton state number and a pointer to a stack top associated with it.

   Process structures are linked into one of two lists. The current process list contains the processes that still require processing for the current input symbol; the pending process list contains processes that will need processing when the next input symbol is read. Every time a new input symbol is read, the pending process list becomes the current process list.

2. Stack nodes. There are two types of stack nodes:

   (a) Data nodes. This type of node contains the actual data of a process' stack. Each data node holds a single automaton state number, and a pointer to a previous stack node (i.e. pointing away from the stack top). If we used *only* this type of stack node, then we would have a tree-structured stack.

   (b) Fan-in nodes. These nodes are used to make the graph-structured stack; each one contains a set of pointers to previous stack nodes. When two process' stacks are merged, a fan-in node is created which holds pointers to both stacks. In our implementation, to bound the amount of effort required to find a data node, we add the constraint that a fan-in node may only point to data nodes.

The pseudocode for the modified GLR algorithm is shown in Figs. 6–7.

4.2 Results

We performed some timing experiments to compare a standard GLR parser with our modified GLR parser. As a basis for comparison, we used the public domain

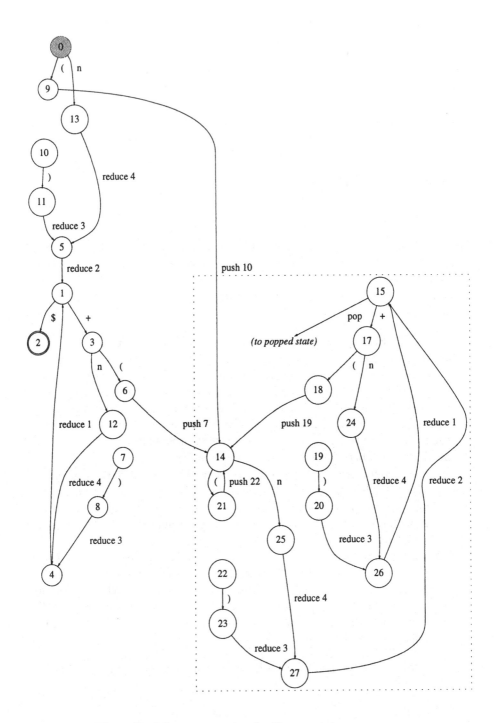

Fig. 4. Pushdown automaton for the expression grammar

Stack	State	Input	Action
	0	((n + n))\$	shift 9
	9	(n + n))\$	push 10, goto 14
10	14	(n + n))\$	shift 21
10	21	n + n))\$	push 22, goto 14
10 22	14	n + n))\$	shift 25
10 22	25	+ n))\$	reduce 4, goto 27
10 22	27	+ n))\$	reduce 2, goto 15
10 22	15	+ n))\$	shift 17
10 22	17	n))\$	shift 24
10 22	24	))\$	reduce 4, goto 26
10 22	26	))\$	reduce 1, goto 15
10 22	15	))\$	pop, goto popped state
10	22	))\$	shift 23
10	23	)\$	reduce 3, goto 27
10	27	)\$	reduce 2, goto 15
10	15	)\$	pop, goto popped state
	10	)\$	shift 11
	11	\$	reduce 3, goto 5
	5	\$	reduce 2, goto 1
	1	\$	shift 2, accept

Fig. 5. Example parser trace

GLR parser available from the `comp.compilers` Usenet newsgroup archive.[3] It uses LR(0) parse tables internally which are computed at startup. Both it and our modified GLR parser are implemented in C.

To ensure a fair comparison, we have modified our parser so that it incurs the same startup penalty and lexical analysis overhead as the public domain parser.

All tests were run on a Sun SPARCsystem 300 with 32M of RAM. Both parsers were compiled using gcc with compiler optimization (-O) enabled. To try and mitigate the effect of unpredictable system conditions on our timings, we ran the tests five times on each input; the results we report are the arithmetic mean of those times.

Our results are shown in Figs. 8–9 along with the grammars used, which we have numbered for convenience of reference. Each grammar is shown both with and without limit points.

Grammar 1 is an ambiguous grammar derived from one in [10]. Reductions in ambiguous grammars by rules with longer and longer right-hand sides are exponentially more expensive for GLR parsers. This is because GLR parsers, upon reduction by a rule $A \rightarrow \alpha$, must find all paths of length $|\alpha|$ from a stack top in the graph-structured stack. On the other hand, our modified GLR algorithm always takes a negligible time for reductions, as reflected in the results.

[3] `http://www.iecc.com` as of this writing.

```
function process(P, input) {
    foreach a ∈ action(input, P.state) {
        switch (a) {
        case SHIFT n:
            mergeInto(pending, n, P.stack)
        case REDUCE A → α, GOTO n:
            mergeInto(current, n, P.stack)
        case PUSH m, GOTO n:
            mergeInto(current, n, push(m, P.stack))
        case POP:
            let S be the set of stack data nodes atop P.stack
            foreach node (state, stack) ∈ S {
                mergeInto(current, state, stack)
            }
        }
    }
}

initialize pending process list to be empty
initialize current process list to be a single process,
    at the automaton's start state with an empty stack

while (current process list is nonempty) {
    input = getNextInputSymbol()
    while (current process list is nonempty) {
        remove a process P from the list
        process(P, input)
    }
    exchange the current and pending process lists
    if (input == EOF) {
        if (process in current process list is in accept state)
            accept input
        else
            reject input
    }
}
reject input
```

Fig. 6. Faster GLR parsing algorithm

```
function mergeInto(list, state, stack) {
    Looks in the specified process list for a process with
    a matching state as that passed in.  If it finds such
    a process, it simply merges its stack with the one
    passed in; if not, it creates a new process structure
    with the given state number and stack pointer, and adds
    it to the specified process list.
}

function push(state, stack) {
    Returns a new stack data node containing the given
    state and stack pointer.
}

function action(inputSymbol, state) {
    Based on its parameters, returns a set containing
    zero or more of:
        SHIFT n
        REDUCE A → α, GOTO n
        PUSH m, GOTO n
        POP
}
```

Fig. 7. Faster GLR parsing algorithm (continued)

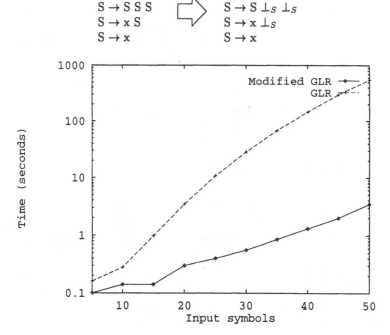

Fig. 8. Timings for Grammar 1

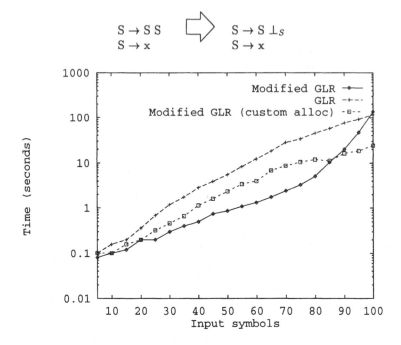

Fig. 9. Timings for Grammar 2

Grammar 2 is another ambiguous grammar from [10]. It is one of the worst cases for our modified GLR algorithm, requiring it to perform numerous stack operations on multiple stacks. This test is also interesting because it underscores the importance of memory management in GLR parsers. Profiling of our parser has shown that over 40% of total run time can be spent doing memory allocation and deallocation when parsing ambiguous grammars. Figure 9 shows our parser having an adversarial relationship with the standard C memory allocator, and the result of adding a custom-built memory allocator.

5 Future Work and Conclusion

There are a number of avenues for further work. Our GLR algorithm should be extended to take lookahead into account, and semantic actions should be supported. In terms of the grammar, the notion of limit points can be generalized so that recursion in the grammar is "unrolled" much as an optimizing compiler might unroll a loop; we have done some preliminary work on this possibility [2]. We would also like to conduct more experiments against other GLR parser implementations, to determine if the results we have obtained are typical.

In this paper, we have presented an alternative way to construct pushdown automata for use in LR parsers. These automata, when used in our modified GLR parsing algorithm, have substantially lowered parsing time when compared to a regular GLR parser. Our timings show an improvement by up to a factor of ten for highly-ambiguous grammars.

By trading space for time — a larger LR parser in exchange for faster execution times — we are able to build GLR parsers which are faster and better suited to more widespread application outside the natural language domain.

References

1. A. V. Aho, R. Sethi, and J. D. Ullman. *Compilers: Principles, Techniques, and Tools.* Addison-Wesley, 1986.
2. J. Aycock. *Faster Tomita Parsing.* MSc thesis, University of Victoria, 1998.
3. A. Bhamidipaty and T. A. Proebsting. Very Fast YACC-Compatible Parsers (For Very Little Effort). Technical Report TR 95–09, Department of Computer Science, University of Arizona, 1995.
4. P. Eades, X. Lin, and W. F. Smyth. A fast and effective heuristic for the feedback arc set problem. *Information Processing Letters*, 47:319–323, 1993.
5. M. R. Garey and D. S. Johnson. *Computers and Intractability: A Guide to the Theory of NP-Completeness.* W. H. Freeman, 1979.
6. D. Grune and C. J. H. Jacobs. *Parsing Techniques: A Practical Guide.* Ellis Horwood, 1990.
7. R. N. Horspool. Recursive Ascent-Descent Parsing. *Journal of Computer Languages*, 18(1):1–16, 1993.
8. R. N. Horspool and M. Whitney. Even Faster LR Parsing. *Software, Practice and Experience*, 20(6):515–535, 1990.
9. R. M. Karp. Reducibility Among Combinatorial Problems. In R. E. Miller and J. W. Thatcher, editors, *Complexity of Computer Calculations*, pages 85–103. Plenum Press, 1972.
10. J. R. Kipps. GLR Parsing in Time $O(n^3)$. In Tomita [24], pages 43–59.
11. D. E. Knuth. On the Translation of Languages from Left to Right. *Information and Control*, 8:607–639, 1965.
12. D. E. Knuth. *The Art of Computer Programming, Volume 3: Sorting and Searching.* Addison-Wesley, 1973.
13. F. E. J. Kruseman Aretz. On a Recursive Ascent Parser. *Information Processing Letters*, 29:201–206, 1988.
14. R. Leermakers. Recursive ascent parsing: from Earley to Marcus. *Theoretical Computer Science*, 104:299–312, 1992.
15. H. R. Lewis and C. H. Papadimitriou. *Elements of the Theory of Computation.* Prentice-Hall, 1981.
16. T. J. Pennello. Very Fast LR Parsing. In *Proceedings SIGPLAN '86 Symposium on Compiler Construction*, volume 21(7) of *ACM SIGPLAN Notices*, pages 145–151, 1986.
17. P. Pfahler. Optimizing Directly Executable LR Parsers. In *Compiler Compilers, Third International Workshop, CC '90*, pages 179–192. Springer-Verlag, 1990.
18. G. H. Roberts. Recursive Ascent: An LR Analog to Recursive Descent. *ACM SIGPLAN Notices*, 23(8):23–29, 1988.
19. G. H. Roberts. Another Note on Recursive Ascent. *Information Processing Letters*, 32:263–266, 1989.
20. E. Speckenmeyer. On Feedback Problems in Digraphs. In *Graph-Theoretic Concepts in Computer Science*, pages 218–231. Springer-Verlag, 1989.

21. M. Tomita. *An Efficient Context-Free Parsing Algorithm for Natural Languages and Its Applications*. PhD thesis, Carnegie-Mellon University, 1985.
22. M. Tomita. *Efficient Parsing for Natural Language*. Kluwer Academic, 1986.
23. M. Tomita. An Efficient Augmented-Context-Free Parsing Algorithm. *Computational Linguistics*, 13(1–2):31–46, 1987.
24. M. Tomita, editor. *Generalized LR Parsing*. Kluwer Academic, 1991.

Interprocedural Path Profiling

David Melski and Thomas Reps

Computer Sciences Department, University of Wisconsin,
1210 West Dayton Street, Madison, WI, 53706, USA,
{melski, reps}@cs.wisc.edu

Abstract. In path profiling, a program is instrumented with code that counts the number of times particular path fragments of the program are executed. This paper extends the *intra*procedural path-profiling technique of Ball and Larus to collect information about *inter*procedural paths (i.e., paths that may cross procedure boundaries).

1 Introduction

In path profiling, a program is instrumented with code that counts the number of times particular finite-length path fragments of the program's control-flow graph — or *observable paths* — are executed. A path profile for a given run of a program consists of a count of how often each observable path was executed. This paper extends the *intra*procedural path-profiling technique of Ball and Larus [3] to collect information about *inter*procedural paths (i.e., paths that may cross procedure boundaries).

Interprocedural path profiling is complicated by the need to account for a procedure's calling context. There are really two issues:

- *What is meant by a procedure's "calling context"?* Previous work by Ammons et al. [1] investigated a hybrid intra-/interprocedural scheme that collects separate *intra*procedural profiles for a procedure's different calling contexts. In their work, the "calling context" of procedure P consists of the *sequence of call sites* pending on entry to P. In general, the sequence of pending call sites is an abstraction of any of the paths ending at the call on P.

  The path-profiling technique presented in this paper profiles true *inter*procedural paths, which may include call and return edges between procedures, paths through pending procedures, and paths through procedures that were called in the past and completed execution. This means that, in general, our technique maintains finer distinctions than those maintained by the profiling technique of Ammons et al.

- *How does the calling-context problem impact the profiling machinery?* In the method presented in this paper, the "naming" of paths is carried out via an edge-labeling scheme that is in much the same spirit as the path-naming scheme of the Ball-Larus technique, where each edge is labeled with a number, and the "name" of a path is the sum of the numbers on the path's edges. However, to handle the calling-context problem, in our method edges are labeled with *functions* instead of *values*. In effect, the use of edge-functions allows edges to be numbered differently depending on the calling context.

At runtime, as each edge *e* is traversed, the profiling machinery uses the edge function associated with *e* to compute a value that is added to the quantity pathNum. At the appropriate program points, the profile is updated with the value of pathNum.

Because edge functions are always of a particularly simple form (i.e., linear functions), they do not complicate the runtime-instrumentation code greatly:

- The Ball-Larus instrumentation code performs 0 or 1 additions in each basic block; a hash-table lookup and 1 addition for each control-flow-graph backedge; 1 assignment for each procedure call; and a hash-table lookup and 1 addition for each return from a procedure.
- The technique presented in this paper performs 0 or 2 additions in each basic block; a hash-table lookup, 1 multiplication, and 4 additions for each control-flow-graph backedge; 2 multiplications and 2 additions for each procedure call; and 1 multiplication and 1 addition for each return from a procedure.

(The frequency with which our technique and the Ball-Larus technique can avoid performing any additions in a basic block should be about the same.) Thus, while interprocedural path profiling will involve more overhead than intraprocedural path profiling via the Ball-Larus technique, the overheads should not be prohibitive.

The specific technical contributions of this paper include:

- In the Ball-Larus scheme, a cycle-elimination transformation of the (in general, cyclic) control-flow graph is introduced for the purpose of numbering paths. We present the interprocedural analog of this transformation.
- In the case of intraprocedural path profiling, the Ball-Larus scheme produces a dense numbering of the observable paths within a given procedure: That is, in the transformed (i.e., acyclic) version of the control-flow graph for a procedure P, the sum of the edge labels along each path from P's entry vertex to P's exit vertex falls in the range [0..number of paths in P], and each number in the range [0..number of paths in P] corresponds to exactly one such path.

The techniques presented in this paper produce a dense numbering of interprocedural observable paths. The significance of the dense-numbering property is that it ensures that the numbers manipulated by the instrumentation code have the minimal number of bits possible.

Our work encompasses two main algorithms for interprocedural path profiling, which we call *context path profiling* and *piecewise path profiling*, as well as several hybrid algorithms that blend aspects of the two main algorithms. Context path profiling is best suited for software-maintenance applications, whereas piecewise path profiling is better suited for providing information about interprocedural hot paths, and hence is more appropriate for optimization applications [4].

This paper focuses on context path profiling, and, except where noted, the term "interprocedural path profiling" means "context path profiling". We chose to discuss the context-path-profiling algorithm because the method is simpler to present than the algorithm for piecewise path profiling. However, the same basic machinery is at the heart of both algorithms (see [4]).

The remainder of the paper is organized into four sections: Section 2 presents background material and defines terminology needed to describe our results. Section 3 gives an overview of interprocedural context path profiling. Section 4 describes the technical details of this approach. Section 5 discusses future work.

2 Background

2.1 Supergraph

As in many interprocedural program-analysis problems, we work with an interprocedural control-flow graph called a *supergraph*. Specifically, a program's supergraph G^* consists of a unique entry vertex $Entry_{global}$, a unique exit vertex $Exit_{global}$, and a collection of control-flow graphs (one for each procedure), one of which represents the program's main procedure. For each procedure P, the flowgraph for P has a unique entry vertex, $Entry_P$, and a unique exit vertex, $Exit_P$. The other vertices of the flowgraph represent statements and predicates of the program in the usual way,[1] except that each procedure call in the program is represented in G^* by two vertices, a *call* vertex and a *return-site* vertex. In addition to the ordinary intraprocedural edges that connect the vertices of the individual control-flow graphs, for each procedure call (represented, say, by call vertex c and return-site vertex r) to procedure P, G^* contains a *call-edge*, $c \to Entry_P$, and a *return-edge*, $Exit_P \to r$. The supergraph also contains the edges $Entry_{global} \to Entry_{main}$ and $Exit_{main} \to Exit_{global}$. An example of a supergraph is shown in Fig. 1(a).

For purposes of profiling, we assume that all branches are logically independent, *i.e.*, the result of one branch does not affect the ability to take any other branch. However, we do not wish to consider paths in G^* that violate the nature of procedure calls (as the path in Fig. 1(b) does). We now develop a language for describing the set of paths in G^* that we wish to consider valid. To do this, let each call site be assigned a unique index between 1 and $NumCallSites$, where $NumCallSites$ is the total number of call sites in the program. Then, for each call site with index i, let the call-edge from the call site be labeled with the symbol "$($_i$", and let the return-edge to the call site be labeled with the symbol "$)$_i$". Let each edge of the form $Entry_{global} \to Entry_P$ be labeled with the symbol "$($_P$" and each edge of the form $Exit_P \to Exit_{global}$ be labeled with the symbol "$)$_P$". Let all other edges be labeled with the symbol e. Then a path p in G^* is a *same-level valid path* if and only if the string formed by concatenating the labels

---

[1] The vertices of a flowgraph can represent individual statements and predicates; alternatively, they can represent basic blocks.

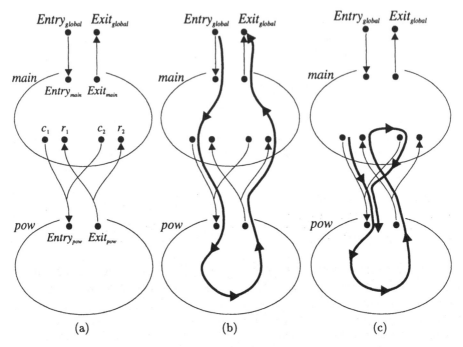

Fig. 1. (a) Schematic of the supergraph of a program in which *main* has two call sites on the procedure *pow*. (b) Example of an invalid path in a supergraph. (c) Example of a cycle that may occur in a valid path.

of p's edges is derived from the non-terminal *SLVP* in the following context-free grammar:

$$SLVP ::= e \ SLVP \quad | \quad SLVP ::= (_i \ SLVP \ )_i \ SLVP \quad \text{for } 1 \leq i \leq NumCallSites$$
$$SLVP ::= \epsilon \quad\quad\quad\quad SLVP ::= (_P \ SLVP \ )_P \ SLVP \quad \text{for each procedure } P$$

Here, ϵ denotes the empty string. A same-level valid path p represents an execution sequence where every call-edge is properly matched with a corresponding return-edge and vice versa.

We also need to describe paths that correspond to incomplete execution sequences in which not all of the procedure calls have been completed. (For example, a path that begins in a procedure P, crosses a call-edge to a procedure Q, and ends in Q.) Such a path p is called an *unbalanced-left path*. The string formed by concatenating the labels on p's edges must be derived from the non-terminal *UnbalLeft* in the following context-free grammar:

$$UnbalLeft ::= UnbalLeft \ (_i \ UnbalLeft \quad \text{for } 1 \leq i \leq NumCallSites$$
$$UnbalLeft ::= UnbalLeft \ (_P \ UnbalLeft \quad \text{for each procedure } P$$
$$UnbalLeft ::= SLVP$$

2.2 Modifying G^* to Eliminate Backedges and Handle Recursion

For purposes of numbering paths, the Ball-Larus technique modifies a procedure's control-flow graph to remove cycles. This section describes the analogous step for interprocedural context profiling. Specifically, this section describes modifications to G^* that remove cycles from each procedure and from the call graph associated with G^*. The resulting graph is called G_{fin}^*. Each unbalanced-left path through G_{fin}^* defines an "observable path" that can be logged in an interprocedural profile. The number of unbalanced-left paths through G_{fin}^* is finite [4], which is the reason for the subscript "fin".

In total, there are three transformations that are performed to create G_{fin}^*. Fig. 3 shows the transformed graph G_{fin}^* that is constructed for the example program in Fig. 2 (the labels on the vertices and edges of this graph are explained in Section 3.1).

Transformation 1: For each procedure P, add a special vertex $GExit_P$. In addition, add an edge $GExit_P \rightarrow Exit_{global}$.

The second transformation removes cycles in each procedure's flow graph. As in the Ball-Larus technique, the procedure's control-flow graph does not need to be reducible; backedges can be determined by a depth-first search of the control-flow graph.

Transformation 2: For each procedure P, perform the following steps:
1. For each backedge target v in P, add a *surrogate* edge $Entry_P \rightarrow v$.
2. For each backedge source w in P, add a *surrogate* edge $w \rightarrow GExit_P$.
3. Remove all of P's backedges.

The third transformation "short-circuits" paths around recursive call sites, effectively removing cycles in the call graph. First, each call site is classified as recursive or nonrecursive. This can be done by identifying backedges in the call graph using depth-first search; the call graph need not be reducible.

Transformation 3: The following modifications are made:
1. For each procedure R called from a recursive call site, add the edges $Entry_{global} \rightarrow Entry_R$ and $Exit_R \rightarrow Exit_{global}$.
2. For each pair of vertices c and r representing a recursive call site that calls procedure R, remove the edges $c \rightarrow Entry_R$ and $Exit_R \rightarrow r$, and add the *summary* edge $c \rightarrow r$. (Note that $c \rightarrow r$ is called a "summary" edge, but not a "surrogate" edge.)

As was mentioned above, the reason we are interested in these transformations is that each observable path—an item we log in an interprocedural path profile—corresponds to an unbalanced-left path through G_{fin}^*. Note that the observable paths should not correspond to just the same-level valid paths through G_{fin}^*: as a result of Transformation 2, an observable path p may end with $\ldots \rightarrow GExit_P \rightarrow Exit_{global}$, leaving unclosed left parentheses. Furthermore, a path in G_{fin}^* that is not unbalanced-left cannot represent any feasible execution path in the original graph G^*.

Indirect Procedure Calls The easiest way to handle indirect procedure calls is to treat them as recursive procedure calls, and not allow interprocedural paths that cross through an indirect procedure call. Another possibility does

```
double pow(double base, long exp) {
    double power = 1.0;
    while( exp > 0 ) {
        power *= base;
        exp--;
    }
    return power;
}
```

```
int main() {
    double t, result = 0.0;
    int i = 1;
    while( i <= 18 ) {
        if( (i%2) == 0 ) {
            t = pow( i, 2 );
            result += t;
        }
        if( (i%3) == 0 ) {
            t = pow( i, 2 );
            result += t;
        }
        i++;
    }
    return 0;
}
```

Fig. 2. Example program used to illustrate the path-profiling technique. (The program computes the quantity $(\sum_{j=1}^{9}(2 \cdot j)^2)) + (\sum_{k=1}^{6}(3 \cdot k)^2).)$

allow interprocedural paths to cross through an indirect procedure call: For purposes of numbering the paths in G_{fin}^*, each indirect procedure call through a procedure variable fp is turned into an if-then-else chain that has a separate (direct) procedure call for each possible value of fp. Well-known techniques (*e.g.*, such as flow insensitive points-to analysis [2, 6]) can be used to obtain a reasonable (but still conservative) estimate of the values that fp may take on.

3 Overview

In this section, we illustrate, by means of the example shown in Fig. 2, some of the difficulties that arise in collecting an interprocedural path profile. Fig. 1(a) shows a schematic of the supergraph G^* for this program. One difficulty that arises in interprocedural path profiling comes from interprocedural cycles. Even after the transformations described in Section 2.2 are performed (which break intraprocedural cycles and cycles due to recursion), G^* will still contain cyclic paths, namely, those paths that enter a procedure from distinct call sites (see Fig. 1(c)). This complicates any interprocedural extension to the Ball-Larus technique, because the Ball-Larus numbering scheme works on acyclic graphs. There are several possible approaches to overcoming this difficulty:

- One possible approach is to create a unique copy of each procedure for each nonrecursive call site and remove all recursive call and return edges. In our example program, we would create the copies *pow1* and *pow2* of the *pow* function, as shown in Fig. 4. *pow1* can be instrumented as if it had been inlined in *main*, and likewise for *pow2*. In many cases, this approach is impractical because of the resulting code explosion.
- A second approach—which is the one developed in this paper—is to parameterize the instrumentation in each procedure to behave differently for different calling contexts. In our example, *pow* is changed to take an extra parameter. When *pow* is called from the first call site in *main*, the value of

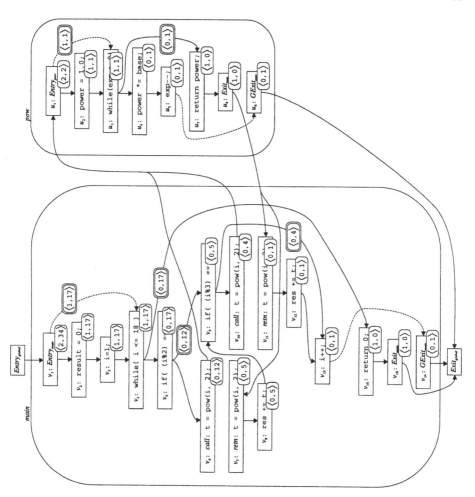

Fig. 3. G_{fin}^* for the code in Fig. 2. Dashed edges represent surrogate edges; the supergraph for the program in Fig. 2 includes the backedges $v_{13} \to v_4$ and $u_5 \to u_3$, which have been removed here by Transformation 2. Here the ordered pair $\langle a, b \rangle$ represents the linear function $\lambda x.a \cdot x + b$. Each vertex v is assigned the linear function ψ_v, which is shown in a rounded box. Each intraprocedural edge e is assigned the linear function ρ_e, which is shown in a doubled, rounded box. Unlabeled intraprocedural edges have the function $\langle 0, 0 \rangle$. Interprocedural edges do not have ρ functions.

the new parameter causes the instrumentation of *pow* to mimic the behavior of the instrumentation of *pow1* in the first approach above; when *pow* is called from the second call site in *main*, the value of the new parameter causes *pow*'s instrumentation to mimic the behavior of the instrumentation of *pow2*. Thus, by means of an appropriate parameterization, we gain the advantages of the first approach without duplicating code.

Section 3.1 gives a high-level description of our path-numbering technique and Section 4 gives a detailed description of the profiling algorithm.

54

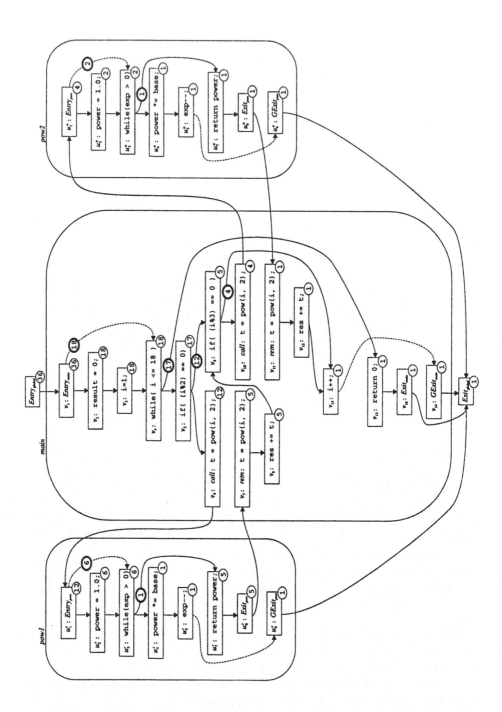

Fig. 4. Modified version of G^*_{fin} from Fig. 3 with two copies of *pow*. Labels on the vertices and edges show the results of applying the Ball-Larus numbering technique to the graph. Each vertex label is shown in a circle, and each edge label are shown in a double circle. Unlabeled edges are given the value 0 by the Ball-Larus numbering scheme.

3.1 Numbering Unbalanced-Left Paths

Extending the Ball-Larus technique to number unbalanced-left paths in G_{fin}^* is complicated by the following facts:

1. While the number of unbalanced-left paths is finite, an unbalanced-left path may contain cycles (such as those in Fig. 1(c)).
2. The number of paths that may be taken from a vertex v is dependent on the path taken to reach v: for a given path p to vertex v, not every path q from v forms an unbalanced-left path when concatenated with p.

These facts mean that it is not possible to assign a single integer value to each vertex and edge of G_{fin}^* as the Ball-Larus technique does. Instead, each occurrence of an edge e in a path p will contribute a value to the path number of p, but the value that an occurrence of e contributes will be dependent on the part of p that precedes that occurrence of e. In particular, e's contribution is determined by the sequence of unmatched left parentheses that precede the occurrence of e in p. (The sequence of unmatched left parentheses represents a calling context of the procedure containing e.)

Consider the example shown in Figs. 2 and 3. Notice that G_{fin}^* in Fig. 3 contains cyclic, unbalanced-left paths. For example, the following path is a cycle from u_1 to u_1 that may appear as a subpath of an unbalanced-left path:

$$u_1 \to u_3 \to u_7 \to u_8 \to v_7 \to v_8 \to v_9 \to v_{10} \to u_1.$$

Fig. 4 shows a modified version of G_{fin}^* with two copies of the procedure *pow*, one for each call site to *pow* in *main*. This modified graph is acyclic and therefore amenable to the Ball-Larus numbering scheme: Each vertex v in Fig. 4 is labeled with *numPaths*$[v]$, the number of paths from v to *Exit*$_{global}$; each edge e is labeled with its Ball-Larus increment [3]. Note that there is a one-to-one and onto mapping between the paths through the graph in Fig. 4 and the unbalanced-left paths through the graph in Fig. 3. This correspondence can be used to number the unbalanced-left paths in Fig. 3: each unbalanced-left path p in Fig. 3 is assigned the path number of the corresponding path q in Fig. 4.

The following two observations capture the essence of our technique:

– Because the labeling passes of the Ball-Larus scheme work in reverse topological order, the values assigned to the vertices and edges of a procedure are dependent upon the values assigned to the exit vertices of the procedure. For instance, in Fig. 4, the values assigned to the vertices and edges of *pow1* are determined by the values assigned to *Exit*$_{pow1}$ and *GExit*$_{pow1}$ (*i.e.*, the values 5 and 1, respectively), while the values assigned to the vertices and edges of *pow2* are determined by the values assigned to *Exit*$_{pow2}$ and *GExit*$_{pow2}$ (*i.e.*, the values 1 and 1, respectively). Note that *numPaths*$[GExit_P] = 1$ for any procedure P (since the only path from *GExit*$_P$ to *Exit*$_{global}$ is the path consisting of the edge *GExit*$_P \to$ *Exit*$_{global}$). Thus, the values on the edges and the vertices of *pow1* differ from some of the values on the corresponding edges and vertices of *pow2* because *numPaths*$[Exit_{pow1}] \neq$ *numPaths*$[Exit_{pow2}]$.

– Given that a program transformation based on duplicating procedures is undesirable, a mechanism is needed that assigns vertices and edges different numbers depending on the calling context. To accomplish this, each vertex u of each procedure P is assigned a linear function ψ_u that, when given a value for $numPaths[Exit_P]$, returns the value of $numPaths[u]$. Similarly, each edge e of each procedure P is assigned a linear function ρ_e that, when given a value for $numPaths[Exit_P]$, returns the Ball-Larus value for e.

Fig. 3 shows G^*_{fin} labeled with the appropriate ψ and ρ functions. Note that we have the desired correspondence between the linear functions in Fig. 3 and the integer values in Fig. 4. For example, in Fig. 3 vertex u_1 has the function $\psi_{u_1} = \lambda x.2 \cdot x + 2$. This function, when supplied with the value $numPaths[Exit_{pow1}] = 5$ from Fig. 4 evaluates to 12, which is equal to $numPaths[u'_1]$ in Fig. 4. However, when $\lambda x.2 \cdot x + 2$ is given the value $numPaths[Exit_{pow2}] = 1$, it evaluates to 4, which is equal to $numPaths[u''_1]$ in Fig. 4.

To collect the number associated with an unbalanced-left path p in G^*_{fin}, as p is traversed, each edge e contributes a value to p's path number. As illustrated below, the value that e contributes is dependent on the path taken to e:

Example 1. Consider the edge $u_1 \rightarrow u_3$ in G^*_{fin}, and an unbalanced-left path s that begins with the following path prefix:

$$Entry_{global} \rightarrow v_1 \rightarrow v_4 \rightarrow v_5 \rightarrow v_6 \rightarrow u_1 \rightarrow u_3 \tag{1}$$

In this case, the edge $u_1 \rightarrow u_3$ contributes a value of 6 to s's path number. To see that this is the correct value, consider the path prefix in Fig. 4 that corresponds to (1):

$$Entry_{global} \rightarrow v_1 \rightarrow v_4 \rightarrow v_5 \rightarrow v_6 \rightarrow u'_1 \rightarrow u'_3$$

In Fig. 4, the value on the edge $u'_1 \rightarrow u'_3$ is 6.

In contrast, in an unbalanced-left path t that begins with the path prefix

$$Entry_{global} \rightarrow v_1 \rightarrow v_4 \rightarrow v_5 \rightarrow v_9 \rightarrow v_{10} \rightarrow u_1 \rightarrow u_3 \tag{2}$$

the edge $u_1 \rightarrow u_3$ will contribute a value of 2 to t's path number. (To see that this is the correct value, consider the path prefix in Fig. 4 that corresponds to (2).)

It can even be the case that an edge e occurs more than once in a path p, with each occurrence contributing a different value to p's path number. For example, there are some unbalanced-left paths in G^*_{fin} in which the edge $u_1 \rightarrow u_3$ appears twice, contributing a value of 6 for the first occurrence and a value of 2 for the second occurrence.

To determine the value that an occurrence of the edge e should contribute to a path number, the profiling instrumentation will use the function ρ_e and the appropriate value for $numPaths[Exit_P]$, where P is the procedure containing e. Thus, as noted above, an occurrence of the edge $u_1 \rightarrow u_3$ may contribute the value $(\lambda x.x + 1)(1) = 2$ or the value $(\lambda x.x + 1)(5) = 6$ to a path number, depending on the path prior to the occurrence of $u_1 \rightarrow u_3$.

```
unsigned int profile[36];      /* 36 possible paths in total */
double pow(double base, long exp,
                unsigned int &pathNum, unsigned int numValidCompsFromExit){
    unsigned int pathNumOnEntry = pathNum; /* Save the calling context */
    double power = 1.0;
    while( exp > 0 ) {
        power *= base;
        exp--;
        profile[pathNum]++;
        /* From surrogate edge u1->u3: */
        pathNum = 1 * numValidCompsFromExit + 1 + pathNumOnEntry;
    }
    pathNum += 0 * numValidCompsFromExit + 1; /* From edge u3->u7 */
    return power;
}
```

Fig. 5. Part of the instrumented version of the program from Fig. 2. Instrumentation code is shown in italics. (See also Fig. 6.)

Figs. 5 and 6 show the program from Fig. 2 with additional instrumentation code — based on the linear functions in Fig. 3 — that collects an interprocedural path profile. The output from the instrumented program is as follows:

0: 0	1: 0	2: 0	3: 0	4: 0	5: 0	6: 0	7: 0	8: 0
9: 0	10: 0	11: 0	12: 0	13: 0	14: 0	15: 0	16: 1	17: 0
18: 9	19: 0	20: 0	21: 0	22: 0	23: 0	24: 9	25: 3	26: 0
27: 3	28: 3	29: 6	30: 3	31: 0	32: 3	33: 3	34: 5	35: 1

Section 4 presents an algorithm that assigns linear functions to the vertices and edges of G^*_{fin} directly, without referring to a modified version of G^*_{fin}, like the one shown in Fig. 4, in which procedures are duplicated.

3.2 What Do You Learn From a Profile of Unbalanced-Left Paths?

Before examining the details of interprocedural path profiling, it is useful to understand the information that is gathered in this approach:

- Each unbalanced-left path p through G^*_{fin} from $Entry_{global}$ to $Exit_{global}$ can be thought of as consisting of a *context-prefix* and an *active-suffix*. The active-suffix q'' of p is a maximal-size, surrogate-free subpath at the tail of p (though the active-suffix may contain summary edges of the form $c \rightarrow r$, where c and r represent a recursive call site). The context-prefix q' of p is the prefix of p that ends at the last surrogate edge before p's active suffix. (The context-prefix q' can be the empty path from $Entry_{global}$ to $Entry_{global}$.)
- The counter associated with the unbalanced-left path p counts the number of times during a program's execution that the active-suffix of p occurs in the context summarized by p's context-prefix.

58

```
int main() {
    unsigned int pathNum = 0;
    unsigned int pathNumOnEntry = 0;
    unsigned int numValidCompsFromExit = 1;
    double t, result = 0.0;
    int i = 1;
    while( i <= 18 ) {
        if( (i%2) == 0 ) {
            t = pow( i, 2, pathNum, 0 * numValidCompsFromExit + 5 );
            /* On entry to pow: pathNum is 0 or 18; fourth arg. always 5 */
            /* On exit from pow: pathNum is 1, 7, 19, or 25 */
            result += t;
        } else
            pathNum += 0 * numValidCompsFromExit + 12;
        if( (i%3) == 0 ) {
            t = pow( i, 2, pathNum, 0 * numValidCompsFromExit + 1 );
            /* On entry to pow: pathNum is 1, 7, 12, 19, 25, or 30; 4th arg. always 1 */
            /* On exit from pow: pathNum is 2, 3, 8, 9, 13, 14, 20, 21, 26, 27, 31, or 32 */
            result += t;
        } else
            pathNum += 0 * numValidCompsFromExit + 4;      /* From edge v9->v13 */
        i++;
        profile[pathNum]++;
        /* From surrogate edge v1->v4: */
        pathNum = 1 * numValidCompsFromExit + 17 + pathNumOnEntry;
    }
    pathNum += 0 * numValidCompsFromExit + 17;             /* From edge v4->v15 */
    profile[pathNum]++;
    for (i = 0; i < 36; i++) {
        cout.width(3); cout << i << ":"; cout.width(2); cout << profile[i] << "  ";
        if ((i+1) % 9 == 0) cout << endl;
    }
    return 0;
}
```

Fig. 6. Part of the instrumented version of the program from Fig. 2. Instrumentation code is shown in italics. (See also Fig. 5.)

Example 2. Consider the path in Fig. 3 with path number 24:

$$24 : Entry_{global} \rightarrow v_1 \rightarrow v_4 \rightarrow v_5 \rightarrow v_6 \rightarrow u_1 \rightarrow u_3 \rightarrow u_4 \rightarrow u_5 \rightarrow u_6 \rightarrow Exit_{global}$$

This path consists of the context-prefix $Entry_{global} \rightarrow v_1 \rightarrow v_4 \rightarrow v_5 \rightarrow v_6 \rightarrow u_1$ and the active-suffix $u_3 \rightarrow u_4 \rightarrow u_5$. The output obtained from running the program shown in Figs. 5 and 6 indicates that the active suffix was executed 9 times in the context summarized by the context-prefix. Note that the context-prefix not only summarizes the call site in *main* from which *pow* was called, but also the path within *main* that led to that call site. In general, a context-prefix (in an interprocedural technique) summarizes not only a sequence of procedure calls (*i.e.*, the calling context), but also the intraprocedural paths taken within each procedure in the sequence.

4 Interprocedural Path Profiling

In this section, we discuss the ψ and ρ functions that serve as replacements for the vertex and edge values of the Ball-Larus technique.

4.1 Assigning ψ and ρ Functions

Solving for ψ Functions For a vertex v in procedure P, the function ψ_v takes the number of valid completions from $Exit_P$ (for an unbalanced-left path p to $Entry_P$ concatenated with any same-level valid path to $Exit_P$) and returns the number of valid completions from v (for the path p concatenated with any same-level valid path to v).

We can find the ψ functions by setting up and solving a collection of equations. For an exit vertex $Exit_P$, ψ_{Exit_P} is the identity function: $\psi_{Exit_P} = id$. For a vertex of the form $GExit_P$, we have the equation $\psi_{GExit_P} = \lambda x.1$. This equation reflects the fact that the number of valid completions from $GExit_P$ is always 1, regardless of the number of valid completions from $Exit_P$. For a call vertex c to a procedure Q associated with the return-site vertex r, where c and r represent a non-recursive call site, we have the equation $\psi_c = \psi_{Entry_Q} \circ \psi_r$. For all other cases, for a vertex m, we have the equation $\psi_m = \sum_{n \in succ(m)} \psi_n$, where $succ(m)$ denotes the successors of m, and the addition $f + g$ of function values f and g is defined to be the function $\lambda x.f(x) + g(x)$.[2]

Because $id(= \lambda x.x)$ and $\lambda x.1$ are both linear functions of one variable, and the space of linear functions of one variable is closed under function composition and function addition, each ψ function is a linear function of one variable. Furthermore, each ψ function $\lambda x.a \cdot x + b$ can be represented as an ordered pair $\langle a, b \rangle$.

To find ψ functions that satisfy the above equations, each procedure P is visited in reverse topological order of the call graph, and each vertex v in P is visited in reverse topological order of P's control-flow graph. (For purposes of ordering the vertices of a procedure P, a return-site vertex r is considered to be a successor of its associated call vertex c.) As each vertex v is visited, the appropriate equation given above is used to determine the function ψ_v.

The order of traversal guarantees that when vertex v is visited, all of the functions that are needed to determine ψ_v will be available. This follows from the fact that the call graph associated with G^*_{fin} is acyclic and the fact that the flow graph of each procedure in G^*_{fin} is acyclic. (The fact that the call graph and flow graphs are acyclic also explains why each vertex needs to be visited only once.)

Solving for ρ functions Each intraprocedural edge e in procedure P is assigned a linear function ρ_e. The function ρ_e, when supplied with the number of valid completions from $Exit_P$ (for an unbalanced-left path p to $Entry_P$ concatenated with any same-level valid path from $Entry_P$ to $Exit_P$), returns the

---

[2] The equations for the ψ functions closely resemble the ϕ functions of Sharir and Pnueli's functional approach to interprocedural data-flow analysis [4, 5].

value that e contributes (to the path number of the path p concatenated with any same-level valid path to e).

Let v be an intraprocedural vertex that is the source of one or more intraprocedural edges. (Note that v cannot be a call vertex for a nonrecursive call site, nor have the form $Exit_P$, nor have the form $GExit_P$.) Let $w_1 \ldots w_k$ be the successors of v. Then we make the following definition:

$$\rho_{v \to w_i} = \begin{cases} \lambda x.0 & \text{if } i = 1 \\ \sum_{j<i} \psi_{w_j} & \text{otherwise} \end{cases} \tag{3}$$

Clearly, each ρ function is a linear function of one variable. Furthermore, (3) can be used to find each ρ function when the ψ functions are known.

4.2 Computing Values for Interprocedural Edges

Unlike intraprocedural edges, an interprocedural edge e always contributes the same value, independent of the path taken to e [4]. For interprocedural edges that are not of the form $Entry_{global} \to Entry_P$, this value is always 0.

For each edge $Entry_{global} \to Entry_P$ and each unbalanced-left path p that starts with this edge, we define the integer value $edgeValue[Entry_{global} \to Entry_P]$ to be the value that $Entry_{global} \to Entry_P$ contributes to p's path number. To find the $edgeValue$ values, it is necessary to use a fixed (but arbitrary) ordering of the edges of the form $Entry_{global} \to Entry_P$. For convenience, we number each edge $Entry_{global} \to Entry_P$ according to this ordering, and use the notation Q_i to refer to the procedure that is the target of the ith edge. We have the following:

$$edgeValue[Entry_{global} \to Entry_{Q_i}] = \begin{cases} 0 & \text{if } i = 0 \\ \sum_{j<i} \psi_{Entry_{Q_j}}(1) & \text{otherwise} \end{cases}$$

4.3 Calculating the Path Number of an Unbalanced-Left Path

In this section, we show how to calculate the path number of an unbalanced-left path p through G_{fin}^* from $Entry_{global}$ to $Exit_{global}$. This is be done during a single traversal of p that sums the values contributed by each edge e for each path prefix p' such that $[p' \parallel e]$ is a prefix of p.

For an interprocedural edge e, the value $edgeValue[e]$ contributed by e is calculated as described in Section 4.2. For an intraprocedural edge e in procedure P, the value contributed by e (for the path p' leading to e) is calculated by applying the function ρ_e to the number of valid completions from $Exit_P$. (The number of valid completions from $Exit_P$ is determined by the path taken to $Entry_P$—in this case a prefix of p'.)

We now come to the crux of the matter: how to determine the contribution of an edge e when the edge is traversed without incurring a cost for inspecting the path p' taken to e. The trick is that, as p is traversed, we maintain a variable, numValidCompsFromExit, that holds the number of valid completions from the exit vertex $Exit_Q$ of the procedure Q that is currently being visited. The number of valid completions from $Exit_Q$ is uniquely determined by p'—specifically, the sequence of unmatched left parentheses in p'. The value numValidCompsFromExit is maintained by the use of a stack, NVCStack, and the ψ functions for return-site vertices. The following steps describe the algorithm to compute the path number for a path p (this number is accumulated in the variable pathNum):

- When the traversal of p is begun, numValidCompsFromExit is set to 1. This indicates that there is only one valid completion from $Exit_R$, where R is the first procedure that p enters: if p reaches the exit of the first procedure it enters, then it must follow the edge $Exit_P \rightarrow Exit_{global}$. The value of pathNum is initialized to the value $edgeValue[e]$ on the first edge e of p (see Section 4.2).
- As the traversal of p crosses a call-edge $c \rightarrow Entry_T$ from a procedure S to a procedure T, the value of numValidCompsFromExit is pushed on the stack, and is updated to $\psi_r(\text{numValidCompsFromExit})$, where r is the return-vertex in S that corresponds to the call-vertex c. This reflects the fact that the number of valid completions from $Exit_T$ is equal to the number of valid completions from r.
- As the traversal of p crosses a return-edge $Exit_T \rightarrow r$ from a procedure T to a procedure S, the value of numValidCompsFromExit is popped from the top of the stack. This reflects the fact that the number of valid completions from the exit of the calling procedure S is unaffected by the same-level valid path through the called procedure T.
- As the traversal of p crosses an intraprocedural edge e, the value of pathNum is incremented by $\rho_e(\text{numValidCompsFromExit})$.
- At the end of the traversal of p, pathNum holds the path number of p.

4.4 Runtime Environment for Collecting a Profile

We are now ready to describe the instrumentation code that is introduced to collect an interprocedural path profile. In essence, the instrumentation code threads the algorithm described in Section 4.3 into the code of the instrumented program. Thus, the variables pathNum and numValidCompsFromExit become program variables. There is no explicit stack variable corresponding to NVCstack; instead, numValidCompsFromExit is passed as a value-parameter to each procedure and the program's execution stack is used in place of NVCstack. The instrumentation also makes use of two local variables in each procedure:

pathNumOnEntry stores the value of pathNum on entry to a procedure. When an intraprocedural backedge is traversed in a procedure P, the instrumentation code increments the count associated with the current observable path and begins recording a new observable path that has the context-prefix indicated by the value of pathNumOnEntry.

pathNumBeforeCall stores the value of pathNum before a recursive procedure call is made. When the recursive procedure call is made, the instrumentation begins recording a new observable path. When the recursive call returns, the instrumentation uses the value in `pathNumBeforeCall` to resume recording the observable path that was executing before the call was made.

Figs. 5 and 6 show an instrumented version of the code in Fig. 2. Reference [4] gives a detailed description of the instrumentation used to collect an interprocedural path profile and describes how the intrumentation can be made more efficient than the code shown in Figs. 5 and 6.

5 Future Work

We are currently in the process of implementing the algorithm described in the paper, and thus do not yet have performance figures to report. The main reasons for believing that the technique described (or a variation on it) will prove to be practical are:

- The Ball-Larus technique for intraprocedural profiling has very low overhead (31% on the SPEC benchmarks [3]). As discussed in the Introduction, although interprocedural path profiling involves more overhead than the Ball-Larus technique, the additional overhead should not be prohibitive.
- In the worst case, the number of paths through a program is exponential in the number of branch statements b, and thus the number of bits required to represent paths is linear in b. However, as in the Ball-Larus approach, it is possible to control the explosion in the number of paths by altering G^*_{fin} to remove paths from it (and adjusting the instrumentation code accordingly). There are a variety of techniques that can be applied without having to fall back on pure intraprocedural profiling [4].

Acknowledgements

This work was supported in part by the NSF under grants CCR-9625667 and CCR-9619219, by an IBM Partnership Award, by a Vilas Associate Award from the Univ. of Wisconsin, and by the "Cisco Systems Wisconsin Distinguished Graduate Fellowship".

References

1. G. Ammons, T. Ball, and J. Larus. Exploiting hardware performance counters with flow and context sensitive profiling. In *PLDI'97*, June 1997.
2. L. O. Andersen. *Program Analysis and Specialization for the C Programming Language*. PhD thesis, DIKU, Univ. of Copenhagen, May 1994. (DIKU report 94/19).
3. T. Ball and J. Larus. Efficient path profiling. In *MICRO 1996*, 1996.
4. D. Melski and T. Reps. Interprocedural path profiling. Tech. Rep. TR-1382, Comp. Sci. Dept., Univ. of Wisconsin, Madison, WI, September 1998. Available at "http://www.cs.wisc.edu/wpis/papers/tr1382.ps".
5. M. Sharir and A. Pnueli. Two approaches to interprocedural data flow analysis. In S.S. Muchnick and N.D. Jones, editors, *Program Flow Analysis: Theory and Applications*, chapter 7, pages 189–234. Prentice-Hall, Englewood Cliffs, NJ, 1981.
6. B. Steensgaard. Points-to analysis in almost-linear time. In *Symp. on Princ. of Prog. Lang.*, pages 32–41, 1996.

Experimental Comparison of *call string* and *functional* Approaches to Interprocedural Analysis

Florian Martin

Universität des Saarlandes, P.O. Box 151150, 66041 Saarbrücken,
martin@cs.uni-sb.de

Abstract. The techniques used to implement (non-trivial) interprocedural data flow analyzers can be generally divided into two subsets: the *call string* approach and the *functional* approach as presented in [Sharir and Pnueli, 1981]. Both differ in time and space complexity as well as in precision due to properties of the abstract domains and transfer functions. We have developed a data flow analyzer generator PAG which is able to produce interprocedural analyzers for both techniques. We specified two variants of constant propagation working in an ANSI-C compiler; a *copy constant* propagation that uses *distributive* transfer function and can be solved precisely, even interprocedurally [Sagiv et al., 1995], and a *full constant* propagator which includes an interpreter for expressions of the language. We present the practical relevant results applying both analyzers to a fair set of real-world programs and compare the space/time consumption of the analyzers versus their precision.

1   Introduction

The need for interprocedural analyses results from a conflict between the goals of software engineering and performance [Metzger and Stroud, 1993]. The usage of procedural and functional abstraction generalizes the code and makes it more extensible and maintainable. Optimizing compilers try to compute information about program points that can be used for code improvements. Intraprocedural analysis assumes the worst case (loss of all information) at procedure boundaries, whereas interprocedural analysis propagates information across procedure/function boundaries or eliminates the calls by inline expansions for non-recursive calls. There exist two different approaches to interprocedural analysis which have been discussed in [Sharir and Pnueli, 1981]: the *call string* and the *functional* approach. The *call string* approach separates call chains (and the related data flow information) to a procedure differing in a suffix of a fixed length. Thus precision may increase with longer call strings. The maximally useful length for non-recursive programs is the height of the call DAG. For recursive programs the number of possible call strings is infinite. If there are no recursive procedures the number of call strings can be exponential in the number of procedures. Thus the call string length has to be limited in any practical implementation to some constant K.

The functional approach, on the other side, computes a function for each procedure describing the "abstract" effect of the procedure. These functions are then used in a standard (intraprocedural-like) algorithm. However, the computation of the abstract functions may not terminate for lattices of infinite cardinality, even if they are of bounded height.

We designed and implemented an interprocedural data flow analyzer generator PAG [Martin, 1998], that produces analyzers using either the call string approach with a length parameter or the functional approach. Using this analyzer generator we generated two analyzers, which have been included in a ANSI-C compiler, and measured the efficiency and precision for practical relevant applications.

By creating PAG we hope to close the gap between the theory of abstract interpretation and practical useful analyzers. PAG is available under a free academic license on request from the author or in form of a simplified WWW interface (www.cs.uni-sb.de/~martin/pag).

The paper is organized as follows: a brief introduction to the framework of dataflow analysis is followed by the discussion of the two interprocedural approaches. Then these are compared based on experimental data for two data flow problems.

2 Techniques

The data flow analysis practiced nowadays is based on the work described in [Kam and Ullman, 1977]. It is uses a *control flow graph CFG=(V,E)* that contains a node for every statement or basic block in a procedure and an edge for a possible flow of control. The set of vertices V is a disjoint union of the set of nodes V_i for each subroutine p_i in the program[1]. Furthermore unique entry nodes s_i and exit nodes e_i for each procedure p_i are added. A *data flow analysis problem (DFP)* is a combination of such a graph with a complete lattice of values, called the *underlying lattice* $(\mathcal{L})$, and a family of functions (one for each node). These functions express the local semantics and are called *transfer functions* ($[\![\bullet]\!] : \mathcal{L} \rightarrow \mathcal{L}$). If every transfer function is monotone (distributive) the problem is called a *monotone (distributive) problem*. To describe the solution of a data flow problem the semantics of a path $\pi = n_1, \ldots, n_k$ in the *CFG* is defined as:

$$[\![\pi]\!] = \begin{cases} id & \text{if } \pi = \epsilon^2 \\ [\![(n_2, \cdots, n_k)]\!] \circ [\![n_1]\!] & \text{otherwise} \end{cases}$$

The desired solution of the *DFP* is the union of the semantics of all paths applied to bottom ($\perp$), called the *merge over all paths solution*:

$$\mathbf{MOP}(n) = \bigsqcup \{[\![\pi]\!](\perp) \mid \pi \text{ is a path from } s_0 \text{ to } n\}$$

---

[1] The existence of a main routine p_0 is assumed.

[2] ϵ denotes the empty path.

for every $n \in V$. As the set of all paths from s to n is usually infinite, this solution is in general not computable. Therefore, the *minimal fixed point solution* was introduced:

$$\mathbf{MFP}(n) = \begin{cases} [\![n]\!](\perp) & \text{if } n = s_0 \\ [\![n]\!] (\bigsqcup \{\mathbf{MFP}(m) \mid m \text{ predecessor } n\}) & \text{otherwise} \end{cases}$$

If $\mathbf{MFP}(n) = \mathbf{MOP}(n)$ for all n, then the $\mathbf{MFP}$ solution is called *precise*. Kam has proved in [Kam and Ullman, 1977] that for every monotone data flow problem the $\mathbf{MFP}$ is greater (with respect to the ordering of the lattice) than the $\mathbf{MOP}$ solution, and is therefore a safe approximation. Moreover, if the *DFP* is distributive the $\mathbf{MFP}$ solution is precise. The interprocedural version of this theorem is presented in [Knoop and Steffen, 1992].

2.1 Call String Approach

This approach considers procedure calls and returns as ordinary transfers of control, but avoids propagation along interprocedurally invalid paths. This can be implemented by tagging the propagated data with a call string, which is a sequence of call nodes, whose calls are still unfinished. As the number of call strings may be infinite their length is bounded by a constant K. This results in an approximate solution by merging the information belonging to call strings with the same K-suffix. For a more practical implementation a vector of data flow elements is used. If a call site c has to be appended to a call string $\gamma = c_1 c_2 \ldots c_K$ which already has length K the first element c_1 of γ is removed, which results in $c_2 \ldots c_K c$. This method is turned into a vector based implementation by encoding the call strings as numbers which will correspond to positions in the data flow array: assign to every call site c a unique number between one and $M - 1$, where M is the number of call sites in the given program plus one. Then a call string $\gamma = c_{i_1} \ldots c_{i_n}$ corresponds to a K digit number m to base M ($m = i_1 \ldots i_n$). Converting this number to the decimal system is done in usual way: multiply the n-th digit by M^n and add this for all digits ($m' = \sum_{1 \le j \le n} i_j * M^j$). This results in a number between zero and M^K where zero denotes the empty call string ϵ. Fortunately not all of these call strings are valid for each procedure. So all invalid numbers can be omitted for a fixed procedure and the array can be compressed, so that every position is used.

As an example consider the flow graph from the left side of Fig. 1 with $K = 1$. Valid call strings for **proc** are $c_1, c_1 c_2, c_1 c_2 c_2, \ldots$. If they are restricted to length one c_1 and c_2 remain. For **main** the empty call string is the only valid call string. So in the procedure **main** position zero of the data flow array of length three is used and in procedure **proc** the positions one and two are used. This results in the graph on the right side of Fig. 1.

If the underlying lattice $\mathcal{L}$ is finite a vector implementation can be constructed that results in the precise solution of the *DFP*. Call chains of length up to $|\mathcal{L}|^2 * M$ must be separated.

The vector based approach can also be used to implement more sophisticated methods which can also be used for the analysis of loops [Martin et al., 1998].

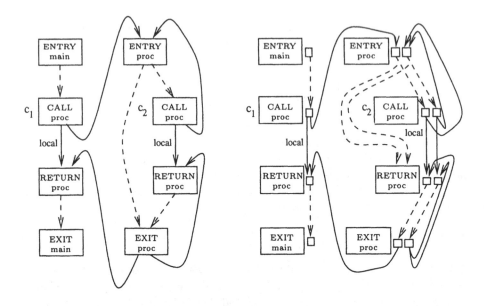

Fig. 1. Example of the vector based call string approach with K=1

2.2 Functional Approach

The functional approach computes for every procedure in the program a function which maps the data flow value at the entry of the procedure to the corresponding data flow value at the exit of the procedure. Because a procedure can be simultaneously recursive it is necessary to do this computation for all procedures in an interleaved fashion. The function is computed by tabulating input/output pairs. This table is guaranteed to be finite if the lattice is of finite cardinality. As an optimization only those input/output pairs are computed for each procedure where the input value actually occurs.

Now a more formal description of this method is given: For each procedure p_i and each node $n \in V_i$ we define an element $\Phi(s_i, n) : \mathcal{L} \to \mathcal{L}$ which describes the effects to elements of $\mathcal{L}$ when they are propagated from the start s_i of procedure p_i to n. These functions are defined by:

$$\Phi(s_i, s_i) = [\![s_i]\!]$$
$$\Phi(s_i, n) = \sqcup_{(m,n) \in E} \; \mathcal{E}(n) \circ \Phi(s_i, m)$$

and $\mathcal{E}$ is defined as either the normal transfer function for intraprocedural edges or Φ for interprocedural ones:

$$\mathcal{E}(n) = \begin{cases} [\![n]\!] & if \; \forall j : n \neq s_j \\ \Phi(s_j, e_j) & if \; \exists j : n = s_j \end{cases}$$

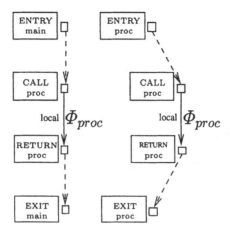

Fig. 2. Functional Approach

The results of the above equation system are used to compute the solution of the data flow problem:

$$\mathcal{F}(s_{main}) = [\![s_{main}]\!](\bot)$$
$$\mathcal{F}(s_i) \quad = \sqcup_{(c,s_i)\in E}\mathcal{F}(c)$$
$$\mathcal{F}(n) \quad = \Phi(s_j,n)(\mathcal{F}(s_j)) \ for \ n \neq s_j, n \in V_j$$

The iteration algorithm in **PAG** is implemented with some optimizations that are specially developed to handle large equation systems with a dynamic number of variables (the elements in the abstract function tables correspond to the variables, so their number is dynamic as the size of the tables is determined in a demand driven way). These optimizations turned out to be very good for this class of equation systems (cf. [Fecht, 1997,Nielson et al., 1998]).

2.3 Comparison

We briefly summarize the properties of both approaches (assuming a language with recursive procedures and table based implementation of the functional approach) for a given lattice $\mathcal{L}$. While the call string approach computes only values of $\mathcal{L}$, the functional approach computes values from $\mathcal{L} \to \mathcal{L}$. In order to guarantee termination it is required that this function space is finite. Thus the call string approach is always guaranteed to terminate, but may deliver worse results. Additionally there is the problem of finding an appropriate length K.
The functional approach is guaranteed to terminate for finite lattices, but may be exponential in the size of the lattice. It delivers best results.

An other point for the reliable use in a compiler is the the speed of the analysis. The speed for interprocedural analyses depends mainly on how often the procedures of the programs are visited during the analysis. In the K call string approach this is the number of K-paths to the procedure in the call graph. In the functional approach it is the number of different data flow values that occur at the beginning of the procedure. In order to keep this number small one tries usually to benefit from the locality properties of the programming language: if it is known that a procedure p can only read and write a certain part of the data flow information, the rest of the data flow information is passed directly from the call to the return of the procedure. This is modeled in PAG by the local edge from Fig. 1 and 2.

But for a constant propagation in C one can not bypass any part of the data flow information since any procedure can modify any other variable through pointer accesses. This is different for other analyses and programming languages. E.g. in Pascal all variables local to the caller can be passed by any call.

3 Practical Evaluation

We generated data flow analyzers for *copy constant propagation* (*ccp*) which is a *distributive* problem and for *full constant propagation* (*fp*) which is not. $\mathcal{L}_{ccp}$ is finite and therefore of bounded height and the $\mathcal{L}_{fp}$ is infinite but has bounded height. The *ccp* only processes assignments of the form $x := y$ or $x := c$ where x, y are variables and c is a constant, whereas *fp* includes a full interpreter for expressions. Furthermore, we use a simplified form of a technique called *downset completion* [Cousot and Cousot, 1992]; instead of combining the data flow information directly where two (or more) control flow edges come together, we first apply the transfer function and combine the results: $f(a \sqcup b)$ is replaced by $f(a) \sqcup f(b)$. This results in better solutions for non distributive $\sqcup$.

Figure 3 shows the structure and size of the used test programs in ANSI C, where most of them are well known everyday life programs (a '*' indicates programs with procedural variables). The columns give from left to right: the name of the program, a short description, the number of lines without comments, the number of procedures, the number of control flow nodes, and the number of variables.

For each of the programs the *functional* analyzer was applied. It finds the precise solution for any program in case of the *copy constant propagation*. This is also true for the *full constant propagation*, but the termination of the functional analyzer is not guaranteed. Also the *call string* analyzers have been applied with call strings up to length two or less if they find the same number of constants as the functional approach.

For each program four mayor columns are printed in Fig. 4 for the copy constant propagation and in Fig. 5 for the full constant propagation: three for call string approach of length zero, one, and two ($\mathcal{C}_0$, $\mathcal{C}_1$, $\mathcal{C}_2$), and one for the functional approach ($\mathcal{F}$). For each analysis method tree numbers are given: as a measurement of (theoretical) precision the number of available constants in the program is used. This is the number of constant variables at all control flow nodes, i.e.

$$\sum_{n \in V} |\{var \mid (\sqcup_{i=1,...,Arity(n)} \, flow(n)[i])(var) \neq \bot, \top\}|$$

program	description	lines	flow nodes	procedures	variables
bison	parser generator	6438	11722	155	3575
cdecl	C++ compiler part	2831	2401	33	841
cloop	benchmark	1488	2176	26	622
dhry	dhrystone	446	319	14	240
ed	editor	1506	2745	47	796
flex	scanner generator	5985	8688	129	2314
flops	benchmark	723	353	3	139
gzip*	compress	4056	6043	47	796
linpack	benchmark	821	796	13	278
twig	code generator	2092	3198	81	1085
xmodem	communication	2060	2965	31	1159

Fig. 3. The set of test programs

Prog	$\mathcal{C}_0$ Prec	Fold	Time	$\mathcal{C}_1$ Prec	Fold	Time	$\mathcal{C}_2$ Prec	Fold	Time	$\mathcal{F}$ Prec	Fold	Time
cdecl	615	10	15,66	627	10	66,41				627	10	113,93
twig	756	6	6,83	865	6	45,13	891	6	308,22	993	6	1746,14
dhry	81	2	1,82	109	2	1,54	109	2	1,45	109	2	2,06
ed	1098	42	7,81	1175	44	26,04	1198	44	37,05	1198	44	27,25
cloop	9839	145	20,95	9865	145	200,30				19649	145	6309,13
flex	3362	22	16,40	3496	22	88,76	9714	22	378,66	9731	22	193,54
flops	6897	107	0,52	7973	119	0,50				7973	119	0,70
bison	2699	10	24,45	2974	10	157,12	2978	10	372,43	2978	10	303,74
linpack	355	78	5,17	355	78	17,60	355	78	24,36	355	78	5,72
gzip	2744	16	9,52	2822	16	91,68	2822	16	1122,28			∞
xmodem	2716	6	88,77	3269	6	256,61	3269	6	326,55	4806	6	802,53

Fig. 4. Copy Constant Propagation

As a measurement of the usability of the calculated information the number of source code transformations is given that can be done with the information obtained by the constant propagation. This is the number of replacements of variables by their values. The last number is the runtime in seconds on a SUN SPARCsystem-600 (Ross-RT625 cpu, 128Mb memory), running SunOS 4.1.4.

To compare the different analysis approaches for each analysis three bar charts are used: Fig. 6, 7, and 8 for the copy constant propagation and Fig. 9, 10, and 11 for the full constant propagation. The first bar charts (Fig. 6, 9) show the relative number of available constants of the call string approaches compared to the functional approach, the second bar charts (Fig. 7, 10) show the same comparison for the number of foldings, and the third bar charts (Fig. 8, 11) show the runtime of the different approaches.

Prog	$\mathcal{C}_0$			$\mathcal{C}_1$			$\mathcal{C}_2$			$\mathcal{F}$		
	Prec	Fold	Time	Prec	Fold	Time	Prec	Fold	Time	Prec	Fold	Time
cdecl	885	10	15,93	903	10	65,08	911	10	135,02	911	10	101,05
twig	995	6	8,31	1130	6	47,05	1156	6	230,13	1258	6	1813,02
dhry	87	3	1,26	141	15	1,49	141	15	1,43	141	15	1,49
ed	2503	50	6,99	2714	52	24,56	2763	52	30,63	2763	52	21,58
cloop	10367	149	21,90	10711	149	260,06	10803	149	728,21	21952	151	2402,53
flex	4329	22	16,82	4597	22	94,54	10890	24	397,14	10911	24	209,26
flops	7080	188	0,74	7306	217	0,58				7306	219	0,67
bison	5591	10	24,03	5960	10	152,13	55973	10	1674,14			∞
linpack	385	80	4,57	385	80	10,15	385	80	16,64	385	80	5,31
gzip	4117	24	8,53	4916	24	83,00	5321	24	1604,51			∞
xmodem	3870	12	94,23	4756	12	226,18	4756	12	323,80	7521	12	593,11

Fig. 5. Full Constant Propagation

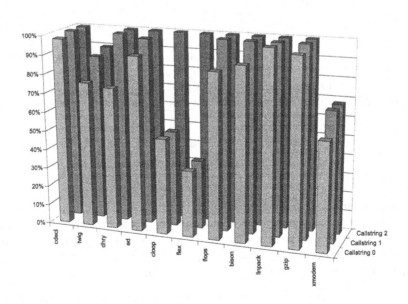

Fig. 6. Copy Constant Propagation: Percentage of available constants compared to the functional approach

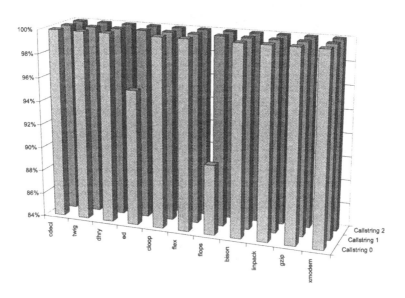

Fig. 7. Copy Constant Propagation: Percentage of constant foldings compared to the functional approach

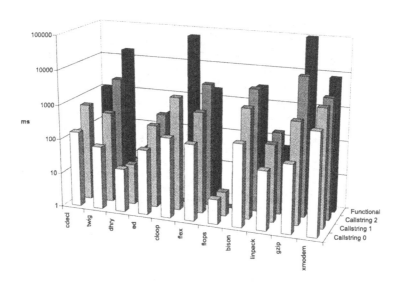

Fig. 8. Copy Constant Propagation: Runtimes

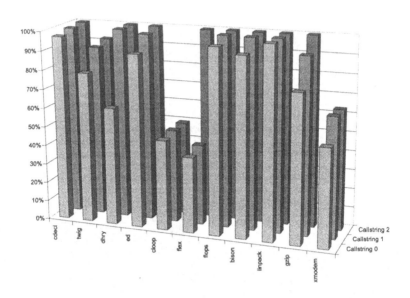

Fig. 9. Full Constant Propagation: Percentage of available constants compared to the functional approach

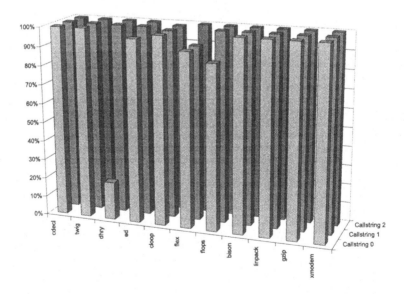

Fig. 10. Full Constant Propagation: Percentage of constant foldings compared to the functional approach

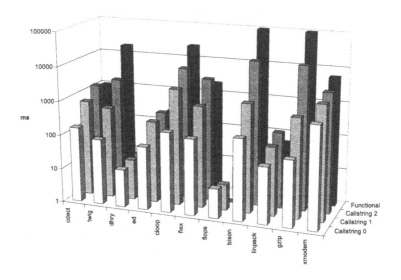

Fig. 11. Full Constant Propagation: Runtimes

3.1 Results

As can be seen in (Fig. 4, 5) the functional analyzers find always the largest number of constants, if they terminate. As termination is not guaranteed for the full constant propagation and the functional approach, one would not use this in a production compiler. One can also see that runtimes of the functional analyzer are unsatisfying for programs like `twig`, `cloop`, `bison`, and `gzip`.

This can be understood by the discussion from Sect. 2.3, where it is stated, that the runtime of the functional analyzer depends on the locality properties of the analysis and the programs, as well as the programming language. And these are very bad for full ANSI C and the constant propagation.

So one can deduce from the theoretical discussion that the functional analyzer may have bad runtimes for some programs, and in fact this claim is supported by the practical measurements.

On the other hand one does not expect runtime explosions for the call string analyzer for K equals zero and one, since then the number of runs through a procedure is determined by one or the number of call sites to the procedure, which is small, at least for hand written programs.

The shortcoming of the call string approach is that it may deliver potentially worse analysis results than the functional approach. Also this claim can be verified by the measurements for the theoretical precision of the analyses (Fig. 6, 9). But the practical use that can be gained from this higher precision is very low. Only for `cloop` and `flex` in the full constant propagation the number of foldings is higher for the functional approach than for the call string 1 approach (Fig. 10).

One can also see from the experiments that the full constant propagation delivers more foldings than a copy constant propagation, and has only a minor impact on the run times (Fig. 4, 5).

4 Conclusion and Further Work

Although no new ideas are presented in this paper, it presents a fair experimental evaluation of the two techniques, *call string-* and *functional approach* for interprocedural data flow analysis applied to two data flow problems.

We have shown that a full constant propagation delivers better results than a simple one (Fig. 4 and 5). Furthermore one can see that the set of call strings which should be kept separately (1) is small for real programs, but leads to similar results as the functional approach.

So we can draw the conclusion that an expensive functional approach can be replaced by a cheaper call string approach, at least for constant propagation in languages similar to C.

In the future we will test if these results also hold for other analyses.

Acknowledgments
I like to thank Martin Alt for contributing to early versions of this article, and Reinhard Wilhelm, Marc Langenbach and Christian Probst for careful proof reading.

References

[Alt et al., 1996] Alt, M., Ferdinand, C., Martin, F., and Wilhelm, R. (1996). Cache Behavior Prediction by Abstract Interpretation. In Cousot, R. and Schmidt, D. A., editors, *SAS'96, Static Analysis Symposium*, volume 1145 of *Lecture Notes in Computer Science*, pages 51–66. Springer. Long version accepted for SAS'96 special issue of Science of Computer Programming.

[Alt and Martin, 1995] Alt, M. and Martin, F. (1995). Generation of Efficient Interprocedural Analyzers with PAG. In Mycroft, A., editor, *SAS'95, Static Analysis Symposium*, volume 983 of *Lecture Notes in Computer Science*, pages 33–50. Springer.

[Cousot and Cousot, 1992] Cousot, P. and Cousot, R. (1992). Abstract interpretation frameworks. *Journal of Logic Computation*, 2(4):511–547.

[Fecht, 1997] Fecht, C. (1997). Abstrakte interpretation logischer programme: Theorie, implementierung, generierung. Dissertation, Universität des Saarlandes, Fachbereich 14.

[Kam and Ullman, 1977] Kam, J. and Ullman, J. D. (1977). Monotone Data Flow Analysis Frameworks. *Acta Informatica*, 7:305–317.

[Knoop and Steffen, 1992] Knoop, J. and Steffen, B. (1992). The Interprocedural Coincidence Theorem. In *Proceedings of the 4th International Conference on Compiler Construction*, volume 641 of *Lecture Notes in Computer Science*, pages 125–140. Springer.

[Martin, 1998] Martin, F. (1998). PAG – an efficient program analyzer generator. *International Journal on Software Tools for Technology Transfer*, Special Issue on Program Analysis. to appear.

[Martin et al., 1998] Martin, F., Alt, M., Ferdinand, C., and Wilhelm, R. (1998). Analysis of Loops. In Koskimies, K., editor, *Proceedings of the 7th International Conference on Compiler Construction*, volume 1383 of *Lecture Notes in Computer Science*, pages 80–94. Springer.

[Metzger and Stroud, 1993] Metzger, R. and Stroud, S. (1993). Interprocedural Constant Propagation: An Empirical Study. *ACM Letters on Programming Languages and Systems*, 2(1–4):213–232.

[Nielson et al., 1998] Nielson, F., Nielson, H. R., and Hankin, C. L. (1998). *Principles of Program Analysis - Flows and Effects*. Preliminary version November 1998; complete version to appear 1999.

[Reps et al., 1995] Reps, T., Horwitz, S., and Sagiv, M. (1995). Precise interprocedural dataflow analysis via graph reachability. In *Conference Record of POPL '95: 22nd ACM SIGPLAN-SIGACT Symposium on Principles of Programming Languages*, pages 49–61, San Francisco, California.

[Sagiv et al., 1995] Sagiv, M., Reps, T., and Horwitz, S. (1995). Precise interprocedural dataflow analysis with application to constant propagation. In *TAPSOFT'95, Arhus, Denmark*, LNCS. Springer-Verlag.

[Sharir and Pnueli, 1981] Sharir, M. and Pnueli, A. (1981). Two approaches to interprocedural data flow analysis. In Muchnick, S. S. and Jones, N. D., editors, *Program Flow Analysis: Theory and Applications*, chapter 7, pages 189–233. Prentice-Hall.

[Thesing et al., 1998] Thesing, S., Martin, F., Lauer, O., and Alt, M. (1998). *PAG User's Manual*.

[Wilhelm and Maurer, 1995] Wilhelm, R. and Maurer, D. (1995). *Compiler Design*. International Computer Science Series. Addison-Wesley.

Link-Time Improvement of Scheme Programs[*]

Saumya Debray   Robert Muth   Scott Watterson

Department of Computer Science
University of Arizona
Tucson, AZ 85721, U.S.A.
{debray, muth, saw}@cs.arizona.edu

Abstract. Optimizing compilers typically limit the scope of their analyses and optimizations to individual modules. This has two drawbacks: first, library code cannot be optimized together with their callers, which implies that reusing code through libraries incurs a penalty; and second, the results of analysis and optimization cannot be propagated from an application module written in one language to a module written in another. A possible solution is to carry out (additional) program optimization at link time. This paper describes our experiences with such optimization using two different optimizing Scheme compilers, and several benchmark programs, via alto, a link-time optimizer we have developed for the DEC Alpha architecture. Experiments indicate that significant performance improvements are possible via link-time optimization even when the input programs have already been subjected to high levels of compile-time optimization.

1 Introduction

The traditional model of compilation usually limits the scope of analysis and optimization to individual procedures, or possibly to modules. This model for code optimization does not take things as far as they could be taken, in two respects. The first is that code involving calls to library routines, or to functions defined in separately compiled modules, cannot be effectively optimized; this is unfortunate, because one expects programmers to rely more and more on code reuse through libraries as the complexity of software systems grows, (there has been some work recently on cross-module code optimization [4, 13]: this works for separately compiled user modules but not for libraries). The second problem is that a compiler can only analyze and optimize code written in the language it is designed to compile. Consider an application that investigates the synthesis of chemical compounds using a top-level Scheme program to direct a heuristic search of a space of various reaction sequences, and Fortran routines to compute reaction rates and yields for individual reactions.[1] With the traditional

---

[*]   This work was supported in part by the National Science Foundation under grants CCR-9502826 and CCR 9711166.
[1] This is a slightly paraphrased account of a project in the Chemistry department at the University of Arizona a few years ago: the project in question used Prolog rather than Scheme, but that does not change the essential point here.

compiler model, analyses and optimizations will not be able to cross the barrier between program modules written in different languages. For example, it seems unlikely that current compiler technology would allow Fortran routines in such an application to be inlined into the Scheme code, or allow context information to be propagated across language boundaries during interprocedural analysis of a Scheme function calling a Fortran routine.

A possible solution is to carry out program optimization when the *entire* program—library calls and all—is available for inspection: that is, at link time. While this makes it possible to address the shortcomings of the traditional compilation model, it gives rise to its own problems, for example:

- Machine code usually has much less semantic information than source code, which makes it much more difficult to discover control flow or data flow information (as an example, even for simple first-order programs, determining the extent of a jump table in an executable file, and hence the possible targets of the code derived from a `case` or `switch` statement, can be difficult when dealing with executables; at the source level, by contrast, the corresponding problem is straightforward).

- Compiler analyses are typically carried out on representations of source programs in terms of source language constructs, disregarding "nasty" features such as pointer arithmetic and out-of-bounds array accesses. At the level of executable code, on the other hand, all we have are the nasty features. Nontrivial pointer arithmetic is ubiquitous, both for ordinary address computations and for manipulating tagged pointers. If the number of arguments to a function is large enough, some of the arguments may have to be passed on the stack. In such a case, the arguments passed on the stack will typically reside at the top of the caller's stack frame, and the callee will "reach into" the caller's frame to access them: this is nothing but an out-of-bounds array reference.

- Executable programs tend to be significantly larger than the source programs they were derived from (e.g., see Figure 2). Coupled with the lack of semantic information present in these programs, this means that sophisticated analyses that are practical at the source level may be overly expensive at the level of executable code because of exorbitant time or space requirements.

This paper describes our experiences with such optimization on a number of Scheme benchmark programs, using a link-time optimizer, called `alto` ("a link-time optimizer"), that we have built for the DEC Alpha architecture. Apart from a variety of more or less "conventional" optimizations, `alto` implements several optimizations, or variations on optimizations, that are geared specifically towards programs that are rich in function calls—in particular, recursion—and indirect jumps (resulting both from higher order constructs and tail call optimization). Experiments indicate that significant performance improvements are possible using link-time optimization, even for code generated using powerful optimizing compilers.

2 Scheme vs. C: Low Level Execution Characteristics

Programs in languages such as Scheme differ in many respects from those written in imperative languages such as C, e.g., in their use of higher order functions and recursion, control flow optimizations such as tail call optimization, and in their relatively high frequency of function calls. However, it is not *a priori* clear that, at the level of executable code, the dynamic characteristics of Scheme programs are still significantly different from C code. To this end, we examined the runtime distributions of different classes of operations for a number of Scheme programs (those considered in Section 7) and compared the results with the corresponding figures for the eight SPEC-95 integer benchmark programs. The results, shown in Figure 1, show some interesting contrasts:

- The proportion of memory operations in Scheme code is 2.5 times larger than that in C code; we believe that this is due to a combination of two factors: the use of dynamic data structures such as lists that are harder to keep in registers, and the presence of garbage collection.
- The proportion of conditional branches is significantly higher (by a factor of almost 1.8) in Scheme code than in C code. This is due at least in part to runtime dispatch operations on tag bits encoding type information.
- The proportion of indirect jumps in Scheme code is close to three times as high as that in C code. This is due, in great part, to the way tail call optimization is handled.
- The proportion of (direct and indirect) function calls is somewhat smaller in the Scheme programs than in the C code. To a great extent, this is because the Scheme compilers try hard to eliminate function calls wherever possible.

Code generated for programs in dynamically typed languages usually also carries out pointer arithmetic to manipulate tagged pointers. We didn't measure the proportion of instructions devoted to tag manipulation (there didn't seem to be a simple and reliable way to do this in the context of our implementation), but we note that Steenkiste's studies indicate that Lisp programs spend between 11% and 24% of their time on tag checking [17]. We expect that the overall conclusion—that programs spend a significant amount of time in tag manipulation—holds for Scheme programs as well.

Most of the prior work on link-time optimization has focused on imperative languages [7, 12, 15, 16, 19]. The differences in runtime characteristics between Scheme and C programs, as discussed above, can have a significant effect on the extent to which systems designed for executables resulting from (human-written) C programs will be effective on code generated from Scheme programs. The reasons for this are the following:

1. The pointer arithmetic resulting from tag manipulation tends to defeat most alias analysis algorithms developed for languages such as C (see, for example, [20]).
2. The higher proportion of memory operations in Scheme programs can inhibit optimizations because, in the absence of accurate alias information,

Operation	Scheme (%)	C (%)	Scheme/C
integer ops	44.81	35.70	1.25
memory ops	34.02	13.63	2.50
floating point ops	0.58	0.76	0.76
conditional branches	10.44	5.89	1.77
indirect jumps	2.89	0.99	2.92
direct calls	0.29	0.44	0.66
indirect calls	1.51	1.72	0.88

Fig. 1. Dynamic distributions for classes of common operations

they greatly limit the optimizer's ability to move code around. The problem is compounded by the fact that pointer arithmetic resulting from tag manipulation adversely affects the quality of alias information available.

3. The higher proportion of indirect branches in Scheme code can interfere with low-level control flow analysis and inhibit optimizations such as profile-directed code layout to improve instruction cache utilization [11].

Our experiments, described in Section 7, show that alto is able to achieve significant speed improvements, even for Scheme programs that have been heavily optimized at compile-time; in this regard it consistently outperforms the OM link-time optimizer [15] from DEC.

3 System Organization

The execution of alto can be divided into five phases. In the first phase, an executable file (containing relocation information for its objects) is read in, and an initial, somewhat conservative, inter-procedural control flow graph is constructed. In the second phase, a suite of analyses and optimizations is then applied iteratively to the program. The activities during this phase can be broadly divided into three categories:

Simplification : Program code is simplified in three ways: dead and unreachable code is eliminated; operations are normalized, so that different ways of expressing the same operation (e.g., clearing a register) are rewritten, where possible, to use the same operation; and no-ops, typically inserted for scheduling and alignment purposes, are eliminated to reduce clutter.

Analysis : A number of analyses are carried out during this phase, including register liveness analysis, constant propagation, and jump table analysis.

Optimization : Optimizations carried out during this phase include standard compiler optimizations such as peephole optimization, branch forwarding, copy propagation, and invariant code motion out of loops; machine-level optimizations such as elimination of unnecessary register saves and restores at function call boundaries; architecture-specific optimizations such as the use of conditional move instructions to simplify control flow; as well as improvements to the control flow graph based on the results of jump table analysis.

This is followed by a function inlining phase. The fourth phase repeats the optimizations carried out in the second phase to the code resulting from inlining. Finally, the final phase carries out profile-directed code layout [11], instruction scheduling, and insertion of no-ops for alignment purposes, after which the code is written out.

4 Control Flow Analysis

Traditional compilers generally construct control flow graphs for individual functions, based on some intermediate representation of the program. The determination of intra-procedural control flow is not too difficult; and since an intermediate representation is used, there is no need to deal with machine-level idioms for control transfer. As a result, the construction of a control flow graph is a fairly straightforward process [1]. Matters are somewhat more complex at link time because machine code is harder to decompile. The algorithm used by alto to construct a control flow graph for an input program is as follows:

1. The start address of the program appears at a fixed location within the header of the file (this location may be different for different file formats). Using this as a starting point, the "standard" algorithm [1] is used to identify leaders and basic blocks, as well as function entry blocks. At this stage alto makes two assumptions: (i) that each function has a single entry block; and (ii) that all of the basic blocks of a function are laid out contiguously. If the first assumption turns out to be incorrect, the flow graph is "repaired" at a later stage; if the second assumption does not hold, the control flow graph constructed by alto may contain (safe) imprecisions, and as a result its optimizations may not be as effective as they could have been.

2. Edges are added to the flow graph. Whenever an exact determination of the target of a control transfer is not possible, alto estimates the set of possible targets conservatively, using a special node $B_{unknown}$ and a special function $F_{unknown}$ that are associated with the worst case data flow assumptions (i.e., that they use all registers, define all registers, etc.). Any basic block whose start address is marked as relocatable is considered to be a potential target for a jump instruction with unresolved target, and has an edge to it from $B_{unknown}$; any function whose entry point is marked as relocatable is considered to be potentially a target of an indirect function call, and has a call edge to it from $F_{unknown}$. Any indirect function call (i.e., using the jsr instruction) is considered to call $F_{unknown}$ while other indirect jumps are considered to jump to $B_{unknown}$.

3. Inter-procedural constant propagation is carried out on the resulting control flow graph, and the results used to determine addresses being loaded into registers. This information, in turn, is used to resolve the targets of indirect jumps and function calls: where such targets can be resolved unambiguously, the edge to $F_{unknown}$ or $B_{unknown}$ is replaced by an edge to the appropriate target.

4. The assumption thus far has been that a function call returns to its caller, at the instruction immediately after the call instruction. At the level of

executable code, this assumption can be violated in two ways. The first involves *escaping branches*, i.e., ordinary (i.e., non-function-call) jumps from one function into another: this can happen either because of tail call optimization, or because of code sharing in hand-written assembly code that is found in, for example, some numerical libraries. The second involves non-local control transfers via functions such as setjmp and longjmp. Each of these cases is handled by the insertion of additional control flow edges, which we call *compensation edges*, into the control flow graph: in the former case, escaping edges from a function f to a function g result in a single compensation edge from the exit node of g to the exit node of f; in the latter case, a function containing a setjmp has an edge from $F_{unknown}$ to its exit node, while a function containing a longjmp has a compensation edge from its exit node to $F_{unknown}$. The effect of these compensation edges is to force the various dataflow analyses to safely approximate the control flow effects of these constructs.

5. Finally, alto attempts to identify indirect jumps through jump tables, which arise from case or switch statements. This is done as part of the optimizations mentioned at the beginning of this section. These optimizations can simplify the control and/or data flow enough to allow the extent of the jump table to be determined. When this happens, the edge from the indirect jump to $B_{unknown}$ is replaced by a set of edges, one for each entry in the jump table. If all of the indirect jumps within a function can be resolved in this way, then any remaining edges from $B_{unknown}$ to basic blocks within that function are deleted.

5   Data Flow Analysis

Alto carries out a variety of inter-procedural data flow analyses, including reachability analysis, constant propagation, register liveness analysis, side effect analysis, etc. The most important of these is inter-procedural constant propagation, which plays a central role in the construction of the control flow graph of the program. A discussion of these analyses is omitted due to space constraints, except for the observation that we find that for Scheme programs, alto is able to determine, on the average, the operands and results for about 29% of the instructions in programs. This is considerably higher than for C and Fortran programs: e.g., for the programs in the SPEC-95 benchmark suite, it is able to evaluate about 17% of the instructions on the average: we are currently looking into the reason for this difference. Note that this does not mean that a third of the instructions of a program can be removed by alto, since in most cases the these represent address computations. This information can, nevertheless, be used to good advantage elsewhere, as discussed above: experiments indicate that for the Scheme benchmarks considered, disabling constant propagation leads to a performance loss of 5%–12% (compared to when all analyses and optimizations are enabled).

6 Program Optimization

The optimizations carried out by `alto` are typically guided by execution profile information and the availability of machine resources. Space constraints preclude a detailed discussion of these optimizations: here we discuss only the most important ones.

6.1 Inlining

Traditionally, Scheme compilers carry out inlining at, or close to, the level of the source program [2, 4, 10, 18]. At this level, the primary benefits of inlining come from specializing and simplifying the inlined function, e.g., by evaluating conditionals and pruning away code that becomes unreachable. Code growth during inlining is usually controlled via syntax-driven techniques, ranging from simple syntax-directed estimates of the size of the callee [2, 4, 10] to more refined estimates based on the residual size of the callee after specializing it to the call site under consideration [18]. At link time, by contrast, it is reasonable to expect that considerable amounts of inlining have already been carried out by the Scheme compiler being used (and then possibly some more by the C compiler, if the compilation is via translation to C). This means that, while some code simplification might occur due to the propagation of constant arguments into library routines, it seems unlikely that link-time inlining will give rise to large amounts of code simplification and pruning. On the other hand, more accurate information is available about object code size, making it easier to consider the effects of inlining on the instruction cache utilization of a program.

The motivations for carrying out inlining within `alto` are three-fold: to reduce the function call/return overhead; to simplify reasoning about aliasing between the caller's code and the callee's code, since after inlining they typically refer to the same stack frame rather than two different frames (see Section 6.2); and to improve branch prediction and instruction cache behavior using profile-directed code layout [11]. In `alto`, code growth due to inlining is controlled by ensuring that (`alto`'s estimate of) the cache footprint of the resulting code does not exceed the size of the instruction cache: in particular, if the call site being considered for inlining lies within any loop, the total size of the "hot" execution paths through the loop is not allowed to exceed the size of the primary instruction cache.

Inlining in the presence of higher order functions has typically been accomplished using sophisticated control flow analyses [10]. We believe that such analyses are too expensive to be practical at the level of machine code. Instead, we use a simple profile-guided inlining technique we call *guarded inlining*—which is conceptually similar to, though somewhat more general than, a technique for optimizing dynamically dispatched function calls in object-oriented languages referred to as "receiver class prediction" [5, 8]—to achieve similar results. Suppose we have an indirect function call whose target we are unable to resolve. We use profiling to identify the most frequent targets at each such indirect call. Suppose that the most frequent target is a function f at address $addr_0$. With guarded inlining, we test whether the target address is $addr_0$: if this is the case, execution drops through into the inlined code for f; otherwise, an indirect function call occurs, as before. It's not too difficult to see, in fact, that in general the transformation can be adapted to any indirect branch. This mechanism allows us to get the benefits of inlining even for call sites that can, in fact, have multiple possible targets, in contrast to schemes that require control flow analysis to identify a unique target for a call site before inlining can take place [10].

6.2 Memory Access Optimizations

We use an intra-basic-block transformation we call *register forwarding* to reduce the number of unnecessary loads from memory. The opportunity for this optimization arises because, in the course of other optimizations such as the elimination of unreachable code, register reassignment and elimination of unnecessary register saves and restores at function boundaries, etc., alto is able to free up registers that can then be reused for other purposes. In the simplest case, a register r_a is stored to a memory location $addr_0$, and a register r_b subsequently loaded from that address, with no redefinition of r_a in between. In this case, assuming that we can verify that the contents of location $addr_0$ have also not been modified, register forwarding replaces the load operation by a register-to-register move from r_a:

$$
\begin{array}{lcl}
\texttt{store } r_a, \ addr_0 & & \texttt{store } r_a, \ addr_0 \\
\ldots & \Rightarrow & \ldots \\
\texttt{load } r_b, \ addr_0 & & \texttt{move } r_a, \ r_b
\end{array}
$$

In general, register r_a may be modified after it has been stored to location $addr_0$ but before r_b is loaded from that location. In this case (again assuming that location $addr_0$ can be guaranteed to not have been modified), if there is a free register r_{tmp}, it can be used to save the original value of r_a before r_a is modified, and eventually moved over to r_b.

In order to guarantee that the memory location $addr_0$ is not modified between the initial store of r_a to it and the subsequent load into r_b, we verify that any intervening stores to memory write to locations other than $addr_0$. For this, we use a slight generalization of a technique called *instruction inspection*, commonly used in compile-time instruction schedulers. we first carry out interprocedural constant propagation to identify references to global addresses. The memory disambiguation analysis then proceeds as follows: two memory reference instructions i_1 and i_2 in a basic block can be guaranteed to not refer to the same memory location if one of the following holds:

1. one of the instructions uses a register known to point to the stack and the other uses a register known to point to a global address; or
2. i_1 and i_2 use address expressions $k_1(r_1)$ and $k_2(r_2)$ respectively, and there are two (possibly empty) chains of instructions whose effects are to compute the value $c_1 + contents\_of(r_0)$ into register r_1 and $c_2 + contents\_of(r_0)$ into r_2, for some register r_0, such that the two chains do not use different definitions of r_0 in the basic block under consideration, and $c_1 + k_1 \neq c_2 + k_2$.

Apart from this transformation, *shrink-wrapping* [6] is used to reduce register save/restore operations at function call boundaries.

Program	Source	Bigloo			Gambit-C		
	lines	functions	blocks	instructions	functions	blocks	instructions
boyer	568	2061	24358	114007	1050	39004	188178
conform	432	2080	24689	115809	1036	39388	190257
dynamic	2318	2202	27633	132576	1050	43716	220461
earley	651	2069	24608	115928	1050	39319	191091
graphs	602	2079	24538	115885	1050	39200	189977
lattice	219	2061	24331	113994	1050	39016	188451
matrix	763	2091	24746	116729	1050	39734	192569
nucleic	3478	2162	27131	126612	1050	40257	199192
scheme	1078	2301	26333	123465	1050	41479	202127

Fig. 2. The benchmark programs used

6.3 Profile-Directed Code Layout

In order to reduce the performance penalty associated with control flow changes and instruction cache misses, alto uses profile information to direct the layout of the code (modern processors typically use dynamic branch prediction, so the effect of code layout on branch misprediction is not considered). The algorithm used here follows that of Pettis and Hansen [11], with a few minor modifications. The code layout algorithm proceeds by grouping the basic blocks in a program into three sets: The *hot set* consists of the set of basic blocks, considered in decreasing order of execution frequency, which account for 2/3 of the total number of instructions executed by the program at runtime; the *zero set* contains all the basic blocks that were never executed; and The *cold set* contains the remaining basic blocks. We then compute the layout separately for each set using a greedy algorithm to construct chains of basic blocks, and concatenate the three resulting layouts to obtain the overall program layout.

7 Experimental Results

We evaluated our link-time optimizer using two optimizing Scheme compilers: Bigloo version 1.8, by M. Serrano [14], and Gambit-C version 3.0 by Marc Feeley. Our experiments were run using nine commonly used Scheme benchmarks: *boyer*, a term-rewriting theorem prover; *conform* is a type checker, written by J. Miller; *dynamic* is an implementation of a tagging optimization algorithm for Scheme [9], applied to itself; *earley* is an implementation of Earley's parsing algorithm, by Marc Feeley; *graphs*, a program that counts the number of directed graphs with a distinguished root and k vertices each having out-degree at most 2; *lattice* enumerates the lattice of maps between two lattices; *matrix* tests whether a given random matrix is maximal among all matrices of the same dimension obtainable via a set of simple transformations of the original matrix; *nucleic* is a floating-point intensive program to determine nucleic acid structure; and *scheme* is a Scheme interpreter by Marc Feeley. The size of each of these benchmarks

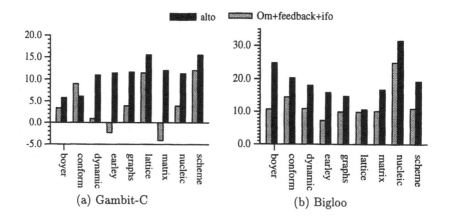

(a) Gambit-C (b) Bigloo

Fig. 3. Speed improvements (%)

is reported in Figure 2.[2] We considered only compiled systems, and restricted ourselves to compilers that translated Scheme programs to C code because `alto` requires relocation information to reconstruct the control flow graph from an executable program, which means that the linker needs to be invoked with the appropriate flags that instruct it to not discard the relocation information; systems that compiled to C seemed to offer the simplest way to communicate the appropriate flags to the linker.

The Bigloo compiler was invoked with options `-O4 -farithmetic -unsafe -cgen`, except for the *nucleic* program, for which the options used were `-O3 -unsafesv -cgen`. The Gambit-C compiler was invoked without any additional compiler options, but the resulting C code had the switch `-D__SINGLE_HOST` passed to the C compiler to generate faster code The resulting C code was compiled with the DEC C compiler V5.2-036 (the highly optimizing GEM compiler system [3], which we found generates faster code than current versions of `gcc`) invoked as `cc -O4`, with additional flags to retain relocation information and produce statically linked executables. The profiling inputs used were the same as that used for the actual benchmarking. The timings were obtained on a lightly loaded DEC Alpha workstation with a 300 MHz Alpha 21164 processor with a split primary cache (8 Kbytes each of instruction and data cache), 96 Kbytes of on-chip secondary cache, 2 Mbytes of off-chip backup cache, and 512 Mbytes of main memory, running Digital Unix 4.0. In each case, the smallest time of 15 runs is considered. Measurements of the number of different kinds of opera-

---

[2] The numbers reported here are for the programs available with the Gambit-C 2.7 distribution (`http://www.iro.umontreal.ca/~gambit`), measured for the "core program", i.e., without system-specific definitions, using the `wc` utility. Of course, "lines of code" is not really an appropriate measure of size for link-time optimization, and these numbers are shown only to provide some intuition: a more appropriate measure, for our purposes, is the number of instructions in the final executable, as reported in this table.

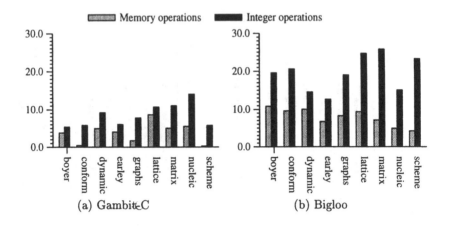

Fig. 4. Reduction in operations executed (%)

tions executed, cache misses, etc., were obtained using hardware counters on the processor, using the best number out of 5 runs.

Figure 3 shows the execution time improvements due to alto, compared to what is achievable otherwise using aggressive compile-time optimization (at level -O4), together with profile-guided and inter-file optimization as well as link-time optimization using the Om link-time optimizer [15]. There are two main points to note from this figure. First, note that in almost all cases—the sole exception is *conform* under Gambit-C—alto produces code that is significantly faster than that produced using Om. The second point is that, even though the programs were subjected to a high degree of optimization by both the Scheme and the C compilers, alto nevertheless succeeds in achieving significant further improvements in performance. The improvements for Bigloo range from about 10% to over 30%, with an average improvement of 19.3%. The improvements are smaller for Gambit-C, ranging from about 6% to about 15.5%, with an average improvement of about 10.2%.[3]

Figure 1 indicates that for the programs considered, there are three main classes of operations executed: memory operations, integer operations, and branch operations. Figure 4 shows the effect of alto on the number of memory and integer operations executed; while alto is able, in some cases, to reduce number of branch operations executed, the reductions are generally not large enough to be significant. It can be seen that for Gambit-C, alto is able to effect a reduction of around 4% in the number of memory operations and 5–10% in the number of integer operations; for Bigloo the improvements are more dramatic, with 5–10% reductions in the number of memory operations and 15–25% reductions in the number of integer operations executed. The vast majority of the memory

---

[3] These averages were computed as follows: for each of the systems considered, we determined the ratio of the execution times after optimization to the original execution time (i.e., Opt./Orig. in Table 3), computed the geometric mean, and subtracted this from 1.00.

Program	ORIGINAL			OPTIMIZED			ΔAccesses
	Accesses $(\times 10^6)$	Misses $(\times 10^6)$	Miss Rate (%)	Accesses $(\times 10^6)$	Misses $(\times 10^6)$	Miss Rate (%)	(%)
boyer	1252.26	1.27	0.10	907.34	0.58	0.06	27.54
conform	453.70	10.10	2.22	398.00	1.19	0.30	12.27
dynamic	395.96	6.43	1.62	338.82	2.14	0.63	14.43
earley	974.06	2.68	0.27	920.58	0.78	0.08	5.49
graphs	1495.59	32.62	2.18	1320.81	6.02	0.45	11.68
lattice	2491.41	3.85	0.15	2443.31	1.55	0.06	1.93
matrix	2637.69	23.64	0.89	2262.69	11.46	0.50	14.21
nucleic	1793.26	164.36	9.16	1447.69	30.37	2.09	19.27
scheme	2767.45	30.47	1.10	2216.75	7.15	0.32	19.89

(a) Bigloo

Program	ORIGINAL			OPTIMIZED			ΔAccesses
	Accesses $(\times 10^6)$	Misses $(\times 10^6)$	Miss Rate (%)	Accesses $(\times 10^6)$	Misses $(\times 10^6)$	Miss Rate (%)	(%)
boyer	1230.11	9.78	0.79	1084.09	1.06	0.09	11.87
conform	913.96	27.24	2.98	866.91	16.95	1.95	5.14
dynamic	1735.13	42.31	2.43	1518.46	14.46	0.95	12.48
earley	1274.87	23.57	1.84	1185.54	0.96	0.08	7.00
graphs	433.58	21.51	4.96	432.86	3.91	0.90	0.16
lattice	2976.57	77.80	2.61	2729.05	1.93	0.07	8.31
matrix	2470.24	71.63	2.89	2213.54	28.21	1.27	10.39
nucleic	377.09	14.76	3.91	358.74	7.97	2.22	4.86
scheme	3126.19	318.07	10.17	3413.83	17.90	0.52	−9.20

(b) Gambit

Table 1. Instruction Cache behavior

operations eliminated turn out to be load operations, which are typically more expensive than store operations.

Table 1 shows the effect of `alto` on the instruction cache behavior of the programs. The group of columns marked 'ORIGINAL' refers to the original program, while those grouped under 'OPTIMIZED' refer to the output of `alto`; the column marked 'Δ Accesses' refers to the percentage improvement in the number of i-cache accesses from the original to the optimized program, relative to the original program. We see, from the ΔAccesses column, that the number of i-cache accesses, i.e., the number of instruction accesses, generally decreases after optimization: the sole exception is the *scheme* benchmark under Gambit-C, which experiences an increase of over 9% in the number of i-cache accesses. We are currently investigating the reason for this anomaly. In all cases, however, both the number of i-cache misses, and the i-cache miss rate, decrease dramatically, primarily due to profile-guided code layout.

Program	ORIGINAL			OPTIMIZED			ΔAccesses (%)
	Accesses ($\times 10^6$)	Misses ($\times 10^6$)	Miss Rate (%)	Accesses ($\times 10^6$)	Misses ($\times 10^6$)	Miss Rate (%)	
boyer	578.28	49.90	8.00	515.76	47.92	9.00	10.81
conform	284.95	18.35	6.00	257.55	21.28	8.00	9.61
dynamic	207.61	26.06	12.00	186.84	25.01	13.00	10.00
earley	649.46	59.11	9.00	605.88	57.47	9.00	6.71
graphs	730.72	128.23	17.00	670.17	96.32	14.00	8.28
lattice	1844.44	46.35	2.00	1671.10	92.60	5.00	9.39
matrix	1463.61	154.46	10.00	1358.69	146.29	10.00	7.16
nucleic	1105.26	79.70	7.00	1051.39	73.54	6.00	4.87
scheme	1331.42	167.60	12.00	1275.19	162.43	12.00	4.22

(a) Bigloo

Program	ORIGINAL			OPTIMIZED			ΔAccesses (%)
	Accesses ($\times 10^6$)	Misses ($\times 10^6$)	Miss Rate (%)	Accesses ($\times 10^6$)	Misses ($\times 10^6$)	Miss Rate (%)	
boyer	728.49	108.08	14.00	700.84	100.10	14.00	3.79
conform	574.35	38.73	6.00	572.06	37.73	6.00	0.39
dynamic	1301.02	101.28	7.00	1237.12	82.82	6.00	4.91
earley	1105.85	50.79	4.00	1061.87	50.23	4.00	3.97
graphs	422.90	20.85	4.00	415.82	20.79	5.00	1.67
lattice	2165.83	76.89	3.00	1979.51	64.55	3.00	8.60
matrix	1816.00	131.53	7.00	1725.56	118.03	6.00	4.98
nucleic	301.20	43.53	14.00	284.68	47.74	16.00	5.48
scheme	2077.62	306.80	14.00	2072.70	302.66	14.00	0.23

(b) Gambit

Table 2. Data Cache behavior

Table 2 shows the effect of `alto` on the data cache behavior of programs tested. While `alto` does not do anything to change data layouts, it can be seen that for most programs there are noticeable reductions in the number of data cache accesses: we believe that this is likely to be due to the elimination of load operations by `alto`. Surprisingly, in a few programs the reduction in data cache accesses is accompanied by an increase in data cache misses: we conjecture that this may be because some load operations, which would have caused nearby memory words to be brought into the cache, were eliminated by `alto`, and that this resulted in cache misses when those nearby words were accessed.

The amount of code growth due to inlining ranges from about 0.5% for the Gambit-C system, where very little inlining takes place, to about 1.5% for Bigloo. For either implementation, the amount of inlining does not seem to vary significantly for the different benchmarks, suggesting that most of the inlining involves library routines; this is not surprising, since the programs used were single-module programs and one would expect the Scheme and C compilers to have inlined most of the obvious candidates at compile time.

We believe that the performance improvements reported here are conservative, because the benchmarks used don't really have the characteristics where link-time optimization can be expected to pay off significantly. Each benchmark consists of a single file; the use of libraries is limited to system primitives (i.e., there is very little code reuse at the user level); and the programs don't use more than one language. In the near future we intend to investigate larger, more realistic, multi-module benchmarks: we believe link-time optimization will offer even greater benefits for such applications.

8 Conclusions

The traditional model of compilation is unable to optimize code that is not available for inspection at compile time. This means that applications that make extensive use of library routines, or where different modules are written in different languages, may incur a performance penalty. One way to address this problem is to apply low level code optimizations at link time. However, the manipulation of machine code has challenges of its own, including increased program size and difficulty in extracting information about program behavior.

This paper describes `alto`, a link-time optimizer we have developed for the DEC Alpha architecture, and our experiences with its application to several Scheme benchmarks, using code generated by three different optimizing Scheme compilers. Even though the benchmarks lack the features that would show off the benefits of link-time optimization, and were compiled with high levels of compiler optimization (both at the Scheme and C level), we find that `alto` is able to achieve significant performance improvements.

Acknowledgements

We are grateful to Jeffrey Siskind and Marc Feeley for their invaluable help with benchmarking. Thanks are also due to Suresh Jagannathan for providing some of the benchmarks.

References

1. A. V. Aho, R. Sethi and J. D. Ullman, *Compilers – Principles, Techniques and Tools*, Addison-Wesley, 1986.
2. J. M. Ashley, "The Effectiveness of Flow Analysis for Inlining", *Proc. 1997 SIGPLAN International Conference on Functional Programming*, June 1997, pp. 99–111.
3. D. Blickstein *et al.*, "The GEM Optimizing Compiler System", *Digital Technical Journal*, 4(4):121–136.
4. M. Blume and A. W. Appel, "Lambda-splitting: A Higher-Order Approach to Cross-Module Optimizations", *Proc. 1997 SIGPLAN International Conference on Functional Programming*, June 1997, pp. 112–124.

5. B. Calder and D. Grunwald, "Reducing Indirect Function Call Overhead in C++ Programs", *Proc. 21st ACM Symposium on Principles of Programming Languages*, Jan. 1994, pp. 397–408.

6. F. C. Chow, "Minimizing Register Usage Penalty at Procedure Calls", *Proc. SIG-PLAN '88 Conference on Programming Language Design and Implementation*, June 1988, pp. 85–94.

7. M. F. Fernández, "Simple and Effective Link-Time Optimization of Modula-3 Programs", *Proc. SIGPLAN '95 Conference on Programming Language Design and Implementation*, June 1995, pp. 103–115.

8. D. Grove, J. Dean, C. Garrett, and C. Chambers, "Profile-Guided Receiver Class Prediction", *Proc. Tenth Annual Conference on Object-Oriented Programming Systems, Languages, and Applications* (OOPSLA '95), Oct. 1995, pp. 108–123.

9. F. Henglein, "Global Tagging Optimization by Type Inference", *Proc. 1992 ACM Symposium on Lisp and Functional Programming*, pp. 205–215.

10. S. Jagannathan and A. Wright, "Flow-directed Inlining", *Proc. SIGPLAN '96 Conference on Programming Language Design and Implementation*, May 1996, pp. 193–205.

11. K. Pettis and R. C. Hansen, "Profile-Guided Code Positioning", *Proc. SIGPLAN '90 Conference on Programming Language Design and Implementation*, June 1990, pp. 16–27.

12. T. Romer, G. Voelker, D. Lee, A. Wolman, W. Wong, H. Levy, B. N. Bershad, and J. B. Chen, "Instrumentation and Optimization of Win32/Intel Executables", *Proc. 1997 USENIX Windows NT Workshop.*

13. V. Santhanam and D. Odnert, "Register Allocation across Procedure and Module Boundaries", *Proc. SIGPLAN '90 Conference on Programming Language Design and Implementation*, June 1990, pp. 28–39

14. M. Serrano and P. Weis, "Bigloo: a portable and optimizing compiler for strict functional languages" *Proc. Static Analysis Symposium (SAS '95)*, 1995, pp. 366–381.

15. A. Srivastava and D. W. Wall, "A Practical System for Intermodule Code Optimization at Link-Time", *Journal of Programming Languages*, pp. 1–18, March 1993.

16. A. Srivastava and D. W. Wall, "Link-time Optimization of Address Calculation on a 64-bit Architecture", *Proc. SIGPLAN '94 Conference Programming Language Design and Implementation*, June 1994, pp. 49–60.

17. P. A. Steenkiste, "The Implementation of Tags and Run-Time Type Checking", in *Topics in Advanced Language Implementation*, ed. P. Lee, 1991. MIT Press.

18. O. Waddell and R. K. Dybvig, "Fast and Effective Procedure Inlining", *Proc. 1997 Static Analysis Symposium* (SAS '97), Sept. 1997, pp. 35–52. Springer-Verlag LNCS vol. 1302.

19. D. W. Wall, "Global Register Allocation at Link Time", *Proc. SIGPLAN '86 Symposium on Compiler Construction*, July 1986, pp. 264–275.

20. R. P. Wilson and M. S. Lam, "Efficient Context-Sensitive Pointer Analysis for C Programs", *Proc. SIGPLAN '95 Conference on Programming Language Design and Implementation*, June 1995, pp. 1–12.

Expansion-Based Removal
of Semantic Partial Redundancies

Jens Knoop, Oliver Rüthing, and Bernhard Steffen

Universität Dortmund, Baroper Str. 301, D-44221 Dortmund, Germany
{knoop,ruething,steffen}@ls5.cs.uni-dortmund.de
http://sunshine.cs.uni-dortmund.de/

Abstract. We develop an expansion-based algorithm for *semantic partial redundancy elimination* (*SPRE*), which overcomes the central drawbacks of the state-of-the-art approaches, which leave the program structure invariant: they fail to eliminate all partial redundancies even for acyclic programs. Besides being optimal for acyclic programs, our algorithm is unique in eliminating *all* partial k-redundancies, a new class of redundancies which is characterised by the number k of loop iterations across which values have to be kept. These optimality results come at the price of an in the worst case exponential program growth. The new technique is thus tailored for optimizing the typically considerably small computational "hot" spots of a program. Here it is particularly promising because its structural simplicity supports extensions to uniformly capture further powerful optimisations like constant propagation or strength reduction in a mutually supportive way.

1 Motivation

Background *Partial redundancy elimination* (*PRE*) is an important, widely used optimisation for performance improvement. Particularly powerful are approaches aiming at the elimination of *semantically* partially redundant computations (for short: SPRE). Intuitively, these are computations whose *values* are computed more than once along some program paths. Instead of recomputing such values, SPRE aims at replacing their (re-) computations by references to the respective values where possible. Intuitively, this is achieved by storing the values of computations for later reuse in temporaries as illustrated in the program fragment of Figure 1 showing the motivating example of [16]: as long as control stays inside the loop-like construct of Figure 1(a), the computations of $x + y$ and $a + b$ always yield the same value meaning that they are *semantically* (not syntactically[1]) partially redundant with respect to each other. These redundancies can be eliminated by computing the values before entering the loop and replacing the original computations by references to the stored values as shown in Figure 1(b).

---

[1] Most commercial implementations consider equivalences on a syntactic basis as proposed e.g. in [13].

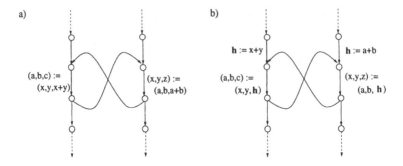

Fig. 1. Illustrating the essence of SPRE.[2]

State-of-the-art algorithms for SPRE (cf. [3, 12, 15, 18, 19]) are characterised by two common major design decisions made on the conceptual and technical side:

- *Conceptually:* the *flow graph* structure must not be modified,
- *Technically:* computations are *moved to* (rather than *placed at*) earlier program points for later reuse of their values.

Unfortunately, this has drawbacks already for *acyclic* programs:

Firstly, under the constraint of structural invariance certain redundancies cannot safely be eliminated at all, i.e., without impairing other program paths. This is illustrated in Figure 2(a). Note that such redundancies are by no means uncommon. Their most prominent manifestation is given by loop invariant code placed on a backedge as depicted in Figure 2(b). Even worse, there are situations like the one in Figure 2(c). Here, even a computation whose value has been computed before on every program path cannot be eliminated. In terms of Figure 2(c) this is because depending on the program path taken, the computation of $a' + b$ is either redundant with respect to the computation of $a + b$ or with respect to the computation of $c + b$. Thus, $a' + b$ cannot statically be replaced by a reference to the value of $a + b$ or $c + b$ as the one actually reused cannot be determined at compile time.

Secondly, SPRE-techniques limited to *moving* computations to earlier program points are inherently weaker than SPRE-techniques being capable of arbitrarily *placing* computations at appropriate program points. This was discussed in detail in [12], and here we only recall an example for illustration. In the program fragment of Figure 3(a) all redundancies can safely be eliminated as shown in Figure 3(c). However, motion-based SPRE-techniques are not capable of doing this and get stuck with the result of Figure 3(b). This is because neither $a+b$ nor $c+b$ are *anticipable* (*down-safe*) at the join point of control, and hence none of them can be hoisted across this point. In [12] we gave reasons why, under the constraint of structural invariance, the problem of designing a general placement-based SPRE-technique cannot satisfactorily be solved: even in acyclic programs

---

[2] For the sake of presentation we allow parallel assignments $(x_1, \dots, x_r) := (t_1, \dots, t_r)$ as a shorthand for an appropriate sequence of assignments.

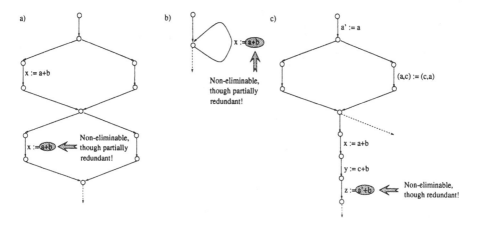

Fig. 2. *Conceptual* design constraint causes non-eliminable redundancies.

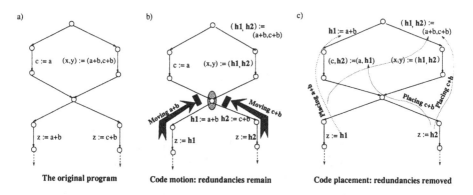

Fig. 3. *Technical* design constraint causes non-eliminable redundancies.

there are redundancies which can only be eliminated at the cost of introducing other ones, which excludes optimality in general. Though the heuristically based extension of a motion-based SPRE-algorithm proposed by Bodík and Anik can be considered a step towards placement-based algorithms (cf. [3]), the general problem of computing an optimal solution where one exists, is still unsolved.

Property-oriented expansion In this article, we present an *expansion-based* algorithm, which preserves the *flow tree* structure, i.e., it preserves the branching structure, but duplicates nodes in order to avoid "destructive joins" (see e.g. Figures 2 and 3 for examples of such joins).

To understand the basic idea behind our approach, note that on the execution tree of a program every redundancy is total and can thus successfully be eliminated. Of course, this insight is merely of theoretical interest because the execution tree is infinite for cyclic programs. However, this observation yields an easy access to the informal understanding of our algorithm. Basically, it

94

works by *expanding* (i.e., unrolling) the program in a *demand-driven* fashion. The expansion is controlled by means of on-the-fly computed semantic equivalence information of program terms. Hence, the algorithm works by means of *property-oriented expansion* in the sense of [17].

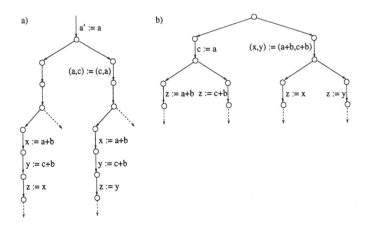

Fig. 4. Optimisations achieved by our approach for the examples of Figure 2(c) and Figure 3(a).

Conceptually, this approach has previously been applied to the *complete* elimination of *syntactic* partial redundancies (cf. [17]), a result which has later been optimized in order to avoid unnecessary code duplication (cf. [4]). The approach here parallels the syntactic approach under a *semantic* perspective leading to substantially stronger optimality results. Its unique power, which will be discussed in detail in the course of this article, is illustrated in Figures 4, 7, and 8.

Contribution While in the syntactic case partial redundancies can be eliminated completely [17] there is no chance for such a result in the semantic setting. Figure 5(a) shows a program containing an unbounded number of redundancies which can only partly be captured by unrolling the program.[3]

The point of this example is that the ith computation of $y + 1$ in the second loop has the same value as x has after executing i iterations of the first loop. Hence, eliminating all partial redundancies would require to unroll both loops infinitely often. On the other hand, there are also situations where redundancies in cyclic programs can be fully eliminated. Figure 5(b) gives an example where even "classical" semantic code motion techniques succeed (cf. Figure 5(c)). The essential difference between both situations is that in case of Figure 5(b) the value of $x + 1$ is immediately available for a usage before it is recomputed while

---

[3] In fact, every process ending with a finite program will fail.

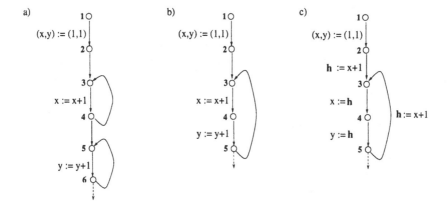

Fig. 5. a) Cyclic program with non-eliminable redundancies b) Cyclic program with eliminable redundancies c) Code motion transformation of b).

in Figure 5(a) the value is possibly rewritten an unbounded number of times while still being usable. The notion of partial k-redundancies (cf. Definition 2) is tuned for taking this phenomenon into account. In essence, a k-redundancy can be eliminated by keeping a value for at most k loop iterations.[4]

In our demand-driven expansion process this is reflected in a mechanism which keeps the semantic equivalence information finite, while being tailored for eliminating all partial k-redundancies. In particular, this assures the termination of the expansion process. Moreover, in acyclic programs every partial redundancy is a partial 0-redundancy. Thus, for *acyclic* programs our algorithm eliminates *all* partial redundancies. This is achieved while simultaneously all the complications associated with semantic code motion and placement are avoided. All this is out of the scope of any structure-preserving[5] approach as demonstrated by the example of Figure 2.

The enormous optimizing power of our algorithm comes at the price of an in the worst case exponential program growth. The new technique is therefore not meant to completely replace previous SPRE-algorithms. Rather it is an extremely powerful means for optimizing the "hot" spots of a program, which can be assumed to be considerably small. Here, our approach is particularly promising because its conceptual and structural simplicity make it easily extensible to uniformly capture further powerful optimisations like partially redundant assignment elimination, constant propagation, or strength reduction.

---

[4] Note that except for the redundancy of Figure 5(a) all other redundancies occurring in the examples discussed so far are partial 0-redundancies.

[5] Here and in the following "structure-preserving" is used as a shorthand for *flow-graph-structure* preserving.

2 Preliminaries

We consider procedures of imperative programs, which we represent by means of directed edge-labelled *flow graphs* $G = (N, E, \mathbf{s}, \mathbf{e})$ with node set N, edge set E, a unique *start node* $\mathbf{s}$ and *end node* $\mathbf{e}$, which are assumed to have no incoming and outgoing edges, respectively. The edges of G represent both the statements and the nondeterministic control flow of the underlying procedure, while the nodes represent program points. We assume that all statements are either the *empty statement* "skip" or a *3-address assignment* of the form $x := y$ or $x := y_1 \; op \; y_2$ where x, y, y_1, y_2 are variables and op a binary operator. However, an extension to assignments involving complex right-hand side terms is straightforward. Unlabelled edges are assumed to represent "skip."

For a flow graph G, let $pred(n)$ and $succ(n)$ denote the set of all immediate predecessors and successors of a node n. Similarly, let $source(e)$ and $dest(e)$ denote the source and the destination node of an edge e. A *finite path* in G is a sequence $\langle e_1, \dots, e_q \rangle$ of edges such that $dest(e_j) = source(e_{j+1})$ for $j \in \{1, \dots, q-1\}$. It is a path from m to n, if $source(e_1) = m$ and $dest(e_q) = n$. $\mathbf{P}[m, n]$ denotes the set of all finite paths from m to n, and for $p \in \mathbf{P}[n, m]$ and $q \in \mathbf{P}[m, n']$ the concatenation of p and q will be written as $p; q$. Without loss of generality we assume that every node $n \in N$ lies on a path from $\mathbf{s}$ to $\mathbf{e}$. An edge of a path p which is labelled by an assignment is called a *constituent* of p. The set of constituents of a path p is denoted by $\mathcal{C}(p)$. Finally, $\#_e(p)$ denotes the number of occurrences of edge e on a path p.

The *semantics* of terms is induced by the *Herbrand interpretation* $\mathbf{H} = (\mathbf{T}, \mathbf{H_0})$, where the data domain is given by the set of terms $\mathbf{T}$ which are inductively composed of variables, constants, and operators, and $\mathbf{H_0}$ is the function which maps every constant c to c and every operator op to the total function $\mathbf{H_0}(op)$: $\mathbf{T} \times \mathbf{T} \to \mathbf{T}$ defined by $\mathbf{H_0}(op)(t_1, t_2) =_{df} op(t_1, t_2)$. $\Sigma = \{\sigma \mid \sigma : \mathbf{V} \to \mathbf{T}\}$ denotes the set of all *Herbrand states* and σ_0 the distinct *start state* which is the identity on $\mathbf{V}$. The *semantics* of terms $t \in \mathbf{T}$ is given by the *Herbrand semantics* $\mathbf{H}$: $\mathbf{T} \to (\Sigma \to \mathbf{T})$ which is inductively defined by:

$$\mathbf{H}(t)(\sigma) =_{df} \begin{cases} \sigma(v) & \text{if } t = v \text{ is a variable} \\ \mathbf{H_0}(c) & \text{if } t = c \text{ is a constant} \\ \mathbf{H_0}(op)(\mathbf{H}(t_1)(\sigma), \mathbf{H}(t_2)(\sigma)) & \text{if } t = op(t_1, t_2) \end{cases}$$

With every edge e a state transformation and a backward substitution function are associated. If $e \equiv x := t$ the corresponding state transformation is defined by $\theta_e(\sigma) =_{df} \sigma[\mathbf{H}(t)(\sigma)/x]$, and the backward-substitution of e for a term t' is defined by $\delta_e(t') =_{df} t'[t/x]$. If e represents skip, the two functions are the identity on their domain. These definitions can inductively be extended to finite paths. The following result describes their relationship:

Lemma 1. $\forall \sigma \in \Sigma \; \forall \, t \in \mathbf{T}. \; \mathbf{H}(t)(\theta_e(\sigma)) = \mathbf{H}(\delta_e(t))(\sigma)$

Now, we can define the notion of (semantically) partially redundant computations:

Definition 1. *Let* $e_1 \equiv x_1 := t_1$ *and* $e_2 \equiv x_2 := t_2$ *be labelled edges and* $n_i =_{df} source(e_i)$, $m_i =_{df} dest(e_i)$ $(i = 1, 2)$.

1. t_2 *at* e_2 *is* partially redundant *with respect to* t_1 *at* e_1 *iff*

$$\exists p \in \mathbf{P}[m_1, n_2] \; \exists q \in \mathbf{P}[\mathbf{s}, n_1]. \; \mathbf{H}(t_1)(\theta_q(\sigma_0)) = \mathbf{H}(t_2)(\theta_{q;\langle e_1 \rangle;p}(\sigma_0))$$

2. t_2 *at* e_2 *is* strong partially redundant *with respect to* t_1 *at* e_1 *iff*

$$\exists p \in \mathbf{P}[m_1, n_2] \; \forall q \in \mathbf{P}[\mathbf{s}, n_1]. \; \mathbf{H}(t_1)(\theta_q(\sigma_0)) = \mathbf{H}(t_2)(\theta_{q;\langle e_1 \rangle;p}(\sigma_0))$$

3. t_2 *at* e_2 *is* (strong) totally redundant *iff every path* $p \in \mathbf{P}[\mathbf{s}, n_2]$ *contains an edge* $e_3 \equiv x_3 := t_3$ *such that* t_2 *at* e_2 *is (strong) partially redundant with respect to* t_3 *at* e_3.

Obviously, strong partial redundancy implies partial redundancy, and strong total redundancy total redundancy. Figure 2 demonstrated that structure-invariant approaches fail to eliminate some partial redundancies and even some total non-strong ones. In fact, they are only complete for the class of strong total redundancies (cf. Definition 1(3)).

As discussed in Section 1 it is impossible to eliminate all partial redundancies because the number of values to be stored for later reuse can be unbounded. The notion of k-redundancy introduced next is tuned to take this into account. Intuitively, k-redundancies can be eliminated by keeping values for at most k loop iterations. This notion of redundancy is not only reasonably general, it is also scalable due its parameterisation in k. In fact, the choice of k provides an easy handle to control the trade-off between power and performance of our algorithm.

Definition 2. *Let* $k \in \mathbb{N}$. *In the situation of Definition 1 we call* t_2 *at* e_2 *partially* k-redundant *with respect to* t_1 *at* e_1 *iff*

$$\exists p \in \mathbf{P}[m_1, n_2]. \; \#_{e_1}(p) \leq k \; \wedge \; \exists q \in \mathbf{P}[\mathbf{s}, n_1]$$
$$\forall q' \in \mathbf{P}[\mathbf{s}, n_1]. \; \mathcal{C}(q) = \mathcal{C}(q') \Rightarrow \mathbf{H}(t_1)(\theta_{q'}(\sigma_0)) = \mathbf{H}(t_2)(\theta_{q';\langle e_1 \rangle;p}(\sigma_0))$$

Essentially, the condition $\#_{e_1}(p) \leq k$ ensures that the value of t_1 has to be preserved for at most k loop iterations. Like the notion of strong partial redundancy also the one of partial k-redundancy rests on a set of paths entering n_1. While, however, in the definition of strong partial redundancy p must fit for all paths entering n_1, p in Definition 2 must only fit for the subset of paths sharing the same constituents. Thus, for acyclic control flow partial k-redundancy coincides for every k with the "weak" variant of partial redundancy of Definition 1(1).

Two expressions t_1 and t_2 are called *Herbrand equivalent* at node n, in symbols $t_1 \stackrel{H}{\sim}_n t_2$, iff $\forall p \in \mathbf{P}[\mathbf{s}, n]. \; \mathbf{H}(t_1)(\theta_p(\sigma_0)) = \mathbf{H}(t_2)(\theta_p(\sigma_0))$. Herbrand equivalences (or *transparent equivalences* (cf. [15])) can be compactly represented by means of structured partition DAGs (SPDAGs). In essence, an SPDAG is a DAG (directed acyclic graph) whose nodes are labelled with constants, operators and variables such that[6]

---

[6] A formal definition can be found in [18].

- leaf nodes are labelled with at most one constant and (possibly many) variables, and
- inner nodes are labelled with at most one operator and (possibly many) variables, and
- constants and variables are assigned to at most one node, and
- two inner nodes with the same operator have different left or right children.

An SPDAG D induces a unique partition on the terms T_D that are represented by D. Figure 6 depicts the partition view of the leftmost SPDAG. We write $t_1 \equiv_D t_2$ to indicate that $t_1, t_2 \in T_D$ are in the same class of D. An instruc-

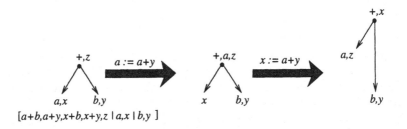

Fig. 6. Sequence of assignments and the associated transformations on SPDAGs

tion ι of the flow graph induces a flow function f_ι on SPDAGs which for a given SPDAG D computes the SPDAG that represents the equalities after executing ι. While f_{skip} is the identity on SPDAGs, computing the effect of $f_{x := t}$ comprises the following three steps:

i) expanding D by t if it is not yet present in D,
ii) changing the variable position of x, and
iii) eliminating unlabelled leaves and their ingoing edges.[7]

Figures 6 illustrates this process by showing the impact of two assignments to an initial SPDAG.

3 The Algorithm

3.1 Overview

Conceptually, our algorithm consists of two stages:

- *Expansion stage*: in this phase the program model is partly unrolled according to a guided demand-driven expansion process. During this stage variables are renamed according to a naming discipline which keeps track of the values computed.

---

[7] This may generate nodes with operator labelling whose operands are (partly) missing. At such nodes the operator labels and outgoing edges are removed. As this possibly generates new unlabelled leaves, the process has to be iterated.

– *Elimination stage*: in this phase redundant computations are replaced by a reference to a variable storing the relevant value.

Note, in an implementation, both stages can be combined, i.e., replacing redundant computations can be done on-the-fly while unrolling. In the following we will describe both stages in detail.

The expansion stage As in the syntactic case the process of expansion is guided by a property-oriented duplication of the original program points (cf. [17]). While, however, in the syntactic setting the properties guiding this process are redundancy sets containing patterns of program assignments, the properties here are given in terms of SPDAGs. The expansion process for programs proceeds in four steps:

1. Set $(\mathbf{s}, \bot)$ to be a reachable node of the expanded program, where $\bot$ denotes the empty SPDAG.
2. Choose a yet non-processed node (n, D) of the expanded program and mark it as processed.
3. For each edge $e = (n, m)$ in the original flow graph (cf. Section 3.2 for details):
   (a) construct a modified edge label ι_{mod} from the label ι of e.
   (b) consider the pair $(m, f^k_{\iota_{mod}}(D))$, and add it to the set of reachable nodes of the expanded flow graph, whenever it is new. $f^k_{\iota_{mod}}$ is the k-restricted flow-function associated with instruction ι_{mod}.
   (c) Draw an edge with label ι_{mod} between (n, D) and $(m, f^k_{\iota_{mod}}(D))$.
4. Continue with the second step until all reachable nodes are processed.

The elimination stage In this stage every labelling $x := x_1 \; op \; x_2$ of an edge e is replaced by $x := y$ if the SPDAG D annotating $source(e)$ contains information on the equality of y and $x_1 \; op \; x_2$, i.e., $y \equiv_D x_1 \; op \; x_2$. In the case that x equals y the complete assignment can be removed.

3.2 Details

The application of the flow functions f_ι as introduced in Section 2 results easily in the construction of annotating SPDAGs of unbounded size when applied to programs with loops. However, by restricting the flow functions it is possible to limit the growth of the SPDAGs while retaining enough information in order to capture partial k-redundancy completely. In essence, this is achieved by using a well-suited naming discipline to keep track of old values, and by carefully cutting SPDAGs.

Naming discipline The name space for values is restricted to the variable names of the original program plus a set of fresh indexed variables $x^{(e,i)}$, where

x is a variable, e an edge of the original program, and $0 \leq i \leq k$ a counter.[8] Intuitively, fresh variables are used to store values generated by different instances of the same statement during the expansion process. To keep track on the current names of variables each generated node (n, D) of the expanded flow graph is associated with

- a mapping $cnt_{(n,D)}[\bullet] : E \to [0, k]$ that maintains for each edge e of the original program the current counter value used to produce the name of the next instance.
- a mapping $curr_{(n,D)}[\bullet]$ from the name space of the original program to the name space of the expanded program. For a variable x of the original program $curr_{(n,D)}[x]$ denotes the current instance of x that is valid at node (n, D).

Initially, for $(\mathbf{s}, \perp)$ all counters $cnt_{(\mathbf{s}, \perp)}[e]$ are set to 0 and $curr_{(\mathbf{s}, \perp)}[x] = x$ for every variable x. Whenever a new edge $e' = ((n, D), (m, D'))$ is constructed the value of its edge counter associated with $e = (n, m)$ is incremented in a cyclic fashion:

$$cnt_{(m,D')}[e] = (cnt_{(n,D)}[e] + 1) \bmod (k + 1)$$

Moreover, if $x^{(e,i)}$ is the left-hand side variable of the edge label of e' then the current instance is updated accordingly:[9]

$$curr_{(m,D')}[x] = x^{(e,i)}$$

All other counters and values of current variables are unalteredly adopted from (n, D). It should be noted that this process is similar to the SSA-naming discipline (cf. [8, 15]). However, it totally avoids the necessity of introducing ϕ-functions.

Modifying edge annotations While processing an edge $e = (n, m)$ of the original flow graph labelled with $x := t$, the constructed transition in the expanded model is labelled with a renamed assignment $x^{(e,i)} := t'$. This happens in two steps. Firstly, all variables in the right-hand side expression t are replaced by their current instances associated with (n, D), i.e., $t' = curr_{(n,D)}[t]$.[10] Secondly, the instance of the left-hand side variable is determined by the associated e-counter at (n, D), i.e., $i = cnt_{(n,D)}[e]$.

k-restricted flow functions The previous steps alone are not sufficient to avoid unbounded growth of SPDAGs. This is achieved by a modification of the flow functions that eliminates "unreferencable" parts of SPDAGs. Let (n, D) be a constructed node of the expanded flow graph and ι an instruction. The k-restricted flow function $f_\iota^k(D)$ is realized through a two-step procedure.

---

[8] For $k = 0$ the second parameter is sometimes omitted for the sake of presentation.

[9] Note that $x^{(e,i)}$ is computed exploiting information on the counters (see paragraph "Modifying edge annotations").

[10] $curr_{(n,D)}[t]$ denotes the straightforward extension of $curr_{(n,D)}[\bullet]$ to terms.

1. *Computing the value flow:* D is subjected to the standard flow function f_ι.
2. *Cutting the resulting SPDAG:* nodes carrying only an operator label are eliminated together with their ingoing and outgoing edges. This may leave some operator labels at leaf nodes which must also be removed.

We demonstrate our algorithm for $k = 0$ using the example of Figure 3(a) for illustration. After the expansion phase we get the program depicted in Figure 7, annotated with SPDAGs at its program points. Instances of a node $\mathbf{n}$ of the original program are numbered $\mathbf{n\text{-}1},\mathbf{n\text{-}2}$, etc. Moreover, e_1 to e_4 refer to the four edges labelled with $c := a$, $(x, y) := (a + b, c + b)$, $z := a + b$ and $z := c + b$, respectively. The results from the elimination phase are emphasized by the grey arrows. Note that the equality of x and $a + b$ at node $\mathbf{7\text{-}2}$ and of y and $c + b$ at node $\mathbf{9\text{-}2}$ allows us to replace the right-hand side expressions on the edges ($\mathbf{7\text{-}2},\mathbf{8\text{-}2}$) and ($\mathbf{9\text{-}2},\mathbf{10\text{-}2}$), which cannot be eliminated by motion-based redundancy elimination techniques.

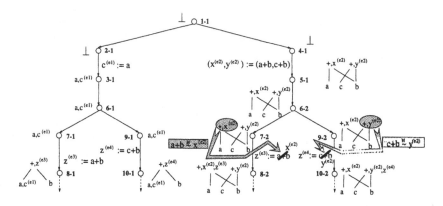

Fig. 7. Illustrating the algorithm for Figure 3(a).

3.3 Results

The algorithm is correct, i.e., it preserves the semantics of its argument programs. The proof of this property benefits from Lemma 2. Its first part is fundamental for proving the correctness of the expansion phase, while the $\Leftarrow$-direction of its second part guarantees the correctness of the replacements of the elimination phase.

The lemma requires the following projections relating the expanded and the original program. A path p in the expanded program has a unique corresponding path p_o in the original one, and a variable x which is part of an edge label in the expanded flow graph has a unique corresponding variable x_o in the original flow graph. It simply results from removing the optional superscript; a process, which applies naturally to terms, too.

Lemma 2. *Let (n, D) be a node in the expanded program (before the elimination phase), and $x := t$ the edge annotation of an outgoing edge of (n, D). Then we have:*

1. $\forall p \in \mathbf{P}[(\mathbf{s}, \perp), (n, D)]$. $\mathbf{H}(t_o)(\theta_{p_o}(\sigma_0)) = \mathbf{H}(t)(\theta_p(\sigma_0))$

2. $\forall t_1 \in T_D \; \forall t_2 \in \mathbf{T}$. $t_1 \overset{\mathbf{H}}{\sim}_{(n,D)} t_2 \iff t_1 \equiv_D t_2$

Both parts can be proved by induction, the first one on the length of path p and the second one on the length of a shortest path leading to (n, D). By means of Lemma 2, we can now prove the main result of this article:

Theorem 1 (k-Optimality). *For a given $k \in \mathbb{N}$ the procedure of Section 3 terminates after eliminating* all *partial k-redundancies of the argument program.*

Suppose there is an instance of a partial k-redundancy in the expanded program before the elimination step has been performed, say between t_1 at edge e_1 and t_2 at edge e_2. The definition of partial k-redundancy ensures that this partial redundancy is a strong one in the expanded program. This is because paths with distinct constituents lead to the construction of different SPDAGs, and hence to different nodes in the expanded program. Let p be the intermediate path between $dest(e_1) =_{df} (n, D_1)$ and $source(e_2) =_{df} (m, D_2)$, and $x^{(e_1, i)}$ the left-hand side variable associated with e_1.

Exploiting that the partial redundancy is strong, Lemma 1 yields that $\delta_p(t_2)$ is Herbrand-equivalent with t_1 at (n, D_1). Hence the $\Rightarrow$-direction of Lemma 2(2) ensures that $\delta_p(t_2)$ is contained in D_1 with $\delta_p(t_2) \equiv_{D_1} x^{(e_1, i)}$. Moreover, the definition of k-redundancy ensures that $x^{(e_1, i)}$ is not rewritten on p. With the definition of the flow functions f^k and with $D_2 = f_p^k(D_1)$ it is easy to see that $\delta_p(t_2) \in T_{D_1}$ implies that $t_2 \in T_{D_2}$. This finally grants $t_2 \equiv_{D_2} x^{(e_1, i)}$ which makes t_2 eliminable at e_2. It can be replaced by $x^{(e_1, i)}$.

Recall that for acyclic programs the notion of partial 0-redundancy coincides with partial redundancy. Thus, we get as an immediate corollary of Theorem 1:

Corollary 1. *On acyclic programs the procedure of Section 3 terminates for $k = 0$ after eliminating* all *partial redundancies of the argument program.*

In particular, this guarantees that our approach resolves for acyclic programs the motion/placement-anomalies of structure-invariant approaches. Moreover, the definition of strong partial redundancies immediately yields:

Corollary 2. *There exists a $k \in \mathbb{N}$ such that the procedure of Section 3 terminates after eliminating* all *strong partial redundancies of the argument program.*

4 Discussion

In this section we discuss some significant characteristics of our algorithm and illustrate them by examples which simultaneously demonstrate the power of the approach.

Initialisation freedom One of the most significant characteristics of our algorithm is that it does not lengthen any execution sequence of the original program. This is in contrast to the structure-invariant setting where optimisations come at the price of inserting initialisation statements. This reflects an abstract cost model, where initialisations are for free. Rosen, Wegman and Zadeck criticised such a model as impractical [15], since even in acyclic programs the elimination of some redundancies requires reinitialisation chains of arbitrary length, whose execution costs may easily exceed those of the saved computations.

Loop unrolling It is well-known that loop-invariant computations like those in the example of Figure 8(a) can be eliminated by unrolling the loop once because the previously partially redundant computations become totally redundant and can therefore be eliminated. Figure 8(b) shows the corresponding final result of this conventional approach. It is worth comparing this result with the

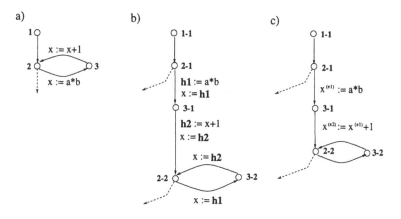

Fig. 8. Loop unrolling vs. expansion.

result of our approach depicted in Figure 8(c). Based on the for code motion typical assumption that reinitialisations are for free, the "classical result" introduces additional assignments to temporaries on program paths. In contrast, our solution (for $k = 0$) does not have any additional assignments and is therefore optimal independently of any simplifying assumptions. In particular, the assignments $x^{(e_1)} := a * b$ and $x^{(e_2)} := x^{(e_1)} + 1$ labeling the edges inside of the loop after the expansion phase are completely removed as they reduce to assignments $x^{(e_1)} := x^{(e_1)}$ and $x^{(e_2)} := x^{(e_2)}$, respectively. In the case of Figure 8(b) obtaining an equivalent effect requires a postprocess, e.g. a combination of dead code elimination [1] and redundant assignment elimination [11].

Loop-carried redundancies "Loop-carried" partial redundancies reveal the function of the parameter k in our algorithm.

The example of Figure 9(a) shows a program that has a loop structure where the computation of $y+1$ is (strongly) redundant with respect to the computation of $x+1$ of the previous iteration. In the structure invariant setting this "loop-carried" redundancy can be eliminated by means of an additional reinitialisation statement as shown in Figure 9(b). By inserting a higher number of x-increments in front of the loop in Figure 9(a) one can easily construct examples where the elimination of a loop carried redundancy requires reinitialisation sequences of arbitrary length.

In contrast, the expansion-based approach is capable of removing redundancies carried over k loop iterations without introducing any additional assignment on a program path. Figure 9(c) shows the result of our algorithm for $k = 1$. Essentially, the expansion process automatically results in a program where two loop iterations of the original program are combined to a single loop with two exits.

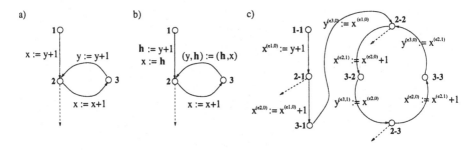

Fig. 9. Elimination of loop-carried (strong) redundancies.

5 Related Work

Semantic redundancy elimination has been pioneered by the *value numbering* approach of Cocke and Schwartz [7], which, however, was tailored for basic block optimisation. Algorithms aiming at the *global* elimination of semantic partial redundancies have been first proposed in [15, 16, 18, 19], and more recently in [3, 12].[11] Common to all of these algorithms is to respect the constraint of structural invariance, and their phase structure. As the impact of structural invariance has been investigated in the previous sections, we here focus on the second point, the phase structure. The algorithm of [12], for instance, consists of three stages each with up to three substeps which require considerably complex analyses.

In comparison, the algorithm proposed here consists only (of a simplified variant) of one of the substeps. This step, the computation of equivalence information by means of an algorithm matching the pattern of Kildall's algorithm

---

[11] The "global" algorithms proposed in [5, 14] have a slightly different accent as they concentrate on motion to dominators.

[10], is significantly simpler.[12] The computation of the meet of equivalence information at merge points, a computational bottleneck, is replaced by the much simpler test of equality, which is used to trigger the node splitting. Hence, our extremely powerful optimisation algorithm is very easy to implement. This comes at the price of an in the worst case exponential program growth. Thus, as discussed below, the practical application of this aggressive algorithm requires some care.

6 Conclusions and Perspectives

Previous approaches for eliminating semantic partial redundancies are all designed under the maxim of structural invariance, i.e., not to affect the program structure. Unfortunately, under this constraint the SPRE-problem lacks a satisfying solution even for acyclic programs. Dropping the constraint, and trading size against efficiency, we developed a new SPRE-algorithm working by property-oriented expansion, which eliminates all partial k-redundancies. In acyclic programs it eliminates even all partial redundancies.

These optimality results come at the price of an in the worst case exponential program growth. The new technique is therefore not meant to completely replace previous SPRE-algorithms. Rather it is an extremely powerful means for optimizing the "hot" spots of a program, which can be assumed to be considerably small. Here, our approach is particularly promising, because of its structural simplicity the new algorithm is open for extensions. Optimisations like partially redundant assignment elimination (cf. [11, 17]), constant propagation (cf. [9, 10]), or strength reduction (cf. [2, 6]) can uniformly be integrated which results in an extremely powerful expansion-based algorithm, where the integrated techniques mutually profit from each other. The integration boils essentially down to exploiting arithmetic properties of term operators and evaluating terms accordingly in the fashion of the strength reduction algorithm of [19]. All this can be done on-the-fly during the expansion process. In this manner it is possible to obtain a demand-driven uniform algorithm capturing the strong interdependencies and their corresponding problem of good application orders (cf. [20]).

References

1. A. V. Aho, R. Sethi, and J. D. Ullman. *Compilers: Principles, Techniques and Tools*. Addison-Wesley, 1985.
2. F. E. Allen, J. Cocke, and K. Kennedy. Reduction of operator strength. In S. S. Muchnick and N. D. Jones, editors, *Program Flow Analysis: Theory and Applications*, chapter 3, pages 79 – 101. Prentice Hall, Englewood Cliffs, New Jersey, 1981.

---

[12] Note that redundancy elimination boils down to locally look up the required value in the respective SPDAG.

3. R. Bodík and S. Anik. Path-sensitive value-flow analysis. In *Conf. Rec. 25th Symp. on Principles of Programming Languages (POPL'98)*, pages 237 – 251. ACM, NY, 1998.

4. R. Bodík, R. Gupta, and M.-L. Soffa. Complete removal of redundant expressions. In *Proc. ACM SIGPLAN Conf. Prog. Lang. Design and Impl. (PLDI'98)*, volume *33* of *ACM SIGPLAN Not.*, pages 1 – 14, 1998.

5. C. Click. Global code motion/global value numbering. In *Proc. ACM SIGPLAN Conf. Prog. Lang. Design and Impl. (PLDI'95)*, volume *30,6* of *ACM SIGPLAN Not.*, pages 246–257, 1995.

6. J. Cocke and K. Kennedy. An algorithm for reduction of operator strength. *Comm. ACM*, 20(11):850 – 856, 1977.

7. J. Cocke and J. T. Schwartz. Programming languages and their compilers. Courant Inst. Math. Sciences, NY, 1970.

8. R. Cytron, J. Ferrante, B. K. Rosen, M. N. Wegman, and F. K. Zadeck. Efficiently computing static single assignment form and the control dependence graph. *ACM Trans. Prog. Lang. Syst.*, 13(4):451 – 490, 1991.

9. J. B. Kam and J. D. Ullman. Monotone data flow analysis frameworks. *Acta Informatica*, 7:305 – 317, 1977.

10. G. A. Kildall. A unified approach to global program optimization. In *Conf. Rec. 1st Symp. Principles of Prog. Lang. (POPL'73)*, pages 194 – 206. ACM, NY, 1973.

11. J. Knoop, O. Rüthing, and B. Steffen. The power of assignment motion. In *Proc. ACM SIGPLAN Conf. on Prog. Lang. Design and Impl. (PLDI'95)*, volume *30,6* of *ACM SIGPLAN Not.*, pages 233 – 245, 1995.

12. J. Knoop, O. Rüthing, and B. Steffen. Code motion and code placement: Just synomyms? In *Proc. 7th European Symp. on Programming (ESOP'98)*, LNCS 1381, pages 154 – 169. Springer-V., 1998.

13. E. Morel and C. Renvoise. Global optimization by suppression of partial redundancies. *Comm. ACM*, 22(2):96 – 103, 1979.

14. J. H. Reif and R. Lewis. Symbolic evaluation and the global value graph. In *Conf. Rec. 4th Symp. Principles of Prog. Lang. (POPL'77)*, pages 104 – 118. ACM, NY, 1977.

15. B. K. Rosen, M. N. Wegman, and F. K. Zadeck. Global value numbers and redundant computations. In *Conf. Rec. 15th Symp. Principles of Prog. Lang. (POPL'88)*, pages 2 – 27. ACM, NY, 1988.

16. B. Steffen. Optimal run time optimization - Proved by a new look at abstract interpretations. In *Proc. 2nd Int. Conf. Theory and Practice of Software Development (TAPSOFT'87)*, LNCS 249, pages 52 – 68. Springer-V., 1987.

17. B. Steffen. Property-oriented expansion. In *Proc. 3rd Stat. Analysis Symp. (SAS'96)*, LNCS 1145, pages 22 – 41. Springer-V., 1996.

18. B. Steffen, J. Knoop, and O. Rüthing. The value flow graph: A program representation for optimal program transformations. In *Proc. 3rd Europ. Symp. Programming (ESOP'90)*, LNCS 432, pages 389 – 405. Springer-V., 1990.

19. B. Steffen, J. Knoop, and O. Rüthing. Efficient code motion and an adaption to strength reduction. In *Proc. 4th Int. Conf. Theory and Practice of Software Development (TAPSOFT'91)*, LNCS 494, pages 394 – 415. Springer-V., 1991.

20. D. Whitfield and M. L. Soffa. An approach to ordering optimizing transformations. In *Proc. 2nd ACM SIGPLAN Symp. on Principles and Practice of Parallel Programming (PPOPP'90)*, volume *25,3* of *ACM SIGPLAN Not.*, pages 137 – 147, 1990.

Register Pressure Sensitive Redundancy Elimination*

Rajiv Gupta and Rastislav Bodík

Dept. of Computer Science, Univ. of Pittsburgh, Pittsburgh, PA 15260, USA

Abstract. *Redundancy elimination* optimizations avoid repeated computation of the same value by computing the value once, saving it in a temporary, and reusing the value from the temporary when it is needed again. Examples of redundancy elimination optimizations include common subexpression elimination, loop invariant code motion and partial redundancy elimination. We demonstrate that the introduction of temporaries to save computed values can result in a significant increase in register pressure. An increase in register pressure may in turn trigger generation of spill code which can more than offset the gains derived from redundancy elimination. While current techniques *minimize* increases in register pressure, to avoid spill code generation it is instead necessary to ensure that register pressure *does not exceed* the number of available registers.

In this paper we develop a redundancy elimination algorithm that is sensitive to register pressure: our novel technique first sets upper limits on allowed register pressure and then performs redundancy elimination within these limits. By setting strict register pressure limits for frequently executed (hot) blocks and higher limits for infrequently executed (cold) blocks, our algorithm permits trade-off between redundancy removal from hot blocks at the expense of introducing spill code in cold blocks. In addition, the program profile is also used to prioritize optimizable expressions; when not enough registers are available, the most profitable redundancies are removed first. To increase redundancy elimination within the allowed register pressure, our algorithm lowers the pressure with two new program transformation techniques: (a) whenever possible, we avoid inserting a temporary and instead access the reused value from existing variables, which reduces the life time of the temporary beyond existing live-range optimal algorithms; and (b) the live ranges of variables referenced by the expressions are shortened by combining expression hoisting with assignment sinking.

Keywords - data flow analysis, code optimization, partial redundancy elimination, partial dead code elimination, code motion, register pressure, spill code.

---

* Supported in part by NSF grants CCR-9808590, EIA-9806525 and a grant from Intel Corporation to the University of Pittsburgh.

1 Introduction

Redundancy elimination is an important commonly implemented optimization. Loop invariant code motion (LICM) eliminates from loops statements that compute the same value in each loop iteration. Global common subexpression elimination (CSE) eliminates an expression that is preceded by an identical computation along all incoming paths. Finally, partial redundancy elimination (PRE) subsumes LICM and CSE by eliminating redundancy from instructions that are redundant along only a subset of incoming paths [1, 6, 7, 9, 13, 14, 16, 17, 19]. Since PRE is the most general redundancy elimination, the focus of this paper is on developing an improved PRE algorithm.

PRE algorithms avoid repeated computation of the same value by computing the value once, saving it in a temporary, and reusing the value from the temporary when it is needed again. In the code below, the recomputation of X+Y is optimized away by remembering its value in the temporary temp.

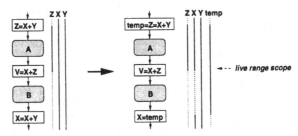

However, an additional register must be allocated for temp, increasing the register pressure in block A. This increase in register pressure may result in generation of memory intensive spill code, which can more than offset the gains derived from redundancy elimination. While it is widely believed that PRE impacts register pressure, and some existing algorithms even attempt to minimize register pressure increase [15, 17], the effects of PRE algorithms on register pressure have not been evaluated.

Let us consider the impact of *lazy code motion* [17] PRE on register pressure (although [15] is the best known algorithm, our implementation currently supports [17]). The algorithm attempts to reduce the increase in register pressure by minimizing the lengths of live ranges for the temporaries introduced to hold values of redundant expressions. Figure 1a illustrates the effect of lazy code motion on register pressure. Plotted in this graph is the average register pressure (y-axis) for all basic blocks that have a given execution frequency (x-axis). The top curve shows the running average of register pressure (i.e., the number of live ranges crossing the basic block entry) prior to the application of PRE. The middle and the bottom curves give the average number of live ranges added and removed due to PRE. For example, block B above has one added and one removed live range (temp vs. X). The overall change in register pressure is the difference of the middle and the bottom curves.

This graph documents that PRE causes a significant (approx. 25%) average increase in register pressure. Most importantly, the increase is not limited to low frequency basic blocks; the resulting spill loads and stores might slow down important, hot basic blocks. The graph reflects only redundancy of expressions that are lexically identical; if our experiments used value numbering techniques to discover additional redundancies [4, 6, 20], significantly higher increases in register pressure would be observed [2, 6].

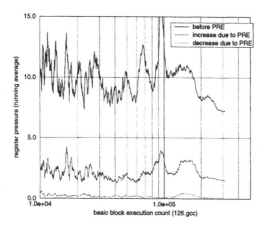

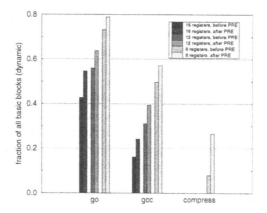

Fig. 1. Effect of lazy code motion PRE on register pressure: (a) Each point corresponds to the average number of live ranges (y) of all basic blocks with a given execution frequency (x). There were about 82,000 executed basic blocks in program 126.gcc from SPEC95. (b) Bars plot the number of executed basic blocks whose register pressure exceeded given limit before and after PRE.

Register pressure changes are harmful only if spill code is generated as a result. Our second experiment aimed to determine whether PRE may indeed increase the pressure above the number of commonly available physical registers, triggering spill code generation. We measured the dynamic number of executed basic blocks whose pressure was above 16, 12, and 8 registers, both before and after PRE. As shown in Figure 1b, the increase in the fraction of basic blocks that exceeded these limits is significant (5–10%). This increase translates to a corresponding increase of basic blocks that will execute some spill code after PRE.

The second experiment exposes the practical inadequacy of the current techniques [15,17], in which minimizing register pressure comes only second to the primary goal of maximizing redundancy removal. Figure 1b convinces us that removing *all* redundancy at any cost may be harmful as it may still cause a significant spill code. We argue that an effective PRE must instead consider redundancy removal and register pressure in balance: when no more registers are available, remaining PRE opportunities must be sacrificed.

Another important observation behind our algorithm is that some PRE opportunities may decrease register pressure (for example, see the live range of X in block B in our example). Therefore, when selecting the subset of PRE opportunities to optimize, these expressions can be used to enable optimization of more important expressions. Furthermore, since numerous basic blocks exceed available register resources already prior to PRE, in addition to minimizing register pressure increases, these pressure releaving expressions might eliminate spill code that was present prior to PRE.

In order to address the above issues we have developed a new register pressure sensitive redundancy elimination algorithm with the following characteristics:

- Our algorithm sets upper limits on allowed register pressure and attempts to maximize elimination of dynamically observed redundancy within these limits. While strict register pressure limits are set for frequently executed (hot) blocks, higher register pressures are permitted in infrequently executed (cold) blocks. Therefore, insufficient registers in cold blocks do not prevent optimization in hot blocks.

- Since under limited register resources our algorithm may exploit only a subset of PRE opportunities, estimates of dynamic PRE benefits are used to give higher priority to the removal of redundancies that yield the most benefit. Moreover, by applying PRE in situations where a reduction in register pressure results, we further enable exploitation of additional PRE opportunities.

- To minimize increase in register pressure, the life time of a *temporary* is reduced beyond existing live-range optimal algorithms [17] by accessing the value from existing program variables that already contain the value. Only when the reused value is not by available in any existing variable, a temporary is introduced to carry the value. In comparison with [17], we reduce temporary live ranges on all paths, rather than only on paths where the value was previously not available. In our example, we would initialize temp from Z after block A, rather than before it, avoiding pressure increase in block A.

- Further reductions in register pressure can be achieved by minimizing the live ranges of *program variables* referenced by optimized expressions through a combination of expression hoisting with assignment sinking. In our example, sinking Z=X+Y to below block A would reduce the live range of Z, without extending live ranges of X and Y. We describe how sinking and hoisting can be used for register pressure sensitive PRE.

2 Register Pressure Guided PRE

We begin by providing an overview of our algorithm, then we discuss the critical steps of the algorithm in greater detail. As shown in Figure 2, our algorithm begins by computing the register pressure and setting an upper limit on the register pressure for each basic block based upon profile information. The register pressure is computed as the maximum number of live variables at any point in the basic block. If the register pressure of a block is already equal to or higher than this limit, no further increases would be allowed. On the other hand if the pressure is lower than the limit, increases up to the limit are allowed.

To uncover opportunities for PRE, anticipability and availability analysis is performed as described in [1]. The dynamic benefit of optimization opportunities associated with each lexical expression is computed using profile data [1]. PRE within the limits of allowed increases in register pressure is performed using a greedy algorithm which prioritizes the expressions according to their benefits and applies PRE to the expression with highest benefit first.

```
for each basic block B
    Determine register pressure RP(B)
    Set register pressure limit, LRP(B), based on freq(B)
end for
for each lexical expression exp
    Perform availability and anticipability analysis on exp
    Compute dynamic benefit of applying PRE to exp
end for
while all expressions have not been considered
    Select the unoptimized expression, uexp,
        with the highest dynamic benefit
    for each basic block B involved in PRE of uexp
        Compute uexp's PRE caused register pressure changes, δRP(B)
        if δRP(B) + RP(B) > LRP(B) then
            Attempt to reduce register pressure of B by
            LRP(B)-δRP(B) + RP(B) by hoisting
            of expressions out of B
            if register pressure is not adequately reduced then
                Inhibit expression hoisting of uexp through B
            end if
        end if
    end for
    Update availability and anticipability information to
        reflect inhibited expression hoisting
    Perform maximal PRE of uexp within register pressure limits
end while
Perform further PRE through assignment sinking
```

Fig. 2. Algorithm for register pressure guided PRE.

Once an expression has been selected for optimization, we compute the changes in register pressure that would result if all of the uncovered PRE opportunities involving that expression are exploited. If changes reflect that for some blocks the increase in register pressure would result in increased spill code, then we attempt to reduce register pressure in those blocks. The reductions are achieved by hoisting expressions out of the blocks with at least one operand that is no longer live after its use by the expression, since the live range of such an operand would be shortened upon hoisting. In other words expression hoisting would continue to shorten the live range of the operand variable until another use of the same operand is encountered. Of course it may not always be possible to achieve the desired reduction in register pressure for a basic block, in which case we inhibit the hoisting of the expression being optimized through that block. For the purpose of analysis, a point at which hoisting is inhibited is essentially viewed as a kill point for the expression. By doing so we inhibit the increase in the register pressure for the block. The affect of inhibiting code hoisting through the block is to disable those opportunities for PRE, involving the current expression, that are enabled by the inhibited code motion. We update the availability and anticipability information to reflect the killing affects of inhibited code motion by treating them as kill points for the current expression. Based upon updated anticipability information and availability information we perform the PRE transformation. In this way we perform PRE to the extent that is allowed by register pressure limits. The above process is similarly repeated for other expressions.

2.1 Using profile data

Profile information serves two important functions in our algorithm. First we use profile information to compute the dynamic benefit of redundancy removal for various expressions. The benefits are used to *selectively* apply PRE during which higher priority is given to redundancy elimination opportunities that result in the most benefit. The second use of profiling is in setting register pressure limits. In particular, strict register pressure limits are set on hot basic blocks while higher register pressure limits are set for cold blocks. In this way we are able to achieve redundancy removal in hot blocks at the expense of allowing spill code in cold blocks.

Setting priorities. Consider the example in Figure 3a in which redundancy exists both in the evaluations of X+Y and A+B. Profile information indicates that X+Y, which is repeatedly computed in the loop, should have priority over A+B. Let us assume that variables X, Y, A and B are live throughout the program and a single register is free. This register can be used to hold the value of T and thus removal of redundancy of X+Y is achieved, as shown in Figure 3b, without generation of additional spill code. Redundancy of A+B is not removed as there are no more free registers.

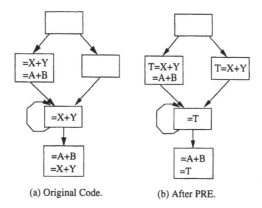

(a) Original Code.   (b) After PRE.

Fig. 3. Selective PRE: optimize high-benefit redundancies in a greedy fashion.

Setting register pressure limits. Next consider the example in Figure 4a. Assuming that the execution frequency of the highlighted path from block 1 to block 2 is very high, we would like to eliminate the redundancy involving X+Y from this path. Furthermore, let us assume that block 3 has a low execution frequency but high register pressure (A is live in block 3 but dead in blocks 1 and 2). If PRE is applied as shown in Figure 4b, the register pressure in block 3 would further increase. On the other hand, if we prevent register-pressure increase in block 3, and thus disable hoisting of X+Y above node 4, PRE along the highlighted path would not be achieved (Figure 4c). Given that the execution frequency of block 3 is low and hence spill code does no harm, it would be preferable to set a higher limit for block 3 and thus enable PRE along the frequently executed path. The register allocator would then either spill the value of T in block 3 as shown in Figure 4d or rematerialize [5] X+Y as shown in Figure 4e. Thus, by setting a higher register pressure limit for cold blocks we can trade-off PRE that benefits hot blocks at the cost of poorer performance for cold blocks.

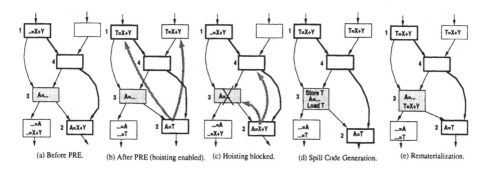

(a) Before PRE.   (b) After PRE (hoisting enabled).   (c) Hoisting blocked.   (d) Spill Code Generation.   (e) Rematerialization.

Fig. 4. Allowing register-pressure increases in cold blocks enables PRE in hot blocks.

2.2 Computing register pressure changes

PRE affects register pressure in two ways. First, because a temporary is introduced to carry the value of the redundant expression, the portions of the program over which the temporary is live experience an increase in register pressure. Second, because the redundant expression itself is hoisted, the live range of a variable referenced in the expression is shortened if the expression represents the last use of the variable, causing a decrease in register pressure. By determining the actual changes in live ranges for the temporary and for the expression operands, we compute the changes in register pressure that would result from PRE of the expression.

Live range of the temporary. Existing live-range optimal algorithms initialize the temporary at the point where the expression is computed for the first time, i.e., X:=A+B is replaced with T:=X:=A+B. The temporary T is then used to provide the value at points where redundant instances of A+B were removed. The temporary is however unnecessary at points where the value of A+B is still held by the left-hand-side variable X. Our approach is to further reduce the live range of the temporary by obtaining the value of the expression from other variables that may also contain its value.

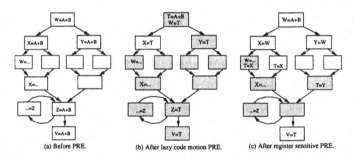

(a) Before PRE. (b) After lazy code motion PRE. (c) After register sensitive PRE.

Fig. 5. Introducing temporary to hold an expression's value.

Consider the example in Figure 5a which after traditional PRE results in the code shown in Figure 5b. As we can see the live range of the temporary T introduced in this case extends over the entire code segment (shown by shaded blocks). We can reduce the increase in register pressure by narrowing this live range as shown in Figure 5c. The reduction is achieved by exploiting the observation that in parts of the code the value of the expression is already available in existing variables. Note that in this approach copy assignments are introduced to initialize the temporary T at points where the live range of T begins. These copy assignments are typically eliminated during register allocation.

Next we present describe the computation of a new optimal live range for PRE which essentially works like the computation of live range in lazy code motion but delays the temporaries. This algorithm performs forward propagation of assignments which compute the expression under consideration. At each program point where at least one such assignment is available along all paths, the value of the expression can be accessed from the variable on the left hand side of that assignment and thus there is no need for a new temporary to hold the expression's value. The copy assignments are introduced at the latest points where the expression's value is available through an existing variable. In the analysis below, $\text{NAVAIL}_{op(x,y)}(n)(\text{XAVAIL}_{op(x,y)}(n))$ represents the must-availability of all program assignments which compute the lexical expression $op(x,y)$ at the entry(exit) of node n (i.e., must-availability for all assignments of the form $v:=op(x,y)$ is computed).

$$\text{NAVAIL}_{op(x,y)}(n) = \bigcap_{p \in Pred(n)} \text{XAVAIL}_{op(x,y)}(n) - \text{DEAD}_{op(x,y)}(n)$$

$$\text{XAVAIL}_{op(x,y)}(n) = (\text{NAVAIL}_{op(x,y)}(n) - \text{KILL}_{op(x,y)}(n)) \sqcup \text{GEN}_{op(x,y)}(n)$$

$$\text{DEAD}_{op(x,y)}(n) = \{\text{stat. } v:=op(x,y): v \text{ is dead at n's entry}\}$$

$$\text{KILL}_{op(x,y)}(n) = \{\text{stat. } v:=op(x,y): n \text{ defines x,y or v}\}$$

$$\text{GEN}_{op(x,y)}(n) = \{\text{stat. } v:=op(x,y): n \text{ computes } v:=op(x,y)\}$$

The above analysis will identify for the example in Figure 5c that the value of the expression A+B is available in variables W, Y and/or X is certain program regions while in others a new temporary T is required. The initialization of T through copying is performed at node exits that are the latest points at which the value of the expression is available in an existing variable (i.e., the value is not available at one of the sucessors of the node).

Live ranges of referenced variables. To track the changes in the live range of a referenced variable x when PRE for expression x+y is carried out, we must take into account the effect of hoisting x+y on x's liveness. We develop the notion of *PRE-liveness* in which the liveness of a variable x is computed in relation to an expression x+y which is being subjected to hoisting. Under this notion of liveness, x is live for x+y at a program point n if and only if even after PRE has been able to hoist x+y above n, x is still live at n. On the other hand if x is not live at n after PRE has hoisted x+y above n, then x is considered to be dead for x+y.

The notion of *PRE-liveness* is illustrated in Figure 6. Consider the situations in which multiple (say two) evaluations of x+y are present on a path and the latest evaluation of x+y represents the last use of x. If both of the evaluations of x+y are hoisted by PRE as shown in Figure 6a, then the live range of x will be shortened. Thus, x is considered to be dead for x+y at the exit of node 2 in Figure 6a. If the last evaluation of x+y cannot be hoisted due to a definition of y, then there is no change in the length of the live range of x. Thus, in Figure 6b x is considered to be live for x+y at the exit of node 2. If after the use of x in x+y, there is another use of x by an expression which is lexically different from x+y, then the length of x's live range will remain the same. Conservatively we consider a variable to be PRE-live if there is at least one path along which it is PRE-live. In Figure 6c x is considered to be live for x+y at the exit of node 2.

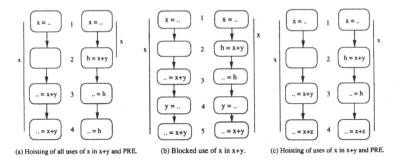

(a) Hoisting of all uses of x in x+y and PRE. (b) Blocked use of x in x+y. (c) Hoisting of uses of x in x+y and PRE.

Fig. 6. PRE-liveness of x: The live ranges after PRE are the PRE live ranges.

Definition: Variable x is *PRE-live* wrt expression op(x,y) at point n if and only if: (i) there exists a path from n to an evaluation of op(x,y) which does not contain any redefinition of x but contains a redefinition of y (see Figure 6b); or (ii) there exists a path from n to an evaluation of an expression op(x,-) (an expression which uses x and is lexically different from op(x,y)) which does not contain any redefinition of x (see Figure 6c).

Next we present the data flow equations for computing the PRE-liveness information. Since both conditions in the above definition require backward flow analysis, we can evaluate them simultaneously as a single data flow problem. For this purpose the data flow solution at a point is represented by one of three values $\top$, USE and $\bot$, where $\top \sqsubseteq$ USE $\sqsubseteq \bot$. The join operator, $\sqcap$, used during data flow is also defined below. Initially the data flow value at a node is $\top$ indicating that no use of the current value of x exists along any path. The value is lowered to $\bot$ if a use by op(x,-) is found indicating the value is to be considered live according to condition (ii) of the definition. The value is lowered from $\top$ to USE if a use of x's value by op(x,y) is found. For points to which op(x,y) cannot be hoisted because of a definition of y, the data flow value is lowered from USE to $\bot$ indicating that the current value of x is live for op(x,y) according to condition (i) of the definition. The PRE-liveness value $NPRELIVE_x^{op(x,y)}(n)$ at the entry of each node n is true if the data flow solution $NEXP_x^{op(x,y)}(n)$ is $\bot$; otherwise it is false. The liveness at exit, $XPRELIVE_x^{op(x,y)}(n)$, is similarly computed from $XEXP_x^{op(x,y)}(n)$.

Liveness analysis for x wrt expression $op(x,y)$ at node n for any path from n to end.

$\top$	x is not used		
USE	x is used only by occurrences of op(x,y) whose hoisting is not blocked by y's definition		
$\bot$	x is used by op(x,-) or by occurrences of op(x,y) whose hoisting is blocked by y's definition		

$\sqcap$	$\top$	USE	$\bot$
$\top$	$\top$	USE	$\bot$
USE	USE	USE	$\bot$
$\bot$	$\bot$	$\bot$	$\bot$

$$NEXP_x^{op(x,y)}(n) = \begin{cases} \bot & \text{if } (XEXP_x^{op(x,y)}(n) = USE \wedge n \text{ defines } y) \\ & \vee (op(x,-) \in n) \\ USE & \text{if } op(x,y) \in n \\ XEXP_x^{op(x,y)}(n) & \text{otherwise} \end{cases}$$

$$XEXP_x^{op(x,y)}(n) = \begin{cases} \top & \text{if } n = \text{exit} \\ \underset{w \in Succ(n)}{\sqcap} NEXP_x^{op(x,y)}(w) & \text{otherwise} \end{cases}$$

$$XPRELIVE_x^{op(x,y)}(n) = (XEXP_x^{op(x,y)}(n) = \bot)$$

$$NPRELIVE_x^{op(x,y)}(n) = (NEXP_x^{op(x,y)}(n) = \bot)$$

Overall register pressure changes. The overall change in register pressure at the entry(exit) of node n due to PRE of op(x,y), denoted by $\delta NRP_{op(x,y)}(n)$ $(\delta XRP_{op(x,y)}(n))$, is computed from the changes in register pressure due to operands (x,y) and the temporary introduced to save the value of op(x,y). The change in register pressure at node n's entry(exit) due to operands of op(x,y), given by $\delta NOPRP_{op(x,y)}(n)$ $(\delta XOPRP_{op(x,y)}(n))$, is computed from the PRE-liveness information. The change in register pressure due to a temporary at node n's entry(exit), given by $\delta NTRP_{op(x,y)}(n)$ $(\delta XTRP_{op(x,y)}(n))$, is computed from must-availability of assignments that compute op(x,y). Note that in the algorithm of Figure 2, the major step was the computation of register pressure changes.

$$\delta XRP_{op(x,y)}(n) = \delta XOPRP_{op(x,y)}(n) + \delta XTRP_{op(x,y)}(n)$$

$$\delta NRP_{op(x,y)}(n) = \delta NOPRP_{op(x,y)}(n) + \delta NTRP_{op(x,y)}(n)$$

$$\delta XOPRP_{op(x,y)}(n) = \begin{cases} 0 & \text{if } XPRELIVE_x^{op(x,y)}(n) \wedge XPRELIVE_y^{op(x,y)}(n) \\ -1 & \text{elseif } XPRELIVE_x^{op(x,y)}(n) \vee XPRELIVE_y^{op(x,y)}(n) \\ -2 & \text{otherwise} \end{cases}$$

$$\delta NOPRP_{op(x,y)}(n) = \begin{cases} 0 & \text{if } NPRELIVE_x^{op(x,y)}(n) \wedge NPRELIVE_y^{op(x,y)}(n) \\ -1 & \text{elseif } NPRELIVE_x^{op(x,y)}(n) \vee NPRELIVE_y^{op(x,y)}(n) \\ -2 & \text{otherwise} \end{cases}$$

$$\delta XTRP_{op(x,y)}(n) = \begin{cases} 1 & \text{if } \exists s \in Succ(n) \text{ st } NAVAILop(x,y)(s) = \text{false} \\ & \text{for all } v:=op(x,y) \\ 0 & \text{otherwise} \end{cases}$$

$$\delta NTRP_{op(x,y)}(n) = \begin{cases} 1 & \text{if } NAVAIL_{op(x,y)}(n) = \text{false for all } v:=op(x,y) \\ 0 & \text{otherwise} \end{cases}$$

The results of applying the above analysis techniques to an example are shown in Figure 7. As we can see, the application of PRE to expression x+y by hoisting results in reduction of register pressure initially. Once the expression is hoisted above uses of x and y the register pressure starts to increase. Assuming the register pressure limits are set such that no increase in register pressure is allowed, the code resulting after PRE is shown in Figure 7b. While PRE due to computation of x+y within the loop and following the loop is removed, still PRE remains due to computation of x+y in the assignment a=x+y. The latter redundancy is not removed because hoisting is disabled to prevent an increase in register pressure.

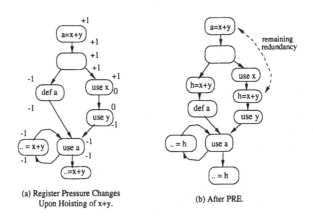

(a) Register Pressure Changes
Upon Hoisting of x+y.

(b) After PRE.

Fig. 7. Example of register pressure changes of operands due to PRE.

3   Register Pressure and Assignment Motion

In this section we show how the PRE algorithm based upon expression hoisting can be further enhanced through assignment motion.

PRE through assignment sinking. As the example in Figure 7 illustrates, after the algorithm of the preceding section has been applied, redundancy may still remain. It may be possible to remove all or part of the remaining redundancy through assignment sinking. In particular if we can sink an assignment that computes some expression op(x,y) to another computation of op(x,y), then the latter computation can be eliminated. We propose that after applying the presented algorithm, a separate phase may be used to remove as much redundancy as possible through assignment sinking. In order to ensure that sinking does not increase register pressure, we may apply sinking only to the extent that it does not cause any increase in register pressure. Furthermore, since assignment sinking may enable partial dead code elimination [3, 11, 18], it can also be performed at the same time.

Given an assignment, the sinking algorithm consists of three major steps: computing register pressure changes, delayability analysis for determining legality of sinking, and insertion point determination. To compute register pressure changes we observe that if an assignment is subjected to sinking, the length of the live range associated with the variable defined by the statement decreases. The changes in the length of the live range associated with a variable used by the *rhs*-expression in the assignment can be predicted using traditional global liveness information for that variable. If the operand variable is not live prior to sinking, then the live range for the operand increases with sinking. On the other hand if the operand variable is live prior to sinking, the length of the live range remains unaffected as long as at the points through which sinking proceeds variable continues to be live. If a partially dead assignment sinks to a point at which it is fully dead, then no change in register pressure occurs at that point since the assignment would neither be inserted at that point nor sunk any further. The delayability analysis is forward analysis that determines points to which an assignment can be sunk. In this analysis sinking is blocked at appropriate program points to prevent register pressure increase. Finally the assignment being sunk is inserted at a node's entry if it can be delayed to its entry but not its exit. It is inserted at a node's exit if it can be delayed to its exit but not to the entries of one of its successors. In both of the above cases insertion is only needed if the variable that the statement defines is live.

Let us illustrate the use of sinking for performing PRE to the example from the preceding section where some PRE had already been applied through hoisting of x+y while some remains. Figure 8a shows the changes in register pressure for sinking a=x+y. The sinking of a=x+y yields the code in Figure 8b in which the remainder of the redundancy is removed. Thus, PRE is achieved without any increase in register pressure through a combination of hoisting and sinking, while neither by itself could have enabled PRE without an increase in register pressure.

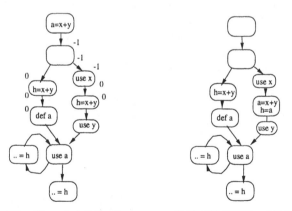

(a) Register Pressure Changes due to Sinking of a=x+y.   (b) After PRE & PDE through Sinking.

Fig. 8. Example.

Live range reduction through assignment hoisting. In some situations assignment hoisting can be used to further reduce the live range of the temporary. In the example of Figure 5a, by performing hoisting of loop invariant assignment instead

120

of simply hoisting loop invariant expressions out of loops. As shown in Figure 9b the live range of temporary T is further shortened if the loop invariant assignment Z=A+B is hoisted out of the loop, instead of simply hoisting expression A+B out of the loop as was done in Figure 9a.

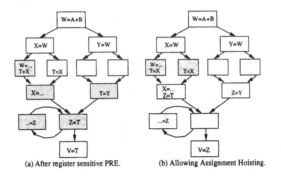

(a) After register sensitive PRE. (b) Allowing Assignment Hoisting.

Fig. 9. Assignment hoisting.

4 Concluding Remarks

In this paper we demonstrated the inadequacy of the current PRE techniques [15, 17] which simply try to minimize the increase in register pressure. Minimization of the increase in register pressure can still lead to a significant increase in spill code. Therefore we proposed an approach to PRE which sets upper limits on allowed register pressures based upon profile information and within the constraints of these limits performs redundancy elimination. In an attempt to maximize redundancy elimination we try to minimize the increase in the register pressure by reducing the range over which a new temporary is introduced and using assignment sinking to perform PRE that was not achieved by hoisting alone. Finally we would like to point out that code reordering performed during instruction scheduling also effects register pressure. Our algorithm can be extended to perform such code reordering. However, for such code reordering to be consistent with good instruction scheduling decisions, it is important to consider pressure on functional unit resources as shown in [12, 10].

References

1. R. Bodik, R. Gupta and M.L. Soffa, "Complete Removal of Redundant Expressions," *ACM SIGPLAN Conference on Programming Language Design and Implementation*, pages 1-14, Montreal, Canada, June 1998.
2. R. Bodik, R. Gupta and M.L. Soffa, "Load-Reuse Analysis: Design and Evaluation," *ACM SIGPLAN Conference on Programming Language Design and Implementation*, Atlanta, Georgia, May 1999.
3. R. Bodik and R. Gupta, "Partial Dead Code Elimination using Slicing Transformations," *ACM SIGPLAN Conference on Programming Language Design and Implementation*, pages 159-170, Las Vegas, Nevada, June 1997.

4. R. Bodik and S. Anik, "Path-Sensitive Value-Flow Analysis," *25th ACM SIGPLAN-SIGACT Symposium on Principles of Programming Languages*, San Diego, California, January 1998.

5. P. Briggs, K.D. Cooper, and L. Torczon, "Rematerialization," *ACM SIGPLAN Conf. on Prog. Language Design and Implementation*, pages 311-321, June 1992.

6. P. Briggs and K.D. Cooper, "Effective Partial Redundancy Elimination," *ACM SIGPLAN Conference on Programming Language Design and Implementation*, pages 159-170, June 1994.

7. F. Chow, S. Chan, R. Kennedy, S-M. Liu, R. Lo, and P. Tu, "A New Algorithm for Partial Redundancy Elimination based upon SSA Form," *ACM SIGPLAN Conference on Programming Language Design and Implementation*, pages 273-286, Las Vegas, Nevada, June 1997.

8. C. Click, "Global Code Motion Global Value Numbering," *ACM SIGPLAN Conference on Programming Language Design and Implementation*, pages 246-257, La Jolla, CA, June 1995.

9. D.M. Dhamdhere, "Practical Adaptation of Global Optimization Algorithm of Morel and Renvoise," *ACM Trans. on Programming Languages*, 13(2):291-294, 1991.

10. R. Gupta, "A Code Motion Framework for Global Instruction Scheduling," *International Conference on Compiler Construction*, LNCS 1383, Springer Verlag, pages 219-233, Lisbon, Portugal, March 1998.

11. R. Gupta, D. Berson, and J.Z. Fang, "Path Profile Guided Partial Dead Code Elimination using Predication," *International Conference on Parallel Architectures and Compilation Techniques*, pages 102-115, San Francisco, Ca, November 1997.

12. R. Gupta, D. Berson, and J.Z. Fang, "Resource-Sensitive Profile-Directed Data Flow Analysis for Code Optimization," *The 30th Annual IEEE/ACM International Symposium on Microarchitecture*, pages 558-568, Research Triangle Park, NC, Dec. 1997.

13. R. Gupta, D. Berson, and J.Z. Fang, "Path Profile Guided Partial Redundancy Elimination using Speculation," *IEEE International Conference on Computer Languages*, pages 230-239, Chicago, Illinois, May 1998.

14. R.N. Horspool and H.C. Ho, "Partial Redundancy Elimination Driven by a Cost-Benefit Analysis," *8th Israeli Conference on Computer Systems and Software Engineering*, pages 111-118, Herzliya, Israel, June 1997.

15. O. Rüthing, "Optimal Code Motion in Presence of Large Expressions," *IEEE International Conference on Computer Languages*, Chicago, Illinois, 1998.

16. E. Morel and C. Renvoise, "Global Optimization by Suppression of Partial Redundancies," *Communications of the ACM*, 22(2):96-103, 1979.

17. J. Knoop, O. Ruthing, and B. Steffen, "Lazy Code Motion," *Proceedings of Conference on Programming Language Design and Implementation*, pages 224-234, 1992.

18. J. Knoop, O. Ruthing, and B. Steffen, "Partial Dead Code Elimination," *Proceedings of Conference on Programming Language Design and Implementation*, pages 147-158, 1994.

19. B. Steffen, "Data Flow Analysis as Model Checking," *Proceedings TACS'91*, Sendai, Japan, Springer-Verlag, LNCS 526, pages 346-364, 1991.

20. B. Steffen, J. Knoop, and O. Rüthing, "The value flow graph: A program representation for optimal program transformations," *Proceedings of the 3rd European Symposium on Programming (ESOP'90)*, LNCS 432, pages 389–405, 1990.

Code Optimization by Integer Linear Programming

Daniel Kästner* and Marc Langenbach

Universität des Saarlandes, Fachbereich Informatik,
Postfach 15 11 50, D-66041 Saarbrücken, Germany
Phone: +49 681 302 5589   Fax: +49 681 302 3065
{kaestner,mlangen}@cs.uni-sb.de
http://www.cs.uni-sb.de/~{kaestner,mlangen}

Abstract. The code quality of many high-level language compilers in the field of digital signal processing is not satisfactory. This is mostly due to the complexity of the code generation problem together with the irregularity of typical DSP architectures. Since digital signal processors mostly are traded on the high volume consumer market, they are subject to serious cost constraints. On the other hand, many embedded applications demand high performance capacities. Thus, it is very important that the features of the processor are exploited as efficiently as possible. By using integer linear programming (ILP), the deficiencies of the decoupling of different code generation phases can be removed, since it is possible to integrate instruction scheduling and register assignment in one homogeneous problem description. This way, optimal solutions can be found—albeit at the cost of high compilation times. Our experiments show, that approximations based on integer linear programming can provide a better solution quality than classical code generation algorithms in acceptable runtime for medium sized code sequences. The experiments were performed for a modern DSP, the Analog Devices ADSP-2106x.

1   Introduction

In the last decade, digital signal processors (DSPs) have established on the high-volume consumer market to be the processors of choice for embedded systems. The high-volume market imposes stringent cost constraints to the DSPs; on the other hand, many embedded applications demand high performance capacities. High-level language compilers often are unable to generate code meeting these requirements [25]. This is mostly due to the complexity of the code generation problem together with the irregularity of typical DSP architectures. Especially, the phase coupling problem between instruction scheduling and register allocation plays an important role.

Since instruction scheduling and register allocation are $\mathcal{NP}$-hard problems, they are mostly solved in separate phases by using heuristic methods. Classical

---

* Member of the Graduiertenkolleg "Effizienz und Komplexität von Algorithmen und Rechenanlagen" (supported by the DFG).

heuristic methods are register allocation by heuristically guided graph coloring [5, 6] or instruction scheduling by *list scheduling* [16], *trace scheduling* [8], *percolation scheduling* [21] or *region scheduling* [12]. These algorithms are very fast, but usually produce only suboptimal solutions without any information about the solution quality.

The task of instruction scheduling is to rearrange a code sequence in order to exploit instruction level parallelism. In register allocation, the values of variables and expressions of the intermediate representation are mapped to registers in order to minimize the number of memory references during program execution. As the goals of these two phases often conflict, that phase which is executed first imposes constraints on the other; this can lead to inefficient code. That problem is known as the *phase ordering problem.*

Formulations based on integer linear programming (ILP) offer the possibility of integrating instruction scheduling and aspects of register allocation in an homogeneous problem description and of solving them together. Moreover, it is possible to get an optimal solution of the considered problems—albeit at the cost of high calculation times. We have shown that by using ILP-based approximations, the computation time can be significantly reduced. The resulting code quality is better than that of conventional graph-based algorithms. Moreover, with integer linear programming, lower bounds on the optimal schedule length can be calculated. This way, the quality of an approximate solution can be estimated, if no optimal solution is available.

The paper is organized as follows: In Section 2, we will give a short overview on related work. After an introduction to integer linear programming, we will present an ILP-formulation for combined instruction scheduling and register assignment. In Section 5, some additional constraints are introduced which are required to adapt the formulation to a real-world target architecture, the ADSP-2106x. Then we will give an overview on some ILP-based approximations in Section 6. The article concludes with a short summary and an outline of future work.

2   Related Work

During the last years, the development of phase coupling code generation strategies has gained increasing attention. In [4], Bradlee has developed a code generation policy where instruction scheduling and register allocation communicate with each other. First, a pre-scheduler is invoked which computes schedule cost estimates which allow the subsequent register allocation phase to quantify the effect of its choices on the scheduler. After the allocation pase, the final schedule is produced.

The AVIV retargetable code generator [13] builds on the retargetable code generation framework SPAM for digital signal processors [26, 27]. It uses a heuristic branch-and-bound algorithm that performs functional unit assignment, operation grouping, register bank allocation, and scheduling concurrently. Register allocation proper is carried out as a second step. Bashford and Bieker [3] are developing a framework for scheduling, compaction, and binding using constraint logic programming. Both approaches are still work in progress, so final results are not available yet.

There have been only few approaches to incorporate ILP-based methods into the code generation process of a compiler. An approach for ILP-based instruction scheduling for vector processors has been presented in [2]. Wilson et al. [28] use an ILP-formulation for simultaneously performing scheduling, allocation, binding, and selection among different code alternatives. However the complexity of the resulting formulations leads to very high computation times. Leupers has developed a retargetable compiler for digital signal processors [18] where local compaction is performed by integer linear programming. However the formulation captures only the problem of instruction scheduling and no approximations or partitioning techniques are considered. Other ILP-based approaches have been developed in the context of software pipelining [24, 11].

3 Basics of Integer Linear Programming

In integer programming problems, an objective function is maximized or minimized subject to inequality and equality constraints and integrality restrictions on some or all of the variables. The calculation of an optimal solution of an integer linear program is $\mathcal{NP}$-hard; yet many large instances of such problems can be solved. This, however, requires the selection of a structured formulation and no ad-hoc approach [7].

In this paper, we will just sketch the basics of integer linear programming, which are essential for the understanding of the presented ILP-approaches. For further information see e.g. [20], [19], [22], or [7].

Let $P_F = \{x \mid Ax \geq b, \ x \in \mathbb{R}^n_+\}$, $c \in \mathbb{R}^n$, $b \in \mathbb{R}^m$, $A \in \mathbb{R}^{m \times n}$. Then Integer linear programming (ILP) is the following optimization problem:

$$\min \quad z_{IP} = c^T x \qquad (1)$$
$$x \in P_F \cap \mathbb{Z}^n$$

The set P_F is called *feasible region*. If some of the variables have to be integral while the others also can take real values, the problem is called *mixed integer linear problem (MILP)*. The feasible area P_F is called integral, if it is equal to the convex hull P_I of the integer points ($P_I = conv(\{x \mid x \in P_F \cap \mathbb{Z}^n\})$); see Fig. 1). In this case, the optimal solution can be calculated in polynomial time by solving its LP-relaxation. This means, that linear programming algorithms can be used, since the solution of the (non-integer) linear program is guaranteed to be integral. Therefore, while formulating an integer linear program, one should attempt to find equality and inequality constraints such that P_F will be integral. It has been shown, that for every bounded system of rational inequalities there is an integer polyhedron [10, 23]. Unfortunately for most problems it is not known how to formulate these additional inequalities—and there could be an exponential number of them [19].

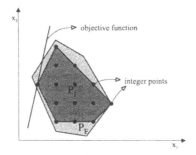

Fig. 1. Feasible Areas.

In general, $P_I \subsetneqq P_F$, and the LP-relaxation provides a lower bound on the objective function. The efficiency of many integer programming algorithms depends on the tightness of this bound. The better P_F approximates the feasible region P_I, the sharper is the bound so that for an efficient solution of an ILP-formulation, it is extremely important, that P_F is close to P_I.

4 The ILP Model

In this section, the problem of instruction scheduling is formally introduced. An ILP formulation for instruction scheduling is presented and is extended to include the problem of register assignment. These formulations work on basic-block level; in [14] it is shown how they can be extended to programs with structured control flow.

4.1 Instruction Scheduling

Basic Definitions
Let a sequence of partially ordered microoperations be given. Then the task of instruction scheduling is to find a schedule which minimizes the execution time of the instruction sequence and respects its partial order. This partial order among the instructions is induced by the data dependences. If a microoperation i is data dependent of another microoperation j, then the ordering of i and j must not be changed; otherwise the semantics of the program would be changed. The data dependences are modelled by the data dependence graph $G_D = (V_D, E_D)$ whose nodes correspond to the microoperations of the input program and whose edges reflect dependences between the adjacent nodes. There are three different types of data dependences:

- true dependence: i defines a resource which is used by j ($(i,j) \in E_D^{true}$)
- output dependence: i defines a resource which is also defined by j ($(i,j) \in E_D^{output}$)
- anti dependence: i uses a resource which is defined by j ($(i,j) \in E_D^{anti}$)

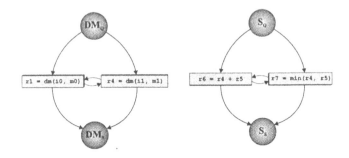

Fig. 2. Resource Flow Graph for two Instructions Executed on an ALU and the Data Memory.

Each operation of the input program can be executed by a certain resource type. In order to describe the mapping of instructions to hardware resources, the resource graph G_R is used [29]. G_R is a bipartite directed graph $G_R = (V_R, E_R)$, where $(j, k) \in E_R$ means that instruction j can be executed by the resources of type k.

An ILP-Formulation for Instruction Scheduling

In the area of architectural synthesis, several ILP-formulations have been developed for the problem of instruction scheduling and resource allocation. We have investigated two well-structured formulations in detail: OASIC [9, 10], which is a time-based formulation[1] and SILP [29, 14], which is an order-based formulation.

In the scope of this paper, we will concentrate on SILP (*Scheduling and Allocating with Integer Linear Programming*); an investigation of OASIC and a comparison of both models can be found in [14, 15]. First we will give an overview of the SILP-terminology:

- The variable t_i indicates the relative position of a microoperation within the instructions of the optimized code sequence; the t_i-values have to be integral.
- w_j describes the execution time of instruction $j \in V_D$.
- z_j denotes the latency of the functional unit executing operation j, i.e. the minimal time interval between successive data inputs to this functional unit.
- The number of available resources of type $k \in V_K$ is R_k.
- τ_j describes the length of the life range of a variable created by operation j.

The ILP is generated from a resource flow graph G_F. This graph describes the execution of a program as a flow of the available hardware resources through the instructions of the program; for each resource type, this leads to a separated flow network. Each resource type $k \in V_K$ is represented by two nodes $k_Q, k_S \in V_F$; the nodes k_Q are the sources, the nodes k_S are the sinks in the flow network to be defined. The first instruction to be executed on resource type k gets an instance

---

[1] In a *time-based* ILP-formulation the choice of the decision variables is based on the time the modelled event is assigned to. In an *order-based* formulation, the decision variables reflect the ordering of the modelled events.

k_r of this type from the source node k_Q; after completed execution, it passes k_r to the next instruction using the same resource type. The last instruction using a certain instance of a resource type returns it to k_S. The number of simultaneously used instances of a certain resource type must never exceed the number of available instances of this type. Fig. 2 shows an example resource flow graph for two resource types of our target processor ADSP-2106x (see Sec. 5); on each resource type, two independent instructions are executed. The *resource flow graph* G_F is a directed graph $G_F = (V_F, E_F)$ with $V_F = \bigcup_{k \in V_K} V_F^k$ and $E_F = \bigcup_{k \in V_K} E_F^k$. The set V_F^k contains the resource nodes for resource type k and all operations of the input program which are executed by k. E_F^k is the set of edges connecting nodes in V_F^k. Each edge $(i, j) \in E_F^k$ is mapped to a flow variable $x_{ij}^k \in \{0, 1\}$. A hardware resource of type k is moved through the edge (i, j) from node i to node j, if and only if $x_{ij}^k = 1$.

The goal of this ILP-formulation is to minimize the execution time of the code sequence to be scheduled. The execution time is measured in control steps (clock cycles). The ILP-formulation for the problem of instruction scheduling reads as follows:

$$\min \quad M_{steps} \tag{2}$$

$$t_j \leq M_{steps} \quad \forall j \in V_D \tag{3}$$

$$t_j - t_i \geq w_i \quad \forall (i, j) \in E_D^{output} \cup E_D^{true} \tag{4}$$

$$t_j - t_i \geq 0 \quad \forall (i, j) \in E_D^{anti} \tag{5}$$

$$\sum_{(i,j) \in E_F^k} x_{ij}^k - \sum_{(j,i) \in E_F^k} x_{ji}^k = 0 \quad \forall j \in V_D, \forall k \in V_k : (j, k) \in E_R \tag{6}$$

$$\sum_{\substack{k \in V_K : \\ (j,k) \in E_R}} \sum_{(i,j) \in E_F^k} x_{ij}^k = 1 \quad \forall j \in V_D \tag{7}$$

$$\sum_{(k,j) \in E_F^k} x_{kj}^k \leq R_k \quad \forall k \in V_K \tag{8}$$

$$t_j - t_i \geq z_i + \left(\sum_{\substack{k \in V_K : \\ (i,j) \in E_F^k}} x_{ij}^k - 1 \right) \cdot \alpha_{ij} \quad \forall (i, j) \in E_F^k \tag{9}$$

The time constraints (equation (3)) guarantee, that for no instruction the start time may exceed the maximal number of control steps M_{steps} (which is to be calculated). Equations (4) and (5) are precedence constraints which are used to model the data dependences. When instruction j depends on instruction i, then j may be executed only after the execution of i is finished. The flow conservation constraints (equation (6)) assert that the value of the flow entering a node equal the flow leaving that node. Moreover, each operation must be executed exactly once by one hardware component. This is guaranteed by equation (7). The Resource constraints (8) are necessary, since the number of available resources of all resource types must not be exceeded. The constraints (9) are called serial constraints. When operations i and j are both assigned to the same resource type k, then j must await the execution of i, when a component of resource type k is actually moved along the edge $(i, j) \in E_F^k$, i.e., if $x_{ij}^k = 1$. The better the feasible region of the relaxation P_F approximates the feasible region of the integral problem P_I, the more efficiently can the integer linear program be solved. In [29], it is shown that the tightest polyhedron is described by using the value $\alpha_{ij} = z_i - asap(j) + alap(i)$.

4.2 Integration of Register Asignment

Up to now, the presented ILP-formulation covers only the problem of instruction scheduling. To take into account the problem of register assignment, this formulation has to be extended. Register assignment is a subtask of register allocation. The goal is to determine the physical register which is used to store a value that has been previously selected to reside in a register. The choice of these registers interacts with the reordering facilities of instruction scheduling.

Again following the concept of flow graphs, the register assignment problem is formulated as register distribution problem. The register flow graph $G_F^g = (V_F^g, E_F^g)$ is a directed graph. The set $V_F^g = V_g \cup G$ is composed of two subsets: $G = \{g\}$ represents a homogeneous register set and the nodes in V_g represent operations performing a write access to a register. Each node $j \in V_g$ is associated with the generated variable whose lifetime is denoted by τ_j. Each arc $(i, j) \in E_F^g$ represents a possible flow of a register from i to j and is mapped a flow variable $x_{ij}^g \in \{0, 1\}$. Then the same register is used to save the variables created by nodes i and j, if $x_{ij}^g = 1$. Lifetimes of variables are associated with true dependences. If an instruction i writes to a register, then the life span of the value created by i has to reach all uses of that value. To model this, additional variables $b_{ij} \geq 0$ are introduced which measure the distance between a defining instruction i and a corresponding use j. The formulation of the precedence relation is replaced by the following equation:

$$t_j - t_i - b_{ij} = w_i \tag{10}$$

Then, for the lifetime of the register defined by instruction i must hold:

$$\tau_i \geq b_{ij} + w_i \qquad \forall \, (i, j) \in E_D^{true} \tag{11}$$

An instruction j may only write to the same register as a preceding instruction i, if j is executed at a time when the lifetime of i, τ_i is already terminated. This is modelled by the *register serial constraints*:

$$t_j - t_i \geq w_i - w_j + \tau_i + (x_{ij}^g - 1) \cdot 2T \tag{12}$$

Here, T represents the number of machine operations of the input program, which is a safe upper bound for the maximal possible lifetime. In order to correctly model the register flow graph, flow conservation constraints, as well as resource constraints and assignment constraints have to be added to the integer linear program. This leads to the following equalities and inequalities:

$$\sum_{(g,j) \in E_F^g} x_{gj}^g \leq R_g \qquad \forall g \in G \tag{13}$$

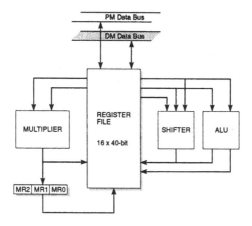

Fig. 3. Simplified Block Diagram.

$$\sum_{(i,j)\in E_F^g} x_{ij}^g = 1 \qquad \forall\, j \in V_g \tag{14}$$

$$\sum_{(i,j)\in E_F^g} x_{ij}^g - \sum_{(j,i)\in E_F^g} x_{j,i}^g = 0 \qquad \forall\, j \in V_F^g \quad \forall g \in G \tag{15}$$

$$t_j - t_i - \tau_i \geq w_i - w_j + (\sum_{g\in G} x_{ij}^g - 1)\cdot 2T \quad \forall (i,j) \in E_F^g \tag{16}$$

The total number of constraints is $\mathcal{O}(n^2)$, where n is the number of operations in the input program. The number of binary variables is bounded by $\mathcal{O}(n^2)$. The proofs are given in [29, 14].

The ILP-formulation as presented here can model only sequential code. However, it is possible to integrate the control structure of the input program into an ILP, so that the movement of instructions across basic block boundaries can be handled internally by the ILPs. This is covered in detail in [15].

5   Adaptation to the ADSP-2106x

We have adapted the investigated formulations to a modern 32-bit digital signal processor with a load/store architecture, the ADSP-2106x SHARC (*Super Harvard Architecture Computer*) [1]. The processor contains three functional units: an ALU, a shifter, and a multiplier. The memory consists of a data memory DM and a program memory PM which can be used to store instructions and data (see Fig. 3). Most arithmetic operations can be executed in parallel with a data memory and a program memory access and in some cases, also the ALU and the multiplier can operate in parallel.

The register file consists of two sets of sixteen 40-bit registers, which are used to store both fixed and floating point data. Furthermore, each set is divided into four groups of four consecutive registers. ALU and multiplier can only operate in parallel if the operands come from the appropriate register group (Fig. 4).

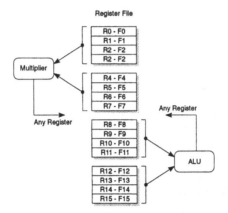

Fig. 4. Register Groups and Usage in Multifunctional Instructions.

The execution of instructions is pipelined. In sequential program flow, when one instruction is being fetched, the instruction fetched in the previous cycle is being decoded, and the instruction fetched two cycles before is being executed. Thus, the throughput is one instruction per cycle.

5.1 Prevention of Incorrect Parallelism

In the presented ILP-formulation, parallel execution of instructions assigned to the same resource type is excluded by the serial constraints. Instructions assigned to different resource nodes can always be executed in parallel. As this parallelism is restricted in the considered architecture, additional constraints are required which explicitly prohibit the parallel execution of a certain pair of operations.

For two operations i and j, which must not be executed in parallel, i.e. for which $t_i \neq t_j$ must hold, constraints are formulated which represent the disjunction $(t_i > t_j) \lor (t_i < t_j)$. Let I denote the number of operations in the input program; then the following inequalities are required:

$$t_i - t_j > -v_{ij}T \tag{17}$$

$$t_i - t_j < (1 - v_{ij})T \tag{18}$$

$$v_{ij} \in \{0, 1\} \tag{19}$$

$$T = 2I + 1 \tag{20}$$

A correctness proof is provided in [14].

5.2 Irregular Register Sets

The operands of multifunction-instructions using ALU and multiplier are restricted to a set of four registers whithin the register file (see Fig. 3). Thus, there are four different register groups to be considered and no homogeneous register set. For each such group, an own register node is inserted into the register flow graph ($G = \{g_1, g_2, g_3, g_4\}$).

When instructions i and j are combined to form a multifunction-instruction, so that for the reaching definition m, the target register set is restricted to exactly one $g \in G$, it must be guaranteed that m in fact uses a register of register set g. Then, a constraint of the form $\sum_{(i,m) \in E_F^g} x_{im}^g \geq 1$ must hold. Since $\sum_g \sum_{(i,m) \in E_F^g} x_{im}^g = 1$, this automatically excludes the use of other register sets. The formulation presented below uses two binary variables p_{ij} and q_{ij} which are defined by following constraints.

$$t_i - t_j \geq -p_{ij}T \tag{21}$$
$$t_i - t_j \leq q_{ij}T \tag{22}$$
$$p_{ij} + q_{ij} = 1 \tag{23}$$

where $T = 2I + 1$. Using these values, the register constraints can be formulated as follows:

$$\sum_{(i,m) \in E_F^g} x_{im}^g \geq 1 - (t_i - t_j) - p_{ij}T \tag{24}$$

$$\sum_{(i,m) \in E_F^g} x_{im}^g \geq 1 + (t_i - t_j) - q_{ij}T \tag{25}$$

The correctness proofs are omitted in this paper; they are explicitly given in [14].

6 Approximations

The computation time required to solve the generated ILPs is high. Therefore, it is an interesting question to know, whether heuristics can be applied which cannot guarantee an optimal solution but can also deal with larger input programs. In this paper, we give an overview of the investigated approximation algorithms; they are treated in detail in [14].

6.1 Approximation by Rounding

Approximation by rounding is a straightforward approach: the flow variables x_{ij}^k are relaxed[2] and the resulting relaxation is solved. Then the variable with a non-integral value closest to 0 or 1 is fixed to that integer and the new mixed integer linear program is solved. This is repeated until an integral solution has been found. However, the solution quality is not convincing enough for this method to be considered promising; moreover the calculation time can be high since usually backtracking steps are required.

---

[2] This means that the integrality constraint $x_{ij}^k \in \{0, 1\}$ is replaced by $0 \leq x_{ij}^k \leq 1$.

6.2 Stepwise Approximation

The algorithm starts by solving the MILP obtained by relaxing all flow variables. Then the following approach is repeated for all control steps. The algorithm checks whether any operations were scheduled to the actual control step in spite of a serial constraint formulated between them and the corresponding variables are redeclared binary. Let M_S^c be the set of these variables. After solving the resulting MILP, the variables $x \in M_S^c$ with $x = 1$ are fixed to their actual value and the next iteration starts. After considering each control step, the set of all flow variables which still have non-integral values is determined. These variables are redeclared binary and the MILP is solved again. This is repeated until a feasible solution has been found. Since in each step optimal solutions with respect to the already fixed variables are calculated, it can be expected that the approximation leads to a good global solution. This is confirmed by the test results.

6.3 Isolated Flow Analysis

In this approach, only the flow variables corresponding to a certain resource type $r \in R$ are declared as binary. The flow variables related to other resources are relaxed. Then, an optimal solution of this MILP is calculated and the flow variables x executed by r are fixed to their actual solution value by additional equality constraints. This approach is repeated for all resource types, so a feasible solution is obtained in the end. This way, in each step, an optimal solution with respect to each individual resource flow is calculated. Since the overall solution consists of individually optimal solutions of the different resource types, in most cases it will be equal to an optimal solution of the entire problem. This optimality, however, cannot be guaranteed, as when analysing an individual resource flow, the others are only considered in their relaxed form. However the computation time is reduced since only the binary variables associated to one resource type are considered at a time.

6.4 Stepwise Approximation of Isolated Flow Analysis

The last approximation developed for the SILP-Formulation is a mixture of the two previously presented approaches. At each step, the flow variables of all resources except the actually considered resource type r are relaxed. For the flow variables x with $res(x) = r$, the stepwise approximation is performed until all these variables are fixed to an integral value. Then the next resource type is considered. Clearly, this approximation is the fastest one, and in our experimental results, the solutions provided by this approximation are as good as the results of the two previously presented approximations. In the following, we denote this approximation by $\mathcal{SF}$.

7 Implementation and Experiments

In our experiments, we use ADSP-2106xassembler programs as input. These programs can be generated by the gcc-based compiler g21k, shipped with the

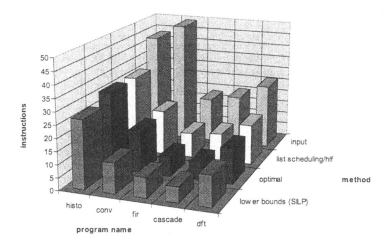

Fig. 5. Comparison of Solution Quality for Different Methods.

ADSP-2106x or can be written by hand. We have chosen as input programs typical applications of digital signal processing: a finite impulse response filter (`fir`), an infinite impulse response filter (`cascade`), a discrete fourier transformation (`dft`), one function of the whetstone-suite (`whetp3`), a histogramm (`histo`), and a convolution algorithm (`conv`). The input programs make no use of the available instruction-level parallelism of the processor. The run times have been measured on a SPARC ULTRA 2x200 with 1024 MB RAM under Solaris 2.5.1.

An overview on the experimental results is given in Fig. 5. The input programs contain between 18 and 49 instructions. In order to oppose the ILP-based techniques to classical algorithms, we have implemented several local scheduling algorithms and a graph-based register allocator. The graph-based algorithm which gave the best results was list scheduling with highest level first heuristic [14, 17]. Even with an optimal register assignment given, the produced code sequences contained on average 13 % more instructions than the optimal code sequences; the solution time was less than one second for each of the input programs. The investigated SILP approximations however produced optimal code for each input program; the only exception was `whetp3`. ILP-based lower bounds could be calculated within several seconds by solving the LP-relaxation of the given problems. These bounds are on average 15 % below the optimal instruction number. The most important characteristics of the ILP-based algorithms are shown in Tables 1 and 2. For reasons of complexity, only instruction scheduling has been performed for the input programs `whetp3, histo` and `conv`; integrated instruction scheduling and register assignment has been performed for `fir, cascade` and `dft` (entry "is+ra" in column "mode"). The generated ILPs contain between 383 and 2143 constraints, between 93 and 946 binary variables and the textual representation of the largest one takes 294.59 KB. As can be seen in Table 2, even for programs whose exact solution (opt) took more than 24 hours, an ILP-based approximation could be calculated in less than 2 minutes

Table 1. Characteristics of the ILPs generated by the SILP-based formulation.

name	mode	constr	bin (expl)	size [KB]
fir	is+ra	422	675 (464)	58.94
cascade	is+ra	606	950 (707)	89.37
dft	is+ra	2143	1201 (946)	294.59
whetp3	is	383	214 (93)	15.26
histo	is	716	434 (168)	29.66
conv	is	963	452 (163)	40.09

(all figures refer to the fastest approximation $\mathcal{SF}$). With exception of `whetp3`, all solutions provided by the approximation were in fact optimal.

Table 2. Runtime characteristics of the SILP-based ILPs.

name	mode	method	instr	CPU-time
fir	is+ra	def	8	1.69 sec
fir	is+ra	app	8	19.58 sec
cascade	is+ra	def	-	> 24 h
cascade	is+ra	app	7	86.72 sec
dft	is+ra	def	-	> 24 h
dft	is+ra	app	14	9 min 20 sec
whetp3	is	def	20	2h 4 min
whetp3	is	app	21	85.96 sec
histo	is	def	-	> 24 h
histo	is	app	31	1 h 2 min
conv	is	def	17	2 h 1 min
conv	is	app	17	53.66 sec

8 Ongoing and Future Work

Even by using ILP-based approximations, the computation time can grow high for large input programs. Thus, when compiling large programs, ILP-based solutions cannot replace the classical methods. However it is profitable to integrate ILP-based methods into conventional algorithms where an ILP-based optimization is only performed for code sequences offering a high degree of potential parallelism and whose efficiency is critical for the application. A typical example are inner loops. Moreover, partitioning techniques have to be developed which allow also for larger code sequences to be optimized by integer linear programming. Up to now, only one target architecture has been considered. However, in the field of digital signal processing, retargetability is an important issue. Currently, a retargetable framework for the presented optimization techniques, called PROPAN (Postpass Retargetable Optimizer and Analyzer) is developed. The goal is to make the described optimizations generic, so that they can be adapted to a new target processor by a concise specification of the important hardware features.

9 Conclusions

We have shown that the the the problem of instruction scheduling and register assignment can be modeled completely and correctly as an integer linear program for an irregular target architecture.

Based on a well-structured ILP-formulation, SILP, several approximations can be calculated while solving the ILPs, leading to good results in relatively low calculation times. The optimality of the result is not guaranteed by such heuristics; yet better results can be obtained than with the conventional, graph-based algorithms [17].

In conventional, graph-based algorithms, it is not possible to estimate the quality of a solution. By solving partial relaxations of the ILP, lower bounds to the optimal solution can be calculated. For the tested programs, the quality of these lower bounds corresponds to the quality of solutions which are calculated by conventional, graph-based algorithms. Thus, it is possible to give an interval which safely contains the optimal solution and to obtain an estimate for the quality of an approximate solution. This holds even when the optimal solution cannot be calculated for reasons of complexity.

References

[1] Analog Devices. *ADSP-2106x SHARC User's Manual*, 1995.

[2] Siamak Arya. An Optimal Instruction Scheduling Model for a Class of Vector Processors. *IEEE Transactions on Computers*, C-34, November 1985.

[3] Ulrich Bieker and Steven Bashford. Scheduling, Compaction and Binding in a Retargetable Code Generator Using Constraint Logic Programming. *4. GI/ITG/GME Workshop "Methoden des Entwurfs und der Verifikation digitaler Systeme"*, March 1996. Kreischa, Germany.

[4] D. G. Bradlee. Retargetable Instruction Scheduling for Pipelined Processors. Phd thesis, Technical Report 91-08-07, University of Washington, 1991.

[5] P. Briggs, K. Cooper, and L. Torczon. Improvements to Graph Coloring Register Allocation. *ACM Transactions on Programming Languages and Systems*, 16(3):428 – 455, 1994.

[6] D. Callahan and B. Koblenz. Register Allocation via Hierarchical Graph Coloring. *Proceedings of the ACM PLDI Conference*, pages 192 – 202, 1991.

[7] S. Chaudhuri, R.A. Walker, and J.E. Mitchell. Analyzing and Exploiting the Structure of the Constraints in the ILP-Approach to the Scheduling Problem. *IEEE Transactions on Very Large Scale Integration (VLSI) System*, 2(4):456 – 471, December 1994.

[8] J.A. Fisher. Trace Scheduling: A Technique for Global Microcode Compaction. *IEEE Transactions on Computers*, C-30(7):478 – 490, July 1981.

[9] C. H. Gebotys and M.I. Elmasry. *Optimal VLSI Architectural Synthesis*. Kluwer Academic, 1992.

[10] C. H. Gebotys and M.I. Elmasry. Global Optimization Approach for Architectural Synthesis. *IEEE Transactions on Computer-Aided Design of Integrated Circuits and Systems*, CAD-12(9):1266 – 1278, September 1993.

[11] R. Govindarajan, Erik R. Altman, and Guang R. Gao. A Framework for Resource Constrained Rate Optimal Software Pipelining. *IEEE Transactions on Parallel and Distributed Systems*, 7(11), November 1996.

[12] Rajiv Gupta and Mary Lou Soffa. Region scheduling: An approach for detecting and redistributing parallelism. *IEEE Transactions on Software Engineering*, 16(4):421–431, 1990.

[13] Silvina Hanono and Srinivas Devadas. Instruction Scheduling, Resource Allocation, and Scheduling in the AVIV Retargetable Code Generator. In *Proceedings of the DAC 1998*, San Francisco, California, 1998. ACM.

[14] Daniel Kästner. Instruktionsanordnung und Registerallokation auf der Basis ganzzahliger linearer Programmierung für den digitalen Signalprozessor ADSP-2106x. Master's thesis, University of the Saarland, 1997.

[15] Daniel Kästner and Marc Langenbach. Integer Linear Programming vs. Graph Based Methods in Code Generation. Technical Report A/01/98, University of the Saarland, Saarbrücken, Germany, January 1998.

[16] David Landskov, Scott Davidson, Bruce Shriver, and Patrick W. Mallet. Local Microcode Compaction Techniques. *ACM Computing Surveys*, 12(3):261–294, 1980.

[17] Marc Langenbach. Instruktionsanordnung unter Verwendung graphbasierter Algorithmen für den digitalen Signalprozessor ADSP-2106x. Master's thesis, University of the Saarland, 1997.

[18] Rainer Leupers. *Retargetable Code Generation for Digital Signal Processors*. Kluwer Academic Publishers, 1997.

[19] G.L. Nemhauser, A.H.G. Rinnooy Kan, and M.J. Todd, editors. *Handbooks in Operations Research and Management Science*, volume 1 of *Handbooks in Operations Research and Management Science*. North-Holland, Amsterdam; New York; Oxford, 1989.

[20] G.L. Nemhauser and L.A. Wolsey. *Integer and Combinatorial Optimization*. John Wiley and Sons, New York, 1988.

[21] Alexandru Nicolau. Uniform parallelism exploitation in ordinary programs. In *International Conference on Parallel Processing*, pages 614–618. IEEE Computer Society Press, August 1985.

[22] C.H. Papadimitriou and K. Steiglitz. *Combinatorial Optimization, Algorithms and Complexity*. Prentice-Hall, Englewood Cliffs, 1982.

[23] C.H. Papadimitriou and K. Steiglitz. *Combinatorial Optimization, Algorithms and Complexity*, chapter 13, pages 318 – 322. Prentice-Hall, Englewood Cliffs, 1982.

[24] John Ruttenberg, G.R. Gao, A. Stoutchinin, and W. Lichtenstein. Software Pipelining Showdown: Optimal vs. Heuristic Methods in a Production Compiler. *Proceedings of the 1996 ACM SIGPLAN Conference on Programming Languages Design and Implementation (PLDI 96)*, 31(5):1 – 11, May 1996.

[25] M.A.R. Saghir, P. Chow, and C.G. Lee. Exploiting Dual Data-Memory Banks in Digital Signal Processors. *http://www.eecg.toronto.edu/˜saghir/papers/asplos7.ps*, 1996.

[26] SPAM Research Group, http://www.ee.princeton.edu/spam. *SPAM Compiler User's Manual*, September 1997.

[27] Ashok Sudarsanam. *Code Optimization Libraries for Retargetable Compilation for Embedded Digital Signal Processors*. PhD thesis, University of Princeton, November 1998.

[28] Tom Wilson, Gary Grewal, Shawn Henshall, and Dilip Banerji. An ILP-Based Approach to Code Generation. In Peter Marwedel and Gert Goossens, editors, *Code Generation for Embedded Processors*, chapter 6, pages 103–118. Kluwer, Boston; London; Dortrecht, 1995.

[29] L. Zhang. *SILP. Scheduling and Allocating with Integer Linear Programming*. PhD thesis, University of the Saarland, Technical Faculty, 1996.

Evaluation of Algorithms for Local Register Allocation*

Vincenzo Liberatore[1], Martin Farach-Colton[2], and Ulrich Kremer[2]

[1] UMIACS, University of Maryland, College Park, MD 20742, USA,
vliberatore@acm.org,
[2] Dept. of Comp. Sc., Rutgers University, New Brunswick, NJ 08903, USA,
{farach,uli}@cs.rutgers.edu

Abstract. Local register allocation (LRA) assigns pseudo-registers to actual registers in a basic block so as to minimize the spill cost. In this paper, four different LRA algorithms are compared with respect to the quality of their generated allocations and the execution times of the algorithms themselves. The evaluation is based on a framework that views register allocation as the combination of boundary conditions, LRA, and register assignment. Our study does not address the problem of instruction scheduling in conjunction with register allocation, and we assume that the spill cost depends only on the number and type of load and store operations, but not on their positions within the instruction stream. The paper discusses the first optimum algorithm based on integer linear programming as one of the LRA algorithms. The optimal algorithm also serves as the base line for the quality assessment of generated allocations. In addition, two known heuristics, namely Furthest-First (FF) and Clean-First (CF), and a new heuristic (MIX) are discussed and evaluated. The evaluation is based on thirteen Fortran programs from the *fmm, Spec, and Spec95X* benchmark suites. An advanced compiler infrastructure (ILOC) was used to generated aggressively optimized, intermediate pseudo-register code for each benchmark program. Each local register allocation method was implemented, and evaluated by simulating the execution of the generated code on a machine with N registers and an instruction set where loads and stores are C times as expensive as any other instruction. Experiments were performed for different values of N and C. The results show that only for large basic blocks the allocation quality gap between the different algorithms is significant. When basic blocks are large, the difference was up to 23%. Overall, the new heuristic (MIX) performed best as compared to the other heuristics, producing allocations within 1% of optimum. All heuristics had running times comparable to live variable analysis, or lower, i.e., were very reasonable. More work will be needed to evaluate the LRA algorithms in the context of more sophisticated global register allocators and source level transformations that potentially increase basic block sizes, including loop unrolling, inlining, and speculative execution (superblocks).

* Research partly supported by NSF Career Development Award CCR-9501942, NATO Grant CRG 960215, NSF/NIH Grant BIR 94-12594-03-CONF and an Alfred P. Sloan Research Fellowship.

1 Introduction

Register allocation can substantially decrease the running time of compiled programs. Unfortunately, register allocation is a hard problem. To overcome the complexity of register allocation and to focus on its most crucial part, we propose a framework that breaks register allocation into a sequence of three distinct phases: *boundary allocation, local allocation,* and *register assignment.* Boundary allocation fixes the set of pseudo-registers that reside in physical registers at the beginning and at the end of each basic block. Local register allocation (LRA) determines the set of pseudo-registers that reside in physical registers at each step of a basic block, while previously chosen boundary conditions are respected. Register assignment maps allocated pseudo-registers to actual registers. The proposed framework has the advantage that (1) each phase is more manageable than the whole register allocation process, (2) it allows the integration of improved local register allocation heuristics with any global framework (e.g. Chaitin-Briggs), and (3) it isolates the register assignment phase, which was found to be the easiest phase of register allocation [20].

The canonical boundary allocation assumes that registers are empty at the beginning and at the end of a basic block. A more sophisticated boundary allocation extracts the boundary conditions from a state-of-the-art global register allocator. For example, a Chaitin-Briggs style allocator [5] could determine the register contents at the basic block boundaries. Once boundary conditions are fixed, any LRA that respects the boundary conditions can be used. In this paper, an optimum algorithm will be presented as well as heuristics to perform LRA under any specified set of boundary conditions. Finally, allocated pseudo-registers will be assigned to physical registers. While register assignment could theoretically add significant overhead, it is in fact the easiest step of register allocation [20].

A first advantage of our framework is that each phase is more manageable than the whole process. Moreover, our approach allows us to replace the local component of any global allocation (e.g. Chaitin-Briggs) with improved LRA heuristics. Our framework puts emphasis on LRA. The basic block in the innermost loop should be the most highly optimized part of the program [1]. Moreover, pseudo-registers are easier to reuse in a basic block [20]. Finally, LRA algorithms are the first and fundamental step in demand-driven register allocation [20]. We do not address the problem of instruction scheduling nor the interplay of register allocation with instruction scheduling. We assume that spill code has a fixed cost that is independent of the position where it is inserted. However, we will account for simple rematerializations.

This paper mostly focuses on the LRA phase. An optimum algorithm and three suboptimal heuristics for LRA are discussed. The optimum algorithm is a novel branch-and-bound method that exploits a special substructure of the integer program. The resulting allocator returns the best possible local allocation and took less than one minute in almost all our benchmarks. Using integer programming formulations for optimal solutions of NP-hard compiler problems has been discussed by a few researchers, in particular in the context of evaluating the quality of heuristic approaches [15, 21]. In addition to the optimal algorithm, we also propose a new heuristic, called MIX, for the same problem. MIX takes polynomial time, returned allocations that were always within 1% of the optimum, and was always more than ten times faster than the optimum. We also analyze previous heuristic for LRA. Previous heuristics always returned allocations that were worse than MIX's. We also measure the time taken by the heuristics, which is part of the total compilation time. If the heuristic running time is considered in isolation, MIX was substantially slower than previous heuristics. However, if we add the heuristic running time to live range analysis time, all heuristics ran in a comparable amount of time. In other words, the total allocation time was dominated by live range analysis rather than by the heuristic running time, and so no great difference was found in the overall running time. In conclusion, MIX returned better allocations than previous heuristics, while the total elapsed time was not seriously affected.

The paper is organized as follows. In §2, LRA is formally defined, followed by a review of relevant literature. In §3, we describe our experimental set-up. In §4, we give a new branch-and-bound algorithm and report experimental results for this algorithm. In §5, we define previous and new heuristics for LRA, report and discuss experimental results. The paper concludes with a summary of its contributions.

2 Register Allocation

The problem of *Register Allocation* is to assign pseudo-registers to actual registers in a basic block so as to minimize the spill cost. Details are specified in the following section.

2.1 Local/Global Register Allocation

For the purpose of this paper, *register allocation* will operate on sequences of intermediate code instructions. Intermediate code instructions define and use *pseudo-registers*. Pseudo-registers contain temporary variables and constants. No aliasing between pseudo-registers is possible. We assume that a pseudo-register represents only one live range, and thus a pseudo-register is defined at most once. We also assume that each pseudo-register can be stored and retrieved in a designated memory location. We denote by $V = \{t_1, t_2, \ldots, t_M\}$ the set of pseudo-registers that appear in the intermediate code, and so $M = |V|$ is the number of distinct pseudo-registers that appear in the code. An example of intermediate code sequence is found in the leftmost column of Figure 1. In the figure, the instructions are ADDI, SUB, etc, and the pseudo-registers are t0, t1, ..., t7.

Register allocation maps pseudo-registers into a set of N actual registers. More precisely, a register allocation is a mapping that specifies which pseudo-registers reside in a register at each step of the program. Formally, a register allocation is a function $ra : V \times \mathbb{N} \to \{\text{True}, \text{False}\}$, where $\mathbb{N}$ is the set of natural

intermediate code	σ	opt LRA code	cost	Registers R1 R2 R3		
				-	-	-
	(read,{0})	LOAD &t0 $\Rightarrow$ R1	2	t0	-	-
ADDI 3 t0 $\Rightarrow$ t1	(write,{1})	ADDI 3 R1 $\Rightarrow$ R2	1	t0	t1	-
	(read,{1,2})	LOADI 4 $\Rightarrow$ R3	1	t0	t1	t2
SUB t1 t2 $\Rightarrow$ t3	(write,{3})	SUB R2 R3 $\Rightarrow$ R1	1	t3	t1	t2
	(read,{3,4})	LOAD &t4 $\Rightarrow$ R3	2	t3	t1	t4
MUL t3 t4 $\Rightarrow$ t5	(write,{5})	MUL R1 R3 $\Rightarrow$ R3	1	t3	t1	t5
	(read,{2,5})	LOADI 4 $\Rightarrow$ R1	1	t2	t1	t5
SUB t2 t5 $\Rightarrow$ t6	(write,{6})	SUB R1 R2 $\Rightarrow$ R1	1	t6	t1	t5
	(read,{1,6})			t6	t1	t5
ADD t1 t6 $\Rightarrow$ t7	(write,{7})	ADD R2 R1 $\Rightarrow$ R1	1	t7	t1	t5

total cost: 11

Fig. 1. Example of optimal LRA with 3 registers. The first column gives a sequence of intermediate code instructions, the second column its representation in terms of pseudo-register usage, the third column the result of applying an optimum allocation, the fourth column gives the cost per operation assuming the spill cost is $C = 2$ and all other operations are unit cost, and the last columns give the register contents after a step has been executed. In the example, the set of live variables at the end of the segment is $L = \{t7\}$ and t2 contains the constant 4.

integers, $ra(t_i, j) =$ True if t_i is in a register at step j and $ra(t_i, j) =$ False otherwise. The register allocation ra function cannot be any mapping $V \times \mathbb{N} \to \{\text{True}, \text{False}\}$, but satisfies the following two additional constraints imposed by register-register architectures:

- If a pseudo-register i is used by an instruction, then i occupies a register immediately before that instruction is executed.
- If a pseudo-register i is defined by an instruction, then i occupies a register immediately after that operation is executed.

There are two issues that are beyond the scope of this paper: instruction scheduling and register assignment. We now show how our functional definition ra of register allocation correctly excludes the two issues. Instruction scheduling is the problem of rearranging the order of execution of instructions. The functional definition of ra excludes any instruction scheduling. We also distinguish between register allocation and *register assignment*: register allocation decides which pseudo-registers reside in actual registers and register assignment maps those pseudo-registers to particular physical registers. Our functional definition for register allocation keeps the two phases distinct. Register assignment could introduce an overhead because the assignment might have to be enforced by swap operations. In particular, at the end of a basic block, different register assignments must be made consistent by means of register swapping.

Since register allocation is, in our definition, a function, we can take its restriction to a subset of its domain. Specifically, we define the *boundary allocation* of a register allocation to be a function that specifies which pseudo-registers occupy actual registers at the beginning and at the end of each basic block. In other words, a boundary allocation fixes register contents at the boundaries of a basic block, and leaves undetermined register contents inside a basic block. We define *Local Register Allocation* (LRA) as the problem of assigning pseudo-registers to registers in a basic block once the boundary allocation is fixed. In other words, LRA is a register allocation for straight-line code that satisfies additional boundary conditions. We can view register allocation as formed by two components: the boundary allocation and the local allocation. Given a register allocation, its local allocation can be replaced with any other local allocation that satisfies the same boundary conditions.

Each intermediate code instruction generates a sequence of reads and writes to pseudo-registers. For example, the instruction SUB t1 t2 => t3 reads the pseudo-registers t1 and t2, subtracts them, and writes the result into t3. We define the *static reference sequence* σ corresponding to the intermediate code to be a sequence of references, each of which is either a read or a write of a subset of V. For example, the instruction SUB t1 t2 => t3 results in the sequence $((\mathsf{read}, \{\mathsf{t1}, \mathsf{t2}\}), (\mathsf{write}, \{\mathsf{t3}\}))$. Formally, a static reference sequence σ is a sequence of elements of $\{\mathsf{read}, \mathsf{write}\} \times V$. In Figure 1, we give a sequence of intermediate code instructions in the first column and the corresponding static reference sequence σ in the second column. Finally, boundary conditions can be cast in the static reference sequence σ by extending the sequence as follows:

- The first element of σ will be a read of the pseudo-registers that are in a register at the beginning of the basic block.
- The last element of σ will be a read of the pseudo-registers that are in a register at the end of the basic block.

Register allocations impose register contents at each step of program execution. Register allocations have to be enforced by loading the appropriate pseudo-registers into registers. Moreover, register allocations often require pseudo-registers to be stored back into their memory location. We now detail how a register allocation is enforced by load and store operations. If the register allocation specifies that a pseudo-register i is in a register at step j, but i is not in any register immediately before step j, then a load operation is inserted in the code to load i into a register. In turn, some other register i' would have to be evicted from the register file to make room for i. Define the set $S = \{\mathsf{clean}, \mathsf{dirty}\}$ as the set of pseudo-register states. We explain S as follows. If i' is clean, then it can be evicted without executing any store. If i' is dirty and live, then i' must be stored when evicted. If i' is clean, then either i' contains a constant or the value in the register is consistent with the value in the memory location assigned to i'. If i' is dirty, then i' does not contain a constant and the value in the registers is not consistent with the value in the location of i'. A pseudo-register i' is dirty when i' has been defined and its contents are maintained in a real register, but have not been stored to the memory location corresponding to i'. Notice that if a pseudo-register is not live, then we do not need to store it regardless of its being clean or dirty. Figure 1 gives an example of register allocation and assignment.

intermediate code	σ	FF LRA code	cost	Registers		
				R1	R2	R3
				-	-	-
	(read,{0})	LOAD &t0 ⇒ R1	2	t0	-	-
ADDI 3 t0 ⇒ t1	(write,{1})	ADDI 3 R1 ⇒ R2	1	t0	t1	-
	(read,{1,2})	LOADI 4 ⇒ R3	1	t0	t1	t2
SUB t1 t2 ⇒ t3	(write,{3})	SUB R2 R3 ⇒ R1	1	t3	t1	t2
		STORE R2 ⇒ &t1	2	t3	t1	t2
	(read,{3,4})	LOAD &t4 ⇒ R2	2	t3	t4	t2
MUL t3 t4 ⇒ t5	(write,{5})	MUL R1 R2 ⇒ R2	1	t3	t5	t2
	(read,{2,5})			t3	t5	t2
SUB t2 t5 ⇒ t6	(write,{6})	SUB R3 R2 ⇒ R1	1	t6	t5	t2
	(read,{1,6})	LOAD &t1 ⇒ R2	2	t6	t1	t2
ADD t1 t6 ⇒ t7	(write,{7})	ADD R1 R2 ⇒ R1	1	t7	t1	t2

total cost: 14

Fig. 2. Example of FF LRA with 3 registers. As compared to the optimal LRA shown in Figure 1, the FF heuristic results in an overall cost of 14 vs. 11 for the optimal allocation.

The leftmost column gives a sequence of intermediate code, and we assume that the code is only a basic block in a larger program. The set of live variables at the end of the basic block is $L = \{t7\}$. The second column reports the static reference sequence σ associated with the intermediate code. The third column gives the final code produced when a register allocation is enforced by (i) interspersing load and store operations in the code and (ii) rewriting pseudo-registers as the assigned actual registers. The last three columns give the register contents immediately after each instruction has been executed.

Since load and store operations are expensive to execute, an objective of register allocation is to minimize the total cost due to loads and stores. Specifically, we assume that load and store operations cost C times as much as any other operation. Notice that load immediates do not involve a memory access and cost $1/C$ as much as a load from memory. Since we assign different costs to different instructions, we will refer to a *weighted* instruction count. In this paper, we assume that the spill cost depends only on the number and type of inserted load and store operations, and not on the position they occupy. An example is given by the fourth column in Figure 1 where the costs of each operation are calculated when $C = 2$. The total cost of this sample allocation is 11, and it is the best possible allocation for this basic block. Different allocations yield different costs. In Figure 2, we report the same intermediate code as in Figure 1, but with a different allocation. Again, $C = 2$ and $L = \{t7\}$, but now the total cost is 14.

2.2 Discussion and Related Work

We study register allocation as the problem of assigning pseudo-registers to registers so as to minimize the spill cost. Other approaches view register allocation as a two step process. Find the minimum number of registers needed to execute the given code without spilling (*register sufficiency*), and if there are less physical registers than needed, introduce spill code, and repeat the previous step. It can be shown that the register sufficiency problem is exactly equivalent to coloring a certain graph, which is called *interference graph* [6]. Several authors put forth compelling arguments against such an approach:

- Some optimizations, like in-line expansion and loop unrolling, complicate the interference graph, and good colorings become hard to find. Hence, the solution to the register sufficiency problem will likely exceed the number of actual registers [13].
- As soon as the the number of registers is exceeded, then spill code must be inserted. Unfortunately, it is hard to decide which pseudo-registers to spill and where to insert spill code [13].
- Coloring addresses the problem of register assignment, but does not deal with the issue of deciding which pseudo-registers should actually be allocated to physical registers [20].

We add the following two observations in support of those arguments. First, the number of registers in the target architecture is fixed, while spill code is not. Therefore, registers are fixed resources and spill code corresponds to a cost. Minimizing a fixed resource is only a very indirect way to minimizing the actual spill cost. Moreover, register sufficiency (or, which is the same, graph coloring) is not only an NP-hard problem [9], but also a problem that is very hard to approximate efficiently [11].

Another approach to register allocation is *demand-driven register allocation* [20]. Demand-driven allocation starts from an inner loop LRA and expands it to a global allocation. Our formulation of LRA and our heuristics can be used in demand-driven register allocation. In demand-driven register allocation, the boundary conditions specify that no pseudo-register resides in a register at the basic block boundary. The subsequent global allocation cleans inefficiencies introduced by such boundary conditions.

Several different models have been proposed to formalize LRA. Historically, the first models are simpler and disregard some feature, whereas subsequent model are more complete. Belady considered a model where there are no boundary conditions, no multiple references in one instructions, and stores can be executed for free [4]. Subsequent work counted each load and store as a unit cost [12,13,19]. Briggs *et al.* give algorithms for global register allocation where each load and store from memory costs $C = 2$ times load immediate or any other operations [5]. Such cost model allows us to keep track of simple rematerializations. In this paper, we also consider the case when one instructions can generate multiple references. Multiple references arise commonly in actual code. For example, the instruction SUB t1 t2 => t3 requires that both t1 and t2 be simultaneously present in registers before the instruction could be executed. Such feature was first considered in [13]. The simplest LRA problem is Belady's, where stores have no cost, loads have unit cost, and there are no multiple references. Belady gave a polynomial-time algorithm for that LRA problem. Subsequently, it was found that, if the cost of a store were zero, the problem would be polynomially solvable even in the presence of different load costs, boundary conditions, and multiple references, but LRA is NP-hard as soon as stores are counted as having positive cost [7]. In conclusion, the hardness of LRA is due to the presence of store operations and not on several other features mentioned above.

We define boundary allocation as a functional restriction of global allocation, and local register allocation as a basic block allocation that respects boundary conditions. To the best of our knowledge, no such formulation had previously been given. The division of register allocation into boundary and local allocations makes possible to integrate an LRA algorithm with any global allocation by simply replacing its local portion. To the best of our knowledge, register allocation and register assignment have been considered as two distinct phases in all previous papers on LRA [3, 12, 13, 19]. Register allocation is more manageable if it is divided into allocation and assignment. Register assignment could conceivably cause the introduction of a large number of register swap operations. Actually, Proebsting *et al.* report that register assignment could almost always be enforced without swaps, and conclude that more emphasis should be placed on allocation rather than on assignment [20].

While we propose a three-phase approach to register allocation, some previous work takes a more compartmentalized approach to register allocation. The register set is partitioned into two sets: one to be used only by pseudo-register live in the basic block and the other only by global pseudo-registers. The former set of register is intended to be used for local allocation, and the latter for global allocation. It will be clear that all LRA algorithms in this paper would work correctly in this framework as well, but we give measurements only for our three-phase approach.

A few heuristics have been proposed for LRA. The oldest is Belady's *Furthest-First* (FF): if no register is empty, evict the pseudo-register that is requested furthest in the future [2]. FF is optimum in the simple Belady's model, which assumes that stores are executed at no cost and that there are no boundary conditions [12]. FF is also optimum when there are multiple references in one step [17], and is a $2C$-approximation algorithm for LRA even in the presence of paid stores and boundary conditions [7]. If stores have a positive cost, FF is not necessarily optimal : Figure 2 gives an FF allocation of cost 14, whereas the optimum is in Figure 1 and costs 11. FF's major problems are that it does not take into account the cost of storing and the effects of rematerialization. In the figure, pseudo-register t1 is stored and later reloaded at a total cost of 4 even though t2 contains a constant and so it could be evicted for free and reloaded at a unit cost. In this case, FF failed to detect that t2 could be rematerialized at a small cost. Another problem arises because FF does not distinguish between clean and dirty registers. In order to fix the latter problem, an heuristic called *Clean-First* (CF) has been introduced [8]. CF evicts a clean pseudo-register that is requested furthest in the future. If no clean pseudo-register exists, CF evicts a dirty pseudo-register that is requested furthest in the future. CF can be arbitrarily worse than the optimum [18]. Finally, Farach *et al.* introduced an algorithm $\mathcal{W}$ that is provably never worse than twice the optimum [7].

Since LRA is NP-hard, no polynomial-time algorithm can be reasonably expected to return an optimum solution in all cases. In particular, all the heuristics above fail to return the optimum solution in some cases. As opposed to heuristics, an optimum algorithm is proposed in [12, 14, 19]. Such optimum algorithm works only when $C = 1$ and takes exponential time and space in the worst case. The optimum algorithm failed to terminate on a few benchmarks due to lack of memory space; those tests were executed as late as 1989 [13].

3 Experimental Set-up

We performed experiments with ILOC, the Intermediate Language for Optimizing Compilers developed at Rice University[1]. We used several ILOC programs from the fmm and SPEC benchmarks. The benchmarks have been heavily optimized by the following passes: reassociation, lazy code motion, constant propagation, peephole analysis, dead code elimination, strength reduction, followed by a second pass of lazy code motion, constant propagation, peephole analysis, and dead code elimination. The resulting ILOC code is similar to that in the first column of tables 1 and 2: it is a sequence of intermediate code instructions that operate on an infinite set of pseudo-registers[2]. We did not have any part in the coding of the benchmark, in the choice of optimization passes, nor in the selection of the input to those benchmarks. We assumed we had N integer registers and N double precision registers. In our experiments, floating point operations are assumed to cost as much as integer ones. We remark that this is only a measurement choice, and that all algorithms in this paper would work if floating point operations were attributed a different cost than integer ones. We performed experiments for a number of registers ranging as $N = 16, 32, 64$, and spill cost $C = 2, 4, 8, 16$. We used a SUN UltraSparc1 (143MHz/64Mb) for algorithm timing experiments. All our allocators were written in C, compiled with gcc -03, and take as input the ILOC programs above. We run our allocators to obtain ILOC code that uses at most N physical registers. We also kept track of the *weighted instruction count* of each basic block, that is, we counted the number of instructions in each basic block weighted by a factor of C if they involve memory accesses, as described above. Then, we transformed that ILOC code into C programs with ILOC's i2c tool in order to simulate its execution. The resulting C program was instrumented to count the number of times each basic block was executed. We ran the resulting C code to obtain a *dynamic weighted instruction count*:

$$\sum_{\text{basic block } B} (\text{number of times } B \text{ was executed}) \times (\text{weighted instruction count for } B) .$$

The count is dynamic because it is collected by a simulation of code execution and it is weighted because spill code count is multiplied by a factor of C, as described above.

---

[1] URL: `http://softlib.rice.edu/MSCP/MSCP.html`

[2] The ILOC benchmarks can be obtained from Tim Harvey (`harv@cs.rice.edu`).

benchmark	prg	Double			Integer		
		blcks	avg len	avg var	blcks	avg len	avg var
fmm	fmin	56	22.93	20	54	4.46	3.70
	rkf45	129	10.85	8.78	132	26.51	23.07
	seval	37	7.81	5	43	19.05	14.44
	solve	96	4.88	3.85	110	27.79	24.14
	svd	214	7.96	6.25	226	38.74	34.77
	urand	10	6.1	4.1	13	18.38	12.62
	zeroin	31	20.10	16.10	30	5.7	4.7
spec	doduc	1898	16.66	12.43	1998	25.59	21.12
	fpppp	433	57.95	44.56	467	60.91	54.47
	matrix300	7	2.57	1.71	62	23.11	17.58
	tomcatv	72	11.68	9.67	73	73.48	68.14
spec95X	applu	493	16.26	10.82	679	55.89	47.32
	wave5X	6444	10.92	7.54	7006	53.25	45.23

Table 1. Characteristics of static reference sequences from optimized code. For each benchmark suite and program, the table gives the number of basic block with references to double (integer) variables, the average number of references to double (integer) variables per basic block, and the average number of distinct double (integer) variables in each block.

Table 1 describes the static reference sequences used in the experiments. Column 1 gives the name of the benchmark suite and column 2 the program name. Column 3, 4, and 5 report data for the static reference sequences of double precision variables. Column 3 gives the number of basic blocks where there is at least one live double precision variable. Column 4 gives the average length of the corresponding reference sequences. Column 5 gives the average number of distinct pseudo-registers referenced in a basic block. Finally, column 6, 7, and 8 report the same quantities for integer sequences. A measure of the size of the double (integer) LRA problem associated with one benchmark can be obtained by the product (number of double (integer) blocks) × (average double (integer) length).

The program fpppp is quite different from the other benchmarks. First, fpppp has on average the longest double and integer reference sequences. Moreover, fpppp contains the longest sequence among all our benchmarks: the basic block _.fpppp_ generates a double precision reference sequence of length 6579 — nearly 5 times longer than any other sequence. The program tomcatv has long integer sequences on average, but not long double sequence. Some optimization passes (e.g. loop unrolling) produce long basic block, but no such optimization is available in the ILOC system and none has been applied to our benchmarks.

We conducted experiments to compare the FF and CF heuristics, our new heuristic called MIX and a new optimum algorithm. We were mostly interested in two quantities: the *quality of the allocation* each algorithm returns and the *speed* of the algorithm itself. Our purpose was to identify possible trade-offs between compiler speed and the speed of generated code. We measured allocation quality by means of a dynamic weighted instruction count, which we described above. The speed of the allocator itself was measured as follows. We inserted rusage routine calls before and after each allocator was actually called. Then, we summed up the user and system time elapsed between the two rusage calls. In this way, we counted only the time needed to execute the LRA allocators, and we disregarded the time for reading the input ILOC files, constructing data structures that represent the associated LRA problems, and performing live range analysis. We also inserted rusage code to estimate the time spent for live range analysis. The live range analysis time was always estimated separately from the allocation time.

LRA performance can be measured only after boundary allocations are fixed. A possible choice is to extract the boundary allocation from a state-of-the-art global allocator. Unfortunately, no such allocator is currently available in the ILOC infrastructure distribution. A *canonical* boundary allocator assumes that all registers are empty at the beginning and end of each basic block [1]. We used this boundary allocation. However, this is only an experimental choice, and that all discussed algorithms would work for any other boundary allocator. More work will be needed to evaluate the different LRA algorithms for other boundary allocators.

4   An Integer Program

We propose a new optimum LRA algorithm that is based on branch-and-bound. The algorithm is slower than some heuristics, but it returns the best possible local allocation. The optimum algorithm is used in this paper as a local allocator and as a definite point of comparison for faster heuristics. Substantial algorithm engineering was required to speed-up a branch-and-bound procedure. Specifically, the network structure of the integer program was isolated and exploited to reduce the number of integer variables and the time needed to solve the initial relaxation. Further details are omitted for lack of space and can be found in [18].

We measured the running time of the optimum in seconds for $C = 2$ and several values of N. As discussed above, measured times do not include I/O, live range analysis, and the time to set-up the problem matrices. The optimum took always less than one minute except for one benchmark (fpppp). We can compare the branch-and-bound time with the size of the benchmark (which has been defined in §3 on the basis of table 1). Broadly speaking, in most cases the optimum took longer on larger programs. The branch-and-bound running time decreases as N increases for all programs but fpppp. An intuitive explanation is that when more registers are available, most allocation problems should become easier.

The fpppp benchmark has a different behavior because it took 25 minutes when $N = 8$ and 3 minutes for $N = 16$, while it was below 30 seconds for all other values of N. We found that fpppp could be explained in terms of its longest sequence of references. The branch-and-bound algorithm does not generate any node for that sequence for all $N \neq 8, 16$, but it visits 12807 nodes for $N = 8$ and 1034 nodes for $N = 16$. Correspondingly, the running time jumps from 26 seconds to 25 minutes. No other basic block exhibits such an extreme behavior. The running time is exposed to the "NP-noise", which the long basic block dramatically amplifies.

5 Heuristics

Heuristic Definition We experimented with three heuristics. Each heuristic specifies which pseudo-register is to be evicted if no empty register is available. *Furthest-First* (FF) determines the set S of pseudo-registers that are requested furthest in the future, and evicts a clean pseudo-register in S. If all pseudo-register in S are dirty, an arbitrary element in S is evicted [2,7]. *Clean-First (CF)* evicts a clean pseudo-register that is used furthest in the future. If no clean pseudo-register exists, a dirty pseudo-register is evicted that is requested furthest in the future [8]. The heuristic *MIX* is based on the algorithm $\mathcal{W}$ [7]. While $\mathcal{W}$ is detailed in [7], we will also report it here for the sake of completeness.

The algorithm $\mathcal{W}$ has an intuitive explanation in terms of the integer program that corresponds to LRA. That program consists of two parts: a network matrix and side constraints. One could wish that the side constraints disappeared, because the network matrix leads to a polynomial-time solution. Unfortunately, it is not possible to simply delete a set of constraints without altering the problem at hand. However, it is possible to perform the following three step procedure, called *Lagrangian relaxation*: (1) Insert a penalty in the objective function with the property that the penalty increases if the side constraints are violated, (2) remove all side constraints, and (3) solve the resulting problem. The idea is that, if the penalty is big enough, the side constraints will not be violated even though they are not explicitly imposed. Finally, the resulting problem is defined only by the network matrix, and so it can be solved in polynomial-time as a network flow problem. The penalty function is to be chosen appropriately: formulas can be found in [7] and are omitted from the present paper. MIX is a new heuristic that invokes selectively either FF or $\mathcal{W}$. The gist is that the computationally more expensive $\mathcal{W}$ algorithm should be invoked only when there is an opportunity to improve significantly on FF. MIX invokes $\mathcal{W}$ when the reference sequence is longer than a certain threshold (1500) and there are a at least 150 dirty variables simultaneously alive [18].

Experimental Results The experimental results can be divided into two broad categories: results for the benchmarks fpppp and tomcatv and results for all other benchmarks. First, we report results for all other benchmarks, and then we give our findings for fpppp and tomcatv. On all benchmarks except fpppp and tomcatv, no heuristic was worse than .5% of the optimum, and, on those instances, FF and MIX took nearly the same time and were faster than CF. Such findings hold with minimal variations for all benchmarks except fpppp and tomcatv. We turn now to fpppp and tomcatv and report our results in Table 2

C	prg		OPT	FF	%	MIX	%	CF	%
2	fpppp	time	145.3	0.3149	0.2167%	0.5205	0.3582%	0.6929	0.4769%
		cost	193357	194858	0.776%	193713	0.184%	209013	8.1%
	tomcatv	time	0.9069	0.0443	4.88%	0.0761	8.388%	0.0992	10.93%
		cost	413779	416380	0.629%	413779	0%	421582	1.89%
4	fpppp	time	151.2	0.3186	0.2107%	0.5218	0.3452%	0.6957	0.4601%
		cost	251322	254325	1.19%	252259	0.373%	282635	12.5%
	tomcatv	time	0.9138	0.0433	4.738%	0.0748	8.182%	0.1055	11.55%
		cost	484108	489310	1.07%	484108	0%	499714	3.22%
8	fpppp	time	140.6	0.3224	0.2293%	0.815	0.5797%	0.709	0.5044%
		cost	367253	373258	1.64%	369222	0.536%	429879	17.1%
	tomcatv	time	0.9064	0.0433	4.775%	0.0747	8.242%	0.0969	10.69%
		cost	624766	635170	1.67%	624766	0%	655978	5%
16	fpppp	time	144.4	0.3198	0.2215%	0.7655	0.5301%	0.7042	0.4877%
		cost	599115	611125	2%	601868	0.459%	724367	20.9%
	tomcatv	time	0.8915	0.0426	4.779%	0.0732	8.212%	0.0974	10.92%
		cost	906082	926890	2.3%	906082	0%	968506	6.89%

Table 2. Performance for $N = 16$ registers. Time is algorithm running time. Cost is weighted dynamic instruction count. Percentage time is fraction of optimum. Percentage cost is variation over optimum.

and 3. Additional results are presented in [18]. The time rows represent the time taken by the heuristics to run in seconds. It does not include the time to read the input file nor the time to perform live range analysis, as discussed above. The cost rows report the total weighted dynamic instruction count in thousands. We make the following observations on the entries in the table. FF, CF, and MIX were always at least ten times faster than the branch-and-bound algorithm. FF and CF are independent of C, and they took the same time for all values of C. In most cases, an increase of C caused MIX to slow down, but in some cases MIX was actually faster for a larger value of C. CF produced allocations that were as much as 23% worse than FF and MIX. FF produced allocations that were up to 4% worse than the optimum for $N = 32$. Moreover, FF and CF produced quite different allocations even in the case $C = 2$, and the gap increased with C.

MIX produced allocations that are up to .9% worse than the optimum and never took much more than 1 second. MIX cost was always better than FF's or CF's in these experiments. The gap between MIX cost and the other heuristics grows larger with C. The time taken by MIX is often less than the time taken by live-variable analysis, a necessary prerequisite to almost all register allocators. The time for live range analysis was 1.58 seconds on fpppp, and .01 seconds on tomcatv.

Discussion We found an interesting correlation between the performance of heuristics and the average length of basic blocks (average basic block length

C	prg		OPT	FF	%	MIX	%	CF	%
2	fpppp	time	19.07	0.3056	1.602%	0.5107	2.678%	0.686	3.597%
		cost	167076	169013	1.16%	167633	0.333%	178557	6.87%
	tomcatv	time	0.8496	0.0417	4.911%	0.0735	8.645%	0.0985	11.59%
		cost	343450	343450	0%	343450	0%	343450	0%
4	fpppp	time	19.22	0.3101	1.613%	0.5134	2.671%	0.6907	3.593%
		cost	198815	202689	1.95%	199928	0.56%	221776	11.5%
	tomcatv	time	0.8568	0.0414	4.829%	0.0731	8.53%	0.1048	12.23%
		cost	343450	343450	0%	343450	0%	343450	0%
8	fpppp	time	18.95	0.3101	1.636%	0.9179	4.844%	0.6943	3.664%
		cost	262293	270040	2.95%	264118	0.696%	308215	17.5%
	tomcatv	time	0.676	0.0293	4.341%	0.0580	8.581%	0.0628	9.285%
		cost	343450	343450	0%	343450	0%	343450	0%
16	fpppp	time	19.73	0.3096	1.57%	0.8418	4.267%	0.6954	3.525%
		cost	389248	404743	3.98%	392802	0.913%	481093	23.6%
	tomcatv	time	0.8336	0.0409	4.909%	0.0718	8.61%	0.0964	11.56%
		cost	343450	343450	0%	343450	0%	343450	0%

Table 3. Performance for $N = 32$ double registers and $N = 32$ integer registers. Time is algorithm running time. Cost is weighted dynamic instruction count. Percentage time is fraction of optimum. Percentage cost is variation over optimum.

is found in table 1). In general, programs with long basic block should be harder to solve due to the NP-hardness of the problem. Indeed, fpppp has the longest average basic block length and the largest gap between the optimum and the heuristics. The program tomcatv has long integer sequences, but not long double sequence. Correspondingly, we observe that heuristics performed better on tomcatv than on fpppp. However, tomcatv still gave rise to substantial performance differences when $N = 16$ and C is large. All other benchmarks have shorter basic blocks, and no significant discrepancy between optimum and heuristics was detected. Long basic blocks are produced by some optimization passes (e.g., loop unrolling, superblock scheduling), but, unfortunately, none is available to us. Since we found that a large average basic block length dramatically increased the difference between heuristics and optimum on our benchmarks, it is easy to conjecture that length-increasing optimizations would widen the heuristic-optimum gap to much more substantial figures than those above for most programs. We notice that the *average static* sequence length affected the hardness of LRA instances. In other words, when we take the average length, we do not weigh the sequence length by the number of times basic blocks were executed. It is not at all obvious *a priori* why a static average should be related to a dynamic instruction count, but we found that this was indeed the case in our benchmarks.

Integer programming is useful for several hard compilation problems; see [15] for a survey. Network flow techniques have been used for intraprocedural register assignment [16]. Lagrangian relaxation was proposed by the mathematician Lagrange in the context of non-linear optimization, and was introduced into discrete optimization by Held and Karp [10]. The gist of Lagrangian relaxation is that, given a complicate problem with many types of constraints, hard constraints should be moved into the objective function so that the remaining problem is easy to solve. In compiler optimization, there are examples where several types of constraints are imposed. If only one type of constraints existed, the problem would be easy, but multiple types of constraints complicate the problem solution. It would be interesting to understand whether Lagrangian relaxation could be exploited to solve those problems efficiently. Finally, we notice that live range analysis takes much longer than any LRA heuristic. As a consequence, live range analysis dominates the time required to perform LRA.

6 Conclusions

In this paper, we have proposed an approach to register allocation that divides an allocator into three successive phases: boundary, LRA, and register assignment. We have studied the problem of local register allocation in the context of four different algorithms. We have given an optimum algorithm and a new heuristic called MIX. The optimum algorithm is based on an integer programming formulation and it was reasonably fast. With the exception of one benchmark program, the optimal solution was always computed in less than a minute. The heuristic MIX combines two previous algorithms FF and $\mathcal{W}$ (the algorithm $\mathcal{W}$ is, in turn, based on a Lagrangian relaxation of the integer program), and returned allocations that were within 1% of the optimum. MIX outperformed FF more significantly when C is larger. All three heuristics, FF, MIX, and CF, computed solutions in less time than typically required for the live variable analysis step within the compiler. For short basic block, the qualities of the generated allocations were comparable across the three heuristics. However, for larger basic block sizes, our findings suggest that MIX should be the best choice for LRA on optimized code, especially when C is large.

More work will be needed to evaluate the LRA algorithms and our three-phase framework in the context of different global register allocators. In addition, since the results suggest that the performance gap between the algorithms will increase with increasing basic block sizes, we are planning to investigate the impact of source level transformations that potentially increase basic block sizes, including loop unrolling, inlining, and speculative execution (superblocks).

Acknowledgments

We gratefully acknowledge helpful conversations with Bill Pugh and Barbara Ryder. We thank Keith Cooper, Tim Harvey, and Taylor Simpson from the Massively Scalar Compiler Group at Rice University for providing us with the ILOC software and benchmark codes.

References

1. A. V. Aho, R. Sethi, and J. D. Ullman. *Compilers: Principles, Techniques, and Tools.* Addison-Wesley, Reading, MA, 1986.
2. J. Backus. The history of FORTRAN I, II, and III. In Richard Wexelblat, editor, *History of Programming Languages*, ACM Monographs Series, pages 25–45. Academic Press, New York, 1981.
3. J. C. Beatty. Register assignment algorithm for generation of highly optimized code. *IBM J. Res. Develop.*, 18:20–39, January 1974.
4. L. A. Belady. A study of replacement algorithms for a virtual storage computer. *IBM Systems Journal*, 5(2):78–101, 1966.
5. P. Briggs, K. Cooper, and L. Torczon. Improvements to graph coloring register allocation. *ACM Trans. on Programming Lang. and Sys.*, 16(3):428–455, May 1994.
6. G. J. Chaitin. Register allocation & spilling via graph coloring. In *Proceedings of the ACM SIGPLAN Symposium on Compiler Construction*, pages 98–105, 1982.
7. M. Farach and V. Liberatore. On local register allocation. In *Proceedings of the 9th Annual ACM-SIAM Symposium on Discrete Algorithms*, pages 564–573, 1998.
8. C. N. Fischer and R. J. LeBlanc, Jr. *Crafting a Compiler*. Benjamin/Cummings, Menlo Park, CA, 1988.
9. M. R. Garey and D. S. Johnson. *Computers and Intractability. A Guide to the Theory of NP-Completeness*. Freeman, San Francisco, 1979.
10. M. Held and R. Karp. The traveling salesman problem and minimum spanning trees. *Operations Research*, 18:1138–1162, 1970.
11. D. S. Hochbaum, editor. *Approximation Algorithms for NP-hard Problems*. PWS Publishing Company, Boston, 1997.
12. L. P. Horwitz, R. M. Karp, R. E. Miller, and S. Winograd. Index register allocation. *Journal of the Association for Computing Machinery*, 13(1):43–61, January 1966.
13. W-C. Hsu, C. N. Fischer, and J. R. Goodman. On the minimization of load/stores in local register allocation. *IEEE Transactions on Software Engineering*, 15(10):1252–1260, October 1989.
14. K. Kennedy. Index register allocation in straight line code and simple loops. In Randall Rustin, editor, *Design and Optimization of Compilers*, pages 51–63. Prentice-Hall, Englewood Cliffs, NJ, 1972.
15. U. Kremer. Optimal and near-optimal solutions for hard compilation problems. *Parallel Processing Letters*, 7(2):371–378, 1997.
16. S. M. Kurlander and C. N. Fischer. Minimum cost interprocedural register allocation. In *Proceedings of the 23rd ACM SIGPLAN-SIGACT Symposium on Principles of Programming Languages*, 1996.
17. V. Liberatore. Uniform multipaging reduces to paging. *Information Processing Letters*, 67:9–12, 1998.
18. V. Liberatore, M. Farach-Colton, and U. Kremer. Evaluation of algorithms for local register allocation. Technical Report TR98-376, Laboratory for Computer Science Research, Rutgers University, 1998.
19. F. Luccio. A comment on index register allocation. *Communications of the ACM*, 10(9):572–574, September 1967.
20. T. A. Proebsting and C. N. Fischer. Demand-driven register allocation. *ACM Trans. on Programming Lang. and Sys.*, 18(6):683–710, November 1996.
21. J. Ruttenberg, G. R. Gao, A. Stoutchinin, and W. Lichtenstein. Software pipelining showdown: Optimal vs. heuristics methods in production compilers. In *Proc. SIGPLAN '96 Conf. on Programming Language Design and Implementation*, pages 1–11, May 1996.

Efficient State-Diagram Construction Methods for Software Pipelining

Chihong Zhang[1], Ramaswamy Govindarajan[2], Sean Ryan[1], and Guang R. Gao[1]

[1] Dept. of Electric and Computer Engineering, Univ. of Delaware, Newark, DE 19711, USA, E-mail:{czhang, ryan, ggao}@capsl.udel.edu
[2] Supercomputer Edn. & Res. Centre, Indian Institute of Science, Bangalore, 560 012, India, E-mail: govind@serc.iisc.ernet.in

Abstract. State diagram based approach has been proposed as an effective way to model resource constraints in traditional instruction scheduling and software pipelining methods. However, the constructed state diagram for software pipelining method (i) is very large and (ii) contains significant amount of replicated, and hence redundant, information on legal latency sequences. As a result, the construction of state diagrams can take very large computation time.

In this paper, we propose two methods for the efficient construction of state diagrams. In the first method, we relate the construction of state diagram to a well-known problem in graph theory, namely the enumeration of *maximal independent sets* of a graph. This facilitates the use of an existing algorithm as a direct method for constructing distinct latency sequences. The second method is a heuristic approach which exploits the structure of state diagram construction to eliminate redundancy at the earliest opportunity in an aggressive fashion. The heuristic method uses a surprisingly simple check which is formally shown to *completely* eliminate redundancy in the state diagram. From our experimental results on two real architectures, both of the two methods show a great reduction in state diagram construction time.

1 Introduction

Recent studies on modulo scheduling, an instruction scheduling method for loops [9, 10, 15, 16, 3], in a production compiler has reported significant improvement (up to 35%) in the overall runtime for a suite of SPEC floating point benchmark programs [17]. On the other hand, rapid advances in VLSI technology and computer architecture present an important challenge for compiler designers: a modulo scheduler must be able to handle machine resource constraints much more complex than before and may need to search for an increasingly larger number of schedules before a desirable one is chosen. Therefore, in exploiting the advantage of modulo scheduling in a production compiler, it is important to be able to handle complex resource constraints efficiently and find a good modulo schedule very quickly.

Proebsting and Fraser proposed an interesting approach that uses finite state automata for modeling complex resource constraints in instruction scheduling [14]. Their approach was based on [12] and subsequently improved and applied to production compilers in [2]. This approach was extended to software pipelining methods in [6, 7]. This paper focuses on the efficient construction of finite state automata for software pipelining methods. In the above methods [2, 6, 7, 12, 14], processor resources are modeled using a finite state automata (or state diagram) which is constructed from the resource usage table for each instruction (class). Each path in the state diagram represents a legal latency sequence which could be directly used by the scheduler for modeling resource contention. The construction of the state diagram is typically done off-line and stored in some form so that the instruction scheduler, at the schedule time, only need to read this information. This has effectively reduced the problem of checking structural hazards in the scheduling method to a fast table lookup, resulting in several fold speedup [2, 7, 12]. In particular, the enhanced Co-Scheduling method, a state diagram based modulo scheduling method, reports a 2-fold speedup in the scheduling time (time to construct the software pipelined schedule) [7].

There are two major challenges facing this Co-scheduling method: (i)the huge size of the state diagram and (ii)the the huge amount of redundant information (paths in the state diagram, which will be used to guide the Co-Scheduling) inside the naively constructed state diagram. A practical solution to the first problem is to construct only a large enough (instead of complete) set of non-redundant state diagram information. However, the huge amount of redundancy makes the construction time extremely long.

To illustrate the above problem, we present several experimental evidences. In one experiment conducted by us, the state diagram for the DEC Alpha 21064 processor with an initiation interval (**II**) equal to 3, contained 224,400 latency sequences, out of which only 30 were distinct. In another experiment, the state diagram for an **II** = 16 contained more than 74 Million (74,183,493) distinct paths[1]. Lastly, to generate 100,000 distinct latency sequences in the above state diagram, it took more than 24 hours on an UltraSparc machine. This obviously makes the Co-Scheduling approach impractical. The previous effort on reduced state diagram [7, 8] has met with only very limited success.

In this paper, we propose two methods to drastically reduce the construction time of state diagrams by eliminating the redundancy cleverly during the construction. The first of these methods relates the construction to a well-known problem in graph theory, namely the enumeration of *maximal independent sets* of an interference graph. This facilitates the use of an existing enumeration algorithm as a direct fast method for constructing *all* latency sequences. We refer to this method as the Enumeration of Maximal Independent Set (E-MIS) method. Two major advantages of this method are that it is a direct method and it generates only distinct (non-redundant) latency sequences.

---

[1] The number of actual paths (including the redundant ones) is far too many to count and generate!

The second method uses a heuristic approach to eliminate redundant paths by exploiting the structure of state diagram construction and by employing an aggressive redundance removal approach. This is accomplished by enforcing a surprisingly simple *redundance constraint* which eliminates *completely* all redundant paths. We refer to this method as the Redundancy Prevention (RP) method, as it identifies, at the earliest in the construction process, states which could cause redundancy and prunes them aggressively. We formally establish that the proposed heuristic results in redundance-free state diagram. However, the redundance constraint used by the heuristic is only a necessary (but not sufficient) condition. As a consequence, the aggressive pruning may eliminate some non-redundant paths as well. However, we find that the RP method to work well in practice.

We compare the efficiency of the proposed methods with that of the reduced state-diagram construction (RD) method in modeling two real processors, namely the DEC Alpha 21064 processor and the Cydra VLIW processor [3]. Our experimental results reveal that the proposed methods result in significant reduction in the construction time by about 3 to 4 orders of magnitude which means we can provide a reasonable amount of distinct paths within minutes instead of days. Another interesting observation made from our experiments is that the RP method, though a heuristic approach which can possibly eliminate non-redundant paths, does reasonably well in enumerating *all* non-redundant paths. In fact, for the two processors modeled and for small values of II less than 16, it did not miss a single path. Lastly, we use the latency sequences constructed by RP and E-MIS methods in the Co-Scheduling framework to construct software pipelined schedules. Initial experiments reveal that the proposed methods do seem to perform competitively, and in a reasonable computation time. This provides an empirical evidence for the use of state diagram approach as a practical and efficient method in software pipelining methods.

In Section 2, we present a brief review of the state diagram based software pipelining method. The problem formulation and the proposed approaches are informally discussed in Section 2.2. Section 3 and 4 respectively present the details of the two proposed methods. In Section 5 we compare the performance of E-MIS and RP methods with the reduced state diagram construction. Concluding remarks are provided in Section 6.

2 Background and Motivation

Software pipelining has been found to be an efficient compilation technique that results in significant performance improvement at runtime [9, 10, 15, 16]. Modeling of resource constraints (or structural hazards) in software pipelining is becoming increasingly complex in modern processor architectures. However, an efficient resource model is crucial for the success of the scheduling method [2, 4, 6, 14]. In this section, first, we review the state diagram based resource model used in software pipelining [6]. Subsequently we motivate our approaches to the efficient construction of state diagram.

2.1 Background

Conventional approaches to model resource constraints uses a simple reservation table (see Figure 1(a)) [13, 10, 9, 15, 16]. The state diagram approach is a systematic and effective way to represent the resource usages and conflicts when multiple operations of a loop are scheduled [6]. Such an approach is efficient as it uses the underlying notions of forbidden (permissible) latencies in the classical pipeline theory.

A state diagram represents legal latency sequences that do not cause structural hazards in the pipeline. Each state in a state diagram represents the current state of the pipeline (operating under software pipelining with an Initiation Interval (**II**)). Associated with each state is the set of permissible latencies at which new initiations can be made from the current state. An edge from state S to S' in the state diagram represents an initiation with a latency l cycles after S. If the current state S has permissible latencies $\{p_1, p_2, \cdots, p_k\}$, then the new state S' will have permissible latencies $p = ((p_i - l) \bmod \mathbf{II})$, for each $i \in [1, k]$, provided p is a permissible latency in the initial state S_0. The state diagram for the above reservation table is shown in Figure 2. For more detailed information on related concepts and the construction of state diagrams see [6–8].

Stage	Time Steps			
	0	1	2	3
1	x			
2		x	x	
3				x

Stage	Time Steps							
	0	1	2	3	4	5	6	7
1	x							
2		x	x					
3			x					

(a) Reservation Table   (b) Resource Usage when **II** = 8.

Fig. 1. A Reservation Table and its Resource Usage for an **II**

A path $S_0 \xrightarrow{p_1} S_1 \xrightarrow{p_2} S_2 \cdots \xrightarrow{p_k} S_k$ in the state diagram corresponds to **a latency sequence** $\{p_1, p_2, \cdots, p_k\}$. The latency sequence represents $k + 1$ initiations that are made at time steps $0, p_1, (p_1 + p_2), \cdots, (p_1 + p_2 + \cdots + p_k)$. In modulo scheduling, these time steps correspond to the **offset values**

$$0, p_1, (p_1 + p_2) \bmod \mathbf{II}, \cdots, (p_1 + p_2 + \cdots + p_k) \bmod \mathbf{II}$$

in a repetitive kernel. For example, the path $S_1 \xrightarrow{2} S_2 \xrightarrow{2} S_3 \xrightarrow{2} S_4$ corresponds to initiations at time steps $(0, 2, 4, 6)$. These offset values for the path are collectively referred to as **offset set**, or in short form OffSet. Once the state diagram is constructed, then the OffSets corresponding to various paths can be used to guide the enhanced Co-Scheduling method to make quick and "good" decision about when (at what offset value) to schedule an instruction in the pipeline [7].

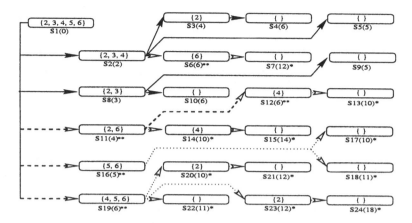

Fig. 2. State Diagram for the Example Reservation Table

2.2 Problem Formulation

The major challenge in the construction of a state diagram is that it can become extremely huge, consisting several million states, even for moderate values of **II**. For example, for the DEC Alpha architecture, the state diagram consists of 10, 648, and 224,400 paths when **II** is varied from 1 to 3! Fortunately, several paths in the state diagram are shown to be redundant [7, 8] in the sense that the corresponding OffSets are equal. In the above 3 state diagrams for DEC Alpha, only 3, 9, and 30 paths are *distinct*.

For the state diagram shown in Figure 2, the paths $S_1 \xrightarrow{2} S_2 \xrightarrow{2} S_3 \xrightarrow{2} S_4$ and the path $S_1 \xrightarrow{4} S_{11} \xrightarrow{6} S_{14} \xrightarrow{4} S_{15}$ correspond to the same OffSet $(0, 2, 4, 6)$, and hence one of them is redundant. The reduced state diagram construction (RD) method proposed in [7] recognizes and eliminates redundant paths by making a simple observation. All states which correspond to initiation times[2] greater than **II** are pruned. Consider the the state S_{14} which corresponds to an initiation at time 10 (shown in brackets adjacent to the state number in Figure 2). In Figure 2, these states (*e.g.*, S_7, S_{13}, and S_{14}) are marked with a '*' and the arcs leading to these states are shown as dotted lines. Those marked with a '**' (the arcs leading to them are dashed lines) are also redundant states. The RD method is unable to recognize them. This makes it somewhat inefficient in removing the redundancy. What's worse for the RD method is that it cannot completely eliminate all redundant paths. This is especially so for architectures involving multiple instruction types where different function units may share some of the resources, a common feature in real architectures.

In order for state diagram based approach to be useful in real compilers, it is important to deal with the redundancy-elimination in an efficient way. Further, even after eliminating all redundant paths, the state diagram may still consist of

---

[2] Initiation time is the sum of the latency values from S_0 to that state along the path. Initiation time modulo **II** corresponds to an offset value.

a large number of distinct paths. Hence, for practical reasons, the most important is to construct a large subset of distinct OffSets within a short time.

In this paper we propose two efficient solutions, the E-MIS method and the RP method, both of which are proved to be successful in attacking the above problem.

3   A Graph Theoretic Approach for OffSets Generation

In this section we relate the generation of OffSets to a well-know graph theory problem which facilitates the use of an existing algorithm as a direct and efficient method. This is based on a correspondence between the set of OffSets and the maximal compatibility classes which was established in [7].

First, we denote the set of permissible offset values by $\mathcal{O} = \{o_0, o_1, \cdots, o_{n-1}\}$ which includes all initial permissible latencies and 0 [7]. For the example discussed in Section 2.1, the set of permissible offset values is $\mathcal{O} = \{0, 2, 3, 4, 5, 6\}$. The following definitions are useful in the discussion.

Definition 1. A path $S_0 \xrightarrow{p_1} S_1 \xrightarrow{p_2} S_2 \cdots \xrightarrow{p_k} S_f$ in the state diagram is called **primary** if the sum of the latency values does not exceed **II**, *i.e.*, $p_1 + p_2 + \cdots + p_k <$ **II**. A path is called **secondary** if $p_1 + p_2 + \cdots + p_k >$ **II**.

Definition 2. A **compatibility class** $\mathcal{C}$ (with respect to $\mathcal{O}$) is a subset of $\mathcal{O}$ such that for any pair of elements c_1 and c_2 in $\mathcal{C}$, $(c_1 - c_2)$ mod **II** is in $\mathcal{O}$. A compatibility class is **maximal** if it is not a proper subset of any other compatibility class.

Two compatible classes for $\mathcal{O}$ are $\{0, 2, 4, 6\}$ and $\{0, 2, 5\}$. These compatibility classes are maximal.

Lemma 3. *The OffSet of any path from the start state S_0 to the final state S_f in the state diagram forms a maximal compatibility class of $\mathcal{O}$.*

Lemma 4. *For each maximal compatibility class C of permissible offset values, there exists a primary path in the state diagrams whose OffSet O is equal to C.*

Hence obtaining all maximal compatible classes is a direct way of obtaining the OffSets. In order to obtain all maximal compatible classes of $\mathcal{O}$, we represent the compatibility information (between pairs of permissible offset values) in the form of an interference graph. The interference graph G for $\mathcal{O}$ has n vertices, each vertex representing one permissible offset value in $\mathcal{O}$. Two vertices v_1 and v_2 in G are connected by an edge, if the corresponding offset values are not compatible. It is possible that a vertex may not share an edge with any other vertex in the graph. The offset value corresponding to such a vertex is compatible with other permissible offset values.

The interference graph for the permissible offset values of our example, $\mathcal{O} = \{0, 2, 3, 4, 5, 6\}$ is shown in Figure 3. The offset value corresponding to each vertex

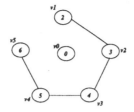

Fig. 3. Interference Graph for Permissible Offset Set {0,2,3,4,5,6}

is shown in circle in the figure. There is an edge between vertex v_1 (corresponding to offset 2) and v_2 (corresponding to offset 3) as 2 and 3 are not compatible in $\mathcal{O}$. Next we state the definitions of maximal independent sets from [5].

Definition 5. A subset S of vertices is an **independent set**, if there exists no edge between any two vertices in S. An independent set is said to be **maximal**, if it is not contained in any other independent set.

In our example graph, $\{v_0, v_1, v_3, v_5\}$ and $\{v_0, v_2, v_4\}$ are maximal independent sets.

From the above definitions and the description of the interference graph, it clearly follows that each maximal independent set in the graph corresponds to a maximal compatibility class, and hence an OffSet in the reduced state diagram. Thus to generate the set of all OffSets of the state diagram, one needs to enumerate all maximal independent sets in the interference graph.

An efficient algorithm for this is reported in [18]. This enumeration of MIS is a direct method for the generation of *all* OffSets. An attractive features of this approach is that it does not incur any redundancy in the generation of OffSets. The complexity of the E-MIS method is $O(\alpha \cdot \beta \cdot \gamma)$ where α, β and γ represent, respectively, the number of vertices, the number of edges, and the number of MIS present in the given graph. The space complexity of the algorithm is $O(\alpha + \beta)$. The number of vertices α in the interference graph is equal to n, the number permissible offset values. Further, since each edge in the graph represents non-compatibility between a pair of offset values, there can be at most $O(n^2)$ edges. Lastly an upper bound for γ can be obtained by further relating maximal compatibility classes to the largest *antichain*[3] of powerset of $\mathcal{O}$ [11]. The cardinality of the largest antichain is given by $\binom{n}{\lfloor n/2 \rfloor}$. Not surprisingly, this bound on γ is exponential in n.

4 Redundancy Prevention Method for State Diagram Construction

In this section, we present the details of the RP method which exploits the the structure of the state diagram construction to identify and eliminate redundancy

---

[3] An antichain A is a subset of S such that for any two elements a_1 and a_2 in A, a_1 is not a proper subset of a_2.

at the earliest opportunity. Further an attractive feature of the RP method is that it follows an aggressive approach for redundance elimination, even though this may mean missing a few OffSets. However our experimental results show that this aggressiveness pays well in state diagrams for real architecture without much loss of information.

4.1 The Redundancy Prevention Algorithm

In this discussion we will assume that the construction of the state diagram proceeds top down, in a depth-first fashion. In our example state diagram (Figure 2), consider the subtrees with their roots at S_6, S_{11}, S_{16}, and S_{19}. All paths in these subtrees are redundant. Thus if our construction method can somehow identify these states and eliminate them before the subtrees rooted on these state are constructed, then the redundant paths through these states can be eliminated.

If we carefully study the example state diagram, we find an interesting characteristic for these four states — the issue time or offset value of a state S appears in the subtree rooted at one of its siblings S'. In particular, the sibling S' is constructed earlier than S in the depth-first construction method. We refer to this sibling S' as a *left sibling* of state S. Notice that there could be more than one left sibling for state S. For convenience, we use the term "*left sibling subtree*" for the tree rooted at a left sibling. For instance, subtrees rooted at S_2 and S_8 are the left sibling subtrees of state S_{11}.

If we inspect this property – the offset value of a state S appearing in the left-sibling subtree — a little more carefully it reveals the fact that the partial OffSet, consisting of offset values for all states from the start state to S, is a subset of the OffSet for another path in the left-sibling subtree. Note that all paths through state S will have this same partial OffSet. Further, as the values in an OffSet are mutually *compatible*, the partial OffSet determines, to a great extent, what other values could be in the OffSets for the paths through S. As a consequence, it is very likely that all these paths could be redundant, and hence can be eliminated by not generating the state S and the subtree rooted at S. The RP method aggressively removes these states to prevent redundancy. Note, however, it is only *likely* that all paths through S are redundant. In other words, a state that satisfies the above property may have a path that is not redundant. We defer a discussion on this to Section 4.2. Based on the above observation, we introduce the following constraint that is used in the RP method.

Definition 6 (Redundancy Constraint). A state S is said to satisfy the redundancy constraint (RC) if the issue time of state S is the same as that of a state S' and S' has occurred in one of the left sibling subtrees of S.

The basic steps in the RP method are:

(1) Follow the depth-first construction rule to construct the state diagram.
(2) If a given state S has already created k child states $S_1, S_2, \cdots, S_k$ and is going to create a new child state S_{k+1} (it should be noted here that, at this time,

all states in the subtrees rooted at $S_1, S_2, \cdots, S_k$ have been constructed), the redundancy constraint checks whether the issue time (offset value) of S_{k+1} has occurred in subtrees rooted at $S_1, S_2, \cdots, S_k$. If so, the state S_{k+1} will not be created; else it is added to the state diagram.

Step 2 sounds time-consuming because for each new child state to be created we need to check all states in the left sibling subtrees. It should be noticed here that the range of offset values is fixed, *i.e.*, from 0 to $\mathbf{II} - 1$. Therefore, it is not difficult to construct an implementation for the RP method the RC check could be done as a simple table lookup. The table, called "`left_sibling_states`" records the issue time of all states in the left sibling subtrees. The size of this table depends on the model, but is very small. Further, for computational efficiency, the RP method constructs the state diagram as a tree rather than as a directed acyclic graph [7]. This means that certain states, *e.g.*, the final state of the state diagram which contains an empty permissible latency set may be repeated several times (states S_5, S_9, and S_{10}) as shown in Figure 2.

The attractive features of this approach are that it exploits the structure of state diagram construction (top-down and left-to-right) to eliminate redundancy at the earliest opportunity. Second, the RP method is aggressive in redundance elimination. Lastly, as a comparison, the E-MIS method is an exact method, and hence has the overhead of having to construct the complete interference graph, before the generation of `OffSets`.

4.2   Properties of RP Method

Note that the RP method uses the redundancy constraint to eliminate states that could possibly lead to redundant paths. This raises two questions: (i) Does the RP method eliminate **all** redundant paths? (ii) Will the RP method ever eliminate a path that is non-redundant? We answer these two questions in this subsection.

Theorem 7. *There are no redundant paths in the state diagram tree constructed by the RP method.*

The proof of this theorem proceeds by showing that, at any point in time, the partial state diagram tree constructed so far does not have any redundancy. Due to the limitation on paper length, we could not give the proof here in this paper.

We remark that the RP method uses the redundancy constraint which is only a necessary, but not sufficient condition. As a result it may miss some non-redundant paths due to the aggressive pruning employed by this method. However, we argue that there is still a good chance that of the "missed" `OffSets` will reappear in some other paths of the state diagram. In Section 5 we study empirically how many non-redundant paths does RP miss in the state diagram and whether they have any influence on the constructed software pipelined schedule.

162

5 Experimental Results

In this section we report our experience in generating the OffSets using the proposed methods for various values of **II** for two real processors, namely the DEC Alpha 21064 superscalar processor and the Cydra VLIW processor. Both architectures have complex resource usage pattern with sharing of resources. The RP and the E-MIS methods have been implemented in our Modulo Scheduling Testbed (MOST) framework [1].

5.1 Construction Time Comparisons

In order to compare the construction speed of RP, E-MIS and RD methods in a fair manner, all the three methods were run to generate a large subset of OffSets, consisting of the first, say, 100,000 *distinct* OffSets. Tables 3 compares the construction time for OffSets generation for the three methods on an Ultra-450 Workstation (with a 250 MHz clock). We observe that the RD method is much slower than RP and E-MIS. For example, the RD method failed to generate 100,000 distinct OffSets even after running for 24 hours for the Alpha architecture, for an **II** = 8. Hence for larger values of **II**, we only compared the RP and the E-MIS methods.

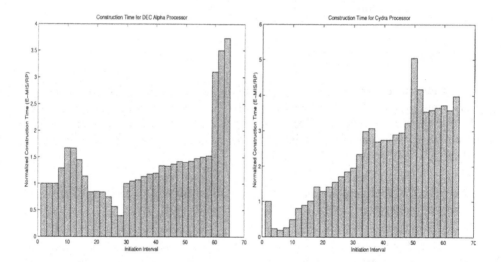

Fig. 4. Comparison of Construction Time for RP and E-MIS Methods

Figure 4 shows the normalized (w.r.t. the RP method) construction time taken by the E-MIS methods for various values of **II** for the two architectures. We observe that the RP and the E-MIS methods are competitive: E-MIS performs better for small values of **II** while RP performs better for moderate to large

IIs. This is not surprising as RP is a very efficient heuristics that we employ to get the OffSets quickly while the E-MIS method, being inherently an exact method, is slow, especially for large values **II**. This is due to the fact that the E-MIS method needs to construct the entire (large) interference graph before the generation of OffSets.

5.2 How many Paths Does RP Miss?

As mentioned earlier the RP method can miss some non-redundant paths during the construction. It is important to verify that RP will not miss too much useful information. On the other hand, since E-MIS is capable of generating all distinct OffSets, we can compare the number of OffSets generated by these two methods if these methods were allowed to complete their execution without any restriction on the maximum number of OffSets generated. The number of distinct OffSets in the state diagram is significantly large, even for small values of **II**. Further the construction time grows exponentially with larger values of **II**. This has limited our experiments to values of **II** less than 16 for the Alpha processor and less than 12 for the Cydra processor. The results are tabulated in Table 1. From the experimental results, we observe that the RP method generates **all** non-redundant paths in the considered cases. It didn't miss a single path! This is somewhat surprising to us, as we anticipated that the RP heuristic to eliminate some non-redundant paths as well. However, we believe that the RP method may still miss some non-redundant paths for large values of **II** and/or for other architectures.

5.3 Application to Co-Scheduling

Lastly we attempt to answer the question how critical are the missed OffSets, if any, in terms of the quality of the constructed software pipelined schedule, when the the enhanced Co-Scheduling method uses the OffSets generated by the RP method. Since the RP method did not miss any path for the DEC Alpha and Cydra processor (for the values of **II** that we could experiment), its application in the enhanced Co-Scheduling should perform at least as good as any other OffSet generation method, *e.g.*, E-MIS or RD methods, applied to Co-Scheduling. What happens if the RP method does miss some OffSets? To answer to this question, we considered the reservation tables used in [7] which model function units with complex resource usage, but without any sharing of resources. In these reservation tables the RP method misses a few paths even for small values of **II**. For example, for one of the reservation tables, the RP method generated only 22 out of 26 distinct OffSets. Also, to reduce the complexity of the enhanced Co-Scheduling method, the scheduling method used all distinct OffSets, up to a maximum of 1000, generated either by RP or E-MIS method. The enhanced Co-Scheduling was applied to a set of 737 loops consisting of single basic block extracted from scientific benchmark programs. We compare the constructed software pipelined schedules, in terms of the initiation interval and the construction time for schedule in Table 2. In order to have a fair comparison,

II	DEC Alpha Processor			Cydra Processor		
	No. of Paths Generated		No. of Missed	No. of Paths Generated		No. of Missed
	RP	E-MIS	Paths	RP	E-MIS	Paths
1	3	3	0	4	4	0
2	9	9	0	16	16	0
3	30	30	0	64	64	0
4	93	93	0	256	256	0
5	288	288	0	1,024	1,024	0
6	894	894	0	4,096	4,096	0
7	2,775	2,775	0	131,072	131,072	0
8	8,613	8,613	0	589,824	589,824	0
9	26,733	26,733	0	7,340,032	7,340,032	0
10	82,974	82,974	0	32,505,856	32,505,856	0
11	257,535	257,535	0	142,606,336	142,606,336	0
12	799,338	799,338	0	N/A	N/A	N/A
13	2,480,988	2,480,988	0	N/A	N/A	N/A
14	7,700,499	7,700,499	0	N/A	N/A	N/A
15	23,900,835	23,900,835	0	N/A	N/A	N/A
16	74,183,493	74,183,493	0	N/A	N/A	N/A

Table 1. Missed Paths in the RP Method

we did not include the time for the generation of OffSets in the scheduling time. We observe that both methods perform more or less alike. This once again establishes that the OffSets missed by the RP method are not really critical in terms of the quality of the constructed schedule.

Measure	RP-Based Co-Scheduling Method Better		E-MIS-Based Co-Scheduling Method Better		Both Same
	# Cases	% Improvement	# Cases	% Improvement	# Cases
Initiation Interval	18	1.11%	16	0.16%	703
Scheduling Time	289	94.18%	448	94.4%	0

Table 2. Effectiveness of RP and E-MIS in Software Pipelining

5.4 Summary of Results

To summarize our experimental results:

- The RD method is too slow in the construction of state diagram for architectures in which function units share resources. Hence it is impractical to apply this for modeling real processors.

- Both the RP and E-MIS methods are much faster than RD, by 3 to 4 orders of magnitude, and their construction time is acceptable for implementation in real compilers.
- In terms of construction speed, the E-MIS method performs better for small values of **II** while RP method performs better for large **II** values.
- Considering the overall performance, for a real compiler, it is better to choose RP method because RP behaves better for large II values. A 3-fold speedup in large II values could mean a reduction of tens of minutes of construction time. For small II values, however, a 3-fold speedup may only mean a reduction of several seconds in construction time.
- Though the RP method can not guarantee to always generate *all* distinct OffSets, we found that it is capable of generating all non-redundant OffSets in the experiments that we conducted. Further, we found that the generated OffSets when applied to the Co-Scheduling method can get equally good performance, in terms of the constructed schedule.

6   Conclusions

In this paper we have proposed two efficient methods to construct distinct paths in the state diagram used for modeling complex pipeline resource usage in software pipelining. The methods proposed in this paper, namely the E-MIS method and the RP method completely eliminate the generation of redundant paths. The first of these methods, the E-MIS method is obtained by relating the OffSets generation to a well-known graph theoretic problem, *viz.*, the enumeration of maximal independent sets of an interference graph. The second method, the RP method, uses a simple but very effective heuristic to prevent the construction of states that may cause redundant paths. We formally establish that this heuristic results in redundance-free state diagram. We compare the performance of RP and E-MIS methods in modeling two real processors, namely the DEC Alpha processor and the Cydra VLIW processor. The RP and E-MIS methods were found to be much superior than the RD method, by 3 to 4 orders of magnitude. When compared between themselves, the RP and the MIS methods perform competitively, the RP performing better for larger values of **II** while the E-MIS performing better for small **II**. Lastly, we have applied the OffSets generated by these methods in the enhanced Co-Scheduling method and reported their performance.

References

1. E. R. Altman. *Optimal Software Pipelining with Function Unit and Register Constraints*. Ph.D. thesis, McGill U., Montréal, Qué., Oct. 1995.
2. V. Bala and N. Rubin. Efficient instruction scheduling using finite state automata. In *Proc. of the 28th Ann. Intl. Symp. on Microarchitecture*, pages 46–56, Ann Arbor, MI, Nov. 29–Dec.1, 1995.

3. G. Beck, D.W.L. Yen, and T. L. Anderson. The Cydra-5 minisupercomputer: Architecture and implementation. *Journal of Supercomputing*, 7, May 1993.

4. A. E. Eichenberger and E. S. Davidson. A reduced multipipeline machine description that preserves scheduling constraints. In *Proc. of the ACM SIGPLAN '96 Conf. on Programming Language Design and Implementation*, pages 12–22, Philadelphia, PA, May 21–24, 1996.

5. M.C. Golumbic. *Algorithmic Graph Theory and Perfect Graphs*. Academic Press, New York, 1980.

6. R. Govindarajan, Erik R. Altman, and Guang R. Gao. Co-scheduling hardware and software pipelines. In *Proc. of the Second Intl. Symp. on High-Performance Computer Architecture*, pages 52–61, San Jose, CA, Feb. 3–7, 1996. IEEE Computer Society.

7. R. Govindarajan, N.S.S. Narasimha Rao, E. R. Altman, and G. R. Gao. An enhanced co-scheduling method using reduced ms-state diagrams. In *Proc. of the 12th Intl. Parallel Processing Symp.*, Orlando, FL, Mar. 1998. IEEE Computer Society. Merged with 9th Intl. Symp. on Parallel and Distributed Processing.

8. R. Govindarajan, N.S.S. Narasimha Rao, Erik R. Altman, and Guang R. Gao. An enhanced co-scheduling method using reduced ms-state diagrams. CAPSL Technical Memo 17, Dept. of Electrical & Computer Engineering, University of Delaware, Newark 19716, U.S.A., Feb. 1998. Also as Tech. Report TR-98-06, Dept. of Computer Science & Automation, Indian Institute of Science, Bangaloe, 560 012, India. (available via http://www.csa.iisc.ernet.in/~govind/papers/TR-98-2.ps.gz).

9. R. A. Huff. Lifetime-sensitive modulo scheduling. In *Proc. of the ACM SIGPLAN '93 Conf. on Programming Language Design and Implementation*, pages 258–267, Albuquerque, New Mexico, June 23–25, 1993.

10. M. Lam. Software pipelining: An effective scheduling technique for VLIW machines. In *Proc. of the SIGPLAN '88 Conf. on Programming Language Design and Implementation*, pages 318–328, Atlanta, Georgia, June 22–24, 1988.

11. C.L. Liu. *Introduction to Combinatorial Mathematics*. McGraw-Hill Book Co., New York, NY, 1968.

12. Thomas Muller. Employing finite state automata for resource scheduling. In *Proc. of the 26th Ann. Intl. Symp. on Microarchitecture*, Austin, TX, Dec. 1–3, 1993.

13. J. H. Patel and E. S. Davidson. Improving the throughput of a pipeline by insertion of delays. In *Proc. of the 3rd Ann. Symp. on Computer Architecture*, pages 159–164, Clearwater, FL, Jan. 19–21, 1976.

14. T. A. Proebsting and C. W. Fraser. Detecting pipeline structural hazards quickly. In *Conf. Record of the 21st ACM SIGPLAN-SIGACT Symp. on Principles of Programming Languages*, pages 280–286, Portland, OR, Jan. 17–21, 1994.

15. B. R. Rau and J. A. Fisher. Instruction-level parallel processing: History, overview and perspective. *Journal of Supercomputing*, 7:9–50, May 1993.

16. B. R. Rau. Iterative modulo scheduling: An algorithm for software pipelining loops. In *Proc. of the 27th Ann. Intl. Symp. on Microarchitecture*, pages 63–74, San Jose, California, November 30–December2, 1994.

17. John Ruttenberg, G. R. Gao, A. Stouchinin, and W. Lichtenstein. Software pipelining showdown: Optimal vs. heuristic methods in a production compiler. In *Proc. of the ACM SIGPLAN '96 Conf. on Programming Language Design and Implementation*, pages 1–11, Philadelphia, PA, May 21–24, 1996.

18. S. Tsukiyama, M. Ide, H. Ariyoshi, and I. Shirakawa. A new algorithm for generating all the maximal independent sets. *SIAM Jl. on Computing*, 6(3):505–517, Sep. 1977.

DEC Alpha Processor

II	Construction time in secs. E-MIS	RP	RD	Normalized time w.r.t. RP method E-MIS/RP	RD/RP
2	0.01	0.01	0.01	1	1
4	0.01	0.01	0.67	1	67
6	0.12	0.12	151	1	1,262
8	1.47	1.14	>24h	1.28	>75k
10	19.52	11.67	N/A	1.67	N/A
12	26.89	16.1	N/A	1.67	N/A
14	25.58	17.65	N/A	1.45	N/A
16	22.24	19.54	N/A	1.14	N/A
18	19.78	23.50	N/A	0.84	N/A
20	25.05	29.52	N/A	0.85	N/A
22	26.58	31.64	N/A	0.84	N/A
24	25.61	34.29	N/A	0.75	N/A
26	20.85	36.72	N/A	0.57	N/A
28	15.69	39.84	N/A	0.39	N/A
30	44.23	44.16	N/A	1	N/A
32	49.94	47.64	N/A	1.05	N/A
34	56.26	52.52	N/A	1.07	N/A
36	62.99	55.53	N/A	1.13	N/A
38	70.04	59.27	N/A	1.18	N/A
40	77.44	64.59	N/A	1.2	N/A
42	90.27	67.3	N/A	1.34	N/A
44	94.91	71.35	N/A	1.33	N/A
46	104.2	76.04	N/A	1.37	N/A
48	114.6	80.59	N/A	1.42	N/A
50	121.4	86.45	N/A	1.51	N/A
52	131.9	92.23	N/A	1.43	N/A
54	142.5	96.35	N/A	1.48	N/A
56	153.9	102.1	N/A	1.51	N/A
58	165.2	108.0	N/A	1.53	N/A
60	402.6	129.9	N/A	3.1	N/A
62	482.3	137.8	N/A	3.5	N/A
64	544.0	145.8	N/A	3.73	N/A

Cydra Processor

II	Construction time in secs. E-MIS	RP	RD	Normalized time w.r.t. RP method E-MIS/RP	RD/RP
2	0.01	0.01	4296	1	429,700
4	0.03	0.13	>24h	1	>664k
6	0.39	2.13	N/A	0.17	N/A
8	15.37	60.4	N/A	0.25	N/A
10	41.03	84.4	N/A	0.48	N/A
12	77.2	95.7	N/A	0.81	N/A
14	95.99	107.4	N/A	0.89	N/A
16	121.2	119.4	N/A	1.01	N/A
18	173.0	122.0	N/A	1.41	N/A
20	180.6	140.1	N/A	1.29	N/A
22	219.4	154.8	N/A	1.42	N/A
24	259.0	166.7	N/A	1.55	N/A
26	302.1	176.7	N/A	1.71	N/A
28	350.3	189.5	N/A	1.84	N/A
30	399.3	203.6	N/A	1.96	N/A
32	511.1	217.3	N/A	2.35	N/A
34	666.3	222.7	N/A	2.99	N/A
36	759.6	247.0	N/A	3.08	N/A
38	713.5	264.4	N/A	2.7	N/A
40	767.3	279.3	N/A	2.74	N/A
42	810.4	294.7	N/A	2.75	N/A
44	893.6	308.3	N/A	2.9	N/A
46	962.6	325.9	N/A	2.95	N/A
48	1106.2	343.1	N/A	3.22	N/A
50	1735.5	343.8	N/A	5.04	N/A
52	1579.5	378.1	N/A	4.18	N/A
54	1392.0	392.9	N/A	3.54	N/A
56	1478.9	412.2	N/A	3.59	N/A
58	1573.4	431.0	N/A	3.65	N/A
60	1675.5	450.0	N/A	3.72	N/A
62	1773.5	495.1	N/A	3.58	N/A
64	1970.5	494.8	N/A	3.98	N/A

Table 3. Comparison of Construction Time for the 3 Methods

A Comparison of Compiler Tiling Algorithms

Gabriel Rivera, Chau-Wen Tseng

Department of Computer Science, University of Maryland, College Park, MD 20742

Abstract. Linear algebra codes contain data locality which can be exploited by tiling multiple loop nests. Several approaches to tiling have been suggested for avoiding conflict misses in low associativity caches. We propose a new technique based on intra-variable padding and compare its performance with existing techniques. Results show padding improves performance of matrix multiply by over 100% in some cases over a range of matrix sizes. Comparing the efficacy of different tiling algorithms, we discover rectangular tiles are slightly more efficient than square tiles. Overall, tiling improves performance from 0-250%. Copying tiles at run time proves to be quite effective.

1 Introduction

With processor speeds increasing faster than memory speeds, memory access latencies are becoming the key bottleneck for modern microprocessors. As a result, effectively exploiting data locality by keeping data in cache is vital for achieving good performance. Linear algebra codes, in particular, contain large amounts of reuse which may be exploited through *tiling* (also known as blocking). Tiling combines strip-mining and loop permutation to create small tiles of loop iterations which may be executed together to exploit data locality [4, 11, 26]. Figure 1 illustrates a tiled version of matrix multiplication of NxN arrays.

```
do KK=1,N,W          // W = tile width
  do II=1,N,H        // H = tile height
    do J=1,N
      do K=KK,min(KK+W-1,N)
        do I=II,min(II+H-1,N)
          C(I,J) = C(I,J) + A(I,K) * B(K,J)
```

Fig. 1. Tiled matrix multiplication

Due to hardware constraints, caches have limited *set associativity*, where memory addresses can only be mapped to one of k locations in a k-way associative cache. *Conflict misses* may occur when too many data items map to the same set of cache locations, causing cache lines to be flushed from cache before they may be reused, despite sufficient capacity in the overall cache. Conflict

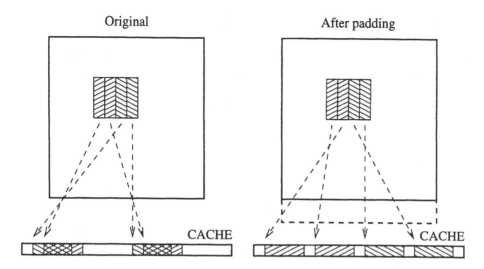

Fig. 2. Example of conflict misses and padding

misses have been shown to severely degrade the performance of tiled codes [13]. Figure 2 illustrates how the columns of a tile may overlap on the cache, preventing reuse. A number of compilation techniques have been developed to avoid conflict misses [6, 13, 23], either by carefully choosing tile sizes or by copying tiles to contiguous memory at run time. However, it is unclear which is the best approach for modern microprocessors.

We previously presented *intra-variable padding*, a compiler optimization for eliminating conflict misses by changing the size of array dimensions [20]. Unlike standard compiler transformations which restructure the computation performed by the program, padding modifies the program's *data layout*. We found intra-variable padding to be effective in eliminating conflict misses in a number of scientific computations. In this paper, we demonstrate intra-variable padding can also be useful for eliminating conflicts in tiled codes. For example, in Figure 2 padding the array column can change mappings to cache so that columns are better spaced on the cache, eliminating conflict misses.

Our contributions include:

- introducing padding to assist tiling
- new algorithm for calculating non-conflicting tile dimensions
- experimental comparisons based on matrix multiply and LU decomposition

We begin by reviewing previous algorithms for tiling, then discuss enhancements including padding. We provide experimental results and conclude with related work.

2 Background

We focus on copying tiles at run-time and carefully selecting tile sizes, two strategies studied previously for avoiding conflict misses in tiled codes. In remaining sections, we refer to the cache size as C_s, the cache line size as L_s, and the column size of an array as Col_s. The dimensions of a tile are represented by H for height and W for width. All values are in units of the array element size.

2.1 Tile Size Selection

One method for avoiding conflict misses in tiled codes is to carefully select a tile size for the given array and cache size. A number of algorithms have been proposed.

- Lam, Rothberg, and Wolf [13] pick the largest non-conflicting square tile using an $O(\sqrt{C_s})$ algorithm for selecting tile size.
- Esseghir [7] picks a rectangular tile containing the largest number of non-conflicting array columns. I.e., $H = Col_s$ and $W = \lfloor C_s/Col_s \rfloor$.
- Coleman and McKinley [6] compute rectangular non-conflicting tiles and select one using their cost model. They applied the Euclidean GCD algorithm to generate possible tile heights, where:

$$H_{next} = H_{prev} \bmod H \qquad (1)$$

  using C_s and Col_s as the initial heights. A complicated formula is presented for calculating non-conflicting tile widths, based on the gap between tile starting addresses and number of tile columns which can fit in that gap.
- Wolf, Maydan, and Chen [24] choose a square tile which uses a small fraction of the cache (5–15%) in order to avoid excessive conflicts. For instance, the tile $H = W = \lfloor \sqrt{0.10C_s} \rfloor$ uses 10% of the cache. The particular fraction of the cache utilized is chosen based on cache characteristics such as associativity and line size.

2.2 Copying

An alternative method for avoiding conflict misses is to copy tiles to a buffer and modify code to use data directly from the buffer [13, 23]. Since data in the buffer is contiguous, self-interference is eliminated. However, performance is lost because tiles must be copied at run time. Overhead is low if tiles only need to be copied once, higher otherwise.

Figure 3 shows how copying may be introduced into tiled matrix multiply. First, each tile of A(I,K) may be copied into a buffer BUF. Because tiles are invariant with respect to the J loop, they only need to be copied once outside the J loop.

It is also possible to copy other array sections to buffers. If buffers are adjacent, then cross-interference misses are also avoided. For instance, in Figure 3

```
do KK=1,N,W
  do II=1,N,H
    copy(A(...),BUF)              // copy A(I,K)
    do J=1,N
      copy(C(...),BUF2)          // copy C(I,J)
      do K=KK,min(KK+W-1,N)
        do I=II,min(II+H-1,N)
          BUF2(...) = BUF2(...) + BUF(...) * B(K,J)
      copy(BUF2,C(...))          // copy back C(I,J)
```

Fig. 3. Tiled matrix multiplication with copying

the column accessed by array C(I,J) in the innermost loop is copied to BUF2 to eliminate interference between arrays C and A. Since the location of the column varies with the J loop, we must copy it on each iteration of the J loop, causing data in C to be copied multiple times [23]. In addition, the data in the buffer must be written back to C since the copied region is both read and written to. Whether copying more array sections is profitable depends on the frequency and expense of cross-interference.

3 Tiling Improvements

We present two main improvements to existing tiling algorithms. First, we derive a more accurate method for calculating non-conflicting tile dimensions. Second, we integrate intra-variable padding with tiling to handle pathological array sizes.

3.1 Non-conflicting Tile Dimensions

We choose non-conflicting tile heights using the Euclidean GCD algorithm from Coleman and McKinley [6]. However, we compute tile widths using a simple recurrence. The recurrences for both height and width may be computed simultaneously using the recursive function *ComputeTileSizes* in Figure 4. The initial invocation is *ComputeTileSizes* $(C_s, Col_s, 0, 1)$.

ComputeTileSizes $(H, H_{next}, W_{prev}, W)$
    $H' = H - L_s + 1$ /* shrink height for long cache lines */
    /* consider tile with dimensions (H', W) */
    if $(H_{next} \geq L_s)$ then
        ComputeTileSizes $(H_{next}, H \bmod H_{next}, W, \lfloor H/H_{next} \rfloor W + W_{prev})$
    endif

Fig. 4. Recursive function for computing nonconflicting tile sizes

Table 1. H and W at invocation i given $C_s = 2048$, $Col_s = 300$

i	1	2	3	4	5	6	7
H	2048	300	248	52	40	12	4
W	1	6	7	34	41	157	512

At each invocation of *ComputeTileSizes*, a new tile size, determined by tile height H and width W, is guaranteed not to conflict when $L_s = 1$. (The proof supporting this result is too long to appear in this paper.) To account for longer cache lines, an adjusted tile height $H' = H - L_s + 1$ is used in place of H. By subtracting most of the cache line size L_s from the tile height H, we slightly under-utilize the cache but guarantee no conflicts will occur. To choose between the different non-conflicting tile dimensions, we select the tile (H, W) minimizing $\frac{1}{H} + \frac{1}{W}$. This cost function favors square tiles over rectangular tiles with the same area; it is similar to that used by Coleman and McKinley [6].

Table 1 illustrates the sequence of H and W values computed by *ComputeTileSizes* at each invocation when $C_s = 2048$ and $Col_s = 300$. An important result is that each of the computed tile sizes are *maximal* in the sense that neither their heights nor widths may be increased without causing conflicts. Moreover, *ComputeTileSizes* computes *all* maximal tile sizes. Note that at invocation 1, (H, W) is not a legal tile size since $H = 2048$ exceeds Col_s. In general, this can occur only at the first invocation, and a simple comparison with Col_s will prevent consideration of such tile sizes. The formula used by *ComputeTileSizes* for finding non-conflicting tile widths is simpler than that of the Coleman and McKinley algorithm. In addition, it avoids occasionally incorrect W values that result from their algorithm.

3.2 Padding

Our second improvement is to incorporate intra-variable padding with tiling. Previously we found memory access patterns common in linear algebra computations may lead to frequent conflict misses for certain pathological column sizes, particularly when we need to keep two columns in cache or prevent self-interference in rows [20]. Bailey [2] first noticed this effect and defined *stride efficiency* as a measure of how well strided accesses (e.g., row accesses) avoid conflicts. Empirically, we determined that these conflicts can be avoided through a small amount of intra-variable padding. In tiled codes a related problem arises, since we need to keep multiple tile columns/rows in cache.

Table 2. H and W at invocation i given $C_s = 2048$, $Col_s = 768$

i	1	2	3	4
H	2048	768	512	256
W	1	2	3	8

Table 3. Tiling Heuristics

Program version	Description
orig	No tiling
ess	Largest number of non-conflicting columns (Esseghir)
lrw	Largest non-conflicting square (Lam, Rothberg, Wolf)
tss	Maximal non-conflicting rectangle (Coleman, McKinley)
euc	Maximal (accurate) non-conflicting rectangle (Rivera, Tseng)
wmc10	Square tile using 10% of cache (Wolf, Maydan, Chen)
lrwPad	lrw with padding
tssPad	tss with padding
eucPad	euc with padding
eucPrePad	euc with pre-copying to padded array
copyTile	Tiles of array A copied to contiguous buffer
copyTileCol	Tiles of array A and column of C copied to contiguous buffer

When *ComputeTileSizes* obtains tile sizes for pathological column sizes, though the resulting tile sizes are nonconflicting, overly "skinny" or "fat" (nonsquare) tiles result, which decrease the effectiveness of tiling. For example, if $Col_s = 768$ and $C_s = 2048$, *ComputeTileSizes* finds only the tile sizes shown in Table 2. The tile closest to a square is still much taller than it is wide. For this Col_s, any tile wider than 8 will cause conflicts. This situation is illustrated Figure 2, in which the column size for the array on the left would result in interference with a tile as tall as shown. On the right we see how padding enables using better tile sizes. Our padding extension is thus to consider pads of 0–8 elements, generating tile sizes by running *ComputeTileSizes* once for each padded column size. The column size with the best tile according to the cost model is selected. By substituting different cost models and tile size selection algorithms, we may also combine this padding method with the algorithms used by Lam, Rothberg, Wolf and Coleman and McKinley.

Padding may even be applied in cases where changing column sizes is not possible. For example, arrays passed to subroutines cannot be padded without interprocedural analysis, since it is not known whether such arrays require preserving their storage order. In many linear algebra codes the cost of pre-copying to padded arrays is often small compared to the cost of the actual computation. For instance, initially copying all of A to a padded array before executing the loop in Figure 1 adds only $O(N^2)$ operations to an $O(N^3)$ computation. We may therefore combine padding with tile size selection by either directly padding columns or by pre-copying.

4 Experimental Evaluation

4.1 Evaluation Framework

To compare tiling heuristics we varied the matrix sizes for matrix multiplication (MULT) from 100 to 400 and applied the heuristics described in Table 3. For each

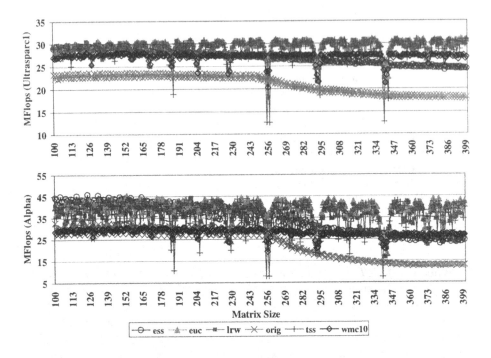

Fig. 5. Matrix multiplication: MFlops of tiling heuristics

heuristic, performance on a Sun UltraSparc I and a DEC Alpha 21064 were measured. Both processors use a 16k direct-mapped Level 1 (L1) cache. In addition, several heuristics were applied to varying problem sizes of LU decomposition (LU). We also computed the percent cache utilization for several heuristics.

4.2 Performance of MULT

Tile Size Selection. We first consider heuristics which do not perform copying or padding. Ultra and Alpha megaflop rates of MULT for these heuristics are graphed in Figure 5. The X-axis represents matrix size and the Y-axis gives Mflops. In the top graph we see that tiled versions usually outperform **orig** versions by 4 or more Mflops on the Ultra, improving performance by at least 20%. We find that for sizes beginning around 200, **ess** and **wmc10**, the heuristics which do not attempt maximality of tile dimensions, obtain a lesser order improvement than **euc**, **lrw**, and **tss**, usually by a margin of at least 2 Mflops. Performance of the latter three heuristics appears quite similar, except at the clusters of matrix sizes in which performance of all heuristics drops sharply. In these cases we see **euc** does not do nearly as bad, and that **tss** drops the most. The lower graph gives the same data with respect to the Alpha. Behavior is similar, though variation in performance for individual heuristic increases, and **ess** is a competitive heuristic until matrix sizes exceed 250.

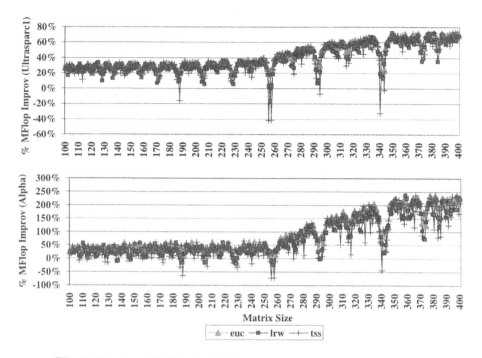

Fig. 6. Matrix multiplication: MFlop improvements of tiling heuristics

These results illuminate the limitations of several heuristics. Lower **ess** performance indicates a cost model should determine tile heights instead of the array column size, as using the column size results in overly "skinny" tiles. Lower **wmc10** performance underscores the need to better utilize the cache. **tss** would benefit from accuracy in computing tile widths. A prominent feature of both graphs is the gradual dip in performance of **orig** and **ess** beginning at 256. This occurs as matrix sizes exceed the Level 2 (L2) cache, indicating **ess** is also less effective in keeping data in the L2 cache than other heuristics.

The top graph in Figure 6 focuses on **euc**, **lrw**, and **tss**, giving percent Mflops improvements on the Ultra compared to **orig**. While all heuristics usually improve performance by about 25%–70%, we again observe clusters of matrix sizes in which performance drops sharply, occasionally resulting in degradations (negative improvement). **euc** does best in these cases, while **lrw** and especially **tss** do considerably worse. The lower graph shows results are similar on the Alpha, but the sudden drops in performance tend to be greater. Also, performance improvements are much larger beyond 256, indicating L2 cache misses are more costly on the Alpha.

Averaging over all problem sizes, **euc**, **lrw**, and **tss** improve performance on the Ultra by 42.1%, 38.0%, and 38.5%, respectively, and by 92.3%, 76.6%, and 76.4% on the Alpha. The advantage of **euc** over **lrw** indicates that using only square tiles is an unfavorable restriction. For instance, at problem size 256,

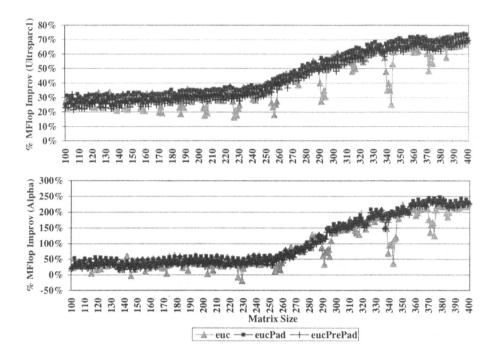

Fig. 7. Matrix multiplication: MFlop improvements of tiling w/ padding

where **euc** selects a 256x8 tile, **lrw** selects an 8x8 tile, at the expense of over 40% of performance on both architectures. Though **euc** handles such problem sizes better than **lrw**, performance still degrades for **euc** since the only tile sizes possible at this column size are too "skinny". Thus, pathological problem sizes adversely affect all three heuristics dramatically.

Padding. To avoid pathological problem sizes which hurt performance, we combine padding with tile size selection. Figure 7 compares **euc** with **eucPad** and **eucPrePad**. In both graphs, **eucPad** and **eucPrePad** improvements demonstrate that padding is successful in avoiding these cases. Moreover, the cost of pre-copying is acceptably small, with **eucPrePad** attaining improvements of 43.3% on the Ultra whereas **eucPad** improves performance by 45.5%. On the Alpha, **eucPrePad** averages 98.5% whereas **eucPad** averages 104.2%. Since pre-copying requires only $O(N^2)$ instructions, the overhead becomes even less significant for problem sizes larger than 400. Improvements for **lrwPad** and **tssPad**, which do not appear in Figure 7, resemble those of **eucPad**. Both are slightly less effective, however. On average, **lrwPad** and **tssPad** improve performance on the Ultra by 44.3% and 43.8% respectively.

Copying Tiles. An alternative to padding is to copy tiles to a contiguous buffer. Figure 8 compares improvements from **copyTile** and **copyTileCol** with those of **eucPad**, the most effective noncopying heuristic. On the Ultra, **copyTile** is as stable as **eucPad**, and overall does slightly better, attaining an average

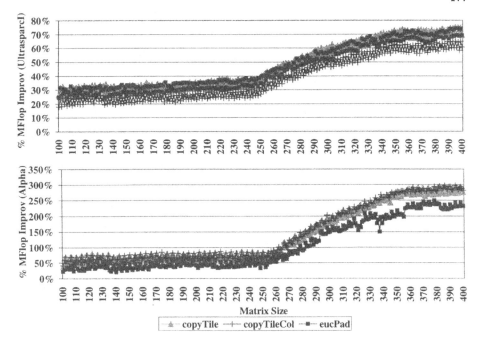

Fig. 8. Matrix multiplication: MFlop improvements of copying heuristics

improvement of 46.6%. Though **copyTileCol** is just as stable, overhead results in improvements consistently worse than both **eucPad** and **copyTile**, and the average improvement is only 38.1%. We find a different outcome on the Alpha, on which both **copyTile** and **copyTileCol** are superior to **eucPad**. This is especially true for larger matrix sizes, where copying overhead is less significant.

Summary. From the above results, we observe that tile size selection heuristics which compute maximal square or rectangular non-conflicting tiles are most effective. Also, padding can enable these heuristics to avoid pathological cases in which substantial performance drops are unavoidable. Moreover, we find copying tiles to be advantageous in MULT.

4.3 Performance of LU

Tile Size Selection. We also compare padding heuristics **euc** and **lrw** on LU. Figure 9 gives percent Mflops improvements for **euc** and **lrw**. As with MULT, on both the Ultra and the Alpha, large drops in performance occur at certain clusters of matrix sizes, and **euc** is again more effective in these cases. However, tiling overhead has a greater impact, leading to frequent degradations in performance until tiling improves both L1 and L2 cache performance at 256. As a result, overall improvements on the Ultra for **euc** and **lrw** are only 17.8% and 11.4%, respectively. On the Alpha, overall performance, even worse for matrix sizes less than 256, is 53.8% and 31.6% for **euc** and **lrw**.

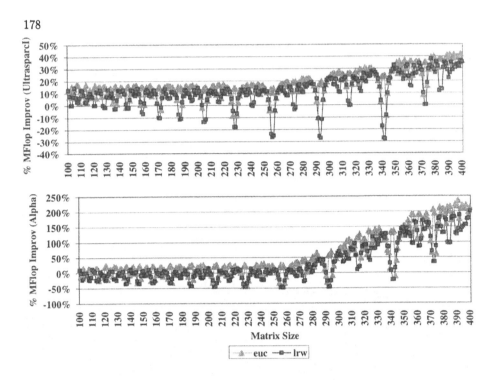

Fig. 9. LU Decomposition: MFlop improvements of tiling heuristics

Padding. We see again that padding helps to stabilize performance in Figure 10. In the top graph, **eucPad** and **eucPrePad** consistently improve Ultra Mflop rates, achieving overall improvements of 19.7% and 15.5% respectively. An interesting feature of this graph are the three spikes in performance of **eucPad** and **eucPrePad** at 128, 256, and 384. These correspond to column sizes containing a large power-of-2 factor, leading to ping-pong conflict misses between references to unpadded arrays [20]. Thus, a side effect of padding to prevent tile self-interference is the elimination of ping-pong cross-interference misses in some cases. The lower graph shows that padding stabilizes performance improvements on the Alpha as well, but large performance increases do not begin until 256. Average improvements for **eucPad** and **eucPrePad** are 58.5% and 49.8% respectively.

4.4 Cache Utilization

Finally, cache utilization, computed as HW/C_s, appears in Figure 11 for four heuristics. The top graph give cache utilization for **euc** and **lrw**. Here, the X-axis again gives problem size while the Y-axis gives percent utilization for a 16k cache. We see that for **lrw**, which chooses only square tiles, utilization varies dramatically for different matrix sizes. Low cache utilization for **lrw** occurs when the largest nonconflicting square tile is very small. For matrix size 256, for instance, **lrw** computes an 8x8 tile. Utilization for **euc** is comparatively high, since it may choose rectangular tiles. The lower graph gives cache utilization

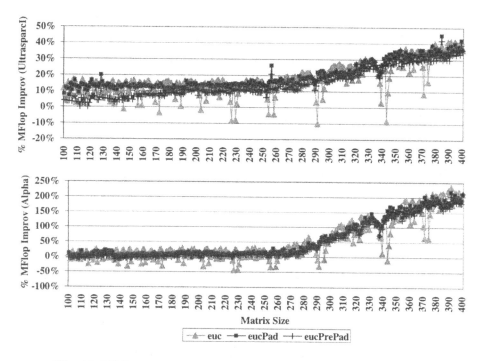

Fig. 10. LU Decomposition: MFlop improvements of tiling w/ padding

for **eucPad** and **lrwPad**. Utilization for **lrwPad** is much higher overall than for **lrw** since padding is used to avoid small tiles. Often we see utilization by both **lrwPad** and **eucPad** remain level for small intervals of problem sizes. This occurs when an especially favorable tile is available at a particular column size N. In these cases, **lrwPad** and **eucPad** will perform the padding necessary to attain that tile in several of the problem sizes leading up to N.

5 Related Work

Data locality has been recognized as a significant performance issue for both scalar and parallel architectures. A number of researchers have investigated tiling as a means of exploiting reuse. Lam, Rothberg, Wolf show conflict misses can severely degrade the performance of tiling [13]. Wolf and Lam analyze temporal and spatial reuse, and apply tiling when necessary to capture outer loop reuse [25], Coleman and McKinley select rectangular non-conflicting tile sizes [6] while others focus on using a portion of cache [24]. Temam *et al.* analyze the program to determine whether a tile should be copied to a contiguous buffer. Mitchel *et al.* study interactions between tiling for multiple objectives at once [16].

In addition to tiling, researchers working on locality optimizations have considered both computation-reordering transformations such as loop permuta-

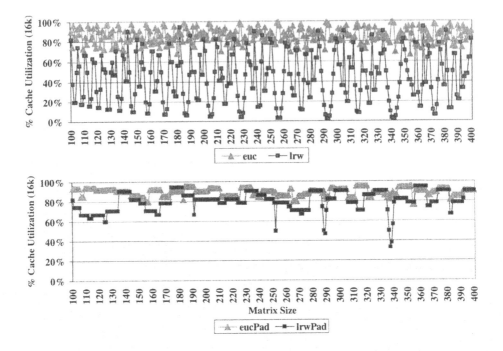

Fig. 11. Matrix multiplication: Cache utilization of tiling heuristics

tion [9, 17, 25] and loop fission/fusion [15, 17]. Scalar replacement replaces array references with scalars, reducing the number of memory references if the compiler later puts the scalar in a register [3]. Many cache models have been designed for estimating cache misses to help guide data locality optimizations [8, 9, 17, 25]. Earlier models assumed fully-associative caches, but more recent techniques take limited associativity into account [10, 22].

Researchers began reexamining conflict misses after a study showed conflict misses can cause half of all cache misses and most intra-nest misses in scientific codes [18]. Data-layout transformations such as array transpose and padding have been shown to reduce conflict misses in the SPEC benchmarks when applied by hand [14]. Array transpose applied with loop permutation can improve parallelism and locality [5, 12, 19]. Array padding can also help eliminate conflict misses [1, 20, 21] when performed carefully.

6 Conclusions

The goal of compiler optimizations for data locality is to enable users to gain good performance without having to become experts in computer architecture. Tiling is a transformation which can be very powerful, but requires fairly good knowledge of the caches present in today's advanced microprocessors. In this paper, we have examined and improved a number of tiling heuristics. We show non-conflicting tile widths can be calculated using a simple recurrence, then demonstrate intra-variable padding can avoid problem spots in tiling. Experimental results on two architectures indicate large performance improvements are possible using compiler heuristics. By improving compiler techniques for automatic tiling, we allow users to obtain good performance without considering machine details. Scientists and engineers will benefit because it will be easier for them to take advantage of high performance computing.

References

1. D. Bacon, J.-H. Chow, D.-C. Ju, K. Muthukumar, and V. Sarkar. A compiler framework for restructuring data declarations to enhance cache and TLB effectiveness. In *Proceedings of CASCON'94*, Toronto, Canada, October 1994.
2. D. Bailey. Unfavorable strides in cache memory systems. Technical Report RNR-92-015, NASA Ames Research Center, May 1992.
3. D. Callahan, S. Carr, and K. Kennedy. Improving register allocation for subscripted variables. In *Proceedings of the SIGPLAN '90 Conference on Programming Language Design and Implementation*, White Plains, NY, June 1990.
4. S. Carr and K. Kennedy. Compiler blockability of numerical algorithms. In *Proceedings of Supercomputing '92*, Minneapolis, MN, November 1992.
5. M. Cierniak and W. Li. Unifying data and control transformations for distributed shared-memory machines. In *Proceedings of the SIGPLAN '95 Conference on Programming Language Design and Implementation*, La Jolla, CA, June 1995.
6. S. Coleman and K. S. McKinley. Tile size selection using cache organization and data layout. In *Proceedings of the SIGPLAN '95 Conference on Programming Language Design and Implementation*, La Jolla, CA, June 1995.
7. K. Esseghir. Improving data locality for caches. Master's thesis, Dept. of Computer Science, Rice University, September 1993.
8. J. Ferrante, V. Sarkar, and W. Thrash. On estimating and enhancing cache effectiveness. In U. Banerjee, D. Gelernter, A. Nicolau, and D. Padua, editors, *Languages and Compilers for Parallel Computing, Fourth International Workshop*, Santa Clara, CA, August 1991. Springer-Verlag.
9. D. Gannon, W. Jalby, and K. Gallivan. Strategies for cache and local memory management by global program transformation. *Journal of Parallel and Distributed Computing*, 5(5):587–616, October 1988.
10. S. Ghosh, M. Martonosi, and S. Malik. Cache miss equations: An analytical representation of cache misses. In *Proceedings of the 1997 ACM International Conference on Supercomputing*, Vienna, Austria, July 1997.
11. F. Irigoin and R. Triolet. Supernode partitioning. In *Proceedings of the Fifteenth Annual ACM Symposium on the Principles of Programming Languages*, San Diego, CA, January 1988.
12. M. Kandemir, J. Ramanujam, and A. Choudhary. A compiler algorithm for optimizing locality in loop nests. In *Proceedings of the 1997 ACM International Conference on Supercomputing*, Vienna, Austria, July 1997.
13. M. Lam, E. Rothberg, and M. E. Wolf. The cache performance and optimizations of blocked algorithms. In *Proceedings of the Fourth International Conference on Architectural Support for Programming Languages and Operating Systems (ASPLOS-IV)*, Santa Clara, CA, April 1991.
14. A. Lebeck and D. Wood. Cache profiling and the SPEC benchmarks: A case study. *IEEE Computer*, 27(10):15–26, October 1994.

15. N. Manjikian and T. Abdelrahman. Fusion of loops for parallelism and locality. *IEEE Transactions on Parallel and Distributed Systems*, 8(2):193–209, February 1997.

16. N. Mitchell, L. Carter, J. Ferrante, and K. Hogstedt. Quantifying the multi-level nature of tiling interactions. In *Proceedings of the Tenth Workshop on Languages and Compilers for Parallel Computing*, Minneapolis, MN, August 1997.

17. K. S. McKinley, S. Carr, and C.-W. Tseng. Improving data locality with loop transformations. *ACM Transactions on Programming Languages and Systems*, 18(4):424–453, July 1996.

18. K. S. McKinley and O. Temam. A quantitative analysis of loop nest locality. In *Proceedings of the Eighth International Conference on Architectural Support for Programming Languages and Operating Systems (ASPLOS-VIII)*, Boston, MA, October 1996.

19. M. O'Boyle and P. Knijnenburg. Non-singular data transformations: Definition, validity, and applications. In *Proceedings of the 1997 ACM International Conference on Supercomputing*, Vienna, Austria, July 1997.

20. G. Rivera and C.-W. Tseng. Data transformations for eliminating conflict misses. In *Proceedings of the SIGPLAN '98 Conference on Programming Language Design and Implementation*, Montreal, Canada, June 1998.

21. G. Rivera and C.-W. Tseng. Eliminating conflict misses for high performance architectures. In *Proceedings of the 1998 ACM International Conference on Supercomputing*, Melbourne, Australia, July 1998.

22. O. Temam, C. Fricker, and W. Jalby. Cache interference phenomena. In *Proceedings of the 1994 ACM SIGMETRICS Conference on Measurement & Modeling Computer Systems*, Santa Clara, CA, May 1994.

23. O. Temam, E. Granston, and W. Jalby. To copy or not to copy: A compile-time technique for assessing when data copying should be used to eliminate cache conflicts. In *Proceedings of Supercomputing '93*, Portland, OR, November 1993.

24. M. Wolf, D. Maydan, and D.-K. Chen. Combining loop transformations considering caches and scheduling. In *Proceedings of the 29th IEEE/ACM International Symposium on Microarchitecture*, Paris, France, December 1996.

25. M. E. Wolf and M. Lam. A data locality optimizing algorithm. In *Proceedings of the SIGPLAN '91 Conference on Programming Language Design and Implementation*, Toronto, Canada, June 1991.

26. M. J. Wolfe. More iteration space tiling. In *Proceedings of Supercomputing '89*, Reno, NV, November 1989.

Implementation Issues of Loop-Level Speculative Run-Time Parallelization

Devang Patel and Lawrence Rauchwerger *

Dept. of Computer Science
Texas A&M University
College Station, TX 77843-3112
http://www.cs.tamu.edu/faculty/rwerger, {dpatel,rwerger}@cs.tamu.edu

Abstract. Current parallelizing compilers cannot identify a significant fraction of parallelizable loops because they have complex or statically insufficiently defined access patterns. We advocate a novel framework for the identification of parallel loops. It speculatively executes a loop as a doall and applies a fully parallel data dependence test to check for any unsatisfied data dependencies; if the test fails, then the loop is re–executed serially. We will present the principles of the design and implementation of a compiler that employs both run-time and static techniques to parallelize dynamic applications. Run-time optimizations always represent a tradeoff between a *speculated* potential benefit and a *certain* (sure) overhead that must be paid. We will introduce techniques that take advantage of classic compiler methods to reduce the cost of run-time optimization thus tilting the outcome of *speculation* in favor of significant performance gains. Experimental results from the PERFECT, SPEC and NCSA Benchmark suites show that these techniques yield speedups not obtainable by any other known method.

1   Run-time Optimization Is Necessary

To achieve a high level of performance for a particular program on today's super-computers, software developers are often forced to tediously hand–code optimizations tailored to a specific machine. Such hand–coding is difficult, increases the possibility of error over sequential programming, and the resulting code may not be portable to other machines. Restructuring, or parallelizing, compilers address these problems by detecting and exploiting parallelism in sequential programs written in conventional languages. Although compiler techniques for the automatic detection of parallelism have been studied extensively over the last two decades, current parallelizing compilers cannot extract a significant fraction of the available parallelism in a loop if it has a complex and/or statically insufficiently defined access pattern. Typical examples are complex simulations such as SPICE [16], DYNA–3D [27], GAUSSIAN [14], CHARMM [1].

* Research supported in part by NSF CAREER Award CCR-9734471 and utilized the SGI systems at the NCSA, University of Illinois under grant#ASC980006N.

It has become clear that static (compile–time) analysis must be comple-
mented by new methods capable of automatically extracting parallelism at *run–
time* [6]. Run–time techniques can succeed where static compilation fails because
they have access to the input data. For example, input dependent or dynamic
data distribution, memory accesses guarded by run–time dependent conditions,
and subscript expressions can all be analyzed unambiguously at run–time. In
contrast, at compile–time the access pattern of some programs cannot be determined, sometimes due to limitations in the current analysis algorithms but often
because the necessary information is just not available, i.e., the access pattern is
a function of the input data. For example, most dependence analysis algorithms
can only deal with subscript expressions that are affine in the loop indices. In the
presence of non–linear expressions, or of subscripted subscripts, compilers generally conservatively assume data dependences. Although more powerful analysis
techniques could remove this last limitation when the index arrays are computed
using only statically–known values, nothing can be done at compile–time when
the index arrays are a function of the input data [12, 25, 28].

We will present the principles of the design and implementation of a compiling system that employs run-time and classic techniques in tandem to automatically parallelize irregular, dynamic applications. We will show that run-time
optimizations always represent a tradeoff between a *speculated* potential benefit
and a *certain* (sure) overhead that must be paid. This work models the com-
peting factors of this optimization technique and outlines a guiding strategy for
increasing performance. We will introduce techniques that take advantage of
classic compiler methods to reduce the cost of run-time optimization thus tilting
the outcome of *speculation* in favor of significant performance gains. [1]

The scope of presented work will be initially limited to loop level parallelization and optimization of Fortran programs in a shared memory environment
using the SPMD programming paradigm. The run–time techniques described
here are designed to be used in the automatic parallelization of 'legacy' Fortran
applications as well as in explicit parallel coding of new, dynamic codes, where
concurrency is a function of the input data.

2 Run-time Optimization

Maximizing the performance of an application executing on a specific parallel
system can be derived from three fundamental optimization principles: (i) maximizing parallelism while minimizing overhead and redundant computation, (ii)
minimizing wait-time due to load imbalance, and (iii) minimizing wait-time due
to memory latency.

Maximizing the parallelism in a program is probably the most important
factor affecting parallel, scalable performance. It allows full concurrent use of all
the resources of any given architecture without any idle (wait) time. At the limit,

---

[1] This paper and the techniques presented in detail here is complimentary to those
recently published in [18].

full parallelism also allows perfect scalability with the number of processors and can be efficiently used to improve memory latency and load balancing.

The most effective vehicle for improving multiprocessor performance has been the restructuring compiler [5, 10, 19, 9]. Compilers have incorporated sophisticated data dependence analysis techniques(e.g., [3, 20]) to detect intrinsic parallelism in codes and transform them for parallel execution. These techniques usually rely on a static (compile time) analysis of the memory access pattern (array subscripts in the case of Fortran programs) and on parallelism enabling transformations like privatization, reduction parallelization, induction variable substitution, etc. [7]. When static information is insufficient to safely perform an optimizing transformation the classic compiler emits conservative code. Alternatively it might delay the decision to execution time, when sufficient information becomes available. This strategy implies that a certain amount of code analysis has to be performed during the time which was initially allocated to useful data processing. This shift of activity will inherently account for *a priori* performance degradation. Only when the outcome of the run-time analysis is a safe optimization can we hope that the overall execution time will decrease. For example, if the parallelization of a loop depends on the value of a parameter that is statically unavailable the compiler can generate a two-version loop (one parallel and one sequential) and code that will test the parameter at run-time and decide which version to execute. While this is a very simple case it shows that time will be 'lost' testing the parameter and, depending on the outcome, may or may not lead to an optimization. Furthermore, even if the loop under question is executed in parallel, performance gains are not certain. All this implies that run-time optimizations always represent a tradeoff which needs a guiding strategy; they represent a *speculation* about a potential benefit for which a *certain* (sure) overhead will have to be paid.

2.1 Principles of Run-Time Optimization

Loop parallelization is the most effective and far reaching optimization for scientific applications. Briefly stated, a loop can be safely executed in parallel if and only if its later iterations do not use data computed in its earlier iterations, i.e., there are no flow dependences. The safety of this and other related transformations (e.g., privatization, reduction parallelization) is checked at compile time through data dependence analysis (i.e., analyzing array subscript functions). When static analysis is not possible the access pattern is analyzed at run-time through various techniques which we will shortly introduce and analyze.

Inspector/Executor vs. Speculative run-time testing. All run-time optimizations in general, and parallelization in particular, consist of at least two activities: *(a)* a test of a set of run-time values (e.g., the values taken by array subscripts) and *(b)* the execution of one of the compiler generated options (e.g., multi-version loops).

If the test phase is performed before the execution of the loop and has no side effects, i.e., it does not modify the state of the original program (shared) variables then this technique is called *inspector/executor* [4]. Its run-time overhead consists only of the time to execute the inspection phase.

If the test phase is done at the same time as the execution of the aggressively optimized loop and, in general, the state of the program is modified during this process, then the technique is called *speculative execution*. Its associated overhead consists at least of the test itself and the saving of the program state (checkpointing). If the optimization test fails, then extra overhead is paid during a program *ante loop* state restoration phase before the conservative version of the code can be executed. In this scenario the the initial optimized loop execution time becomes additional overhead too.

Although it might appear that the more 'sedate' *inspector/executor* method is a better overall strategy than the *speculative* technique, there is in fact a much more subtle trade-off between the two. An inspector loop represents a segment of code that must always be executed before any decision can be made and always adds to the program's critical path. However, if the test is executed concurrently with the actual computation (it is always quasi-independent of it – computation cannot possibly depend on the test) then some of the overhead may not add additional wall-clock time. The same is true if checkpointing is done 'on-the-fly', just before a variable is about to be modified. In other words *with respect to performance alone* the two methods are competitive.

A potential negative effect of speculative execution is that the optimization test's data structures are used concurrently with those of the original program, which could increase the working set of the loop and degrade its cache performance.

The previous comparison assumes an important principle: *any run-time parallelization technique must be fully parallel* to scale with the number of processors. For the speculative method this is always implicitly true – we test during a speculative parallel execution. Inspectors may be executed sequentially or in parallel – but, with the exception of simple cases, only parallel execution can lead to scalable performance. Inspector loops cannot always be parallelized. If there exists a data or control dependence cycle between shared data and its address computation then it is not possible to extract an address inspector that can be safely parallelized and/or that is side effect free. In fact the inspector would contain most of the original loop, in effect degenerating into a *speculative* technique (will need checkpointing) without its benefits.

In summary we conclude that both run-time techniques are generally competitive but that the speculative method is the only generally applicable one.

2.2 Obtaining Performance

Run-time optimization can produce performance gains only if the associated overhead for its validation is outweighed by the obtained speedup or,

$$Speedup = SuccessRate \times (Optimization\_Speedup - Testing\_Overhead) > 0$$

This *Speedup* function can be maximized by increasing the power of the intended optimization and decreasing the time it takes to validate it. Because run-time optimizations are speculative, their success is not guaranteed and therefore, their *SuccessRate*, needs to be maximized.

Performance through Run-time Overhead Reduction. The optimization representing the focus of this paper is loop parallelization within a SPMD computation. This transformation generally scales with data size and number of processors and its overall potential for speedup is unquestionable. Its general profitability (when and where to apply it) has been the topic of previous research and its conclusions remain valid in our context.

Thus, the task at hand is to decrease the second term of our performance objective function, the testing-overhead. Regardless of the adopted testing strategy (inspector/executor or aggressive speculation) this overhead can be broken down into (a) the time it takes to extract data dependence information about the statically un-analyzable access pattern, and (b) the time to perform an analysis of the collected data dependence information.

The first rule we have adopted is that all run-time processing (access tracing and analysis) must be performed in parallel — otherwise it may become the sequential bottleneck of the application. The access pattern tracing will be performed within a parallel region either before the loop in case of the inspector approach or during the speculative execution of the transformed loop. The amount of work can be upper bounded by the length of the trace but (see Section 5) can be further reduced (at times dramatically) through reference aggregation and elimination of duplicated (redundant) address records. This type of optimization can be achieved through the use of static, i.e., compile time information. Usually, when a compiler cannot prove independence for all referenced variables, the partial information obtained during static analysis is discarded. In such a case our run-time compiler phase will retrieve all previously considered useless, but valid information and complement it with only the really dynamic data. This tight integration of the run-time technique with the classic compiler methods is the key to the reduction of tracing overhead.

Another important tool in reducing overhead is the development of static heuristics for uncovering the algorithms and data structures used in the original program. For example, pattern matching a reduction can encourage the use of a run-time reduction validation technique. An inference about the use of structures may reduce the number of addresses shadowed.

Increasing the Success Rate of Speculation. Collecting the outcome of every speculation and using this data in the computation of a *statistic* could drastically alter the success rate of speculation. The use of *meaningful* statistics about the parallelism profile of dynamic programs will require some evidence that different experiments on one application with different input sets produces similar results (with respect to parallelism). Feeding back the results of speculative parallelization during the same execution of a code may be, for the moment, a more practical approach. For example, after failing speculation on loop several consecutive times a more conservative approach can adopted 'on-the-fly'.

A more difficult but more effective strategy in enhancing both the success rate of speculation as well as lowering run-time overhead is to find heuristics that can 'guess' the algorithmic approach and/or data structure used by the original program and drive the speculation in the right direction. A simple example is reduction recognition: if a statement 'looks' like a reduction then it can be verified by generating a speculative test for it – the chances of success are very high. Making the correct assumption at compile time whether an access pattern is sparse or dense or whether we use linked lists or arrays (regardless of their implementation) can go a long way in making run-time optimization profitable (see Section 5).

3 Foundational Work: Run-Time Parallelization

We have developed several techniques [21–24] that can detect and exploit loop level parallelism in various cases encountered in irregular applications: (i) a speculative method to detect fully parallel loops (The LRPD Test), (ii) an inspector/executor technique to compute wavefronts (sequences of mutually independent sets of iterations that can be executed in parallel) and (iii) a technique for parallelizing while loops (do loops with an unknown number of iterations and/or containing linked list traversals). We now briefly describe a simplified version of the speculative LRPD test (complete details can be found in [21, 22]).

The LRPD Test. The LRPD test speculatively executes a loop in parallel and tests subsequently if any data dependences could have occurred. If the test fails, the loop is re-executed sequentially. To qualify more parallel loops, *array privatization* and *reduction parallelization* can be speculatively applied and their validity tested after loop termination.[2] For simplicity, reduction parallelization is not shown in the example below; it is tested in a similar manner as independence and privatization. The LRPD test is fully parallel and requires time $O(a/p + \log p)$, where p is the number of processors, and a is the total number of accesses made to A in the loop.

Consider a do loop for which the compiler cannot statically determine the access pattern of a shared array A (Fig. 1(a)). We allocate the shadow arrays for marking the write accesses, A_w, and the read accesses, A_r, and an array A_{np}, for flagging non-privatizable elements. The loop is augmented with code (Fig. 1(b)) that will mark during speculative execution the shadow arrays every time A is referenced (based on specific rules). The result of the marking can be seen in Fig. 1(c). The first time an element of A is written during an iteration, the corresponding element in the write shadow array A_w is marked. If, during any iteration, an element in A is read, but never written, then the corresponding element in the read shadow array A_r is marked. Another shadow array A_{np} is

---

[2] *Privatization* creates, for each processor cooperating on the execution of the loop, private copies of the program variables. A shared variable is privatizable if it is always written in an iteration before it is read, e.g., many temporary variables. A *reduction variable* is a variable used in one operation of the form $x = x \otimes exp$, where $\otimes$ is an associative and commutative operator and x does not occur in exp or anywhere else in the loop. There are known transformations for implementing reductions in parallel [26, 15, 13].

used to flag the elements of A that *cannot* be privatized: an element in A_{np} is marked if the corresponding element in A is both read and written, and is read first, in any iteration.

A post-execution analysis, illustrated in Fig. 1(c), determines whether there were any cross-iteration dependencies between statements referencing A as follows. If $\mathrm{any}(A_w(:) \wedge A_r(:))$[3] is true, then there is at least one flow- or anti-dependence that was not removed by privatizing A (some element is read and written in different iterations). If $\mathrm{any}(A_{np}(:))$ is true, then A is not privatizable (some element is read before being written in an iteration). If Atw, the total number of writes marked during the parallel execution, is not equal to Atm, the total number of marks computed after the parallel execution, then there is at least one output dependence (some element is overwritten); however, if A is privatizable (i.e., if $\mathrm{any}(A_{np}(:))$ is false), then these dependencies were removed by privatizing A.

```
do i=1,5
   z = A(K(i))
   if (B1(i) .eq. .true.) then
      A(L(i)) = z + C(i)
   endif
enddo

B1(1:5) = (1 0 1 0 1)
K(1:5) = (1 2 3 4 1)
L(1:5) = (2 2 4 4 2)

      (a)
```

```
do i=1,5
   markread(K(i))
   z = A(K(i))
   if (B1(i) .eq. .true.) then
      markwrite(L(i))
      A(L(i)) = z + C(i)
   endif
enddo

      (b)
```

Operation	Value				
	1	2	3	4	5
Aw	0	1	0	1	0
Ar	1	1	1	1	0
Anp	1	1	1	1	0
Aw(:) ∧ Ar(:)	0	1	0	1	0
Aw(:) ∧ Anp(:)	0	1	0	1	0
Atw	3				
Atm	2				

(c)

Fig. 1. Do loop (a) transformed for speculative execution, (b) the `markwrite` and `markread` operations update the appropriate shadow arrays, (c) shadow arrays after loop execution. In this example, the test fails.

4 Variations of the LRPD Test

Static compilation can generate a wealth of incomplete information that, by itself, is insufficient to decide whether parallelization is safe but can be exploited to reduce run-time overhead. When we can establish statically that, for example, all iterations of a loop first read and then write a shared array (but nothing else) then we can conclude that privatization is not possible, and therefore should not test for it. This approach of using partial information has led to the development of simplified variants of the LRPD test. The overall purpose of the various specialized forms of the LRPD test presented in this section is (a) to reduce the overhead of run-time processing to the minimum necessary and sufficient to achieve safe parallelization (but without becoming conservative), and (b) to extend the number of access patterns that can be recognized as parallelizable. We will now enumerate some of the more frequently used variants of the LRPD

---

[3] any returns the "OR" of its vector operand's elements, i.e., $\mathrm{any}(v(1:n)) = (v(1) \vee v(2) \vee \ldots \vee v(n))$.

test that we have developed and elaborate on those that have not been presented in our earlier paper [18]. Further refinements and related issues (such as choice of marking data structures) are discussed in Section 5.

- Processor–wise LRPD test for testing cross-processor instead of cross-iteration dependences, qualifying more parallel loops with less overhead.
- A test supporting copy-in of external values to allow loops that first read-in a value to be executed in parallel.
- Early failure detection test to reduce the overhead of failed speculation.
- Early success detection test with on-demand cross-processor analysis.
- A test that can distinguish between fully independent and privatizable accesses to reduce private storage replication for privatized arrays.
- An Aggregate LRPD test – aggregates individual memory the references in contiguous intervals or sets of points.

4.1 A processor–wise version of the LRPD test

The LRPD Test determines whether a loop has any cross–*iteration* data dependences. It turns out that essentially the same method can be used to test whether the loop, as executed, has any cross–*processor* data dependences [2]. The only difference is that all checks in the test refer to processors rather than to iterations, i.e., replace "iteration" by "processor" in the description of the LRPD test so that all iterations assigned to a processor are considered as one "super–iteration" by the test. It is important to note that a loop that is not fully parallel (it has cross-iteration dependences) could potentially pass the processor–wise version of the LRPD test because data dependences among iterations assigned to the same processor will not be detected. This is desirable (and correct) provided that each processor executes its assigned iterations in increasing order. The processor–wise version of the test can therefore parallelize more loops and, at the same time incur less time and space costs: the shadow structures need to be initialized only once and can use boolean values (bits) for marking. When last value assignment is required, i.e., when the last written value needs to be copied out from the privatized array to the original shared array, the needed last–write timestamps can be expressed implicitly in the value of the processor identifier if static scheduling of iterations is used.

4.2 Supporting Copy-In of External Values

Suppose that a loop is determined as fully parallel by the LRPD test except for the accesses to one element a. If the first time(s) a is accessed it is read, and for every later iteration that accesses a it is always written before it is read, then the loop could be executed as a doall by having the initial accesses to a *copy–in* the global value of a, and the iterations that wrote a used private copies of a. In this way a loop with a $(read)^*(write|read)^*$ access pattern can be safely transformed into a doall. The LRPD test can be augmented to detect this situation by keeping track of the maximum iteration i_r^+ that read a (before it was ever written), and the minimum iteration i_w^- that wrote a. Then, if $i_r^+ \leq i_w^-$, the loop can be executed in parallel. Two additional private shadow structures are needed to verify this condition. In the processor–wise LRPD test, these additional shadow structures are not necessary because the information is available implicitly if static scheduling is employed. If the iteration space is assigned to the processors in contiguous chunks, i.e., processor i gets iterations $(n/p) * i$ through $(n/p) * (i + 1) - 1$, $0 \leq i < p$, then, we need only check that the first write to a appears on a processor with an id that is not less than the last processor id in which a is marked as non-privatizable or read-only.

4.3 Aggregate LRPD test

The simple, and rather naive way to insert the marking code into a loop is to simply add a markwrite, markread, markredux macro for every occurrence of a write and read access to the shadowed array.

There are however many programs that although irregular in general have a specific 'local' or partial regularity. These types of access patterns can be classified in the following manner:

- Arrays in nested loops accessed by an index of the form *(ptr, affine_fcn)*. The innermost loop index generates points for the affine function, and the outermost loop for the pointer. Generally the first dimension of the array is relatively small and is often traversed in an innermost loop or, for very small loop bounds, completely unrolled. It usually represents the access to the components of an n-dimensional vector. The bounds of this inner loop never change throughout the program.
- Multi-dimensional access patterns described by complex but statically determined functions, but where one more of the inner dimensions are simple functions.

A commonality in these cases is the fact that they all perform portion-wise contiguous accesses. The length of this regular interval can be either fixed (vectors with n-components, structures) or of variable length (e.g., in sparse matrix solvers). This characteristic can be exploited by marking contiguous intervals rather than every element accessed. Depending on the actual length of the intervals this technique can lead to major performance improvements. In the case of fixed-size intervals the information is kept implicitly (not stored in the shadow structures themselves) and the analysis phase needs only minor adjustment to the generic LRPD test. When intervals are variable in size within the context of the tested loop, their length will be kept explicitly and the shadow structures adapted accordingly into *shadow interval structures* (e.g., interval trees). The analysis phase will change to a more complex algorithm to reflect the parallel merge of complex data structures. While the asymptotic complexity increases the problem size can decrease dramatically (depending on the average length of intervals). We detect of these types of semi-irregular access patterns by using recently developed array region analysis techniques [17].

5 Implementation Issues

Merging the Phases of LRPD Test

In Section 3 we have presented the LRPD test as a sequence of phases: initialization, checkpointing, speculative execution, analysis and possible sequential re-execution. Every phase adds its contribution to the critical path of the program and may negatively affect the state of the caches. Some of the steps of a speculative execution can be merged, i.e., they can be executed concurrently. The major advantage of merging the various steps is that without increasing the working set, they add fine grain parallelism and thus may hide communication latencies.

Through **on-demand copy-in** we can copy-in values that are read from the original shared array and write them into their private counterparts by taking advantage of the shadow information. (If an element has not been written before, then read from the original array, else read from the private array; always write to the private array) **On-demand checkpointing** allows us to copy 'on-the-fly', to a private storage area, only the memory elments modified by the loop instead of saving entire data structures (e.g., arrays), a significant saving in the case of sparse access patterns. **Cross-processor last value assignment, merge-out and reduction**, when necessary, can be done concurrently after a successful speculation. For example, the shadow structures give the needed information on the processors contributing to the reductions (those that have their elements marked as reductions) to schedule the update of the shared arrays without contention.

Choosing Shadow Structures

The choice of shadow structures is dictated by the characteristics of the access pattern and the data structures used (implicitly or explicitly) of the original program. From our experience we have seen arrays used as arrays, C-like structures, linked lists, etc. The access pattern can be regular dense, regular sparse (fixed strides), or irregular sparse. Heuristics (omitted here for brevity but explained in final version of the paper) are used to guess the character of the access pattern. In the following, we will give a few examples of how these choices are made in our implementation.

Sparse/Dense access pattern can be inferred from the ratio between array dimension and number of references (distinct references if known). If the ratio is much larger than unity, then we can conclude that we have a sparse access. For the dense case we choose shadow arrays where the Write / Read / NotPrivate / NotReduction tags are represented by a maximum of 4 bits for the processor-wise test. For the sparse case we choose hash-table shadow structures or other specialized data structures.

Irregular/regular access pattern. Use of pointers (subscripted subscripts) is an indication of irregular accesses. If it is also sparse, then hash tables can be useful.

Portion-wise contiguous regular accesses. If intervals are fixed size, then regular arrays are chosen. Alternatively, when intervals are loop variant, interval trees are a better choice.

Repetitive Program Behavior

Schedule reuse, inspector decoupling. If the speculatively executed loop is re-executed during the program with the same data access pattern, then the results of the first LRPD test can be reused (this is an instance of *schedule reuse* [25]). If the defining parameters of an inspector loop are available well before the loop will be executed, then the test code can be executed early, perhaps during a portion of the program that does not have enough (or any) parallelism, possibly hiding the run-time testing overhead completely.

Use of statistics. One of the most effective ways to reduce the cost of failed parallelization attempts is to 'guess' correctly when a loop might be parallel. A powerful heuristic could be using statistics collected during past instantiations of the loop. Simply put, if the loop has been found to be parallel in the past, then there is a good chance that it will be parallel in the future. Such techniques have been extensively used in predicting paging behavior, cache misses and branch outcome. Unfortunately there is no experimental evidence that statistics about loop data dependence structure are significant.

5.1 The Run-time Pass in Polaris

Based on the previously presented techniques, we have implemented a first version of run-time parallelization in the Polaris compiler infrastructure [8] that is loosely based on the experimental work described in [22] and [11]. Due to space limitations we only give a very general overview of this 'run-time pass'.

Currently, candidate loops for run-time parallelization are marked by a special directive in the Fortran source code. Alternatively, all loops that Polaris leaves sequential are run-time parallelized. As a statistical model of loop parallelism in irregular applications will be developed we will be able to automatically select the candidates which have the highest possibility of success.

The bulk of the run-time pass is placed after all other static analysis has been completed and just before the post-pass (code generation). It can therefore use all the information uncovered by the existing Polaris analysis. In this pass the compiler proceeds as follows:

1. From all candidate loops, all those containing I/O statements, premature exits and while loops will be removed (these last two limitation will be soon relaxed).
2. For every loop we filter from the list of all their variables found independent or privatizable by previous Polaris analysis. The remainder will be run-time tested.

194

3. The selection of the appropriate LRPD test variant will be made based on a heuristic. If a reduction has been pattern matched then we apply reduction test. If it cannot be proven that a memory element is read before it is written the we test for privatization.

4. All references to variables under test will be instrumented with a call to the marking (shadowing) routines. These subroutines have been developed in a separate parallel Fortran library. A significant effort is made to remove redundant shadowing. For instance, any reference with the same subscript may have its shadow removed if its dominator has already been instrumented.

5. Finally, the code is generated by cloning the loop into a speculative parallel version (with shadowing instrumentation) and a serial loop. Calls for memory allocation, initialization, checkpointing and analysis are inserted.

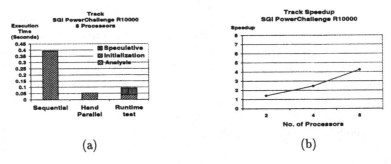

(a)   (b)

Fig. 2. Loop TRACK_NLFITL_DO_300: (a) Timing of test phases, (b) Speedup

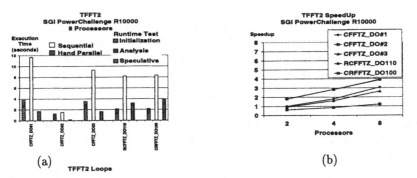

(a)   (b)

Fig. 3. Major Loops in TFFT2: (a) Timing of test phases, (b) Speedup

6   Experimental Results of Run-time Test in Polaris

We will now present experimental results obtained on several important loops from three applications that Polaris could not parallelize, namely, **TFFT2**, **P3M** and **TRACK**. After inserting run-time test directives before the loop, the codes have been automatically transformed by the compiler and executed in dedicated mode on an SGI Power Challenge with R10K processors at NCSA,

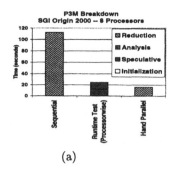 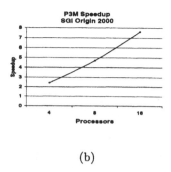

(a)   (b)

Fig. 4. Loop P3M_PP_DO_100: (a) Timing of test phases, (b) Speedup

University of Illinois. All test variant selections and other optimizations are automatic and no special, application specific compiler switches have been used.

TFFT2, a SPEC code has a fairly simple structure and all access patterns are statically defined, i.e., they are not dynamic or input dependent. Nevertheless, difficulties in its analysis arise due to (1) five levels of subroutine calls within a loop, (2) array reshaping between subroutine calls , (3) exponential relations between inner and outer loop bounds, and (4) array index offsets that depend on outer loop index. We have transformed all important loops of this program for speculative execution.

The speedups shown in Figure 3 reflect the application of the speculative LRPD test to the five most important loops of the program: CFFTZ_DO#1, CFFTZ_DO#2, CFFTZ_DO_#3, RCFFTZ_DO_110, CRFFTZ_DO_100. While speedups are generally good Loop CFFTZ_DO_#2 performs poorly because we allocated a shadow array four times larger than the actual access region (allocation based on dimension rather than access region) and because the loop itself is relatively small. The overall speedup of the TFFT2 program is 2.2 on 8 processors.

From the **P3M**, NCSA benchmark, a N-body simulation we have considered the triply nested loop in subroutine pp which takes about 50% of the actual sequential execution time. For better load balancing we have coalesced the loop nest and then applied speculative parallelization to several arrays that could not be proven privatizable by Polaris. For the best result we have employed the processor-wise privatization test (with dynamic scheduling) with shadow arrays and early success detection. No checkpointing was necessary because all arrays are privatized and the final reduction is performed on private arrays that are merged after loop execution. Figure 4 shows good speedup and scalability. The obtained speedup is significantly less than the manually parallelized version because the initialization phase, though short, has a cache flushing effect, thus causing the speculative loop to slow down; misses are experienced on all read-only arrays.

TRACK, a PERFECT code that simulates missile tracking, is one of the more interesting programs we have encountered. The tested loop, NLFILT_DO_300, has cross-iteration dependences in some of its instantiations and their frequency is input dependent. For the data set presented in Figure 2 the loop fails the cross-iteration dependence once in its 60 instantiations. However, the processor-wise test 'hides' the dependences and passes every time. The checkpointing overhead is quite important when array sizes are large with respect to the actual work that the loops performs. We believe that an improved on-demand checkpointing scheme will reduce this overhead. Note: The hand-parallel speedup in Figure 2 is in fact an *ideal* speedup because the loop cannot be manually parallelized (because its parallelism is input dependent). The value shown is still correct because the hand-parallel version has been statically scheduled and there are no cross-processor dependences.

7 Conclusion

While the general LRPD algorithm has been extensively presented in [24] and briefly shown here for clarity of the presentation, this paper emphasizes the practical aspects of its application and integration in a compiler. In essence we advocate a very tight connection between static information obtained through classical compiler methods and the run-time system. This resulting optimized code will make use of all available static information and test only the necessary and sufficient conditions for safe parallelization. This interplay between compiler and run-time system results in testing methods that are tailored to a particular application (within limits) and that perform better.

A major source of optimization in speculative parallelization is the use of heuristics for inferring the data structure and access pattern characteristics of the program. Once a hypothesis is made, it can be tested at run-time much faster than a general method. For example, guessing the use of linked list or a structure and testing accordingly can improve performance dramatically.

Reducing run-time overhead may also require the speculative application of known code transformations, e.g., loop distribution, forward substitution. Their validity will be checked simultaneously with the previously presented run-time data dependence test, without incurring any additional overhead.

References

1. Charmm: A program for macromolecular energy, minimization, and dynamics calculations. *J. of Computational Chemistry*, 4(6), 1983.
2. Santosh Abraham. *Private Communication.* Hewlett Packard Laboratories, 1994.
3. Utpal Banerjee. *Loop Parallelization.* Norwell, MA: Kluwer Publishers, 1994.
4. H. Berryman and J. Saltz. A manual for PARTI runtime primitives. Interim Report 90-13, ICASE, 1990.
5. W. Blume, *et. al.* Advanced Program Restructuring for High-Performance Computers with Polaris. *IEEE Computer*, 29(12):78–82, December 1996.
6. W. Blume and R. Eigenmann. Performance Analysis of Parallelizing Compilers on the Perfect Benchmarks^{TM} Programs. *IEEE Trans. on Parallel and Distributed Systems*, 3(6):643–656, November 1992.

7. W. Blume et. al. Effective automatic parallelization with Polaris. *IJPP*, May 1995.
8. W. Blume et al. Polaris: The next generation in parallelizing compilers, In *Proc. of the 7-th Workshop on Languages and Compilers for Parallel Computing*, 1994.
9. K. Cooper et al. The parascope parallel programming environment. *Proc. of IEEE*, pp. 84–89, February 1993.
10. M. Hall et. al. Maximizing multiprocessor performance with the Suif compiler. *IEEE Computer*, 29(12):84–89, December 1996.
11. T. Lawrence. Implementation of run time techniques in the polaris fortran restructurer. TR 1501, CSRD, Univ. of Illinois at Urbana-Champaign, July 1995.
12. S. Leung and J. Zahorjan. Improving the performance of runtime parallelization. In *4th PPOPP*, pp. 83–91, May 1993.
13. Z. Li. Array privatization for parallel execution of loops. In *Proceedings of the 19th International Symposium on Computer Architecture*, pp. 313–322, 1992.
14. M. J. Frisch et. al. *Gaussian 94*. Gaussian, Inc., Pittsburgh PA, 1995.
15. D. E. Maydan, S. P. Amarasinghe, and M. S. Lam. Data dependence and dataflow analysis of arrays. In *Proc. 5th Workshop on Programming Languages and Compilers for Parallel Computing*, August 1992.
16. L. Nagel. *SPICE2: A Computer Program to Simulate Semiconductor Circuits*. PhD thesis, University of California, May 1975.
17. Y. Paek, J. Hoeflinger, and D. Padua. Simplification of Array Access Patterns for Compiler Optimizat ions. In *Proc. of the SIGPLAN 1998 Conf. on Programming Language Design and Implementation, Montreal, Canada*, June 1998.
18. D. Patel and L. Rauchwerger. Principles of speculative run–time parallelization. In *Proceedings 11th Annual Workshop on Programming Languages and Compilers for Parallel Computing*, pp. 330–351, August 1998.
19. C. Polychronopoulos et. al. Parafrase-2: A New Generation Parallelizing Compiler. *Proc. of 1989 Int. Conf. on Parallel Processing, St. Charles, IL*, II:39–48, 1989.
20. W. Pugh. A practical algorithm for exact array dependence analysis. *Comm. of the ACM*, 35(8):102–114, August 1992.
21. L. Rauchwerger, N. Amato, and D. Padua. A scalable method for run-time loop parallelization. *IJPP*, 26(6):537–576, July 1995.
22. L. Rauchwerger. Run–time parallelization: A framework for parallel computation. UIUCDCS-R-95-1926, Univ. of Illinois, Urbana, IL, September 1995.
23. L. Rauchwerger and D. Padua. Parallelizing WHILE Loops for Multiprocessor Systems. In *Proc. of 9th International Parallel Processing Symposium*, April 1995.
24. L. Rauchwerger and D. Padua. The LRPD Test: Speculative Run-Time Parallelization of Loops with Privatization and Reduction Parallelization. In *Proc. of the SIGPLAN 1995 Conf. on Programming Language Design and Implementation, La Jolla, CA*, pp. 218–232, June 1995.
25. J. Saltz, R. Mirchandaney, and K. Crowley. Run-time parallelization and scheduling of loops. *IEEE Trans. Comput.*, 40(5), May 1991.
26. P. Tu and D. Padua. Array privatization for shared and distributed memory machines. In *Proc. 2nd Workshop on Languages, Compilers, and Run-Time Environments for Distributed Memory Machines*, September 1992.
27. R. Whirley and B. Engelmann. *DYNA3D: A Nonlinear, Explicit, Three-Dimensional Finite Element Code For Solid and Structural Mechanics*. Lawrence Livermore National Laboratory, Nov., 1993.
28. C. Zhu and P. C. Yew. A scheme to enforce data dependence on large multiprocessor systems. *IEEE Trans. Softw. Eng.*, 13(6):726–739, June 1987.

Compilation and Memory Management for ASF+SDF

Mark van den Brand[1] and Paul Klint[1,2] and Pieter Olivier[2]

[1] CWI, Department of Software Engineering, Kruislaan 413, NL-1098 SJ Amsterdam, The Netherlands
[2] University of Amsterdam, Programming Research Group, Kruislaan 403, NL-1098 SJ Amsterdam, The Netherlands

Abstract. Can formal specification techniques be scaled-up to industrial problems such as the development of domain-specific languages and the renovation of large COBOL systems?
We have developed a compiler for the specification formalism ASF+SDF that has been used successfully to meet such industrial challenges. This result is achieved in two ways: the compiler performs a variety of optimizations and generates efficient C code, and the compiled code uses a run-time memory management system based on maximal subterm sharing and mark-and-sweep garbage collection.
We present an overview of these techniques and evaluate their effectiveness in several benchmarks. It turns out that execution speed of compiled ASF+SDF specifications is at least as good as that of comparable systems, while memory usage is in many cases an order of magnitude smaller.

1 Introduction

Efficient implementation based on mainstream technology is a prerequisite for the application and acceptance of declarative languages or specification formalisms in real industrial settings. The main characteristic of industrial applications is their *size* and the predominant implementation consideration should therefore be the ability to handle huge problems.

In this paper we take the specification formalism ASF+SDF [5, 19, 15] as point of departure. Its main focus is on language prototyping and on the development of language specific tools. ASF+SDF is based on general context-free grammars for describing syntax and on conditional equations for describing semantics. In this way, one can easily describe the syntax of a (new or existing) language and specify operations on programs in that language such as static type checking, interpretation, compilation or transformation. ASF+SDF has been applied successfully in a number of industrial projects [9, 11], such as the development of a domain-specific language for describing interest products (in the financial domain) [4] and a renovation factory for restructuring of COBOL code [12]. In such industrial applications, the execution speed is very important, but when processing huge COBOL programs memory usage becomes a critical issue as well. Other applications of ASF+SDF include the development of a GLR parser generator [26], an unparser generator [13], program transformation tools [14], and the compiler discussed in this paper. Other components, such as parsers, structure editors, and interpreters, are developed in ASF+SDF as well but are not (yet) compiled to C.

What are the performance standards one should strive for when writing a compiler for, in our case, an algebraic specification formalism? Experimental, comparative, studies are scarce, one notable exception is [18] where measurements are collected for various declarative programs solving a single real-world problem. In other studies it is no exception that the units of measurement (rewrite steps/second, or logical inferences/second) are ill-defined and that memory requirements are not considered due to the small size of the input problems.

In this paper, we present a compiler for ASF+SDF that performs a variety of optimizations and generates efficient C code. The compiled code uses a run-time memory management system based on maximal subterm sharing and mark-and-sweep garbage collection. The contribution of this paper is to bring the performance of executable specifications based on term rewriting into the realm of industrial applications.

In the following two subsections we will first give a quick introduction to ASF+SDF (the input language of the compiler to be described) and to μASF (the abstract intermediate representation used internally by the compiler). Next, we describe the generation of C code (Section 2) as well as memory management (Section 3). Section 4 is devoted to benchmarking. A discussion in Section 5 concludes the paper.

1.1 Specification Language: ASF+SDF

The specification formalism ASF+SDF [5, 19] is a combination of the algebraic specification formalism ASF and the syntax definition formalism SDF. An overview can be found in [15]. As an illustration, Figure 1 presents the definition of the Boolean datatype in ASF+SDF. ASF+SDF specifications consist of modules, each module has an SDF-part (defining lexical and context-free syntax) and an ASF-part (defining equations). The SDF part corresponds to signatures in ordinary algebraic specification formalisms. However, syntax is not restricted to plain prefix notation since arbitrary context-free grammars can be defined. The syntax defined in the SDF-part of a module can be used immediately when defining equations, the syntax in equations is thus *user-defined*.

The emphasis in this paper will be on the compilation of the equations appearing in a specification. They have the following distinctive features:

- Conditional equations with positive and negative conditions.
- Non left-linear equations.
- List matching.
- Default equations.

It is possible to execute specifications by interpreting the equations as conditional rewrite rules. The semantics of ASF+SDF is based on innermost rewriting. Default equations are tried when all other applicable equations have failed, because either the arguments did not match or one of the conditions failed.

One of the powerful features of the ASF+SDF specification language is list matching. Figure 2 shows a single equation which removes multiple occurrences of identifiers from a set. In this example, variables with a *-superscript are list-variables that may match zero or more identifiers. The implementation of list matching may involve backtracking to find a match that satisfies the left-hand side of the rewrite rule as well as all its conditions. There is only backtracking within the scope of a rewrite rule, so if the right-hand side of the rewrite rule is normalized and this normalization fails *no* backtracking is performed to find a new match.

```
imports Layout
exports
  sorts BOOL
  context-free syntax
    true                    → BOOL {constructor}
    false                   → BOOL {constructor}
    BOOL "|" BOOL           → BOOL {left}
    BOOL "&" BOOL           → BOOL {left}
    BOOL "xor" BOOL         → BOOL {left}
    not BOOL                → BOOL
    "(" BOOL ")"            → BOOL {bracket}
  variables
    Bool [0-9']∗ → BOOL
  priorities
    BOOL "|"BOOL → BOOL < BOOL "xor"BOOL → BOOL <
    BOOL "&"BOOL → BOOL < notBOOL → BOOL
equations
```

[B1]	true | $Bool$	= true	[B5]	not false	= true
[B2]	false | $Bool$	= $Bool$	[B6]	not true	= false
[B3]	true & $Bool$	= $Bool$	[B7]	true xor $Bool$	= not $Bool$
[B4]	false & $Bool$	= false	[B8]	false xor $Bool$	= $Bool$

Fig. 1. ASF+SDF specification of the Booleans.

The development of ASF+SDF specifications is supported by an interactive programming environment, the ASF+SDF Meta-Environment [23]. In this environment specifications can be developed and tested. It provides syntax-directed editors, a parser generator, and a rewrite engine. Given this rewrite engine terms can be reduced by interpreting the equations as rewrite rules. For instance, the term true & (false|true) reduces to true when applying the equations of Figure 1.

```
imports Layout
exports
  sorts ID Set
  lexical syntax
    [a-z][a-z0-9]∗ → ID
  context-free syntax
    "{" {ID ","}∗ "}" → Set
hiddens
  variables
    Id "∗"[0-9]∗ → {ID ","}∗
    Id [0-9']∗    → ID
equations
[1]  {Id₀∗, Id, Id₁∗, Id, Id₂∗}
   = {Id₀∗, Id, Id₁∗, Id₂∗}
```

Fig. 2. The Set equation in ASF+SDF.

```
module Booleans
signature
  true;      or(_,_);
  false;     xor(_,_);
  and(_,_);  not(_);
rules
  and(true,B) = B;
  and(false,B) = false;
  or(true,B) = true;
  or(false,B) = B;
  not(true) = false;
  not(false) = true;
  xor(true,B) = not(B);
  xor(false,B) = B;
```

Fig. 3. The Booleans in μASF.

1.2 Intermediate Representation Language: μASF

The user-defined syntax that may be used in equations poses two major implementation challenges.

First, how do we represent ASF+SDF specifications as parse trees? Recall that there is no fixed grammar since the basic ASF+SDF-grammar can be extended by the user. The solution we have adopted is to introduce the intermediate format ASFIX (ASF+SDF fixed format) which is used to represent the parse trees of the ASF+SDF modules in a format that is easy processable by a machine. The user-defined syntax is replaced by prefix functions. The parse trees in the ASFIX format are self contained.

Second, how do we represent ASF+SDF specifications in a more abstract form that is suitable as compiler input? We use a simplified language μASF as an intermediate representation to ease the compilation process and to perform various transformations before generating C code. μASF is in fact a single sorted (algebraic) specification formalism that uses only prefix notation. μASF can be considered as the abstract syntax representation of ASF+SDF. ASFIX and μASF live on different levels, μASF is only visible within the compiler whereas ASFIX serves as exchange format between the various components, such as structure editor, parser, and compiler.

A module in μASF consists of a module name, a list of functions, and a set of equations. The main differences between μASF and ASF+SDF are:

- Only prefix functions are used.
- The syntax is fixed (eliminating lexical and context-free definitions, priorities, and the like).
- Lists are represented by binary list constructors instead of the built-in list construct as in ASF+SDF; associative matching is used to implement list matching.
- Functions are untyped, only their arity is declared.
- Identifiers starting with capitals are variables; variable declarations are not needed.

Figure 3 shows the μASF specification corresponding to the ASF+SDF specification of the Booleans given earlier in Figure 1[1]. Figure 4 shows the μASF specification of sets given earlier in Figure 2. Note that this specification is not left-linear since the variable Id appears twice on the left-hand side of the equation. The {list} function is used to mark that a term is a list. This extra function is needed to distinguish between a single element list and an ordinary term, e.g., {list}(a) *versus* a or {list}(V) *versus* V. An example of a transformation on μASF specifications is shown in Figure 5, where the non-left-linearity has been removed from the specification in Figure 4 by introducing new variables and an auxiliary condition.

2 C Code Generation

The ASF compiler uses μASF as intermediate representation format and generates C code as output. The compiler consists of several independent phases that gradually simplify and transform the μASF specification and finally generate C code.

---

[1] To increase the readability of the generated code in this paper, we have consistently renamed generated names by more readable ones, like true, false, etc.

```
module Set
signature
  {list}(_);
  set(_);
  conc(_,_);
  t;

rules
set({list}(conc(*Id0,
  conc(Id,conc(*Id1,
    conc(Id,*Id2)))))) =
set({list}(conc(*Id0,
  conc(Id,conc(*Id1,*Id2)))));
```

```
module Set
signature
  {list}(_);
  set(_);
  conc(_,_);
  t;
  term-equal(_,_);
rules
term-equal(Id1,Id2) == t ==>
set({list}(conc(*Id0,
  conc(Id1,conc(*Id1,
    conc(Id2,*Id2)))))) =
set({list}(conc(*Id0,
  conc(Id1,conc(*Id1,*Id2)))));
```

Fig. 4. μASF specification of Set.   **Fig. 5.** Left-linear specification of Set.

A number of transformations is performed to eliminate "complex" features such as removal of non left-linear rewrite rules, simplification of matching patterns, and the introduction of "assignment" conditions (conditions that introduce new variable bindings). Some of these transformations are performed to improve the efficiency of the resulting code whereas others are performed to simplify code generation.

In the last phase of the compilation process C code is generated which implements the rewrite rules in the specification using adaptations of known techniques [22, 17]. Care is taken in constructing an efficient matching automaton, identifying common and reusable (sub)expressions, and efficiently implementing list matching. For each μASF function (even the constructors) a separate C function is generated. The right-hand side of an equation is directly translated to a function call, if necessary. A detailed description of the construction of the matching automaton is beyond the scope of this paper, a full description of the construction of the matching automaton can be found in [10]. Each generated C function contains a small part of the matching automaton, so instead of building one big automaton, the automaton is split over the functions. The matching automaton respects the syntactic specificity of the arguments from left to right in the left-hand sides of the equations. Non-variable arguments are tried before the variable ones.

The datatype ATerm (for Annotated Term) is the most important datatype used in the generated C code. It is provided by a run-time library which takes care of the creation, manipulation, and storage of terms. ATerms consist of a function symbol and zero or more arguments, e.g., and(true, false). The library provides predicates, such as check_sym to check whether the function symbol of a term corresponds to the given function symbol, and functions, like make_nfi to construct a term (normal form) given a function symbol and i arguments ($i \geq 0$). There are also access functions to obtain the i-th argument ($i \geq 0$) of a term, e.g., arg_1(and(true, false)) yields false.

The usage of these term manipulation functions can be seen in Figures 6 and 7. Figure 6 shows the C code generated for the and function of the Booleans (also see

```
ATerm and(ATerm arg0, ATerm arg1) {
  if(check_sym(arg0,truesym))
    return arg1;
  if(check_sym(arg0,falsesym))
    return arg0;
  return make_nf2(andsym,arg0,arg1);
}
```

Fig. 6. Generated C code for the and function of the Booleans.

Figures 1 and 3). This C code also illustrates the detection of reusable subexpressions. In the second if-statement a check is made whether the first argument of the and-function is equal to the term false. If the outcome of this test is positive, the first argument arg0 of the and-function is returned rather than building a new normal form for the term false or calling the function false(). The last statement in Figure 6 is necessary to catch the case that the first argument is neither a true or false symbol, but some other Boolean normal form.

Figure 7 shows the C code generated for the Set example of Figure 2. List matching is translated into nested while loops, this is possible because of the restricted nature of the backtracking in list matching. The functions not_empty_list, list_head, list_tail, conc, and slice are library functions which give access to the C data structure which represents the ASF+SDF lists. In this way the generated C code needs no knowledge of the internal list structure. We can even change the internal representation of lists *without adapting the generated C code*, by just replacing the library functions. The function term_equal checks the equality of two terms.

When specifications grow larger, *separate compilation* becomes mandatory. There are two issues related to the separate compilation of ASF+SDF specifications that deserve special attention. The first issue concerns the identification and linking of names appearing in separately compiled modules. Essentially, this amounts to the question how to translate the ASF+SDF names into C names. This problem arises since a direct translation would generate names that are too long for C compilers and linkage editors. We have opted for a solution in which each generated C file contains a "register" function which stores at run-time for each defined function defined in this C file a mapping between the address of the generated function and the original ASF+SDF name. In addition, each C file contains a "resolve" function which connects local function calls to the corresponding definitions based on their ASF+SDF names. An example of registering and resolving can be found in Figure 8.

The second issue concerns the choice of a unit for separate compilation. In most programming language environments, the basic compilation unit is a file. For example, a C source file can be compiled into an object file and several object files can be joined by the linkage editor into a single executable. If we change a statement in one of the source files, that complete source file has to be recompiled and linked with the other object files.

In the case of ASF+SDF, the natural compilation unit would be the module. However, we want to generate a single C function for each function in the specification (for efficiency reasons) but ASF+SDF functions can be defined in specifications using multiple equations occurring in several modules. The solution is to use a single function

```
ATerm set(ATerm arg0) {
  if(check_sym(arg0,listsym)) {
    ATerm tmp0 = arg_0(arg0);
    ATerm tmp1[2];
    tmp1[0] = tmp0; tmp1[1] = tmp0;
    while(not_empty_list(tmp0)) {
      ATerm tmp3 = list_head(tmp0);
      tmp0 = list_tail(tmp0);
      ATerm tmp2[2];
      tmp2[0] = tmp0; tmp2[1] = tmp0;
      while(not_empty_list(tmp0)) {
        ATerm tmp4 = list_head(tmp0);
        tmp0 = list_tail(tmp0);
        if(term_equal(tmp3,tmp4))
          return set(list(conc(slice(tmp1[0],tmp1[1]),
                      conc(tmp3,conc(slice(tmp2[0],tmp2[1]),
                                     tmp0))))));
        tmp2[1] = list_tail(tmp2[1]);
        tmp0 = tmp2[1];
      }
      tmp1[1] = list_tail(tmp1[1]);
      tmp0 = tmp1[1];
    }
  }
  return make_nf1(setsym,arg0);
}
```

Fig. 7. C code for the Set specification.

as compilation unit and to *re-shuffle* the equations before translating the specification. Equations are thus stored depending on the module they occur in as well as on their outermost function symbol. When the user changes an equation, only those functions that are actually affected have to be recompiled into C code. The resulting C code is then compiled, and linked together with all other previously compiled functions.

3 Memory Management

At run-time, the main activities of compiled ASF+SDF specifications are the creation and matching of large amounts of terms. Some of these terms may even be very big (more than 10^6 nodes). The amount of memory used during rewriting depends entirely on the number of terms being constructed and on the amount of storage each term occupies. In the case of innermost rewriting a lot of redundant (intermediate) terms are constructed.

At compile time, we can take various measures to avoid redundant term creation (only the last two have been implemented in the ASF+SDF compiler):

– Postponing term construction. Only the (sub)terms of the normal form must be constructed, *all* other (sub)terms are only needed to direct the rewriting process.

```
void register_xor() {
    xorsym = "prod(Bool xor Bool -> Bool {left})";
    register_prod("prod(Bool xor Bool -> Bool {left})",
                  xor, xorsym);
}
void resolve_xor() {
    true = lookup_func("prod(true -> Bool)");
    truesym = lookup_sym("prod(true -> Bool)");
    false = lookup_func("prod(false -> Bool)");
    falsesym = lookup_sym("prod(false -> Bool)");
    not = lookup_func("prod(not Bool -> Bool)");
    notsym = lookup_sym("prod(not Bool -> Bool)");
}
ATerm xor(ATerm arg0, ATerm arg1) {
    if (check_sym(arg0, truesym))
        return (*not)(arg1);
    if (check_sym(arg0, falsesym))
        return arg1;
    return make_nf2(xorsym,arg0,arg1);
}
```

Fig. 8. Generated C code for the `xor` function of the Booleans.

By transforming the specification and extending it with rewrite rules that reflect the steering effect of the intermediate terms, the amount of term construction can be reduced. In the context of functional languages this technique is known as *deforestation* [27]. Its benefits for term rewriting are not yet clear.

- Local sharing of terms, only those terms are shared that result from non-linear right-hand sides, e.g., $f(X) = g(X, X)$. Only those terms will be shared of which the sharing can be established at compile-time; the amount of sharing will thus be limited. This technique is also applied in ELAN [8].
- Local reuse of terms, i.e., common subterms are only reduced once and their normal form is reused several times. Here again, the common subterm has to be determined at compile-time.

At run-time, there are various other mechanisms to reduce the amount of work:

- Storage of all original terms to be rewritten and their resulting normal forms, so that if the same term must be rewritten again its normal form is immediately available. The most obvious way of storing this information is by means of pairs consisting of the original term and the calculated normal form. However, even for small specifications and terms an explosion of pairs may occur. The amount of data to be manipulated makes this technique useless.

  A more feasible solution is to store only the results of functions that have been explicitly annotated by the user as "memo-function" (see Section 5).
- Dynamic sharing of (sub)terms. This is the primary technique we use and it is discussed in the next subsection.

3.1 Maximal Sharing of Subterms

Our strategy to minimize memory usage during rewriting is simple but effective: we only create terms that are *new*, i.e., that do not exist already. If a term to be constructed already exists, that term is reused thus ensuring maximal sharing. This strategy fully exploits the redundancy that is typically present in the terms to be build during rewriting. The library functions to construct normal forms take care of building shared terms whenever possible. The sharing of terms is invisible, so no extra precautions are necessary in the code generated by the compiler.

Maximal sharing of terms can only be maintained when we check at every term creation whether a particular term already exists or not. This check implies a search through all existing terms but must nonetheless be executed *extremely fast* in order not to impose an unacceptable penalty on term creation. Using a hash function that depends on the internal code of the function symbol and the addresses of its arguments, we can quickly search for a function application before creating it. The (modest but not negligible) costs at term creation time are hence one hash table lookup.

Fortunately, we get two returns on this investment. First, the considerably reduced memory usage also leads to reduced (real-time) execution time. Second, we gain substantially since the equality check on terms (term_equal) becomes very cheap: it reduces from an operation that is linear in the number of subterms to be compared to a constant operation (pointer equality). Note that the compiler generates calls to term_equal in the translation of patterns and conditions.

The idea of subterm sharing is known in the LISP community as *hash consing* and will be discussed below.

3.2 Shared Terms versus Destructive Updates

Terms can be shared in a number of places at the same time, therefore they cannot be modified without causing unpredictable side-effects. This means that all operations on terms should be *functional* and that terms should effectively be *immutable* after creation.

During rewriting of terms by the generated code this restriction causes no problems since terms are created in a fully functional way. Normal forms are constructed bottom-up and there is no need to perform destructive updates on a term once it has been constructed. When normalizing an input term, this term is not modified, the normal form is constructed independent of the input term. If we would modify the input term we would get graph rewriting instead of (innermost) term rewriting. The term library is very general and is *not* only used for rewriting; destructive updates would therefore also cause unwanted side effects in other components based on this term library.

However, destructive operations on lists, like list concatenation and list slicing, become expensive. For instance, the most efficient way to concatenate two lists is to physically replace one of the lists by the concatenation result. In our case, this effect can only be achieved by taking the second list, prepending the elements of the first list to it, and return the new list as result.

In LISP, the success of hash consing [1] has been limited by the existence of the functions rplaca and rplacd that can destructively modify a list structure. To support destructive updates, one has to support two kinds of list structures "mono copy" lists with maximal sharing and "multi copy" lists without maximal sharing. Before destructively changing a mono copy list, it has to be converted to a multi copy list. In the 1970's, E. Goto has experimented with a Lisp dialect (HLisp) supporting hash consing and list types as just sketched. See [25] for a recent overview of this work and its applications.

In the case of the ASF+SDF compiler, we *generate* the code that creates and manipulates terms and we can selectively generate code that copies subterms in cases where the effect of a destructive update is needed (as sketched above). This explains why we can apply the technique of subterm sharing with more success.

3.3 Reclaiming Unused Terms

During rewriting, a large number of terms is created, most of which will not appear in the end result. These terms are used as intermediate results to guide the rewriting process. This means that terms that are no longer used have to be reclaimed in some way.

After experimentation with various alternatives (reference counting, mark-and-compact garbage collection) we have finally opted for a mark–and–sweep garbage collection algorithm to reclaim unused terms. Mark-and-sweep collection is more efficient, both in time and space than reference counting [20]. The typical space overhead for a mark-sweep garbage collection algorithm is only 1 bit per object.

Mark-and-sweep garbage collection works using three (sometimes two) phases. In the first phase, all the objects on the heap are marked as 'dead'. In the second phase, all objects reachable from the known set of root objects are marked as 'live'. In the third phase, all 'dead' objects are swept into a list of free objects.

Mark-and-sweep garbage collection is also attractive, because it can be implemented efficiently in C and can work without support from the programmer or compiler [7]. We have implemented a specialized version of Boehm's conservative garbage collector [6] that exploits the fact that we are managing ATerms.

4 Benchmarks

Does maximal sharing of subterms lead to reductions in memory usage? How does it affect execution speed? Does the combination of techniques presented in this paper indeed lead to an implementation of term rewriting that scales-up to industrial applications?

To answer these questions, we present in Section 4.1 three relatively simple benchmarks to compare our work with that of other efficient functional and algebraic language implementations. In Section 4.2 we give measurements for some larger ASF+SDF specifications.

Compiler	Time (sec)
Clean (strict)	32.3
SML	32.9
Clean (lazy)	36.9
ASF+SDF (with sharing)	37.7
Haskell	42.4
Opal	75.7
ASF+SDF (without sharing)	190.4
Elan	287.0

Table 1. The execution times for the evaluation of 2^{23}.

4.1 Three Small Benchmarks

All three benchmarks are based on symbolic evaluation of expressions $2^n \bmod 17$, with $17 \leq n \leq 23$. A nice aspect of these expressions is that there are many ways to calculate their value, giving ample opportunity to validate the programs in the benchmark [2].

Note that these benchmarks were primarily designed to evaluate *specific* implementation aspects such as the effect of sharing, lazy evaluation, and the like. They cannot (yet) be used to give an overall comparison between the various systems. Also note that some systems failed to compute results for the complete range $17 \leq n \leq 23$ in some benchmarks. In those cases, the corresponding graph also ends prematurely. Measurements were performed on an ULTRA SPARC-5 (270 MHz) with 512 Mb of memory. So far we have used the following implementations in our benchmarks:

- The ASF+SDF compiler as discussed in this paper: we give results *with* and *without* maximal sharing.
- The Clean compiler developed at the University of Nijmegen [24]: we give results for standard (*lazy*) versions and for versions optimized with strictness annotations (*strict*).
- The ELAN compiler developed at INRIA, Nancy [8].
- The Opal compiler developed at the Technische Universität Berlin [16].
- The Glasgow Haskell compiler [21].
- The Standard ML compiler [3].

The `evalsym` **Benchmark** The first benchmark is called `evalsym` and uses an algorithm that is CPU intensive, but does not use a lot of memory. This benchmark is a worst case for our implementation, because little can be gained by maximal sharing. The results are shown in Table 1. The differences between the various systems are indeed small. Although, ASF+SDF (with sharing) cannot benefit from maximal sharing, it does not loose much either.

---

[2] The actual source can be obtained at
http://adam.wins.uva.nl/~olivierp/benchmark/index.html

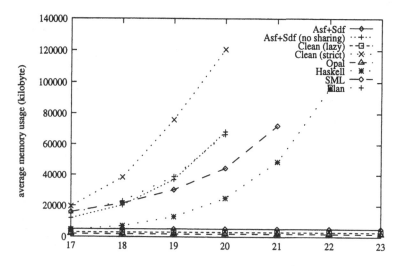

Fig. 9. Memory usage for the `evalexp` benchmark

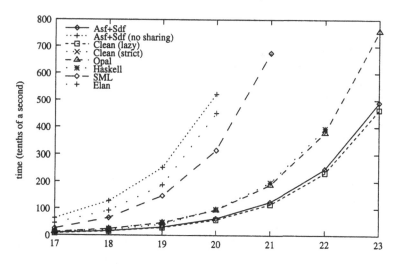

Fig. 10. Execution times for the `evalexp` benchmark

The `evalexp` Benchmark The second benchmark is called `evalexp` and is based on an algorithm that uses a lot of memory when a typical eager (strict) implementation is used. Using a lazy implementation, the amount of memory needed is relatively small.

Memory usage is shown in Figure 9. Clearly, normal strict implementations cannot cope with the excessive memory requirements of this benchmark. Interestingly, ASF+SDF (with sharing) has no problems whatsoever due to the use of maximal sharing, although it is also based on strict evaluation

Execution times are plotted in Figure 10. Only Clean (lazy) is faster than ASF+SDF (with sharing) but the differences are small.

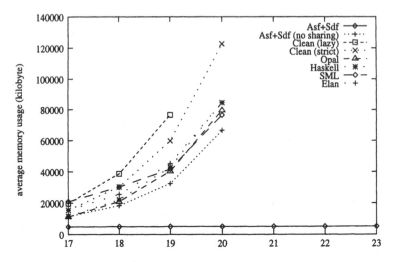

Fig. 11. Memory usage for the `evaltree` benchmark

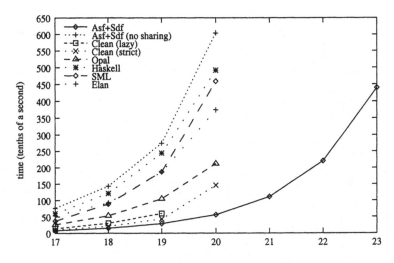

Fig. 12. Execution times for the `evaltree` benchmark

The `evaltree` Benchmark The third benchmark is called `evaltree` and is based on an algorithm that uses a lot of memory both with lazy and eager implementations. Figure 11 shows that neither the lazy nor the strict implementations can cope with the memory requirements of this benchmark. Only ASF+SDF (with sharing) can keep the memory requirements at an acceptable level due to its maximal sharing. The execution times plotted in Figure 12 show that only ASF+SDF scales-up for $n > 20$.

4.2 Compilation Times of Larger ASF+SDF Specifications

Table 2 gives an overview of the compilation times of four non-trivial ASF+SDF specifications and their sizes in number of equations, lines of ASF+SDF specification, and gen-

Specification	ASF+SDF (equations)	ASF+SDF (lines)	Generated C code (lines)	ASF+SDF compiler (sec)	C compiler (sec)
ASF+SDF compiler	1876	8699	85185	216	323
Parser generator	1388	4722	47662	106	192
COBOL formatter	2037	9205	85976	208	374
Risla expander	1082	7169	46787	168	531

Table 2. Measurements of the ASF+SDF compiler.

Application	Time (sec)	Memory (Mb)
ASF+SDF compiler (with sharing)	216	16
ASF+SDF compiler (without sharing)	661	117
Risla expansion (with sharing)	9	8
Risla expansion (without sharing)	18	13

Table 3. Performance with and without maximal sharing.

erated C code. The ASF+SDF compiler is the specification of the ASF+SDF to C compiler discussed in this paper. The parser generator is an ASF+SDF specification which generates a parse table for an GLR-parser [26]. The COBOL formatter is a pretty-printer for COBOL, this formatter is used within a renovation factory for COBOL [12]. The Risla expander is an ASF+SDF specification of a domain-specific language for interest products, it expands modular Risla specifications into "flat" Risla specifications [4]. These flat Risla specifications are later compiled into COBOL code by an auxiliary tool. The compilation times in the column "ASF+SDF compiler" give the time needed to compile each ASF+SDF specification to C code. Note that the ASF+SDF compiler has been fully bootstrapped and is itself a compiled ASF+SDF specification. Therefore the times in this column give a general idea of the execution times that can be achieved with compiled ASF+SDF specifications. The compilation times in the last column are produced by a native C compiler (SUN's cc) with maximal optimizations.

Table 3 gives an impression of the effect of maximal sharing on execution time and memory usage of compiled ASF+SDF specifications. We show the results (with and without sharing) for the compilation of the ASF+SDF to C compiler itself and for the expansion of a non-trivial Risla specification.

5 Concluding Remarks

We have presented the techniques for the compilation of ASF+SDF to C, with emphasis on memory management issues. We conclude that compiled ASF+SDF specifications run with speeds comparable to that of other systems, while memory usage is in some cases an order of magnitude smaller. We have mostly used and adjusted existing techniques but their combination in the ASF+SDF compiler turns out to be very effective.

It is striking that our benchmarks show results that seem to contradict previous observations in the context of SML [2] where sharing resulted in slightly increased execution speed and only marginal space savings. On closer inspection, we come to the conclusion that both methods for term sharing are different and can not be compared easily. We share terms immediately when they are created: the costs are a table lookup and the storage needed for the table while the benefits are space savings due to sharing and a fast equality test (one pointer comparison). In [2] sharing of subterms is *only* determined during garbage collection in order to minimize the overhead of a table lookup at term creation. This implies that local terms that have not yet survived one garbage collection are not yet shared thus loosing most of the benefits (space savings and fast equality test) as well. The different usage patterns of terms in SML and ASF+SDF may also contribute to these seemingly contradicting observations.

There are several topics that need further exploration. First, we want to study the potential of compile-time analysis for reducing the amount of garbage that is generated at run-time. Second, we have just started exploring the implementation of *memo-functions*. Although the idea of memo-functions is rather old, they have not be used very much in practice due to their considerable memory requirements. We believe that our setting of maximally shared subterms will provide a new perspective on the implementation of memo-functions. Finally, our ongoing concern is to achieve an even further scale-up of prototyping based on term rewriting.

Acknowledgments

The discussions with Jan Heering on ASF+SDF compilation are much appreciated. The idea for the benchmarks in Section 4.1 originates from Jan Bergstra. Reference [2] was pointed out to us by one of the referees.

References

1. J.R. Allen. *Anatomy of LISP*. McGraw-Hill, 1978.
2. A.W. Appel and M.J.R. Goncalves. Hash-consing garbage collection. Technical Report CS-TR-412-93, Princeton University, 1993.
3. A.W. Appel and D. MacQueen. A standard ML compiler. In G. Kahn, editor, *Functional Programming Languages and Computer Architecture*, LNCS, pages 301–324, 1987.
4. B.R.T. Arnold, A. van Deursen, and M. Res. An algebraic specification of a language for describing financial products. In M. Wirsing, editor, *ICSE-17 Workshop on Formal Methods Application in Software Engineering*, pages 6–13. IEEE, April 1995.
5. J.A. Bergstra, J. Heering, and P. Klint, editors. *Algebraic Specification*. ACM Press/Addison-Wesley, 1989.
6. H. Boehm. Space efficient conservative garbage collection. In *Proceedings of the ACM SIG-PLAN '91 Conference on Programming Language Design and Implementation*, SIGPLAN Notices 28, 6, pages 197–206, June 1993.
7. H. Boehm and M. Weiser. Garbage collection in an uncooperative environment. *Software - Practice and Experience (SPE)*, 18(9):807–820, 1988.
8. P. Borovanský, C. Kirchner, H. Kirchner, P.-E. Moreau, and M. Vittek. ELAN: A logical framework based on computational systems. In José Meseguer, editor, *Proceedings of the First International Workshop on Rewriting Logic*, volume 4 of *Electronic Notes in Theoretical Computer Science*. Elsevier Science, 1996.
9. M.G.J. van den Brand, A. van Deursen, P. Klint, S. Klusener, and A.E. van der Meulen. Industrial applications of ASF+SDF. In M. Wirsing and M. Nivat, editors, *Algebraic Methodology and Software Technology (AMAST '96)*, volume 1101 of *Lecture Notes in Computer Science*. Springer-Verlag, 1996.

10. M.G.J. van den Brand, J. Heering, P. Klint, and P.A. Olivier. Compiling rewrite systems: The asf+sdf compiler. Technical report, Centrum voor Wiskunde en Informatica (CWI), 1999. In preparation.

11. M.G.J. van den Brand, P. Klint, and C. Verhoef. Term rewriting for sale. In C. Kirchner and H. Kirchner, editors, *Proceedings of the First International Workshop on Rewriting Logic and its Applications*, volume 15 of *Electronic Notes in Theoretical Computer Science*, pages 139–161. Elsevier Science, 1998.

12. M.G.J. van den Brand, M.P.A. Sellink, and C. Verhoef. Generation of components for software renovation factories from context-free grammars. In I.D. Baxter, A. Quilici, and C. Verhoef, editors, *Proceedings of the Fourth Working Conference on Reverse Engineering*, pages 144–153, 1997.

13. M.G.J. van den Brand and E. Visser. Generation of formatters for context-free languages. *ACM Transactions on Software Engineering and Methodology*, 5:1–41, 1996.

14. J.J. Brunekreef. A transformation tool for pure Prolog programs. In J.P. Gallagher, editor, *Logic Program Synthesis and Transformation. Proceedings of the 6th International Workshop, LOPSTR'96*, volume 1207 of *LNCS*, pages 130–145. Springer-Verlag, 1996.

15. A. van Deursen, J. Heering, and P. Klint, editors. *Language Prototyping: An Algebraic Specification Approach*, volume 5 of *AMAST Series in Computing*. World Scientific, 1996.

16. K. Didrich, A. Fett, C. Gerke, W. Grieskamp, and P. Pepper. OPAL: Design and implementation of an algebraic programming language. In J. Gutknecht, editor, *International Conference on Programming Languages and System Architectures*, volume 782 of *Lecture Notes in Computer Science*, pages 228–244. Springer-Verlag, 1994.

17. C.H.S. Dik. A fast implementation of the Algebraic Specification Formalism. Master's thesis, University of Amsterdam, Programming Research Group, 1989.

18. P.H. Hartel et al. Benchmarking implementations of functional languages with 'pseudoknot', a float-intensive benchmark. *Journal of Functional Programming*, 6:621–655, 1996.

19. J. Heering, P.R.H. Hendriks, P. Klint, and J. Rekers. The syntax definition formalism SDF — Reference manual. *SIGPLAN Notices*, 24(11):43–75, 1989. Most recent version available at URL: http://www.cwi.nl/~gipe/.

20. R. Jones and R. Lins. *Garbage Collection: Algorithms for Automatic Dynamic Memory Management*. Wiley, 1996.

21. S.L. Peyton Jones, C.V. Hall, K. Hammond, W.D. Partain, and P.L. Wadler. The glasgow haskell compiler: a technical overview. *Proc. Joint Framework for Information Technology (JFIT) Technical Conference*, pages 249–257, 1993.

22. S. Kaplan. A compiler for conditional term rewriting systems. In P. Lescanne, editor, *Proceedings of the First International Conference on Rewriting Techniques*, volume 256 of *Lecture Notes in Computer Science*, pages 25–41. Springer-Verlag, 1987.

23. P. Klint. A meta-environment for generating programming environments. *ACM Transactions on Software Engineering and Methodology*, 2:176–201, 1993.

24. M.J. Plasmeijer and M.C.J.D. van Eekelen. *Concurrent Clean - version 1.0 - Language Reference Manual, draft version*. Department of Computer Science, University of Nijmegen, Nijmegen, The Netherlands, 1994.

25. M. Terashima and Y. Kanada. HLisp—its concept, implementation and applications. *Journal of Information Processing*, 13(3):265–275, 1990.

26. E. Visser. *Syntax Definition for Language Prototyping*. PhD thesis, University of Amsterdam, 1997.

27. P. Wadler. Deforestation: Transforming programs to eliminate trees. *Theoretical Computer Science*, 73(2):231–248, 22 June 1990.

The Design of the PROMIS Compiler*

Hideki Saito[1], Nicholas Stavrakos[1], Steven Carroll[1],
Constantine Polychronopoulos[1], and Alex Nicolau[2]

[1] Center for Supercomputing Research and Development,
University of Illinois at Urbana-Champaign,
1308 W. Main St., Urbana, IL 61801
FAX: 217-244-1351
{saito, stavrako, scarroll, cdp}@csrd.uiuc.edu
[2] Department of Information and Computer Science,
University of California at Irvine,
Irvine, CA, 92697-3425
nicolau@ics.uci.edu

Abstract. PROMIS is a multilingual, parallelizing, and retargetable compiler with an integrated frontend and backend operating on a single unified/universal intermediate representation. This paper describes the organization and the major features of the PROMIS compiler.
PROMIS exploits multiple levels of static and dynamic parallelism, ranging from task- and loop-level parallelism to instruction-level parallelism, based on a target architecture description. The frontend and the backend are integrated through a unified internal representation common to the high-level, the low-level, and the instruction-level analyses and transformations. The unified internal representation propagates hard to compute dependence information from the semantic rich frontend through the backend down to the code generator. Based on conditional algebra, the symbolic analyzer provides control sensitive and interprocedural information to the compiler. This information is used by other analysis and transformation passes to achieve highly optimized code. Symbolic analysis also helps statically quantify the effectiveness of transformations. The graphical user interface assists compiler development as well as application performance tuning.

1 Introduction

Most systems under design and likely to be built in the future will employ hierarchical organization with many levels of memory hierarchy and parallelism. While these architectures are evolutional and meet advances in hardware technology, they pose new challenges in the design of parallelizing compilers.

The PROMIS compiler tackles these challenges through its hierarchical internal representation (IR), the integration of the frontend and the backend, extensive symbolic analysis, and aggressive pointer analysis. The hierarchical IR

---

* This work is supported in part by DARPA/NSA grant MDA904-96-C-1472, and in part by a grant from Intel Corporation.

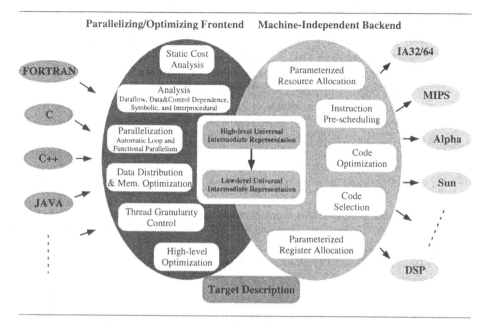

Fig. 1. Overview of the PROMIS Compiler

provides a natural mapping for exploitation of multi-level memory hierarchy and parallelism[8]. The frontend-backend integration via the unified IR enables the propagation of more information from the frontend to the backend, which in turn helps achieve a synergistic effect on the performance of the generated code[5]. Symbolic analysis not only produces control flow sensitive information to improve the effectiveness of the existing analysis and optimization techniques, but also quantitatively guides program optimizations to resolve many tradeoffs[9]. Pointer analysis uses information provided by symbolic analysis to further refine aliasing information.

The PROMIS compiler is a multilingual, parallelizing, and retargetable compiler with an integrated frontend and backend operating on a single unified and universal IR (or UIR). Unlike most other compilers, PROMIS exploits multiple levels of static and dynamic parallelism ranging from task- and loop-level parallelism to instruction-level parallelism, based on a target architecture description.

Fig. 1 shows the organization of the PROMIS compiler. The core of the compiler is the unified and universal hierarchical representation of the program. Both the frontend and the backend analysis and optimization techniques, driven by the description of the target architecture, manipulate this common UIR. Support for symbolic analysis is an integral part of the UIR, which provides control sensitive information throughout the compilation process. The current implementation of PROMIS supports C, C++, FORTRAN77, and Java bytecode as input languages and can target wide variety of systems, such as CISCs, RISCs, and DSPs.

PROMIS is an on-going research project with many parts of its optimizer and backend still under development. In this paper, we focus on the design aspects of the compiler, while we anticipate to obtain the first performance results by the time this paper is published (i.e., in early 1999).

The rest of the paper is organized as follows: Section 2 focuses on the frontend-backend integration. Section 3 describes the PROMIS IR. Analysis and optimization issues are discussed in Section 4. The PROMIS GUI is introduced in Section 5. Section 6 discusses related work on compiler development. Finally, Section 7 summarizes the paper.

2   Motivation for the Frontend-Backend Integration

Conventional compilation frameworks use abstract syntax information (typically represented in the form of source or intermediate code) to connect the frontend and the backend. Examples include restructuring tools (such as Parafrase-2[13], Polaris[2], and KAP[11]) and system vendors' backend compilers. This conventional approach makes the development of the frontend and the backend independent and modular. However, the inability to transfer dependence information from the frontend to the backend results in performance degradation[5].

For example, suppose the backend is a multiprocessor-aware compiler which is capable of dealing with parallel directives (such as C$DOACROSS and C$OPENMP PARALLEL DO). In this case, the frontend usually augments a parallel loop with a parallel directive and leaves other optimizations to the backend. However, since dependence analysis in the backend is usually less accurate than in the frontend,[1] intra-iteration dependence information becomes less accurate. If the loop is not parallelizable, both inter- and intra-iteration dependences are lost during the transition from the frontend to the backend. In both of these cases, the loss of accuracy makes many backend optimizations less effective, and therefore leads to lower application program performance.[2] Backend compilers can also perform equally extensive dependence analysis in the high-level representation before optimizing in the low-level representation (but still after the high-level transformations in the frontend). However, performing time-consuming dependence analysis both in the frontend and in the backend would simply slow down the compiler. Furthermore, due to high-level program transformations, some loss of accuracy is inevitable[15].

In cases where the backend is a uniprocessor-oriented compiler (such as GCC), the situation is even worse. A typical frontend replaces a parallel loop with a call to a runtime library routine (such as DOALL()), creates a function for the loop body, and uses the pointer to this loop body function as an argument to the runtime library call[7]. Since the loop body is now a separate function

---

[1] Program transformations performed by the frontend usually makes the program harder to analyze. The backend may complicate the program by itself by linearizing multi-dimensional arrays. Also, many backend compilers simply have less powerful dependence analyzers than many frontends.

[2] For example, more data dependence edges usually result in less ILP.

requiring interprocedural analysis, the backend optimization is unlikely to be as effective.

Furthermore, there are cases where inter-processor parallelism and intra-processor parallelism can be exchanged[5]. A frontend which is independently developed from the backend may package what could best be exploited as ILP parallelism into iteration level parallelism. This not only leads to lower functional unit utilization, but can also increase the total execution time.

In PROMIS, these problems are tackled by integrating the frontend and the backend via the common IR. The following section describes the PROMIS IR and how it is used to address these problems.

3 The PROMIS IR

In the PROMIS compiler, the frontend and the backend operate on the same internal representation, which maintains all vital program structures and provides a robust users' and developers' IR interface. The IR interface makes most transformations and optimizations independent of the implementation details of the IR data structures. The PROMIS IR is capable of dealing with multiple input languages and output ISAs (instruction set architectures). The IR structures are semantic entities, rather than syntactic constructs. Therefore, transformations and optimizations views and accesses the semantics of the program, rather than the statements of a particular language or the instructions of a target architecture.

The PROMIS IR is based on the Hierarchical Task Graph (HTG)[8]. The HTG is a hierarchical control flow graph (HCFG) overlayed with hierarchical data- and control-dependence graphs (HDDG and HCDG). The HTG has been successfully used both in a frontend parallelizer[13] and in a backend compiler[12]. In the HTG, hierarchical nodes capture the hierarchy of program statements, and hierarchical dependence edges represent the dependence structure between tasks at the corresponding level of hierarchy. Therefore, parallelism can be exploited at each level of the HTG: between statements (or instructions), between blocks of statements, between blocks of blocks of statements, and so on. This flexibility promotes a natural mapping of the parallelism onto the hierarchy of the target architecture. The entire IR framework consists of the following:

- Symbol Table
- Expression Trees
- Control Flow Edges (CFEs)
- Control Dependence Edges (CDEs)
- Data Dependence Edges (DDEs)
- Hierarchical Task Graphs (HTGs)
  - HTG nodes[3]

---

[3] Each top-level node summarizes the entire procedure, providing a support for interprocedural analysis. This also provides a support for optimizing across multiple input files.

- Hierarchical Control Flow Edges (HCFEs)
- Hierarchical Control Dependence Edges (HCDEs)
- Hierarchical Data Dependence Edges (HDDEs)
  - Call Graphs

3.1 Multilingual Frontend

Unlike previous attempts at a multilingual IR (such as UNCOL), PROMIS does not try to accommodate all programming languages. Instead, PROMIS aims at generating high performance code for the mainstream imperative programming languages, such as C, C++, and FORTRAN. The current version of the PROMIS IR represents a subset of the union of the language features of C++, FORTRAN, and Java. This subset includes (but certainly is not limited to) assignments, function calls, multi-dimensional array accesses, and pointers arithmetic. Performance critical features of these languages are directly supported, and thus represented in the PROMIS IR. On the other hand, syntax sugar is still supported in the input program but must be converted during the IR construction process. For example, virtual function calls are directly supported, while some of the operators, such as, comma, increment, and decrement are converted.

PROMIS translates stack-based Java bytecode into register-based statements and applies language independent analyses and optimizations. Two major challenges in optimizing Java are exceptions and concrete type inference. In PROMIS, both of these challenges are tackled by symbolic analysis. For example, exception detection code can be eliminated as deadcode if the compiler can prove the lack of exception. Such proof usually involves evaluation of symbolic expressions. Another example is exception handlers. If the compiler can prove all the exceptions handled in a catch block are actually caught by other handlers, the catch block can be eliminated. If all catch blocks of a try block are eliminated, the compiler may be able to convert the try block into a normal block.[4]

3.2 Frontend-Backend Integration

Enhanced support for integrated compilation in PROMIS is enabled by the UIR. The UIR propagates vital dependence information obtained in the frontend to the backend. The backend, for example, does not need to perform memory disambiguation since the data dependence information from the frontend substitutes it at a higher accuracy. Backend optimization techniques that rely on accurate memory disambiguation can work more effectively in the integrated compiler.

The PROMIS IR has three distinctive levels of representation: high-level (HUIR), low-level (LUIR), and instruction-level (IUIR). Although the UIR can be at any arbitrary sub-level between the HUIR and the LUIR during the course of the IR lowering process (and also between the LUIR and IUIR), the focus of the current development effort is given to the three major levels. In the PROMIS IR, statements are represented as HTG nodes.

---

[4] Note that this is not always possible, for example, due to a *finally* block.

The abstract syntax trees from the parser can have arbitrarily complex expression trees. During the construction of the HUIR, expression trees are normalized to have a single side effect per statement. Function calls and assignments to pointer dereferences are identified and isolated as separate statements. Since an original statement may have multiple side effects, possibly to the same memory location, it is non-trivial to normalize it without adding extraneous dependencies[15]. This problem is due to the semantics (i.e., lack of strict evaluation ordering of expressions) of the language. Therefore, it is also applicable to any other compilers.

During IR lowering (from HUIR to LUIR), complex expression trees are broken down to collections of simple expression trees, each of which is similar to quadruples. Data dependence information is maintained and propagated throughout the lowering process. Therefore, the PROMIS backend utilizes the same quality of dependence information as the frontend, unlike conventional compilers.

Fig. 2(a) shows a HUIR representation of the statement a[i] = b * c. At the leaf-level of the HTG, there is an `AssignStmt` node corresponding to this assignment statement. The associated expression tree gives the semantics of the statement. For the sake of simplicity, the left hand side of an assignment operator is always an address. This is also true when the value is assigned to a virtual (or physical) register that technically doesn't have an address. DDEs connect the source and the destination expressions of data dependence for this expression tree. HDDEs connect the source and the destination HTG nodes, summarizing detailed data dependence information provided by the DDEs. Fig. 2(b) is a part of the LUIR corresponding to Fig. 2(a). In this example, IR lowering is performed for register-register type architectures. During the lowering process, local dependence information is generated and non-local dependence information is updated to reflect the lowering. Since the statements are already normalized during HUIR construction, it is straightforward to perform IR lowering while maintaining the accuracy of dependence information.

In addition to providing detailed dependence information to the backend, the UIR also enables sharing of compiler passes between the frontend and the backend. For example, tools such as the available expression analyzer and the constant propagator can work on the HUIR dealing with complex expressions, on the LUIR dealing with simple expressions, and the IUIR dealing with simple expressions, opcodes, and side effects. The ability to raise the IR from IUIR to LUIR and from LUIR to HUIR (again, without loss of dependence information) is unique to the PROMIS IR. Since the LUIR is a proper subset of the HUIR, high-level analysis and transformation techniques can be seamlessly applied to the LUIR. Raising from the IUIR to the LUIR is simply performed by removing the opcodes and transforming each node to a set of single side-effect nodes. Extraneous operations and dependences produced from the side effects of opcode (e.g., many zero-flag assignments and dependences on it) can be easily eliminated afterwards.

220

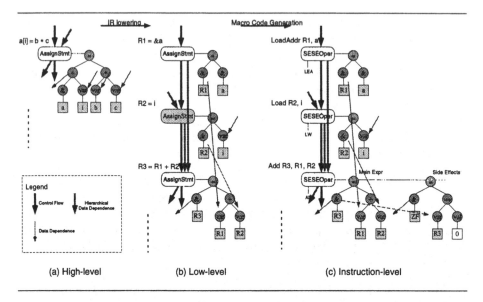

Fig. 2. High-level, low-level, and instruction-level IR

3.3 Multitarget Backend

Macro code generation on the PROMIS IR converts the LUIR into the IUIR. This involves the conversion of generic simple expression trees to a restricted set of simple expression trees, the assignment of a macro opcode to each of the converted expression trees, and expression tree construction for the side-effects of the opcodes. As in IR lowering, macro code generation maintains and propagates dependence information. It also generates dependence information for the side effects so that they can be handled in a uniform manner. The target-level backend optimizer operates on the IUIR, and eventually all macro opcodes are replaced by actual opcodes of the target. The target system information is automatically or manually generated from the target architecture description, which is common to the compiler and the simulator.[5]

Fig. 2(c) shows the IUIR of Fig. 2(b) for a pseudo instruction set architecture. During the macro code generation process, dependences to and from side effects and the transformed main expressions are generated and updated, respectively. The first instruction in Fig. 2(c) corresponds to the first statement in Fig. 2(b). The instruction is still an assignment statement representing R1 = &a. However, the HTG node is changed from AssignStmt to SESEOper (Single-Entry Single-Exit operator) in order to attach an opcode LEA and side-effects (in this case, none). The third instruction ADD has side effects, of which the zero-flag (ZF) assignment is presented. ZF is assigned based on the result of the addition. Therefore there is a data dependence (within the instruction, shown as a dashed

---

[5] A VLIW simulator developed at UCI is used to quantitatively evaluate various transformations and optimizations during the development phase.

line) from the assignment to R3 and the use of its value. In this example, there are dependence arcs from R3 and ZF to elsewhere, indicating that the values are used later.

3.4 Support for Symbolic Analysis

As will be shown in the next section, symbolic analysis plays a dominant role within PROMIS. To increase the efficiency of the symbolic interpreter the IR has been extended in two ways.

First, variable versioning, which is similar to the SSA (Static Single Assignment)[6], has been implemented directly into the IR. Scalar variables and scalar fields of a structure can be versioned. Second, conditional algebra[9] operators have been included in the IR. The conditional operator $\tau(e)$ returns 1 if $e \neq 0$ and 0 otherwise. With this simple operator, control sensitive information can be encoded into the expressions of the IR. For example, encoding the situation where X_3 is dependent on the outcome of a branch with condition C_1 would yield: $X_3 = X_1\tau(C_1) + X_2\tau(!C_1)$. In this expression X_3 gets the value X_1 if C_1 is true, else it gets the value X_2. This technique is similar to the GSA (Gated Single Assignment)[1]. However, these conditional operators can be used in any expressions, and its algebraic theory provides a foundation for simplifying such expressions.

3.5 IR Extensibility

The core IR is designed to provide the basic functionality that is required by the majority of passes in the compiler. In addition to this core functionality many additional data structures are used during the compilation process (e.g. connectivity matrix, dominator tree, etc). Although these data structures are useful in many compiler passes, they are transient and not a necessary part of the IR; rather they are data structures built upon the core IR. Allowing these transient data structures to be placed within the IR would clutter the IR unnecessarily. Another problem is maintaining them across multiple passes. It may not be possible (or extremely difficult) to maintain them across passes that were developed before the addition of such transient data structures, and thus not aware of them. Development of a new pass would also be difficult if the pass has to maintain transient data structures it does not use.

To alleviate both these problems PROMIS provides an API called External Data Structure Interface (EDSI). EDSI allows compiler developers to register data with each HTG node (e.g. each node can contain the immediate predecessor and successors of a dominator tree). In addition, a data structure can register a call-back function to be called during certain IR events (e.g. control flow arc removal/insertion, node addition/removal, etc). These call back functions allow the data structures to perform the necessary tasks to maintain their consistency with the IR.

4 Analysis and Optimization

4.1 Symbolic Analysis

Ever since the benefits of symbolic analysis were first demonstrated for compilers[13], many commercial and research compilers have adopted the use of symbolic analysis. The number of analysis and transformation techniques using symbolic analysis has increased greatly, due to the symbolic analysis capabilities of modern compilers. In light of this, support for symbolic analysis has been integrated within the internal representation of PROMIS. This integration provides a mechanism for extending the symbolic analysis framework, thus allowing new analysis and transformation techniques to be easily added into the framework.

The symbolic analysis framework uses a symbolic kernel that allows symbolic expressions to be handled in a manner similar to numeric values. Symbolic expressions consist of either scalar variables, scalar fields of structures, and/or arrays. Symbolic expression types include integer, floating point, and complex. Because the values a variable can possess may be dependent on the control flow of the program, control sensitive values of a variable are encoded within a symbolic expression. Control sensitive value extraction and symbolic expression simplification are also performed by the symbolic kernel.

In PROMIS, symbolic analysis is performed via symbolic interpretation. Values (or ranges of values) for each variable are maintained by the interpreter in environments. These environments are propagated to each statement. Each statement is interpreted, and its side effects are computed. These side effects are applied to the incoming environment of a statement, resulting in new versions for the affected variables. Successive application of these side effects simulates the execution of the program. Pointer analysis is performed during interpretation. This tight integration between symbolic and pointer analysis allows for efficient information flow to occur between the two passes.

Fig. 3 shows a section of code along with the corresponding interpreted HTG. Interpretation begins with a new environment initialized with the formal parameters. The first node assigns 10 to the variable x. Since x is yet to be versioned, the new version 1 is assigned to x, and x_1 is added to the symbolic environment. For the next node, y = a, the interpreter searches for the current version of the variable a in the current environment and finds a_1. The variable y in this node also needs a version, and it becomes y_1, just like the variable x in the previous node. The variable y_1 is added to the symbolic environment.

The next node is a branch statement. The conditional expression of the branch is evaluated, and then two child environments are created (corresponding to the true and false paths of the branch). Variable lookup requests, when they cannot be satisfied by these child environments, are forwarded to their parent environments. In addition, control flow tags are assigned for each child environment. A control flow tag corresponds to the condition that must be satisfied in order for a section of code to execute.

The true and false portions of the IF-THEN-ELSE structure are evaluated. As control flow converges, the two incoming environments into the RETURN statement

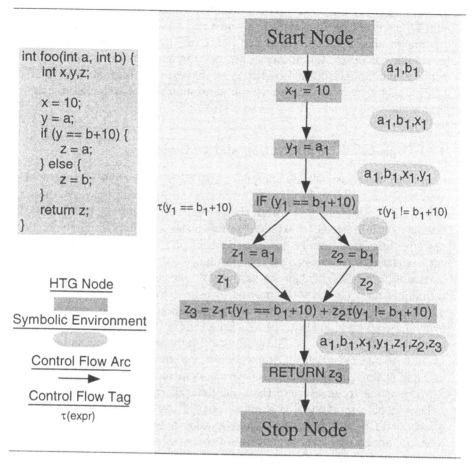

Fig. 3. Symbolic Interpretation Example

must be merged. In this example, the variables z_1 and z_2 are merged into the new variable z_3. Finally, the expression to be returned gets versioned to z_3.

Interprocedural analysis seamlessly integrates into the symbolic analysis framework. When a function call is encountered by the interpreter, its side effects are calculated and applied to the incoming environment, like any other expression. Once calculated, the side effects of a function call can be saved for subsequent interpretations or discarded to alleviate the memory footprint of the compiler. This method of handling function calls eliminates the need for special case function call handling in many analysis and transformation techniques. The only caveat is that function calls are interpreted for a specific alias pattern. Aliasing between parameters and global variables, which are used within the function call, must be properly identified and handled.

Alias information improves the accuracy of other analysis techniques, the effectiveness of optimizations, and the compilation time. Alias information is first gathered during IR construction. Static aliases (e.g. Fortran EQUIVALENCE and C/C++ unions) are analyzed, and their alias patterns are saved. Formal parameter aliases are then analyzed iteratively before symbolic interpretation. Although not exact, this iterative process eliminates many possible alias patterns. Symbolic interpretation is then applied to the program. The interpreter utilizes this alias information and points-to information collected during interpretation.

4.2 High-Level Parallelization and Optimization

Similar to most parallelizing compilers, PROMIS will include a number of classical analysis and transformation techniques. In PROMIS however, these techniques will be implemented within the symbolic analysis framework. This allows classical optimizations to exploit the full power of symbolic analysis. Several optimizations have been re-engineered within the symbolic analysis framework, such as strength reduction, static performance analysis, induction variable elimination[9], symbolic dependence analysis[3], and array privatization[16]. Other techniques need not be re-engineered to benefit from symbolic analysis. These optimizations, which include constant propagation, dead code elimination, and available expression analysis, benefit from the control sensitive information provided by symbolic analysis. The application of these techniques can be controlled by an integrated symbolic optimizer, which determines the ordering of the analysis and optimization techniques for each segment of code.

A quantitative measure of the synergistic effect of the combination of symbolic and pointer analysis is a major goal of the PROMIS project. Symbolic analysis will benefit from the disambiguation power of pointer analysis. Likewise, pointer analysis will benefit from the control sensitive value information of pointer expressions provided to it by symbolic analysis.

4.3 Instruction-Level Parallelization and Optimization

The PROMIS backend is divided into machine independent and machine dependent phases. The former works on the LUIR, while the latter works on the IUIR. As in the frontend, symbolic information plays an important role throughout the backend.

The machine independent phase includes classical optimizations, such as, common subexpression elimination, copy propagation, and strength reduction. The conversion from the LUIR to IUIR involves instruction selection and preliminary code scheduling. The mutation scheduler[12] performs instruction mutation, instruction scheduling, register allocation, loop unrolling, and code compaction on the IUIR. The machine dependent phase derives target specific information from the target machine description, and therefore the optimizer code itself is target independent. The PROMIS backend can also be guided by the results of an architectural simulator, which shares the target machine description with the compiler.

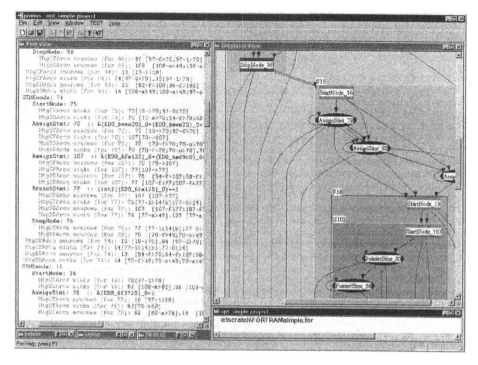

Fig. 4. Screen Capture of the PROMIS Compiler

Unlike other backend compilers, PROMIS does not perform memory disambiguation because data dependence information from the frontend is available in the backend.

5 Graphical User Interface

Graphical user interfaces (GUIs) have become a necessity for developers and users of any compiler. The PROMIS GUI aids in compiler development and user program optimization. Both of these tasks benefit greatly from the graphical representation of information.

For compiler development, PROMIS provides both textual and graphical views of the IR (Fig. 4). Since the PROMIS IR is hierarchical, both views (textual and graphical) are also hierarchical. Users can expand or collapse a compound node to display more or less information about the node. This is useful for preventing unnecessary information from drowning out the needed information that the compiler developer is seeking.

The IR can be viewed in two modes: online and offline. An offline view takes a simplified snapshot of the IR, and saves it in a separate data structure. This allows compilation to continue while the compiler developer explores the

IR. Offline views are particularly useful to compare the IR before and after an operation. Online views require the compilation of a program to stop (or pause). While the compilation is paused, the IR can be inspected and modified (e.g. removal of superfluous data dependence arcs). Compilation continues when the view is closed. The offline view can be saved to disk and retrieved for comparison to later compiler runs.

The GUI also provides a mechanism to set breakpoints at specific points in the compilation of a program. This functionality allows compiler developers to dynamically pause compilation and perform an offline or online view of the IR.

The PROMIS status bar informs the compiler user of the current phase of the compiler. It also gives feedback to the compiler developer as to the time spent in each module of the compiler. The compiler developer can use this information to identify performance bottlenecks in the compiler.

External data structures can be added to the compiler to implement new analysis and transformation techniques. It would be helpful if these external data structures used the GUI in a similar manner as the IR. To promote the use of this common interface, an API has been developed for compiler developers. By defining several functions in the new external data structure, which the GUI can call, the graphical display for the new data structure will be integrated within the existing GUI. Also, the API allows new PROMIS developers to quickly use the power of the GUI without having to spend time learning GUI programming.

Application programmers using PROMIS for performance tuning will be able to give and receive information about the program under compilation. Programmers will be able to receive information, such as profiling information, which they can then use to optimize time consuming portions of the code. Programmers will also be able to give information to the compiler to aid compilation. This information will include dependence arc removal, dead code identification, and value (or range of values) specification for variables.

6 Related Work

PROMIS is the successor of the Parafrase-2 Compiler[13] and the EVE Compiler[12]. The PROMIS Proof-Of-Concept (POC) Prototype[5] is the combination of these two compilers. The POC compiler uses semantics retention assertions to propagate data dependence information from Parafrase-2 (frontend) to EVE (backend). Experimental results on the POC compiler indicate that propagating high-level data dependence information to the backend leads to higher performance and underscore the significance of tradeoffs between inter-processor and intra-processor parallelism[4]. The unified PROMIS IR propagates all dependence information computed at the frontend to the backend, and static/dynamic granularity control is used to achieve better parallelism tradeoffs.

Another compiler effort aiming at similar goals is the National Compiler Infrastructure[14]. The infrastructure is based on the intermediate program format called SUIF[10], and analysis and optimization modules which operate on SUIF. These modules communicate using intermediate output files. SUIF is based on the abstract syntax information of the program, and data dependence information can be represented in the form of annotations[17]. The SUIF compiler system aims at independent development of compiler modules while PROMIS compiler employs an integrated design approach. Zephyr[18] is the other component of the National Compiler Infrastructure. Zephyr is a toolkit that generates a compiler from the input language specification, the target machine description, and a library of analyses and transformations.

7 Summary

As computer systems adopt more complex architectures with multiple levels of parallelism and deep memory hierarchies, code generation and optimization becomes an even more challenging problem. With the proliferation of parallel architectures, automatic or user-guided parallelization becomes relevant for systems ranging from high-end PCs to supercomputers. In this paper we presented the PROMIS compiler system, which encompasses automatic parallelization and optimization at all granularity levels, and in particular at the loop and instruction level. Based on the preliminary results obtained from the Proof-of-Concept prototype, we believe that our unique approach to full integration of the frontend and the backend through a common IR, together with aggressive pointer and symbolic analysis will amount to significant performance improvements over that achieved by separate parallelizers and ILP code generators using equally powerful algorithms. Moreover, our design approach does not compromise retargetability and it further facilitates the ability to compile different imperative languages using the same compiler.

PROMIS is an on-going research project with many parts of its optimizer and backend still under development. In this paper, we focused on the design aspects of the compiler. The first performance results on the PROMIS compiler are anticipated to become available in early 1999. As of this writing, PROMIS identifies parallel loops and also generates VLIW instructions.

Ackknowledgements

The authors are grateful to Peter Grun, Ashok Halambi, and Nick Savoiu of University of California at Irvine for their work on the trailblazing part of the backend and pointer analysis contribution to PROMIS. We would also like to thank Chris Koopmans and Peter Kalogiannis of CSRD for their contribution.

References

1. Robert A. Ballance, Arthur B. Maccabe, and Karl J. Ottenstein. The program dependence web: A representation supporting control-, data-, and demand-driven interpretation of imperative languages. In *Proceedings of the ACM SIGPLAN Conference on Programming Language Design and Implementation*, pages 257–271, June 1990.

2. William Blume et al. Effective automatic parallelization with polaris. *International Journal of Parallel Programming*, May 1995.

3. William J. Blume. *Symbolic Analysis Techniques for Effective Automatic Parallelization*. PhD thesis, University of Illinois at Urbana-Champaign, 1995. Also available as CSRD Technical Report No.1433.

4. Carrie Brownhill, Alex Nicolau, Steve Novack, and Constantine Polychronopoulos. Achieving multi-level parallelization. In *Proceedings of the International Symposium on High Performance Computing (ISHPC)*, 1997. Also in LNCS No. 1336.

5. Carrie Brownhill, Alex Nicolau, Steve Novack, and Constantine Polychronopoulos. The PROMIS compiler prototype. In *Proceedings of the International Conference on Parallel Architectures and Compilation Techniques (PACT)*, 1997.

6. Ron Cytron, Jeanne Ferrante, Barry K. Rosen, Mark N. Wegman, and F. Kenneth Zadeck. Efficiently computing static single assignment form and the control dependence graph. *ACM transactions on Programming Languages and Systems*, 13(4):451–490, October 1991.

7. Milind Girkar, Mohammad Haghighat, Paul Grey, Hideki Saito, Nicholas Stavrakos, and Constantine Polychronopoulos. Illinois-Intel Multithreading Library: Multithreading support for iA-based multiprocessor systems. *Intel Technology Journal*, 1998. 1st Quarter '98.

8. Milind Girkar and Constantine D. Polychronopoulos. The hierarchical task graph as a universal intermediate representation. *International Journal of Parallel Programming*, 22(5):519–551, 1994.

9. Mohammad R. Haghighat. *Symbolic Analysis for Parallelizing Compilers*. Kluwer Academic Publishers, 1995.

10. Mary Hall et al. Maximizing multiprocessor performance with the SUIF compiler. *IEEE Computer*, December 1996.

11. Kuck and Associates, Inc. Kuck and Associates, Inc. Home Page. http://www.kai.com.

12. Steve Noback. *The EVE Mutation Scheduling Compiler: Adaptive Code Generation for Advanced Microprocessors*. PhD thesis, University of California at Irvine, 1997.

13. Constantine D. Polychronopoulos, Milind Girkar, Mohammad Reza Haghighat, Chia Ling Lee, Bruce Leung, and Dale Schouten. Parafrase-2: An environment for parallelizing, partitioning, synchronizing, and scheduling programs on multiprocessors. *International Journal of High Speed Computing*, 1(1):45–72, 1989.

14. The National Compiler Infrastructure Project. The national compiler infrastructure project. http://www-suif.stanford.edu/suif/NCI, January 1998. Also at http://www.cs.virginia.edu/nci.

15. Hideki Saito. Frontend-backend integration for high-performance compilers. Technical report, Center for Supercomputing Research and Development, University of Illinois at Urbana-Champaign, December 1998. *In Preparation*.

16. Peng Tu. *Automatic Array Privatization and Demand-Driven Symbolic Analysis*. PhD thesis, University of Illinois at Urbana-Champaign, 1995. Also available as CSRD Technical Report No.1432.

17. Robert Wilson et al. SUIF: An infrastructure for research on parallelizing and optimizing compilers. Technical report, Computer Systems Laboratory, Stanford University.

18. Zephyr Compiler Group. Zephyr: Tools for a national compiler infrastructure. http://www.cs.virginia.edu/zephyr.

Floating Point to Fixed Point Conversion of C Code

Andrea G. M. Cilio and Henk Corporaal

Delft University of Technology
Computer Architecture and Digital Techniques Dept.
Mekelweg 4, 2628CD Delft, The Netherlands
A.Cilio@its.tudelft.nl   H.Corporaal@its.tudelft.nl

Abstract. In processors that do not support floating-point instructions, using fixed-point arithmetic instead of floating-point emulation trades off computation accuracy for execution speed. This trade-off is often profitable. In many cases, like embedded systems, low-cost and speed bounds make it the only acceptable option. We present an environment supporting fixed-point code generation from C programs. It allows the user to specify the position of the binary point in the source code and let the converter automatically transform floating-point variables and operations. We demonstrate the validity of our approach on a series of experiments. The results show that, compared to floating-point, fixed-point arithmetic executed on an integer datapath has a limited impact on the accuracy. In the same time the fixed-point code is 3 to 8 times faster than its equivalent floating-point emulation on an integer datapath.

1 Introduction

In order to meet the increasingly tight time-to-market constraints, code generation for complex embedded systems is shifting towards high level languages and code compilation. The C language, although not ideal for embedded applications, is a popular imperative specification language as it combines the capabilities of a typical HLL with low-level assembly language features like bit manipulation. Furthermore, C has become the *de facto* standard specification language of several international standards: for example MPEG (IEC 13838)[9] and ADPCM (G.722)[7].

One of the limitations of C is that it does not support fixed-point integer types. For embedded systems in which tight cost constraints do not allow the use of floating-point hardware, using a fixed-point version of the algorithm to implement is an attractive alternative to floating-point software emulation, for which the reported overhead ranges between a factor of 10 and 500 [6]. Often, the trade-offs between an algorithm implementation using floating-point software emulation and a fast, albeit less accurate, fixed-point algorithm favor the latter solution.

In manual fixed-point programming the designer replaces the floating point variables with fixed-point ones, encoded as integers. To avoid overflows and reduce the loss of precision he must scale the integer words. Determining the number of shifts is known to be error prone and time consuming. Automatic conversion from floating-point to fixed-point is an attractive alternative, addressing these problems.

This paper presents a design environment that supports semi-automatic conversion of floating-point code into fixed-point. The user is allowed to specify the fixed-point

Fig. 1. Signed fixed-point representation ($WL = 32, IWL = 4$) of the floating-point number 14.631578947368421. The accuracy of the fractional part is equivalent to 13 decimal digits.

representation of selected, critical floating-point variables; a tool called *float2fix* automatically performs floating- to fixed-point conversion of the remaining floating-point variables and inserts the appropriate scaling operations. The code generator can then map the converted intermediate representation (IR) into a target instruction set that supports only integer arithmetic.

The rest of this paper is organized as follows. Section 2 reviews the basic concepts of fixed-point arithmetic and introduces our approach to the specification of the fixed-point type of a variable in C source code. Section 3 describes the code transformations performed by *float2fix*. In Sec.4 the code transformations are tested on a number of benchmarks. Section 5 presents a survey of research on automatic fixed-point code generation from C. Finally, Sec.6 concludes this paper and summarizes its contributions.

2 Representation and Specification of Fixed-point Numbers

In this section we review some basic concepts related to fixed-point arithmetic and we address the issue of how to specify the fixed-point format in the C source.

2.1 Fixed-point representation

A fixed-point number can be thought of as an integer multiplied by a two's power with negative exponent. In other words, the weight 1 is assigned to a bit other than the LSB of the word, and the bits to the right of that bit represent the fractional part of the value. We can associate a fixed-point type to this representation. The minimal set of parameters that determine a fixed-point type are the signedness, the total length of the word WL and the length of its integer part, IWL. The fractional word length of a 2's complement number n is thus[1] $FWL = WL - IWL - 1$ and the value represented by its bits, $a_{WL-1}, \ldots, a_0$ is:

$$a = \left(-a_{WL-1} 2^{WL-1} + \sum_{i=0}^{WL-2} a_i 2^i \right) \cdot 2^{FWL} \tag{1}$$

Figure 1 shows the signed fixed-point representation of a number. The values of WL and IWL determine two important properties of the fixed-point representation: the range of representable numbers R and the quantization step Q:

$$R = [-2^{IWL}, 2^{IWL}); \qquad Q = 2^{-(WL-1-IWL)}$$

---

[1] Note that we do not consider the sign bit a part of IWL.

Two more parameters must be specified to describe at source level the bit-true behavior of a fixed-point type: *casting mode* and *overflow mode*. The casting mode specifies what happens to a fixed-point number when it is shifted to right. The least significant bits can be ignored *(truncate mode)* or used to round off the number. The overflow mode specifies how to handle the result of a fixed-point operation that overflows. The most significant bits can be discarded *(wrap-around mode)* or the result can be replaced with the maximum value that can be represented with that fixed-point type *(saturation mode)*.

In our opinion, a bit-true specification at the source level, which must include overflow and rounding mode, has little use; the target machine dictates what are the most efficient type parameters and thus the behavior of fixed-point operations. In practice, if a particular behavior is not supported in hardware, it must be emulated in software, and this is highly inefficient. Emulation is thus hardly acceptable in applications where the focus is on performance. On the other hand, if the designer can explore the target architecture solution space, he might want to change the specifics of casting mode or overflow mode of the target machine without having to change the source code in order to adapt it to the new fixed-point parameters. For these reasons, we decided to let casting and overflow be target-dependent aspects and define a fixed-point type only by its WL and IWL.

In the following discussion, we will consider only signed fixed-point numbers and a unique value of WL. In [1] we discuss how to implement code generation for types with user-definable WL. We consider supporting unsigned fixed-point types a straightforward extension that adds little to the approach presented in the following sections.

2.2 Fixed-point arithmetic rules

The following rules specify the format of the result of a fixed-point arithmetic operation $c = a \star b$. The IWL of the result is derived from the fixed-point representation (1).

Addition and comparison. Two fixed-point numbers can be added or compared by a normal integer unit, provided the position of their binary points is the same. If the source operands have different IWL, the word with the smaller IWL must be scaled so as to align the binary point positions:

$$IWL_c = \max\{IWL_a, IWL_b\} \tag{2}$$

Multiplication. The two's complement integer multiplication of two words yields a result of $2WL$ bits. The IWL of the result is given by:

$$IWL_c = IWL_a + IWL_b + 1 \tag{3}$$

Notice that the second most significant bit of the result is normally just a duplicate of the sign bit and $IWL_a + IWL_b$ bits are sufficient to represent the integer part of the result.[2] In many processors, integer multiplication returns only the lower WL bits. The

---

[2] It is easy to verify that the two most significant bits of the result are not equal only if both source operands are -2^{WL}.

upper part is discarded and overflows can be signaled. The reason for this is that in high-level languages multiplication maps two source operands of integer type into a destination of the same type, therefore compilers do not generate code that exploits the precision of a full result. In a fixed-point multiplication this behavior is not acceptable, because the upper WL bits of the result contain the integer part of the number. There are three alternatives to obtain the upper half of the result:

1. Make the upper part of the result accessible in the source code.
2. Scale the source operands before multiplying so that the result will fit in WL bits.
3. Implement the fixed-point multiplication as a macro computing the upper part.

The first alternative, used in [13], is convenient when the target architecture upper word is also accessible. However, this approach requires custom adaptations to the compiler. The second approach, called *integer multiplication*, shows poor accuracy. The last approach can be very accurate at the price of additional computation. Our converter supports the latter two alternatives, but leaves the possibility to efficiently map multiplications to target processors in which the upper part of the result is accessible.

Division. Two fixed-point numbers can be divided using a normal integer divider. From (1) follows that the IWL of the result is:

$$IWL_c = WL - 1 + IWL_a - IWL_b = \qquad (4)$$

The division is the trickiest of the fixed-point arithmetic operations. Without careful scaling of the source operands, the chances to loose accuracy are very high. Notice that if the IWL of the denominator IWL_b is small, then the accuracy of the result is poor. If $IWL_a > IWL_b$, the result cannot even be represented with a WL-bit word. In this case, we must clearly insert scaling operations to reduce the resulting IWL. In Subsec.3.3 we present some strategies to limit the loss of accuracy in fixed-point divisions.

2.3 Fixed-point specification

Our fixed-point specification does not require special adaptations to the compiler front-end and is *transparent* to the compiler. The user specifies the value for IWL of `float` and `double` variables by means of annotations introduced by a reserved `#pragma` directive. This directive is ignored by a compiler that does not recognize it, thus the same source file can be used for both floating-point and fixed-point compilation. The user can also specify the IWL of arguments of external functions, as shown in the example below.

Example 1 (Specification of fixed-point variables and functions).
```
double sin(double);
float signal_out[100], *in_ptr;
#pragma suif_annote "fix" signal_out 5
#pragma suif_annote "fix" sin 8 1
```
The base type of the array `signal_out` is a fixed-point integer with $IWL = 5$. The fixed-point type of the pointer `in_ptr` will be determined by the converter using data-flow information. The function `sin()` takes a fixed-point argument with $IWL = 8$ and returns a fixed-point result with $IWL = 1$. □

The user is expected to annotate all floating-point variables for which the fixed-point format cannot be determined by the converter using the static analysis of the program described in Sec.3. Note that floating-point variables initialized with a constant need not be annotated by the user, because *float2fix* can determine their fixed-point format from the constant value. For all the intermediate values, like compiler defined temporaries, the fixed-point format can be determined from the format of the other operands.

3   Fixed-point conversion and code generation

In this section we present a general view of our code generation environment, with special attention for the aspects specifically related to floating-point to fixed-point code conversion. Then we describe in more detail our conversion tool, *float2fix*, and we demonstrate the code transformations involved through an example.

3.1   The code generation environment

The conversion to fixed point uses the SUIF (Stanford University Intermediate Format) compiler [4] and takes advantage of its flexible intermediate representation. In SUIF new unique types can be defined by adding annotations to existing types. This enables us to extend the IR with a fixed-point type system without any change to the compiler. Figure 2 shows the passes necessary to generate fixed-point code for our target architecture, called *MOVE*, from a C source. The designer starts with the manual annotation of float and double variables, as explained in Sec.2. This annotated source file is translated into SUIF IR by the front-end. Our converter, *float2fix*, is run immediately after the front-end. It reads the annotated IR and translates it to a fixed-point (integer encoded) IR (see (a) in Fig.2) that can be converted back to a C integer source. This source can be compiled by *gcc-move* into fixed-point MOVE code (b). The annotated source file can also be directly compiled by *gcc-move* into floating-point code (c) (either hardware-supported or software emulated). This allows to run simulations and perform comparisons between the two versions of the algorithm. The user can evaluate the performance and the accuracy of the fixed-point code and adjust the fixed-point format of the variables. An alternative path to code generation (d), not yet fully implemented, will use the SUIF based back-end and will be able to recognize fixed-point instruction patterns (like shift-operation-shift) and map them into dedicated instructions.

3.2   Fixed-point conversion

Float2fix is implemented as an IR-to-IR transformation pass that translates the SUIF representation of a floating-point program annotated by the user into a fixed-point equivalent in the following steps:

1. It generates and installs the fixed-point types specified by the user's annotations. The type of the annotated variable is updated to the new type.

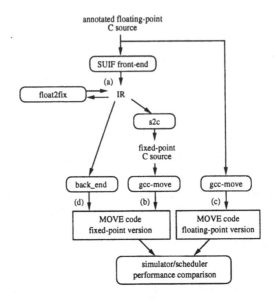

Fig. 2. Code generation trajectory.

2. It converts floating-point constants to fixed-point format and installs the corresponding types. If the constant is not linked to an annotated variable definition, its fixed-point format is determined by:

$$IWL = \max\{\lceil \log_2 |constant| \rceil, 0\}^3$$

For initialized arrays, $|constant|$ is replaced with $\max_i \{|constant_i|\}$ where i is the index of the array element.

3. It propagates the fixed-point format along the instruction trees. The objects that may need type conversion are: variables that the user did not annotate, compiler generated temporary variables, and single definition-use values (edges of the instruction tree). The IWL of these objects is determined by applying rules (2, 3, 4) and the techniques to be presented in Subsec. 3.3.

4. It inserts the appropriate scaling instructions to align the binary point of source operands or to convert from one fixed-point type to another.

Figure 3 illustrates the last two transformations on a statement taken from one of the test programs of Sec. 4: `acc += (*coef_ptr)*(*data_ptr)`. This expression is shown as a graph in which the nodes represent instructions and the boxes represent variables. Edges represent definition-uses of data. Next to every edge is the type of the transferred datum; the first letter indicates whether the type is floating-point (f) or integer (i), the following number indicates the wordlength, WL. Enclosed in square brackets is the value of IWL. Note that a 32-bit `int` type would be described with

---

[3] Notice that we could allow *negative* values of IWL, i.e. numbers whose binary point falls out of the word. An analogoue extension is possible to represent numbers for which $IWL \geq WL$.

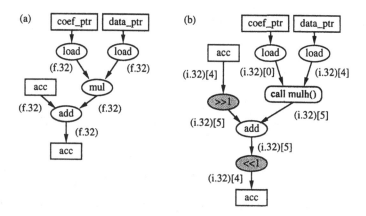

Fig. 3. Example of code transformation on a SUIF instruction tree, representing: `acc +=` `(*coef_prt)*(*data_ptr)`. (a) Original tree. (b) Transformed tree.

(i.32)[31]. The fixed-point multiply is translated to the macro invocation $\text{mulh}(a, b)$, that computes the upper part of the integer multiplication using one of the following formulae[4]

$$a_h * b_h + ((a_h * b_l + a_l * b_h) \gg 16) \tag{5}$$
$$a_h * b_h + (((a_h * b_l + a_l * b_h) + (a_l * b_l \gg 16)) \gg 16) \tag{6}$$

where

$$a_h = a \gg 16; \qquad a_l = a \ \& \ 0x\text{FFFF}$$

Note that (5) introduces some approximation due to the fact that the product between the lower parts is disregarded; in (6) the first shift is unsigned.

3.3 Precision-improving techniques

Hereby we present a number of heuristics that improve the precision attainable with fixed-point arithmetic operations.

Multiplication. As stated in Sec. 2, one bit of the result's integer part is a copy of the sign bit and conveys no additional information. We can therefore scale down the result by one position. This gives us one additional bit for the fractional part. Moreover, a chain of multiplications automatically converted to fixed-point can produce a result with unnecessarily high IWL and therefore little accuracy. By scaling the result we alleviate this problem.

Another important improvement is possible for macro (6) when the destination of the multiply is a fixed-point variable d, and the IWL of the result, as computed by (3), is higher than IWL_d. In this case, we can modify the macro so that it computes exactly

---

[4] These formulae are valid for $WL = 32$.

the bits that are to be found in d. Given $D = IWL_a + IWL_b + 1 - IWL_d$, the modified macro $\text{mulh}(a, b, D)$ is

$$((a_h * b_h) \ll D) + (((a_h * b_l + a_l * b_h) + ((a_l * b_l) \gg 16)) \gg (16 - D)) \quad (7)$$

Division. Equation (4) summarizes the difficulty of fixed-point division: a denominator with small IWL_b with respect to IWL_a yields very poor accuracy. The solution is to scale the denominator and increase IWL_b before performing the division. This is necessary when $IWL_b > IWL_a$, as the division would otherwise produce an overflow. When the denominator is a constant value B, it is possible to shift out the least significant bits that are '0' without introducing any loss of accuracy. We can extend this idea by computing Err_{denom}, the error caused by shifting out the n least significant bits of the denominator:

$$Err_{denom} = B_{n-1:0}/(B - B_{n-1:0})$$

where $B_{n-1:0}$ is the unsigned integer value represented by the n least significant bits. We can then compare this error with the maximum quantization error of the result, Err_Q, and estimate an amount of shifting that minimizes both Err_{denom} and the potential quantization error. This approach can be further generalized into a heuristic that can be applied to variable denominators. We compute the amount of shifting using the following expression

$$\lfloor (FWL_b) \cdot \alpha \rfloor \quad (8)$$

α is a parameter representing the aggressiveness of scaling; it is the fraction of bits of the fractional part that have to be shifted out. The above expression takes into account both Err_{denom} and Err_Q. Although this technique is risky, in that it may introduce spurious divisions by zero, it turned out to work very well in practice, as shown in Sec.4. Example 2 demonstrates the idea

Example 2 (Scaling the denominator to improve division accuracy). Consider the operation $c = a/b$ where a, b are the fixed-point numbers whose value and IWL are shown in Fig.4. An integer division delivers zero as quotient, and thus a 100% error. The same result is obtained if b is shifted one position right. If we scale b by 2 to 5 positions, we are shifting out zeroes and we cannot loose accuracy. Shifting out the first 4 bits gives invariably 0.25, which corresponds to an error of 12%; shifting by 5 position drastically improves the accuracy: 0.28125 (1.72% error). Shifting out the first '1', in the sixth position, does not affect the result. Shifting out all the subsequent '0' bits steadily improves the accuracy: by shifting 8 positions the error becomes 0.35%, by shifting 11 positions 0.01%. By shifting out 12 bits the error increases to 0.42%. From this point on, shifting more bits makes the accuracy smaller, because the new least significant bits computed are erroneous. Only when we start to shift out the three most significant '1' bits Err_{denom} increasingly offsets the reduction of quantization error, and the overall error rises up to 76%. If also the last non-zero bit of b is shifted out we have a division by zero. The macro that we implemented will replace it with the largest number that can be represented with WL bits. □

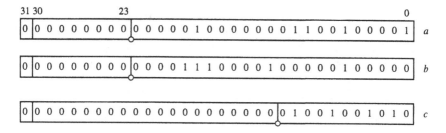

Fig. 4. Example of fixed-point division between $a = 0.015720487$ and $b = 0.054935455$; the fixed-point format of the result $c = 0.28616285$ is the most accurate one among the many that are possible for a/b.

4 Experimental results

In this section we present experimental results of our fixed-point code generation trajectory and we compare them with two possible floating-point implementations. The chosen test applications are FIR, a 35th-order fir filter and IIR, a 6th-order iir filter [3]. Both have been coded using `float` variables and then converted to fixed-point C, compiled, scheduled and simulated. We tested four versions of the programs:

1. **fp-hw** Floating-point implementation using floating-point unit.
2. **fp-sw** Floating-point implementation using software emulation.
3. **fix-s** Fixed-point implementation using integer multiplication (see Sec.2).
4. **fix-m** Fixed-point implementation using invocation to multiply macro (5).

Table 1 shows the accuracy and performance of these four versions. Each row shows the results for the version whose name is in the first column. The cycle counts in columns 2 and 6 were obtained by scheduling the code on a processor with 2 load-store units, 2 immediate units, 2 integer units an a floating-point unit (FPU). In this architecture the FPU supports double-precision only. The `float` source operands are extended when loaded from memory. Columns 3 and 7 show the number of moves. This relates to a peculiar characteristic of our target architecture: data transports, or moves, are explicitly programmed [2]; we roughly need 2 moves per basic (RISC-like) operation. Our target machine has 8-move busses and therefore can execute around 4 instructions per cycle. The fundamental unit of 'control' of the processor is the data transport, as opposed to the machine instruction. Columns 4 and 8 show the code static size. As accuracy metric we chose the Signal to Quantization Noise Ratio (SQNR), defined as follows:

$$\mathrm{SQNR} = 10 \log_{10}\left(\frac{S}{N}\right)$$

where S is the average of the signal's absolute value and N is the average of the error, defined as the difference between the original signal and the quantized signal. Column 5 and 9 show the SQNR of the last three implementations in comparison to fp-hw. From these results we can draw the following conclusions:

Version	FIR Filter				IIR Filter			
	Cycles	Moves	Instr.	SQNR	Cycles	Moves	Instr.	SQNR
fp-hw	32826	86862	66	–	7422	22367	202	–
fp-sw	151849	542200	170	70.9 dB	39192	107410	258	64.9 dB
fix-s	23440	102426	58	33.1 dB	5218	27861	61	20.3 dB
fix-m	39410	175888	68	74.7 dB	8723	51899	81	55.1 dB

Table 1. Performance and accuracy results for the test applications.

1. For both programs, the speedup factor of fixed-point implementations relative to fp-sw is large, above 6 for fix-s, above 3 for fix-m. Good resource utilization contributes to this result: in fix-m, for example, the machine buses were busy 55% of the execution time in FIR and 74% in IIR.

2. The SQNR of fix-s implementations is poor, whereas fix-m FIR shows a ratio of 74dB, which is acceptable in most applications. For IIR the accuracy of the results is not completely satisfactory.

3. The SQNR ratio of fp-sw implementation shows that it introduces some error compared to fp-hw. This is due to the fact that the software really emulates `float` values, whereas the FPU uses double precision.

4. Remarkably, in FIR the SQNR of fix-m is higher than that of fp-sw. This is due to the fact that, for floating-point numbers that have a small exponent, the fixed-point representation can use up to 31 bits for the fractional part, whereas in a `float` (IEEE 754) only 24 bits are used to represent the significand.

5. The execution overhead due to macro (5) is 68% respect to fix-s. This indicates that the compiler and the scheduler were effective at optimizing the code and reducing the impact of the macro computations. In particular, a feature related to the explicit programming of moves, namely *software bypassing*,[5] reduced the register pressure to a level very close to that of fix-s.

6. In IIR the scheduler did not find enough parallelism to keep the 8 busses busy in the fp-hw implementation. As a result, fix-m is only slightly slower, while fix-s outperforms fp-hw. These cases suggest the use of more accurate macros, like (6) and (7).

We tested some of the precision improvements presented in Subsec.3.3. By scaling down the result of (5) by one bit we obtained a 9% cycle count reduction and at the same time measured an improvement of accuracy of 1.1dB. More tests remain to be done using macros (6) and (7).

Scalability of converted fixed-point code The high level of parallelism allowed by the target configuration used in the tests is somewhat biased towards fixed-point code,

---

[5] Software bypassing is a technique whereby a transport from the result register of a functional unit to the functional unit that uses it is explicitly programmed, bypassing the write and read of a general purpose register.

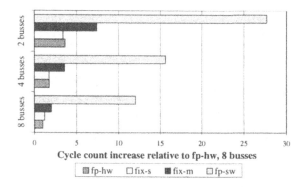

Fig. 5. Scalability of the four program versions.

which shows a higher amount of inherent parallelism. To verify this, we run a number of tests with smaller target configurations on FIR, to see how much impact do restricted resources have on the overhead of the fixed-point implementations (see Fig.5). Reducing the number of busses and integer units by half increased the cycle count by 76% and 44% in fix-m and fix-s, respectively, whereas fp-sw resulted only 30% slower. This suggests that fp-sw does not scale with the machine resources as effectively as a fixed-point implementation. One of the reasons is that floating-point operations are implemented by function calls, which reduce the scope of the scheduler. On the other hand, fixed-point conversion introduces operations in the expression trees without affecting the scheduling scope. As a result, fix-m is still 4.4 times faster than fp-sw. Even on a minimal configuration with two busses, fix-m is 3.7 times faster.

Notice that the tests of all versions were performed on the same processor configuration. Since the integer versions do not use the FPU, this choice is biased towards the fp-hw version, since the expensive resources utilized by the FPU, or part of them, could be invested in more busses and integer units.

Accuracy of division. Although the test programs did not contain fixed-point divisions, we also measured the accuracy attainable with the heuristic (8). We performed a large number of fixed-point divisions on random values and collected statistical data. Usually floating-point operands of real programs are not randomly distributed over the entire range; to account in part for this, we added a parameter that determines the ratio between range of the random distribution for the numerator and the denominator. Figure 6 shows the results when the largest number is smaller than 2.0 ($IWL = 1$ bit). On the X axis is the value of the heuristic's parameter, α. On the Y axes is the error introduced by the fixed-point conversion, expressed in dB. As one can see, the precision steadily increases for all versions up to $\alpha = 0.4$. For high values of α, the error due to coarse quantization of the denominator offsets the accuracy gained due to a smaller IWL for the result. The effect of the heuristic is less pronounced when IWL is larger. As a limit case, the heuristic gracefully degrades to integer division when the range of both operands is

$WL - 1$, and we obtain flat curves with integer precision, which entirely depend on the ratio.

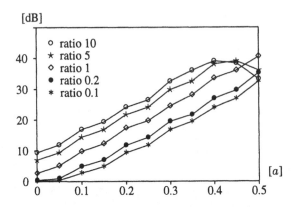

Fig. 6. Effect of heuristic (8) on division's accuracy.

5 Related work

In the last years the field of automatic conversion of C programs from floating-point to fixed-point has gained much attention. This is due to the appearance of digital signal processors offering hardware support for fixed-point arithmetic (like the popular Texas Instruments' TMS320C50). Usually, the design of a fixed-point algorithm starts with floating-point code which is then converted to fixed-point, manually or in a semi-automatic fashion. Two alternatives have been considered regarding instantiation of the fixed-point format of a floating-point variable:

1. *Instantiation at definition time* involves a unique instantiation at the location where the variable is defined.
2. *Instantiation at assignment time* requires that the optimal format be determined every time the variable is assigned.

According to Willems et al.[14], the implementation of algorithms for specific target machines requires a bit-true specification at source level. This specification can then be transferred into a HDL or a programming language. In [11] he proposes a non-ANSI extension to C in which two fixed-point parameterized types are introduced. The first allows the user to instantiate the fixed-point format of a variable at definition time. With the second, more flexible type the converter determines the best format at assignment time. This approach leads to very accurate fixed-point conversion. The behavior of the operators on the new types is fully specified, including overflow handling and rounding mode[6] . The user is free to specify the fixed-point format for some variables and let the

---

[6] In ANSI-C these aspects are dependent on the implementation.

converter determine the format for the remaining ones. This result is achieved by propagating the known formats along the data-flow graph and by profiling the floating-point variables left unspecified by the user. Statistics of these variables are collected by means of a hybrid (floating-point and fixed-point) simulator and are used to estimate the optimal number of bits for the integer and the fractional parts. The process is interactive: the converter can ask the user to supply additional data when the information available is not sufficient. Once the fixed-point format of all the variables has been determined, the conversion tool can generate new ANSI-C code based only on integers types, with the appropriate scaling and masking operations. An open question is how well can compiler optimizations reduce the overhead due to integer bit-true transformations when generating code for a specific target. Also, it is questionable whether a bit-true control of the algorithm at the source level is "cost-effective". The target machine in fact dictates what are the most efficient overflow and rounding modes. Software emulation of a different behavior is inefficient, hardly acceptable in implementations for which execution speed is critical.

One disadvantage of the instantiation at assignment time used by Willems is that it requires two specific simulators: a hybrid and a bit-true simulator. The former, as mentioned above, is needed for profiling, the latter to simulate the accuracy of the application on the target processor. Another complication comes from pointers. The converter must estimate the result of loads and the values that might have been stored into a location. The fixed-point format of all the possible values must then be combined.

In [13][8] Sung, Kum et al. propose an automated, fixed-point transformation methodology based on profiling. Also in this case, the user can specify the fixed-point format of selected variables. The range, mean and variance of the remaining variables are measured by profiling. A range estimator [12] uses the collected statistical data to determine the optimal fixed-point format. The conversion uses the concept of *definition time instantiation* only. The authors focus on specific target architectures (TSM320C5x) with dedicated hardware for fixed-point arithmetics. Moreover, their approach requires custom adaptations to existing compilers. Their results show that fixed-point programs using 16-bit integer words are 5 to 20 times faster than the software floating point simulation. The speedup drops to a factor 2 when 32-bit fixed-point words are used.

The simulation based format determination, used in both mentioned approaches, has two disadvantages. One of them is that it depends on the profiling input data. A more serious problem is that it is slow, as the optimal fixed-point format is determined running several simulations for every single variable. The estimator is typically implemented by means of C++ classes, which introduce a severe overhead compared to a base type [10].

Our approach differs in several aspects from the above described ones. The choice of *definition time instantiation*, substantially simplifies the algorithm. Also, it contributes to more efficient code, as the number of shift operations is likely to be smaller. Although we do not support profiling to determine the fixed-point format, the results showed that static analysis and the described heuristics can deliver the same accuracy. Finally, and differently from the other approaches, we generate machine code for a wide target space [5].

6 Conclusions

Data type conversion of a floating-point specification to a fixed-point specification has been implemented and tested on two digital filter algorithms. We devised several alternatives for fixed-point multiplication. The results show that the loss of accuracy due to the fixed-point representation is highly dependent on the implementation of the multiplication. With the most accurate alternatives, we obtain a Signal to Quantization Noise Ratio of 74dB and 55dB with respect to a double-precision, hardware supported implementation. For one test program, the comparison with a floating-point implementation on an integer datapath (software emulation) showed that, depending on the level of parallelism sustainable by the target machine, a speedup factor from 3.7 to 5.9 is achieved with the more accurate fixed-point version, and a speedup from 8.2 to 9.9 with the less accurate one, compared to floating-point software emulation.

The accuracy and the execution speed attained in the experiments show that the approach presented in this paper is promising. The results encourage us to continue in the direction of fine-tuning the heuristics and generating code for specialized targets with direct support for fixed-point, like shifters at the functional unit inputs and access to the upper part of the integer multiplication result.

References

[1] Andrea G. M. Cilio. Efficient Code Generation for ASIPs with Different Word Sizes. In *proceedings of the third conference of the Advanced School for Computing and Imaging*, June 1997.

[2] Henk Corporaal. *Microprocessor Architectures; from VLIW to TTA*. John Wiley, 1997. ISBN 0-471-97157-X.

[3] Paul M. Embree. *C Algorithms for Real-Time DSP*. Prentice Hall, 1995.

[4] Stanford Compiler Group. *The SUIF Library*. Stanford University, 1994.

[5] Jan Hoogerbrugge. *Code Generation for Transport Triggered Architectures*. PhD thesis, Technical University of Delft, February 1996.

[6] Loughborough Sound Images. Evaluation of the performance of the c6201 processor & compiler, 1997. Internal paper: http://www.lsi-dsp.co.uk/c6x/tech.

[7] International Telegraph and Telephone Consultative Committee. General Aspects of Digital Transmission Systems. Terminal Equipments Recommendations G.700–G.795. International standard, CCITT, Melbourne, November 1988.

[8] Wonyong Sung Jiyang Kang. Fixed-point C compiler for TMS320C50 digital signal processor. In *proceedings of ICASSP'97*, 1997.

[9] Joint Technical Committee ISO/IEC JTC1/SC29/WG11. ISO/IEC 13818 "Information technology – Generic coding of moving pictures and associated audio. International standard, ISO/IEC, June 1995.

[10] Stanley B. Lippman. *Inside the C++ Object Model*. Addison-Wesley, 1996.

[11] Thorsten Grötker Markus Willems, Volker Bürsgens and Heinrich Meyr. FRIDGE: An Interactive Fixed-point Code Generator Environment for HW/SW CoDesign. In *proceedings of the IEEE International conference on Acoustic, Speech and Signal Processing*, pages 687–690, München, April 1997.

[12] Ki-Il Kum Seehyun Kim and Wonyong Sung. Fixed-point Optimization Utility for C and C++ Based Digital Signal processing Programs. In *proceedings of IEEE Workshop on VLSI Signal Processing*, October 1995.

[13] Wonyong Sung and Jiyang Kang. Fixed-Point C Language for Digital Signal Processing. In *Twenty-Ninth Annual Asilomar Conference on Signals, Systems and Computers*, October 1995.

[14] Markus Willems, Volker Bürsgens, Holger Keding, Thorsten Grötker, and Heinrich Meyr. System Level Fixed-point Design Based on an Interpolative Approach. In *Design Automation Conference*, 1997.

Optimizing Object-Oriented Languages Through Architectural Transformations

Tom Tourwé* and Wolfgang De Meuter

{Tom.Tourwe,wdmeuter}@vub.ac.be
Programming Technology Lab
Vrije Universiteit Brussel
Pleinlaan 2, 1050 Brussel, Belgium

Abstract. Certain features of the object-oriented paradigm are a serious impediment for the runtime performance of object-oriented programs. Although compiler techniques to alleviate this problem were developed over the years, we will present some real-world examples which show that these solutions fall short in making any significant optimizations to systems that are required to be very flexible and highly reusable. As a solution, we propose a radically different approach: using an open compiler to "compile away" whole designs by performing architectural transformations based on programmer annotations. We will discuss this approach in detail and show why it is more suited to solve the efficiency problems inherently associated with object-oriented programming.

1 Introduction

It is well known that certain distinguishing features of the object-oriented paradigm are a serious impediment for the runtime performance of an object-oriented system. The most important and powerful feature of object-oriented programming languages which is hard to implement efficiently is polymorphism, or the ability to substitute any object for another object which understands the same set of messages in a certain context. Due to this feature, a compiler cannot predict at compile time which method will be executed at runtime by a particular message. Thus, so called *dynamic dispatch* code has to be generated for message sends, which looks up the appropriate method based on the runtime type of the receiver. In comparison to code for a normal function call, dynamic dispatch code is clearly much slower. Apart from this *direct cost*, polymorphism is also responsible for the fact that traditional compiler optimizations can no longer be performed. For example, inline substitution of method bodies is no longer possible, because the compiler cannot statically determine which method will be invoked by a particular message. This is called the *indirect cost*. It is stated in [6] that some programs spend up to 47 % of their time executing dynamic dispatch code, and that this number is still expected to increase in the

---

* Author financed with a doctoral grant from the Institute for Science and Technology (IWT), Flanders.

future. One of the main reasons thereof is that object-oriented programming encourages a programmer to write many small methods (a few lines of code) that get polymorphically invoked by each other. Unfortunately, recent insights in the programming style fostered by the object-oriented paradigm precisely encourage the use of these features. Proof thereof is the tremendous success of programming conventions such as design patterns [7] and idioms [1, 3].

Of course, the reason for the success of these programming techniques is that there currently exists a trend to make a software system comply to many important non-functional requirements, such as reusability, extendability and adaptability, enabling the developers to reuse major parts of it. This leads to systems in which a lot of attention is paid to the global *architecture*. How the different classes in a system are combined and the specific ways in which their objects interact becomes very important in order to be able to easily reuse or extend the system. The techniques that support fulfilling this goal however, encourage the use of the specific features of object-oriented languages even more. Thus, more often than not, system developers are confronted with a dilemma: should a system be written in a very flexible and highly reusable way (thereby heavily relying on late binding polymorphism), which may lead to inefficient code, or should they take into account the efficiency of a system and not care about the non-functional aspects of the code? As a result, developers are often tempted to avoid using inefficient features, which clearly does not contribute much to the quality of the software.

Not surprisingly, techniques have been developed over the years which focus on trying to eliminate dynamic dispatch code. This is achieved by trying to predict the exact type an object will have at runtime, which then allows the compiler to statically bind the messages sent to this object. Although the results are encouraging, we will argue why these techniques in isolation are not sufficient to significantly optimize future object-oriented systems. The main deficiency is that they only have a narrow local view of the system. We will show that they fail to incorporate global knowledge about the system's structure and architecture and are therefore forced to make local and more conservative optimizations. To alleviate this problem, we propose to use an open compiler, which is able to reason about programs at the meta level and which can perform architectural transformations based on the information gathered this way. The compiler is open so that developers can annotate their source code and provide the compiler with detailed architectural knowledge about their system. Further, it is able to reason about a system at the meta level in order to deduce even more knowledge about its architecture.

The paper is structured as follows. The next section discusses existing techniques for improving the performance of object-oriented systems, while section 3 provides a representative example and an in-depth discussion as to why these techniques on their own are not capable to improve performance of (future) object-oriented systems significantly. In section 4, we present our approach and explain the framework we use for reasoning about programs and using programmer annotations. Section 5 explains how our approach enables significant optimization of, amongst others, the example introduced in section 3, while section 6 describes future work and section 7 concludes.

2 Current Optimization Techniques

This section presents some of the most important techniques developed to overcome the efficiency problem of object-oriented languages. More specifically, *class hierarchy analysis, customization* and *exhaustive class testing* will be discussed. We present the overall picture and elaborate only on the properties needed to understand the discussions in the following sections. We refer the reader to [5, 2] for detailed descriptions of these techniques and a detailed report of the results.

2.1 Class Hierarchy Analysis

Class hierarchy analysis tries to avoid dynamic dispatch code by providing the compiler with the class hierarchy of the whole program. It is based on the observation that sometimes, when compiling a class, knowledge about its superclasses and subclasses can help in determining which method will be invoked by a particular message send. An example will make this more clear. Consider the inheritance hierarchy in Figure 1 and suppose that method p of class G performs a self send of the message m. When straightforwardly compiling the method p, dynamic dispatch code will have to be generated for this message send, since there are different implementations of the method m in the hierarchy. However, if the compiler takes into account the class hierarchy of class G, it is able to statically bind the message. The method m is never overridden: not in class G, nor in any of its subclasses. Thus, the method m that will be executed at runtime by method p is the one that is defined in class C.

2.2 Customization

Customization statically binds message sends by compiling different versions of the method in which they occur. Each version is specialized for one particular receiver. Since the receiver is thus statically bound in each of these different versions, the compiler is able to avoid dynamic-dispatch code for each self send occurring in that method.

Consider again the class hierarchy in Figure 1. The method o of class B has three different types of possible receivers: the classes B, D and E. Thus, the method o is compiled to three different versions, corresponding to each of the three possible receivers. In each of these three versions, the receiver of the message is statically bound. If method o of class B performs a self send of message m, the specialized method o for class B will bind this message to method m of class B and the specialized version for class D will bind this message to method m of class D. Note that class hierarchy analysis would not be able to statically bind this self send, since the method m is overridden in subclass D of B.

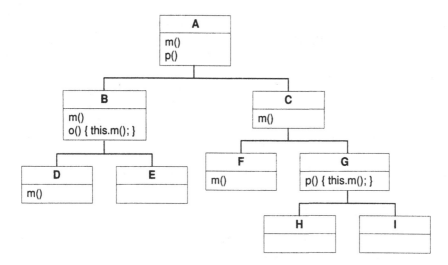

Fig. 1. Class A and its subclasses.

A disadvantage of this technique is the risk of code explosion: when a large number of classes are possible receivers for a certain message, many specialized versions of the corresponding method need to be generated. Also, methods are only specialized for the receiver of a message, which only enables statically binding self sends. Other message sends occurring in the method body, for example messages sent to an argument or to an instance variable, are not taken into account. For these reasons, an extension of the customization technique, called *specialization* was developed. However, the problem of code explosion becomes even worse using this technique, since even more different versions need to be generated for a method. Also, specialization requires support for multi-methods in the runtime environment, something popular languages as C++ or Java lack.

2.3 Exhaustive Class Testing

Exhaustive class testing is a technique which statically binds a message by inserting appropriate class tests around it, taking into account the class hierarchy. Consider again the hierarchy in Figure 1. Instead of specializing the method o for each of its possible receivers, the compiler could generate the following code for the message m:

```
if(receiver instanceof D) { <code of method m in class D> }
else if(receiver instanceof B || receiver instanceof E} {
    <code of method m in class B>
}
else { receiver.m(); } // send the message
```

At first sight, it might seem that this code can be optimized even further by using a switch-statement (e.g. a dispatch table). This is however not the case, since most of the time this table would be sparse. The problem of finding a numbering scheme for the classes in the system so that for every message send a dense table can be constructed is very hard, or even impossible. For this reason, class testing is very efficient only if the number of possible receivers for a message send is small and if the execution of dynamic dispatch code is more costly then the execution of a class test and all tests that failed before. This means that there can be a loss in performance when there are many possible receivers, since many tests will have to be performed. Furthermore, it is always possible that the same method is executed each and every time, which means that the other tests will never succeed, but they still have to be executed.

2.4 Conclusion

This section presented some of the techniques developed recently in order to alleviate the efficiency problem of object-oriented languages. The primary focus of all these techniques lies in trying to avoid the generation of expensive dynamic dispatch code. This is achieved by statically binding as much message sends as possible. An important observation that can be made is that no one technique is able to solve the problem on its own. Depending on the situation and the context of a message send, one certain technique is better suited than another.

3 An Illustrating Example

In this section, we will present a representative example which shows how writing software in a flexible and reusable way often incurs an inherent performance loss. Also, it will become clear that, in order for software to be reusable, heavy reliance on late binding polymorphism is required. Furthermore, we will point out why the techniques discussed in the previous section are not sufficient to significantly optimize code for this and other examples.

A generally accepted collection of techniques for writing reusable and adaptable software today is design patterns [7]. Given their popularity and widespread use, it is extremely relevant to discuss the efficiency of systems using these patterns. The example presented here is thus taken from [7]. For a more in-depth discussion of the use, the advantages and the disadvantages of design patterns, we refer the reader to this book.

3.1 The Visitor Design Pattern

Problem Statement and Solutions. The prototypical example of the use of the Visitor pattern is the architecture of a compiler that needs to traverse the abstract syntax tree (AST) of a program many times in order to pretty-print, typecheck or generate code for it. Instead of implementing these operations on the elements that make up the AST, as is depicted in Figure 2, we could implement each operation in a different class, called a *Visitor* class, and pass objects of this class to the elements of the AST. These elements then call the appropriate method in the Visitor object. This solution is depicted in Figure 3. This way of defining operations on element classes has several advantages. Clearly, the code becomes much easier to understand, maintain and reuse, since element classes are not cluttered with code for different operations. Also, adding new operations becomes much easier, as this simply boils down to implementing the appropriate subclass of the Visitor class and no element classes need to be changed.

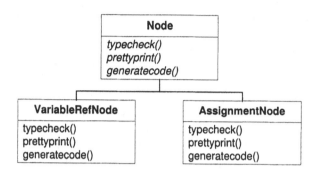

Fig. 2. The straightforward solution.

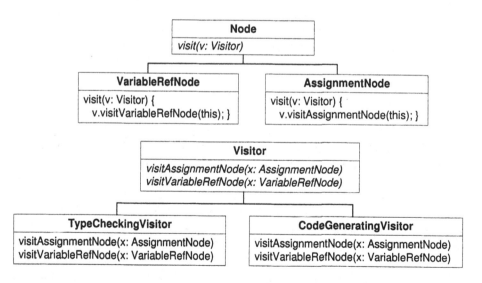

Fig. 3. The Visitor design pattern solution.

The Visitor pattern relies on a technique called *double dispatch* [1]. By using this technique, one can ensure that the method that will eventually get executed by a message send not only depends on the runtime value of the receiver, but also on the value of the message's argument. The `visit` method in the `Node` class and its subclasses is an example of this technique. The method that will get called is dependent on both the type of the receiver of the `visit`-method and the type of the `Visitor` argument passed to it.

Why Current Optimization Techniques Fail. Clearly, since current optimization techniques only focus on statically binding the receiver of the message, they fall short in optimizing methods that use double dispatch. In order to arrive at the method that will perform the actual work, at least two message sends need to be statically bound. This is not a trivial task, since these two messages are nearly always subject to late binding, because many subclasses of the `Node` and the `Visitor` classes exist. Often, simply sending the message will thus be more efficient then inserting many class tests or compiling many specialized methods. A more important reason for the failure of these techniques, however, is that they do not take into account the specific architecture of this pattern. The whole idea behind it is to separate the operations that classes need to define from these classes themselves. As a result, many more messages need to be sent. Instead of trying to statically bind these messages, a better approach would consist of avoiding these message sends altogether. A significant performance gain can be achieved, for example, by moving the operations back to the specific subclasses of class `Node`, avoiding at least half the total number of messages sent[1]. The result of this operation would then be the architecture depicted in Figure 2. Of course, as already mentioned, this architecture is much less flexible and reusable. Therefore, the compiler should be able to perform the transformation of the architecture automatically, so that developers can still produce flexible code. Current techniques do not make this possible, however.

3.2 Conclusion

Similar observations can be made for other design patterns, but other examples were left out due to space limitations. These observations lead us to conclude that compliance to many important non-functional requirements, such as reusability and flexibility, incur an inherent performance loss. The primary reason for this is that developers have to rely heavily on features which are hard to compile efficiently. Furthermore, current compiler techniques are not capable of optimizing such systems significantly, as the example we presented clearly showed. This is because those techniques focus only on statically binding messages and do not incorporate a more architectural view of a system. Design patterns and other techniques for writing flexible software often introduce extra abstractions and make clever use of inheritance and delegation in order to make objects more interchangeable and to prepare for future extensions. Since current techniques

---

[1] In reality, the performance gain will even be higher as it is a characterizing property of a visitor to access the state variables of the visited object through accessors. These can also be removed easily.

fail to recognize these extra abstractions, it is clear that they are not able to eliminate them, thereby reducing the number of message sends. For a compiler to be able to optimize such systems, it should incorporate some techniques to transform one architecture into another more efficient one, eliminating redundant message sends instead of trying to statically bind them.

4 Architectural Optimization Through Transformations

The main reason why current compilers are not able to significantly optimize highly flexible systems is because they cannot automatically infer the intentions of the developer. A compiler does not know, for example, why a specific abstraction is introduced, so it cannot eliminate it to produce better code. Therefore, in our approach, these intentions are made explicit. For this purpose, an *annotation* language is provided in which these intentions can be expressed. In order for the compiler to be able to use this information in a useful way, it should incorporate some knowledge on how to optimize a certain intention. Again, this knowledge should be provided by the developer and can be expressed in the *transformation* language.

A drawback of our approach is that a lot of user intervention is required for the optimization of a system. We believe this is unavoidable however, as systems tend to get more complex and because there are limits to the amount of information that can be deduced automatically by dataflow analysis techniques [11]. It should be stressed however, that we strive to minimize developer intervention as much as possible. First of all, some work has been published recently in the area of the automatic detection of design principles, such as design patterns [10]. By integrating this work into our framework, the burden of manually specifying intentions becomes obsolete. Second, popular techniques for constructing flexible systems, such as design patterns, are used over and over again. This means a library of commonly used transformations can be constructed, which can be reused for compiling different systems and which releaves developers from specifying the same transformations over and over again. Furthermore, the fact that the intentions of a developer are made explicit in the software can also aid in other areas besides performance. First of all, documentation and understandability can be improved upon. Second, the information revealed by the intentions can be used to study the evolution conflicts of object-oriented systems in more detail [9].

It is important to note that the transformations performed by our compiler are source-to-source transformations. This has two main advantages. First of all, the code our compiler outputs can still be optimized by current optimization techniques in order to achieve even better performance. Second, current techniques will benefit from the fact that unnecessary abstractions are removed by our compiler, as this allows them to statically bind even more messages.

In what follows, we will explain how all these different aspects can be integrated into one uniform framework which allows for architectural optimization of object-oriented systems.

4.1 A Uniform Framework

The transformational approach we propose poses some important requirements. In order to be able to specify and perform the transformations on a program easily, a suitable representation of it has to exist. Surely, the transformations can be performed on the abstract syntax tree of the program, although it has been argued that this representation is not very well suited for this purpose [8]. Also, the representation should be designed in such a way that it allows for easy recognition of specific (user defined) patterns in a program, which the AST certainly is not. The work done in [10] and the conceptual framework introduced in [4] inspired us to represent a program in a special-purpose logic language. For our purposes, the declarative nature of such languages and the builtin matching and unification algorithms are very important features.

Following [4], we represent a program in the logic language *TyRuBa* by means of a set of logic propositions. How constructs of the base-language (the language in which the program is implemented) are represented in the logic language is specified by the *representational mapping*. We will discuss this in more detail below. A *code generator* is associated with the representational mapping, specifying how code should be generated from the logic propositions representing the program. It can be seen as the inverse function of the representational mapping.

We will now describe some important properties of TyRuBa, the logic language we use, and will then continue explaining in more detail how a base-level program is represented in this language and what the annotation and the transformation language look like.

TyRuBa. The TyRuBa system is basically a simplified Prolog variant with a few special features to facilitate code generation. We assume familiarity with Prolog and only briefly discuss the most important differences.

TyRuBa's lexical conventions differ from Prolog's. Variables are identified by a leading "?" instead of starting with a capital. This avoids confusion between base-language identifiers and variables. Some examples of TyRuBa variables are: ?x, ?Abc12, etc. Some examples of constants are: x, 1, Abc123, etc. Because TyRuBa offers a quoting mechanism which allows intermixing base-language code and logic terms, the syntax of terms is also slightly different from Prolog's. To avoid confusion with method calls, TyRuBa compound terms are written with "<" and ">" instead of "(" and ")".

TyRuBa provides a special kind of compound term that represents a piece of "quoted" base-language code. Basically this is simply a special kind of string delimited by "{" and "}". Instead of characters however, the elements of such quoted code blocks may be arbitrary tokens, intermixed with logic variables or compound terms. The following is an example of a quoted term, in Java-like syntax. Note the variables and logic terms that occur inside the code.

```
{ void foo() {
    Array<?El> contents = new ?El[5];
    ?El anElement=contents.elementAt(1); }
}
```

The Representational Mapping. The representational mapping specifies how a program is represented in the logic language. This basically means that constructs of the base-language are represented in the logic language by means of a set of logic propositions. The mapping scheme between logic representation and base-language may vary and determines the kind of information that is accessible for manipulation. For our purpose, a fine-grained mapping is necessary, since we want to be able to manipulate a program at every level of detail. Furthermore, more structural and higher-level information, such as the relationship between different classes and their specific interaction, also needs to be modeled in the logic language to enable easy reasoning about the architecture of the program. It should be stressed that the representation of a program is generated automatically by the compiler and that it is thus not the task of the developer.

We will explain this representational mapping by using the following running example:

```
class Test extends SuperTest {
    boolean b;
    int m(int i) {
        if(b)
            return i;
        else
            return 0;
    }
}
```

The presence of a class and its position in the inheritance hierarchy is made explicit by the following facts:

```
class(Test).
extends(Test,SuperTest).
```

Classes are regarded as being composed out of instance variables, methods and constructors. The instance variables of a class are represented as follows:

```
field(Test,boolean,b).
```

The *field* predicate thus always indicates to which class the field belongs and specifies the type and the name of the variable. The presence of methods and constructors is asserted in a different way: their declarations are chopped up into little pieces, each of which represents one particular aspect. It is the responsibility of the code-generator to assemble the various parts and generate code accordingly. The method m can be represented as follows:

```
method(Test,m,[int],method1).
returntype(method1,int).
formalparameter(method1,int,i).
body(method1,blocknode).
```

These predicates specify the returntype, the formal parameters and the body of the method. The first argument of each predicate specifies to which method the particular feature belongs. This is necessary for the code generator so that it can assemble all parts of a specific method in order to generate code for it. Note that the *method* predicate not only lists the name of the class and the name of the method, but also the type of the formal parameters. This is needed in order to uniquely identify the method, as it can possibly be overloaded.

Bodies of methods and constructors consist of statements and expressions and can thus be represented by a normal parse tree. The nodes of this parse tree need to be unique, and we need to be able to refer to them in an easy way. Therefore, a proposition representing a node has an extra argument, which specifies its (unique) name. The body of the method m, for example, will be represented as follows:

```
blockstatementnode(blocknode,[ifnode1]).
ifstatementnode(ifnode1,expr-node,then-node,else-node).
fieldaccessnode(expr-node,this,b).
returnstatementnode(then-node,ret-expr).
returnstatementnode(else-node,litnode0).
variableaccessnode(ret-expr,i);
literalnode(litnode0,0).
```

As should be clear, all nodes point to their child nodes via their specific names. The `ifstatementnode`, for example, mentions its three child nodes, a condition node, a then node and an else node, by their respective names. Furthermore, the two `returnstatementnodes` picture why nodes need to have a name: two nodes of the same kind can exist and we need to be able to make a distinction between them, because they can occur in different parts of the program. Again, this representation is generated automatically by our compiler.

The Annotation Language. The declarative nature of a logic language allows developers to straightforwardly provide the compiler with architectural knowledge by means of logic facts. When annotating a particular design pattern in a system, for example, the developer should state which classes are the primary participants in the architecture of that pattern. Consider for example the annotated occurrence of a visitor design pattern below:

```
/** ConcreteVisitor(PrettyPrintVisitor).
    operationname(PrettyPrintVisitor,prettyprint).
 */
public class PrettyPrintVisitor extends Visitor { ... }

/** ConcreteElement(AssignmentNode). */
public class AssignmentNode extends Node { ... }

/** ConcreteElement(VariableRefNode). */
public class VariableRefNode extends Node { ... }
```

The assertions, which are embedded in `javadoc`-like comments, state that the classes `AssignmentNode` and `VariableRefNode` are instances of the concrete element participants and that the class `PrettyPrintVisitor` is an instance of the concrete visitor participant of this pattern. The predicate `operationname` specifies the name of the operation that is implemented by the particular concrete visitor. The reason for its presence will become clear soon. Using this information, together with the rules expressing which transformations should be performed, our compiler is able to transform the visitor architecture into a more efficient architecture (this will be shown in section 5). Of course, apart from classes, individual methods, fields and constructors can also be annotated in this way.

An advantage of specifying this information through javadoc-like comments is that the source code of the system is not mixed with the annotations that handle its performance. This is important because mixing the code with directives makes it less readable. Also, current compilers will treat annotations as comments and can thus still be used to compile this code, although the result will not be as efficient as when the program is compiled with our optimizing compiler.

The Transformation Language. A transformation that should be performed on a program basically expresses "if this particular pattern occurs then replace it by this pattern". An intuitive way to express a transformation is thus via a logic rule: the condition of the rule corresponds to the condition of the if and the head of the rule corresponds to the then part of the if. Consider the following example:

```
messagenode(?nodename,?rec,?var,[]):-fieldaccessnode(?nodename,?rec,?var).
```

The result of this rule is that the compiler will replace all direct variable references, such as this.b, by message sends, such as this.b()[2]. Note that the name of the messagenode predicate is copied from the fieldaccessnode predicate. This is to ensure that the code generator will generate code for the message send only. Remember that node names need to be unique, so the code generator has special provisions so that code is generated only once for a specific node.

5   The Illustrating Example Revisited

In this section, we will show how the example presented in section 3 can be optimized by using architectural transformations. The main idea upon which this revisited example relies is that the complete architecture of the particular design pattern is compiled away. This is achieved by transforming the solution it proposes into a more straightforward solution for the same problem. As already shown in previous sections, the result of this operation will be more efficient, as a straightforward solution is often much less flexible and does not rely on polymorphism as much. As a consequence, much less messages will need to be sent and thus the performance of the system will be improved significantly.

---

[2] Note that this is only an illustrative example. Expressions of the form this.b = 2 will be replaced by this.b() = 2 which is of course not correct.

The Visitor pattern defines an architecture in which Visitor classes implement an operation over some object structure. As already explained, this architecture can be optimized by implementing the operation defined by a specific Visitor class on the elements that make up this object structure. A concrete example should make this more clear. Consider a visitIfStatementNode method in a PrettyPrintVisitor class, which could look like this:

```
void visitIfStatementNode(IfStatementNode x) {
    this.printOnOutputStream(''if('');
    x.getCondition().visit(this);
    this.printOnOutputStream('') '');
    x.getThenPart().visit(this);
    this.printOnOutputStream('' else '');
    x.getElsePart().visit(this);
}
```

This method should be moved to the IfStatementNode class and the code should be changed so that it looks like this:

```
void prettyprint(PrettyPrintVisitor x) {
    x.printOnOutputStream(''if('');
    this.getCondition().prettyprint(x);
    x.printOnOutputStream('') '');
    this.getThenPart().prettyprint(x);
    x.printOnOutputStream('' else '');
    this.getElsePart().prettyprint(x);
}
```

A number of changes needs to be made to the first code fragment in order to arrive at the second. First of all, the visitIfStatementNode method should be moved to the class of its formal parameter (e.g. the IfStatementNode class) and its name should be changed to prettyprint. Note that, since the method is moved and not copied, the original visitIfStatementNode method will be deleted from the PrettyPrintVisitor class. Second, the type of the formal parameter of the method should be changed to the concrete visitor class (e.g. PrettyPrintVisitor). This is necessary so that methods and instance variables of this visitor class can still be accessed. Third, since the method is moved to the class of its formal parameter, all references to the formal parameter should be replaced by self-references. All self-references in turn have to be changed to references to the formal parameter, as this now points to the visitor class where the method was originally defined. Finally, recursive calls to the visit method of child nodes should be replaced by calls to the prettyprint method of these nodes. The following rules can be used to describe these changes:

```
method(?concreteElement,?operationname,[?visitor],?methodid) :-
    ConcreteVisitor(?visitor),ConcreteElement(?concreteElement),
    method(?visitor,?methodname,[?concreteElement],?methodid),
    operationname(?visitor,?operationname).
formalparameter(?methodid,?concreteVisitor,?name) :-
    formalparameter(?methodid,?concreteElement,?name),
```

```
    concreteVisitor(?concreteVisitor),concreteElement(?concreteElement).
thisexpressionnode(?node) :- variableaccessnode(?node,x).
variableaccessnode(?node,x) :- thisexpressionnode(?node).
messagenode(?node,?rec,?operationname,?args)
  :- messagenode(?node,?rec,visit,?args),
     ConcreteVisitor(?visitor),operationname(?visitor,?operationname).
```

These rules make use of the architectural knowledge provided by the developer, as is described in 4.1. Note, for example, how the rules make use of the `operationname` predicate in order to provide a meaningful name to the methods that implement the operation of the visitor. Given these rules and this knowledge, the compiler is able to remove the extra indirections and abstractions introduced by this architecture. The code it emits can then be further optimized by already existing techniques, enabling even better optimization conditions.

6 Future Work

Further investigation into different areas is needed in order to complete the work presented in this paper. First of all, we only tested our approach on some small but prototypical systems, which showed good results. The next step thus consists of trying to optimize real-world object-oriented systems. Second, we will study the impact of our techniques on current optimization techniques. We hold the position that the latter can benefit from our optimizations, as unnecessary abstractions and indirections are removed, which enables better conditions for statically binding and inlining messages. Third, we will integrate our work with the work of [10] and develop a library of transformations in order to automate the optimization process and eliminate developer intervention as much as possible.

7 Conclusion

In this paper, we showed that current techniques for optimizing object-oriented systems fall short when applied to systems which conform to important non-functional requirements such as reusability, adaptability and extendability. This is mainly due to the fact that these techniques only try to statically bind message sends by predicting the exact type of an object at runtime. They do not incorporate global knowledge about the architecture of a system, with all its specific abstractions and relationships between classes and methods. As a consequence, they fail to see that it is the architecture of such systems that is the principal reason for the performance loss. To alleviate this problem, we proposed to use a compiler incorporating architectural knowledge which is able to transform one architecture into another, more efficient one, thereby reducing the total number of messages sent, instead of simply statically binding them. In order to achieve this, a uniform framework was presented, consisting of a representation for a program suited for our purpose, an annotation and a transformation language. Using this framework, developers are able to provide the compiler with architectural information and can specify rules to manipulate and transform the internal representation of the program. We showed how to use this framework for performing architectural optimizations on systems implemented using design patterns.

8 Acknowledgements

The authors would like to thank Theo D'Hondt for promoting the work presented in this paper. Special thanks to Kris De Volder for fruitful discussions about and important contributions to this work. Many thanks to Carine Lucas, Kris De Volder and Kim Mens for proofreading. Thanks to all other members of the Programming Technology Lab for making it an inspiring place to work.

References

[1] Kent Beck. *Smalltalk Best Practice Patterns*. Prentice Hall, 1997.

[2] Craig Chambers. *The Design and Implementation of the SELF Compiler, an Optimizing Compiler for Object-Oriented Programming Languages*. PhD thesis, Stanford University, 1992.

[3] James O. Coplien. *Advanced C++ programming styles and idioms*. Addison-Wesley Publishing Company, 1992.

[4] Kris De Volder. *Type-Oriented Logic Meta Programming*. PhD thesis, Vrije Universiteit Brussel, 1998.

[5] Jeffrey Adgate Dean. *Whole Program Optimization of Object-Oriented Languages*. PhD thesis, University of Washington, 1996.

[6] Karel Driesen and Urs Holzle. The direct cost of virtual function calls in c++. In *Proceedings of the OOPSLA 96 Conference*, pages 306–323. ACM Press, 1996.

[7] Erich Gamma, Richard Helm, Ralph Johnson, and John Vlissides. *Design Patterns, Elements of Reusable Object-Oriented Software*. Addison-Wesley Professional Computing Series, 1995.

[8] William G. Griswold. *Program Restructuring as an Aid to Software Maintenance*. PhD thesis, University of Washington, 1991.

[9] Carine Lucas. *Documenting Reuse and Evolution with Reuse Contracts*. PhD thesis, Vrije Universiteit Brussel, 1997.

[10] Roel Wuyts. Declarative reasoning about the structure of object-oriented systems. In *Technology of object-oriented languages and systems*, 1998.

[11] Hans Zima and Barbara Chapman. *Supercompilers for Parallel and Vector Computers*. Addison Wesley, 1990.

Virtual Cache Line: A New Technique to Improve Cache Exploitation for Recursive Data Structures

Shai Rubin, David Bernstein, Michael Rodeh

IBM Research Lab in Haifa, MATAM – Advanced Technology Center
Haifa 31905, Israel
{rubin, bernstn}@haifa.vnet.ibm.com
IBM Research Lab in Haifa and Computer Science Department
The Techion, Haifa Israel
rodeh@us.ibm.com

Abstract. Recursive data structures (lists, trees, graphs, etc.) are used throughout scientific and commercial software. The common approach is to allocate storage to the individual nodes of such structures dynamically, maintaining the logical connection between them via pointers. Once such a data structure goes through a sequence of updates (inserts and deletes), it may get scattered all over memory yielding poor spatial locality, which in turn introduces many cache misses. In this paper we present the new concept of Virtual Cache Lines (VCLs). Basically, the mechanism keeps groups of consecutive nodes in close proximity, forming virtual cache lines, while allowing the groups to be stored arbitrarily far away from each other. Virtual cache lines increase the spatial locality of the given data structure resulting in better locality of references. Furthermore, since the spatial locality is improved, software prefetching becomes much more attractive. Indeed, we also present a software prefetching algorithm that can be used when dealing with VCLs resulting in even higher data cache performance. Our results show that the average performance of linked list operations, like scan, insert, and delete can be improved by more than 200% even in architectures that do not support prefetching, like the Intel Pentium. Moreover, when using prefetching one can gain additional 100% improvement. We believe that given a program that manipulates certain recursive data structures, compilers will be able to generate VCL-based code. Also, until this vision becomes true, VCLs can be used to build more efficient user libraries, operating-systems and applications programs.

1. Introduction

When dealing with recursive data structures the problem of high latencies in accessing memory is well recognized. Significant efforts have been directed in the past on reducing its harmful effects. Advanced memory designs have been developed [2], e.g., by way of cache memories and prefetch instructions, and offer partial remedy to this problem. Actually, Mowry [1] showed that many scientific programs spend more than half of their time waiting for data. In [1,6] software methods and tools to overcome this problem for scientific code are proposed.

Memory latency impacts both the instruction stream and the data stream. The locality of the instruction stream may be improved by code reorganization [14,18]. Also, code usually has natural locality by itself. Therefore, larger instruction caches reduce the instruction cache miss ratios considerably.

Data locality is more difficult to cope with as data can grow in size to magnitudes which do not fit into cache (or even into memory) for any practical cache size. Even worse, data may be scattered in memory in a rather random way unless measures are taken to cluster related pieces. A common approach, especially for scientific programs, *is to reorganize the computation while leaving the data layout intact* [20]. Unfortunately, this approach is only marginally applicable to scattered data since the machine stalls while the next piece of data to be processed is fetched. Prefetching offers only partial remedy – it is the data layout itself, which should be optimized for better spatial locality.

Spatial locality can be achieved by storing neighboring nodes in close proximity. When seeking a solution to this problem, three measures have to be balanced: (a) The data structure operations have to be efficient. For example, if a linked list is stored in consecutive locations in memory, search is fast but insert and delete operations become inefficient. (b) Memory has to be utilized effectively. For example, by allowing gaps between nodes, update operations may become more efficient, at the expense of lower memory utilization. (c) The machine architecture should be exploited. For instance, in machines that support memory prefetch instructions, they should be used to reduce memory latency. Examples of such balance between these three measures are B-trees [13]; special data structures designed to cope with long disk latencies when using virtual memory. The technique presented in this paper takes the intuition from this basic data structure, however it deals with memory latencies rather than disk latencies.

1.1 Recursive Data Structures (RDS)

Recursive Data Structures (RDSs) are usually defined in terms of nodes and links connecting them. Only in rare cases do they specify the relative positioning of the nodes. It is this degree of freedom which we try to exploit.

Consider a program which manipulates an RDS. The nodes of the RDS are typically dynamically allocated on the run-time heap and are, in general, scattered in memory. Therefore, cache hit ratio is rather low, and frequent calls to the memory manager are time consuming. To improve, Luk and Mowry [5] have suggested to linearize the data, namely, to map heap-allocated nodes that are likely to be accessed closely in time into contiguous memory locations.

We extend this notion of data linearization by dynamically grouping nodes into Virtual Cache Lines (VCLs) – a software concept that is a generalization of the hardware-oriented structure of cache lines. This grouping have four major positive effects: (a) The number of cache misses decreases. (b) The number of calls to the memory manager is reduced. (c) Memory fragmentation improves. (d) Ability to use prefetching when dealing with RDS is much higher than before. One negative effect is that managing the VCLs is somewhat more complicated. The good news are that compared with the common implementation of the linked list the VCLs overall performance can be improved by 300%.

In order to confirm the fact that VCLs might be useful regardless the architecture one uses, we measured the performance for two common platforms. The first is a non-prefetching architecture of Intel's Pentium [3] and the second architecture is the IBM PowerPC [4] that supports prefetching instructions.

1.2 Compilers techniques for handling RDSs.

While improving spatial locality is a clear objective, finding ways to achieve this goal is quite a challenge:

1. The problem is global, namely, the entire program has to be taken into account. A data layout, which is good for one segment of the code, may be suboptimal for another portion of the program. This introduces heavy dependency on interprocedural analysis.

2. Discovering the data structure that a program uses is a very hard problem. Moreover – what we really need is to discover not only the nature of the data structure, but also the code segments which implement the data structure operations. For example – not only do we have to find that a program manipulates a binary tree, but we also have to identify the code sections that implement the insert and delete operations.

In view of recent research results in the area of shape analysis [9,10,15] we do believe that the above mentioned difficulties may be circumvented for many programs. We hope that this paper will encourage shape-analysis researchers to focus not only on discovering the data structures layout the program manipulates, but also to find the places (in the program) where certain operations are performed. For example, in order to fully automate the process of replacing the user-defined data structures with more sophisticated structures (like ours), we need to know where in the program the user does an insert or a delete operation.

However, this paper takes a more pragmatic approach, the method is simply to implement data structures in a cache-aware way. The paper presents this new idea from two different aspects. First, it suggests a new software data layout technique that exploits a given memory hierarchy regardless the processor one uses. Second, it points to a more sophisticated design to highly optimize the original basic technique, by using prefetching instructions that exist in some of the more common architectures such as PowerPC [4].

Several compiler related applications might gain from using the proposed technique:

1. User libraries. Recently user libraries become part of the official C++ language [8]. Our technique for cache optimization can be easily integrated into specific structures (e.g. singly-linked lists, doubly-linked lists) of these libraries.

2. Memory allocators and garbage collectors . A lot of research work was conducted investigating the way to improve the cache conscious data placement of memory allocators. Additionally the importance of garbage collectors is increasing in the recent years as Java becomes more popular. Since lists are basic part of these mechanisms, it might be very useful to take into account cache consideration when

building these parts of the compiler. Actually first signs of such research can be found in [16,17,21].

The rest of this paper concentrates on presenting our novel data layout technique and the exploitation of prefetching in the context of this data layout. It is our plan to carry this research all the way to automatic generation of efficient data layouts of recursive data structures by optimizing compilers.

1.3 Outline of the paper

Section 2 reviews the VCL model in more details and presents a linked list implementation that uses it. This section also presents an evaluation of the VCL technique when it was tested on Intel's Pentium. Section 3 discusses and presents a prefetching algorithm that further improves the cache behavior of the linked list data structure. This time the evaluation is done by using an existing prefetching architecture - the IBM PowerPC. This section also presents a comparison between the known Greedy-Prefetch [5] and our new proposed technique. Section 4 concludes the paper, presents future work, and introduces the new research opportunities the VCL idea opened for the compiler and program analysis researchers.

2. Virtual Cache Lines - A Cache-Aware Data Structure

This section presents the concepts behind the Virtual Cache Lines model. First, it discusses the relation between the configuration of the physical cache lines (currently only the L1 cache) on a given system and the virtual cache lines arrangement. The last sub-section presents performance evaluation of the proposed model implemented on the popular Intel's Pentium architecture.

2.1 Aggregating nodes of a linked list

Consider a linked list with nodes which span 8 bytes[1], and assume that the machine has cache lines of size 64. Let us start with a VCL size which is equal to that of a physical cache line. Therefore, each VCL can contain 8 or fewer nodes. If we break the linked list into sublists each of which contains 8 consecutive nodes (except, possibly, for the last sublist), the cache miss ratio is reduced by up to a factor of 8 (Figure 1). Moreover, prefetching becomes very attractive since in this data layout, it is rather easy to find the address of the next VCL prior to processing the current one, thereby leaving as many as 8 nodes to be visited and processed before accessing the next VCL.

---

[1] Throughout this paper we limit ourselves to relatively small nodes. The motivation behind this assumption is that large nodes can, in many cases, be split into two sections: (a) the *key* section which contains the node's identifier. (b) The *data* section. If we store the second part separtly from the first, then the first becomes rather small. It is the first section which is visited more often. This method is partially adopted in the STL [8] library.

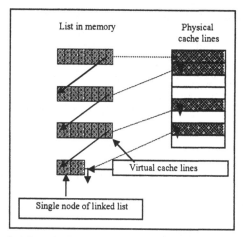

Figure 1. Organization of nodes of a link list in the VCL mechanism. The links between nodes inside the VCL are omitted for readability.

2.1.1 Relaxing memory density

While a dense layout such as the one shown in Figure 1 is indeed very effective for traversal operations, it performs rather poorly when it comes to update operations such as insert and delete, since every such operation will invoke massive re-organization of the entire list. A way out of this trap is to trade memory density for performance, namely, allow gaps in the data layout. In the case of linked lists, let us allow the number of nodes per VCL to vary between min and max (Figure 2), except maybe the last VCL. The next section shows that the mechanism to keep the number of nodes between these limits is fairly simple and efficient.

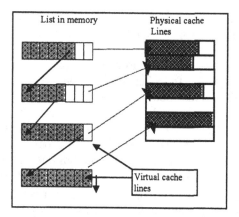

Figure 2. Practical implementation of the VCL model. The number of nodes in each VCL varies between min and max (in this case min=5, max=8).

2.1.2 Supporting insert/delete operations efficiently

Two situations may arise: Either an update operation can be done within the min/max imposed limits, or multiple VCLs have to be involved to resolve either a VCL overflow situation or VCL underflow situation. In case of a VCL overflow (max is exceeded), either some nodes of the current VCL are spilled into the next VCL(s), or a new VCL (or maybe more) is allocated dynamically. Similarly in cases of underflow – either we rebalance or we delete a VCL by invoking the memory manager (Figure 3).

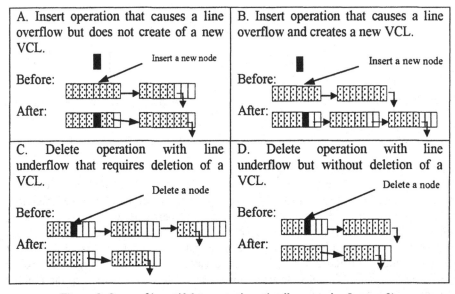

Figure 3. Cases of insert/delete operations (in all cases min=5, max=8).

The insert[2] algorithm of a new node to the list is shown in Figure 4. This procedure is being invoked each time a node should be inserted to a line and the line is full, meaning the VCL already contains max nodes.

We will save from the reader the formal details proving inductively that after performing the code derived from Figure 4 each VCL (except, maybe, the last one) contains between min and max nodes. However, intuitively it is easy to see that in all cases this inductive invariant holds. In Case 1 we found a VCL with at least one empty place so, shifting the nodes towards this empty place will enable us to insert the new node. Since we did not add any new line it is obvious that each line contains between min and max nodes. In Case 2 we scan min lines, each contains max nodes. This means we have seen min×max nodes. Since we created (max-min) new lines, it is clear that dividing the min×max original nodes to max lines yields min nodes in each line. Clearly in the first line we will have an extra node – the one we intended to insert. Case 3 is an end case. Since we allowed the last line to contain less then min nodes, it is possible to divide the original nodes in the desired fashion.

---

[2] The algorithm for the delete operation is completely analog. In order to increase readability we will save the details from the reader.

It is important to realize two major points: (a) In all cases, VCL overflow and VCL underflow require constant time only. (b) The two parameters - min and max - have to be chosen carefully. If they are too close to each other, then the number of memory allocations and deallocations caused by VCL overflow and underflow situations will increase and performance will degrade. In the other extreme, when min is much smaller than max, memory utilization diminishes, potentially introducing high overhead by way of paging.

```
Scan the list from the overflowed line till one of
the following is true:

Case 1: You reached a line that contains less then
max nodes.

Case 2: You scanned min lines and all of them
contain max nodes.

Case 3: You reached the end of the list.

In Case 1:
Reorganize the nodes in the lines you have just
scanned (including the one that has less than max
nodes) such that each line will have at least min
nodes

In Case 2:
Create (max - min) new VCLs. Reorganize the nodes
in the lines you have just scanned and the new
lines such that each line will have at least min
nodes.

In Case 3:
Reorganize the nodes in the lines you have just
scan such that each line will have at least min
nodes except the last one - if necessary create a
new VCL.
```

Figure 4. The insert algorithm in case of line overflow.

2.2 Performance evaluation of the VCL model in non-prefetching architecture

To assess the performance of the VCL scheme, the efficiency of a simple scan on the list was evaluated. It is easy to realize the importance of a highly efficient scan operation on the list. Since the linked list is a very basic data structure, most of its common operations like insert (after specific item), delete (a specific item) and find require at least partial scanning of the list.

We have measured the performance of three implementations of linked lists:

1. Scattered lists -- the standard implementation of linked lists, where each node is individually allocated by the memory manager. We were careful and constructed these lists by doing a large number of random insert and delete operations. In this way we promised that the nodes are truly scattered in memory, a typical situation to programs that manipulate large number of heap objects. This model is widely used in programs and user libraries [8].

2. Smart lists -- a linked list that uses the VCL mechanism.

3. Compressed lists -- a linked list that is mapped to an array. This can serve as a reference model since it offers optimal spatial locality. While this model is of no interest when it comes to update operations, it may be used as a lower bound when assessing performance of scan operations.

For convenience we assumed that the linked lists to be studied are sorted by a specific field called key. The Scattered and Smart lists implementations present the same interface to the invoking applications.

As a representative of non-prefetching architectures we chose the Intel Pentium. Moreover, testing the proposed model on such a popular processor is tempting. Intel's Pentium processor has an on-chip 8Kb data cache and a 256Kb L2 cache (instruction and data). Both caches have line size of 32 bytes. The operating system that we used was Windows 95. The Pentium architecture does not support prefetch instructions.

One last remark should be noted. Our main purpose is to show the potential improvement when using VCLs. We performed our experiments on lists that are constructed from nodes that span 8 bytes. It should be cleared that the improvement percentage (relatively to the Scattered list) one might gain when dealing with larger nodes is smaller. However, this improvement percentage is not the right way to light out results. The correct view is measuring the performance difference between the Smart list and the best performance one might achieve - the Compressed list. This difference is small regardless the nodes size.

2.2.1 Performance of list scanning operation

To assess the performance of scanning the list we ran 15,000 experiments. In each such experiment we randomly selected a value to be searched for, and then performed the search on the three list implementations. Since the search is a linear process, searching is actually scanning of the list. The code that we ran in all three cases is shown in Figure 5. In all cases lists with the same number of nodes are identical, meaning the contents of the nodes and the order between them is the same. The only difference between lists with the same length is their memory layout.

```
1.    current = list->head_address();
2.    while (current) {
3.        if (current->key == key_to_find)
4.            return current;  // End of the current
search
5.        current = current->next;
6.    }
```

Figure 5. The code for a single search operation. This code was performed for each of the lists' models.

We measured the time it took to complete the 15,000 searches in each of the implementation of the linked list. The test was repeated for several list sizes. We used a VCL with min=8 and max=10. The size of a single node (including the next pointer) was 8 bytes. Therefore, each VCL consumed 80 bytes out of which at least 64 were used. On the Pentium processor these numbers mean that the "busy" part of each VCL consumes 2-3 physical cache lines.

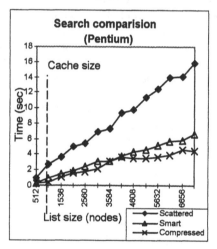
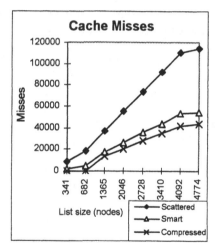

Figure 6. Time measured when performing 15,000 continuous searches on various sizes of lists using the three implementations of the linked list (Scattered, Compressed and VCLs).

Figure 7. Number of cache misses which occurred during a search operation using the three implementations of the linked list.

Figure 6 shows the performance results that we obtained. On average, Smart lists perform 2.48 times better than Scattered lists. For comparison reasons, observe that Scattered lists perform 3.4 times worse than Compressed lists. It is clear that when the list is smaller than the cache size, say 512 nodes which require 4Kb, the performance of the repeated searches through the list in the three implementations is similar.

Figure 7 presents the total number of cache misses which occurred during the run. The cache misses where measured by using Vtune® - commercial tool shipped by Intel. Two main observations are worth mentioning:

Observation 1: There is a high correlation between run-time performance and cache misses in the three implementations of the linked list.

Observation 2: The performance (time and cache misses) of Smart lists is close to that of Compressed lists.

The last observation is somewhat surprising. We see that the Smart list achieves a very close performance to the compressed list. However, the smart list is still scattered around in memory. In this case the nodes of the Smart list are allocated in groups of tens, which means we have a large number of independent groups (between 50 and 710 in the case of Figure 6. It seems that in order to get an 'array' performance small groups are enough.

2.2.2 Performance evaluation of insert/delete operations

Next, let us see how does insert and delete perform. The following experiment shows that maintaining linked lists is more efficient in the VCL model. In this experiment we compared the performance of Scattered and Smart lists (min=8, max=10). The two lists were built, by performing the same sequence of insert and delete operations. Obviously, the number of inserts was bigger than the number of deletes. Figure 8 presents the time it takes to build these lists with various sizes. The most important observation from this experiment is:

Observation 3: It is more efficient to maintain linked list in the VCL model than in the scattered implementation due to reduced number of memory manager invocations as well as lower number of cache misses (because of the implicit search operation).

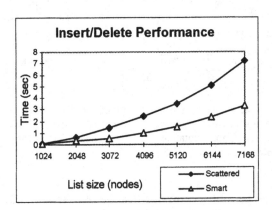

Figure 8. Comparison of the time it takes to maintain Scattered and Smart lists.

One point should be cleared. The relation between min and max values will influence the results of this experiment. If the difference between min and max will be large, then the number of node reorganizations (as described in 2.1.2) will decrease and the performance gap between the smart and the scattered list will widen. We choose these specific values for min and max for two main reasons:

1. These values were discovered as the appropriate values when trying to optimize the scan operation.
2. We want to demonstrate that even when the gap between min and max is small, the improvement in the performance of the insert and the delete operation is still measurable.

3. Prefetching Techniques for the VCL Model

This section presents an algorithm that improves the performance of the VCL scheme by using various aspects of the software prefetch mechanism. As a representative for architectures that support prefetching we choose the IBM PowerPC processor (model 604e) that implements the 'dcbt' (Data Cache Byte Touch) non-interrupted prefetch instruction. Another advantage of the PowerPC 604e processor is the fact that it has a prefetch queue that can tolerate up to four consecutive prefetch operations. The processor has an on-chip 32Kb data cache and a 512Kb L2 cache (instruction and data). Both caches have line size of 32 bytes. The operation system is AIX ver 4.1.

3.1 The Prefetch algorithm

The most popular prefetch technique in the case of recursive data structures is the Greedy-Prefetching [5]. The basic idea is very simple; when traversing the data structure, prefetch the nodes that are directly pointed by the current node. Figure 9 illustrates Greedy-Prefetch when traversing a linked list.

```
1. current := list->head_address();
2. while (current != NULL) {
3.         PREFETCH(current->next)
4.         WORK(current);
5.         current := current->next;
6. }
```

Figure 9. Greedy-Prefetching on a linked list.

Our prefetch approach takes a similar direction. However, instead of performing inter-prefetching between the nodes of the data structure, we perform inter prefetching between the VCLs. The prefetch method uses the fact that the VCLs themselves can be arranged in a linked list data structure. Therefore, when traversing the current VCL, the algorithm performs a prefetch to the next VCL. VCL prefetching means not only bringing a specific physical cache line into the cache, but using an arbitrary number of bytes starting from a specific address. This can be achieved by the new prefetch queue implemented on the PowerPC processor model 604e. This model supports a prefetch queue of up to four prefetch instructions, where each instruction refers to a single physical cache line. Therefore, prefetching the next VCL can be achieved by several sequential prefetches that refer to a small linear part of memory (our VCL). Figure 10 shows how to achieve a prefetch of a single VCL that is 128 bytes long using four 'regular' prefetch instructions.

```
1.    address = start_of_VCL
2.    prefetch(address,0);
3.    prefetch(address,32);
4.    prefetch(address,64);
5.    prefetch(address,96);
```

Figure 10. Prefetching a VCL with length of 128 bytes by applying 4 regular prefetch instructions each of 32 bytes.

By prefetching VCLs instead of the original nodes of the data structure, the proposed approach should overcome the main disadvantage of Greedy-Prefetching. As mentioned above, the Greedy-Prefetch performs prefetch to the 'closest' nodes. In some cases this prefetch will be done too late and hence fails to hide the memory latency caused by a cache miss. Actually, our results (in the next section), show that the Greedy-Prefetch can degrade performance in cases where a small amount of work is done on each node. By prefetching VCLs instead of nodes, the algorithm increases the gap between the prefetch instruction and the data usage. For example, assume that a single VCL consists of 12 original nodes; we can prefetch 12 nodes ahead instead of one. Figure 11 presents the code that traverses the list of VCLs and performs prefetch one VCL ahead.

```
1.  current_VCL = list->first_VCL();
2.  current = list->head_address();
3.  while (current_VCL) {
4.      prefetch_next_VCL(current_VCL->next));
5.      num = current_VCL->num_of_items();
6.      for (I=0 ; I< num ; I++) {
7.              WORK(current);
8.              current = current->next;
9.      }
10. current_VCL = current_VCL->next;
11.}
```

Figure 11. Prefetch of VCLs instead of original nodes.

Determining the length of the VCL is done by taking into account several architectural features. The number of nodes in each VCL is determined as follows: the time it takes to perform lines 6-9 in Figure 11 should be (approximately the same as) the time it takes to bring the following VCL into the cache. Hence, the optimal number of nodes in the VCL is directly influenced by an architectural feature; the time it takes to bring data into the cache. The second architectural component that we should consider when building the VCLs is the depth of the prefetch queue. As mentioned, prefetch of a single VCL is performed by several sequential physical cache line prefetches (Figure 10). Hence, the length of a VCL (in bytes) should be smaller than the maximal number of bytes that can be simultaneously prefetched by the prefetch queue.

3.2 Performance evaluation of the VCL model in prefetching architecture

To evaluate the suggested prefetching mechanism, we repeated the scan test on the three types of lists. We also compared our prefetch algorithm with the known Greedy-Prefetch (Figure 9). We repeated the comparison in several cases where the program performed a different amount of work in each node when traversing the list. The amount of work is measured in clock cycles and determined in the function call WORK (Figures 9,11). Again, each node is 8 bytes long and since the 604e processor supports up to four sequential prefetches, we built the VCLs with a maximum length of 128 bytes. This way we could simulate a VCL prefetch using up to four prefetch instructions.

Figure 12 presents the results we got. Some major points should be noted:

1. The Smart list with prefetching behaves better (approximately 25% improvement) than the Smart list without prefetching.
2. When the amount of work is small (less than 16 cycles per node) Greedy-Prefetch degrades performance.
3. The proposed prefetch method is better than Greedy-Prefetching in most cases and performs equally to it when we perform considerable amount of work on each node. This means that one can use the proposed method and achieve performance at least as good as the Greedy-Prefetch.

From these last points we can conclude the following main observation:

Observation 4: The combination of the VCL data layout and the prefetching technique improves the cache behavior of the Scattered linked list between 100% to 300%.

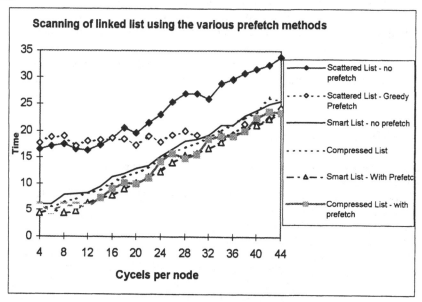

Figure 12. Evaluation of the prefetch algorithm

4. Future work and conclusions

Based on the lessons we learned from these preliminary results, we intend to continue our research in the following directions. First, we intend to find the precise connections between the length of the physical cache line and the virtual cache line. This connection is related to correctly choosing the values for the min and max parameters. Second, this research might be extended higher in the memory hierarchy and to more sophisticated data structures such as trees. However, we believe that the promising research direction is found in the shape analyses area. The opportunity to automatically transform a naive data structure and its implementation programmed by the user to more sophisticated structures and methods would enable us to insert the cache-aware data structures by the compiler without any assistance from the programmer.

Programs that use Recursive Data Structures (RDSs) usually suffer from poor cache behavior due to the lack of locality in their data layout. One of the most common ways to deal with memory latency is to use prefetching. While this approach wins a success in numeric applications [1,11], in a pointer intensive environment the prefetch solution is more complex and not widely applicable [5]. This paper presents a new method to deal with this challenging problem. The Virtual Cache Line mechanism groups together sequential nodes of a linked list. This grouping concept results in a notably higher spatial locality of the linked list and therefore improves its cache performance. Our results show that not only it is possible to handle the linked list in the VCL manner, it is even more efficient to do so. The insert/delete operation becomes more efficient, but the main result is that even without prefetching scanning the list improves by 200%. Combining the VCL method with our two new prefetching algorithms further improves the performance gain by an average factor of 300%.

We believe that these preliminary results provide motivation to keep and develop prefetching methods and mainly to make compilers to use them automatically.

References

1. Todd C. Mowry. Tolerating-Latency Through Software-Controlled Data Prefetching. Ph.D. thesis, Stanford University, 1994.
2. J. E. Bennet and M. J. Flynn. Reducing Cache Miss Rates Using Prediction Caches. Stanford University, CSL-TR-96-707, 1996.
3. Pentium Processor Family Developer Manual Vol 3. Intel, 1995 Edition.
4. Tom Shanley. PowerPc 601 Architecture. MindShare Press, 1994.
5. Chi-Keung Luk and Todd C. Mowry. Compiler-Based Prefetching for Recursive Data structures. In Proceeding of the 7th International Conference on Architectural Support for Programming Languages and Operating Systems, 1996.
6. Gupta, J. Hennessy, K. Gharachorloo, T. Mowry, and D. Weber. Comparative Evaluation of Latency Reducing and Tolerating Techniques. In Proceedings of the 18th Annual International Symposium on Computer Architecture, 1991.
7. Alvin R. Lebeck, D. A. Wood. Cache Profiling and the SPEC Bencmark: A Case Study. IEEE Computer, vol. 27, No. 10 Oct 1994

8. R. Musser, A. Saini. STL Tutorial and Reference Guide. Addison Wesley 1995.
9. Shapiro and S. Horwitz. Fast and Accurate Flow-Intensive Points to Analysis. Conference Record of the 24th ACM Symposium on Principles of Programming Languages, 1997.
10. Sagiv, T. Reps, R. Wilhem. Solving Shape-analysis Problems in Languages with destructive Updating. Conference Record of the 23th ACM Symposium on Principles of Programming Languages, 1996.
11. D. Bernstein, D Cohen, A Freund, D Mayden. Compiler Techniques for Data Prefetching on the PowerPC. In Proceedings of the International Conference of Parallel Architectures and Compilation Techniques. June 1995.
12. D. Callahan, K. Kennedy, A. Porterfield. Software Prefetching. In Proceeding of the 2sc International Conference on Architectural Support for Programming Languages and Operating Systems, 1991
13. R. Bayer and E. M. McCreight. Organization and Maintenance of Large Ordered Indexes. Acta Informatica 1(3): 173-189, 1972.
14. K. Pettis, R. C. Hansen. Profile Guided Code Positionig. In proceeding of the ACM SIGPLAN Conference on Programming Language Design and Implementation, 1990.
15. Sagiv, M., Reps, T., and Wilhelm, R., Parametric shape analysis via 3-valued logic. To appear in Conference Record of the Twenty-Sixth ACM Symposium on Principles of Programming Languages, New York, 1999.
16. Trishul Chilimbi, James Larus, and Mark Hill. Improving Pointer-Based Codes Through Cache-Conscious Data Placement, Wisconsin University Technical Report CS-TR-98-1365, 1998.
17. Brad Calder, Chandra Krintz, Simmi John, and Todd Austin, Cache-Conscious Data Placement, 8th International Conference on Architectural Support for Programming Languages and Operating Systems, 1998.
18. W. W. Hwu and P. P. Chang. Achieving High Instruction Cache Performance with an Optimizing Compiler. Proceedings of the 16th International Symposium on Computer Architecture, 1989.
19. M. Lam. Software Pipelining: An Effective Scheduling Technique for VLIW Machines. Proceedings of the SIGPLAN Annual Symposium, 1988.
20. Monica S. Lam, Edward E. Rothberg, Michael E. Wolf. The Cache Performance and Optimizations of Blocked Algorithms. In Proceeding of the 2sc International Conference on Architectural Support for Programming Languages and Operating Systems, 1991.
21. Trishul M. Chilimbi and James R. Larus. Using Generational Garbage Collection to Implement Cache-Conscious Data Placement. The International Symposium on Memory Management, 1998.

Extending Modulo Scheduling
with Memory Reference Merging

Benoît Dupont de Dinechin

ST Microelectronics, CMG/MDT Division
Benoit.Dupont-de-Dinechin@st.com

Abstract. We describe an extension of modulo scheduling, called "memory reference merging", which improves the management of cache bandwidth on microprocessors such as the DEC Alpha 21164. The principle is to schedule together memory references that are likely to be merged in a read buffer (LOADs), or a write buffer (STOREs). This technique has been used over several years on the Cray T3E block scheduler, and was later generalized to the Cray T3E software pipeliner. Experiments on the Cray T3E demonstrate the benefits of memory reference merging.

Introduction

As a result of the increasing gap between microprocessor processing speed, and memory bandwidth, cache optimization techniques play a major role in the performance of scientific codes. Cache optimization, like many other performance-improving optimizations, can be classified as high-level, or as low-level:

- High-level cache optimizations apply on a processor-independent program representation. High-level cache optimizations include loop restructuring transformations such as distribution, fusion, blocking, tiling, unimodular transformations [19], and unroll-and-jam [2].
- Low-level cache optimizations occur after instruction selection, when the program is represented as symbolic assembly code with pseudo-registers. The main motivation for low-level cache optimizations is that they may cooperate closely with instruction scheduling.

An important cache optimization, which is applied at high-level, low-level, or both, is prefetching / preloading [20] (non-binding / binding prefetching [10]):

- Prefetching describes the insertion of an instruction that has no architectural effects, beyond providing a hint to the hardware that some designated data should be promoted to upper levels of the memory hierarchy.
- Preloading consists in the execution of a some LOAD instructions early enough so that the corresponding datum has time to move through the memory hierarchy up to a register before its value is actually used.

A typical application of preloading as a low-level loop optimization is the static prediction of hit / miss behavior, so as to provide instruction schedulers with realistic LOAD latencies [4].

In the case of the Cray T3E computer, the interplay between instruction scheduling (block scheduling and software pipelining), and low-level cache optimizations, appears as a challenging problem. The processing nodes of this machine are based on DEC Alpha 21164 microprocessors, backed up by a significant amount of Cray custom logic, including hardware stream prefetchers [25]. As we developed the software pipeliner of the Cray T3E [5-7], we assumed that the subject of low-level cache optimizations would reduce to: insertion of prefetching instructions, conversion of some LOADs into preloading instructions, and scheduling of these with the suitable latency.

However, a number of prefetching and preloading experiments conducted on the Cray T3E revealed a complex behavior: neither the insertion of prefetching instructions, nor preloading with the off-chip access latency, yield consistent results [14]: a few loops display significant performance improvements, while most others suffer performance degradations. Currently, software prefetching on the Cray T3E is limited to library routines that were developed and optimized in assembly code. Compiler preloading amounts to scheduling LOADs that are assumed to miss with the level-2 (on-chip) cache latency.

Among the explanations is the fact that prefetching and preloading consume additional entries in a read buffer called "Miss Address File" on the DEC Alpha 21164. For a number of codes, MAF entries end up being the critical resource of inner loops. Performance of such loops used to be quite unpredictable, as merging of memory references in the read buffer and the write buffer happened as an uncontrolled side-effect of instruction scheduling. On these loops, block scheduling[1] would often perform better than software pipelining, because the latter technique spreads unrolled memory references across the loop schedule, eventually resulting in a lower amount of memory reference merging.

In this paper, we describe the "memory reference merging" optimization, which evolves from the simple "LOAD grouping" technique originally implemented in the block scheduler of the Cray T3D by Andrew Meltzer. Section 1 states the performance problem presented by memory hierarchies such as found on the DEC Alpha 21164, which motivates the memory reference merging optimization. Section 2 describes the design and implementation of this technique in the scheduling engine of the Cray T3E software pipeliner. Section 3 presents some of the experimental results of the memory reference merging optimization, obtained with the current Cray T3E production compilers.

1 Motivating Problem

1.1 Read and Write Buffers of the DEC Alpha 21164

Modern microprocessors have non-blocking data caches [9]: a LOAD instruction that misses in cache does not prevent subsequent instructions from being

---

[1] On the Cray T3E this includes "bottom-loading", a loop pipelining technique where the loop body is rotated before block scheduling so as to schedule LOADs with a longer latency.

issued, at least up to the first read reference to the LOAD's destination register. A restricted support for non-blocking LOADs was found on the DEC Alpha 21064 microprocessor, whose "load silo" could hold two outstanding level-1 cache misses, while servicing a third LOAD hit. In the DEC Alpha 21164 microprocessor [8], the load silo has been generalized to a Miss Address File, which is in fact a MSHR (Miss Status Holding Register) file as defined by Kroft [15].

More precisely, the DEC Alpha 21164 microprocessor includes [11]: a memory address translation unit or "Mbox"; a 8 KB level-1 data cache (Dcache), which is write-through, read-allocate, direct-mapped, with 32-byte blocks; a 96 KB level-2 instruction and data cache (Scache), which is write-back, write-allocate, 3-way set-associative, and is configured with either 32-byte or 64-byte blocks. The Dcache sustains two reads or one write per processor cycle. Maximum throughput of the Scache is one 32-byte block read or write per two cycles.

The Mbox itself contains several sections: the Data Translation Buffer (DTB), the Miss Address File (MAF), the Write Buffer (WB), and Dcache control logic [11]. When a LOAD instruction executes, the virtual address is translated, and Dcache access proceeds. In case of a Dcache miss, the six entries of the MAF are associatively searched for an address match at the 32-byte block granularity. If a match is found, and other implementation-related rules are satisfied, the new miss is merged in the matching MAF entry. If no match is found, or if merging cannot take place due to some reason, a new entry is allocated in the MAF. In case the MAF is full, the processor stalls until a new entry is available.

On the DEC Alpha 21164, the MAF is the read counterpart of a write buffer [26]: its purpose is to buffer unsatisfied read requests directed to a given 32-byte cache block, so that they can all be served in a single 2-cycle transaction when data returns from the Scache (or from external memory). Indeed, the WB on the DEC Alpha 21164 also maintains a file of six associative 32-byte blocks, and may store any of them to the Scache in a single 2-cycle transaction. Write buffer merging rules are less constrained than MAF merging rules though, mainly because a WB entry does not have to maintain a list of destination registers.

The performance implications of the MAF are quite significant: assuming all data read by a loop fits into the Scache, and that the access patterns and the instruction schedule are such that four 64-bit LOAD misses merge in every MAF entry, then the loop runs without memory stalls, provided that LOADs are scheduled with a suitable latency. On the other hand, if MAF merging is not exploited due to poor spatial locality, or because the LOADs to the same cache blocks are scheduled too many cycles apart, or due to some MAF implementation restriction, then the memory throughput cannot be better than one LOAD every other cycle, a fourfold decrease compared to Dcache bandwidth.

The ability to run at full speed when data is in Scache and not in Dcache is especially important on the DEC Alpha 21164. Indeed, there is no guarantee that floating-point data ever reaches Dcache when it is LOADed into a register from the Scache. The reason is that floating-point Dcache refills have the lowest priority when it comes to writing into Dcache [11]. In fact, for instruction scheduling purposes, Dcache behavior regarding to floating-point data is so unpredictable that it is better to assume it is not there [14]. In this respect the DEC Alpha 21164 appears quite similar to the MIPS R8000, whose memory system bypasses level-1 cache in case of floating-point references [12].

Just like the MAF, correct exploitation of the write buffer on DEC Alpha like processors yields significant performance improvements, as reported in [26].

1.2 Problem Statement

As discussed in the previous section, careful exploitation of the merging in a read buffer and/or a write buffer, such as the MAF and the WB of the DEC Alpha 21164, can significantly improve performance. The stage of compilation where such exploitation best takes place is instruction scheduling, as merging behavior ultimately depends on the relative issue dates of the mergeable instructions.

In this paper, we shall focus on modulo scheduling [21, 16, 3, 22], a widely used software pipelining technique which encompasses block scheduling as a degenerate case. Modulo scheduling is a software pipelining technique where all the loop iterations execute the same instruction schedule, called the *local schedule* [22, 16], and such that the execution of any two successive iterations is separated by a constant number of cycles, called the *Initiation Interval* (II). The general process of modulo scheduling can be summarized as follows:

1. Compute the lower bound *recMII* on the II, which makes scheduling possible as far as recurrence constraints are concerned. Compute the lower bound *resMII* on the II set by the resource constraints. This provides an initial value $\min(recMII, resMII)$ for the II.
2. Schedule the instructions, subjected to: (a) the modulo resource constraints at the current II must not be violated; (b) each instruction must be scheduled within its *margins*, that is, its current earliest and latest possible schedule dates (called Estart and Lstart by Huff [13]).

When all the instructions can be scheduled this way, the local schedule of the software pipeline is obtained. From this local schedule, the complete software pipeline code is constructed [23, 7].

In case the current instruction to schedule modulo resource conflicts with the already scheduled instructions for all dates within its margins, a *failure condition* is detected. Although failure at the current II can be handled in a variety of ways, the last resort is to increase the II, and to restart scheduling from scratch. Eventually this strategy succeeds, as modulo scheduling degenerates to block scheduling when the II grows large enough.

Within the framework of modulo scheduling and block scheduling, we state the problem of memory reference merging as follows:

- Compute the *merge intervals* associated to pairs of memory references. A merge interval is defined to contain the relative issue dates of the two references in the pair such that merging is possible, assuming that an entry is available in the read buffer (LOADs) or the write buffer (STOREs).

- While scheduling instructions, assume suitable read buffer or write buffer resource conflicts for any pair of mergeable memory references whose relative issue dates do not belong to one of the merge intervals of that pair.

Still the purpose of the instruction scheduler is to reduce execution times, either by minimizing the length of the instruction schedule (block scheduling), or by maximizing the loop throughput (software pipelining).

Although motivated by the DEC Alpha 21164 memory hierarchy, memory reference merging has wider applications than optimizing instruction schedules for that microprocessor. In particular, the recently available DEC Alpha 21264 microprocessor extends the number of entries in the read buffer and the write buffer to eight, while the block size of the individual buffer entries increases from 32 to 64 bytes. Unlike the Scache of the DEC Alpha 21164, the level-2 cache of the DEC Alpha 21264 is not on-chip. As a result, memory reference merging is likely to become a key optimization on the DEC Alpha 21264.

On the MIPS R8000, best performing instruction schedules are obtained by "pairing" memory references. The principle of pairing is to allow dual-issuing of memory references only in cases they are guaranteed to access distinct cache banks [27]. Pairing is implemented in the MIPSpro heuristic-based modulo scheduler, which betters the MIPS R8000 optimum integer linear programming modulo scheduler [24] by as much as 8% geometric performance mean on SPEC FP benchmark. It was not until after the latter was extended to include pairing that performance of the two software pipeliners became comparable [27]. As we shall see, pairing is a special case of memory reference merging.

Other simple forms of memory reference merging apply to other processors, such as fusing pairs of LOADs on the IBM POWER 2 to take advantage of the higher cache bandwidth available from quad-word (128 bits) LOAD instructions.

2 Memory Reference Merging

2.1 Approximating Merge Intervals

Memory reference merging is an optimization that applies during instruction scheduling of inner loops. At this stage of the compilation process, memory references can be partitioned into three classes:

- memory references whose effective address is a loop-invariant expression;
- memory references whose effective address is an inductive expression with a compile-time constant step (*simple inductions* [7]);
- memory references whose effective address is a complex loop-variant expression, including inductive expressions with a symbolic step.

Let k be the normalized loop counter of the inner loop. We shall abstract the effective address of memory reference i in the loop body as $(r_i + k\delta_i + o_i)$, where r_i is a base value, δ_i is the induction step, and o_i is a constant offset. In cases of complex loop-variant effective address expressions, we shall assume that the induction step value δ_i is $\perp$ (undefined). Merge buffer entry block size is denoted b (32 bytes on the DEC Alpha 21164). All the quantities r_i, δ_i, o_i, b are expressed in the lower addressable unit of the machine, typically a byte.

The first step of memory reference merging is to partition the memory references of the loop body into *base groups*. A base group contains all the references that can share the same base value and induction step, perhaps after some adjustments of the offset values. As a matter of illustration, let us consider the following cases, where the value of j is unknown at compile-time:

```
while (i < n) {          while (i < n) {          while (i < n) {
    ... = a[i];              ... = a[i];              ... = a[i];
    i = i + 1;               i = i + j;               ... = a[i-3];
    ... = a[i-3];            ... = a[i-3];            i = i + j;
}                        }                        }
```

In the first case, the two memory references to a belong to the same base group, with respective offsets 0 and -2. In the second case, the unknown value of j forces the two memory references into different base groups. In the third case, even though the induction step is a compile-time unknown, the two memory references to a can again be folded into the same group, with offsets 0 and -3.

Once base groups are available, we define the *mergeable* memory references as those that will use an entry in the read buffer or the write buffer. On the DEC Alpha 21164, this rules out Dcache hits, which we assume only for integer LOADs with a loop-invariant effective address. Then, among the mergeable memory references, we identify the *incompatible* pairs:

- Any two memory references from different base groups do not merge.
- A LOAD and a STORE cannot merge, since they go respectively to the read buffer (MAF on the DEC Alpha 21164), and to the write buffer.
- The read buffer may rule out merging for implementation-related limitations. For instance the MAF of the DEC Alpha 21164 prevents LOADs of different data sizes, data types, or 4-byte alignment, from merging [11].

The merge intervals of incompatible pairs are obviously the empty set. For the other (compatible) pairs, we assume that merging is possible provided that:

(1) the two effective addresses fall in the same merge buffer entry, which is an aligned block of b addressable units;
(2) in the case of LOADs, the two effective addresses must not refer to the same word[2], which is an aligned block of w addressable units;
(3) the two issue dates t_i and t_j are no more than m cycles apart.

This value m represents the upper limit on the number of cycles below which the hardware may consider two memory references as candidates for merging.

Absolute alignments are impractical to manage at compile-time, since the number of cases to consider grows exponentially with the number of memory reference streams in the loop. Thus we approximate conditions (1) and (2) as:

---

[2] This is an implementation-related restriction. On the DEC Alpha 21164, w is 8 bytes.

(1') the two effective addresses differ by no more than b addressable units.
(2') the two LOAD effective addresses differ by more than w addressable units.

Although conditions (1'), (2'), and (3), are accurate enough for the purposes of block scheduling, they miss many opportunities of merging in the case of modulo scheduling. Indeed modulo scheduling works by overlapping the execution of successive loop iterations. For any two memory references i and j of the loop body, we must account for the possibility of merging between $i_{k'}$ and $j_{k''}$, where $i_{k'}$ and $j_{k''}$ denote respectively the k'-th and k''-th instances of memory references i and j. Conditions (1'), (2'), (3) then become:

(a) $(r + k''\delta + o_j) - (r + k'\delta + o_i) \in [-b+1, b-1]$
    ($r_i = r_j = r$, and $\delta_i = \delta_j = \delta$, since i and j are in the same base group)
(b) $(r + k''\delta + o_j) - (r + k'\delta + o_i) \notin [-w+1, w-1]$
    (assume $w = 0$ in case of STOREs, so that $[-w+1, w-1] = \emptyset$)
(c) $(t_j + k''\lambda) - (t_i + k'\lambda) \in [-m+1, m-1]$
    (λ is the current value of the initiation interval of the software pipeline)

Computing merge intervals for memory references i and j now reduces to:

- Find the set K_{ij} of all values $k \stackrel{\text{def}}{=} k' - k''$ that satisfy (a), (b), and (c).
- The merge intervals are $[k\lambda - m + 1, k\lambda + m - 1] \cap [t_{ij}^-, t_{ij}^+], k \in K_{ij}$.

Here $[t_{ij}^-, t_{ij}^+]$ denotes the admissible range of $t_j - t_i$ while scheduling instructions.

The set K_{ij} associated to a memory reference pair (i, j) is actually straightforward to compute using interval arithmetic. Let us first define, for any integers a, b, c, the *reduce* operation on interval $I \stackrel{\text{def}}{=} [a, b]$ as:

$$\text{reduce}([a,b], c) \stackrel{\text{def}}{=} \begin{vmatrix} c > 0 & \rightarrow [\lceil \frac{a}{c} \rceil, \lfloor \frac{b}{c} \rfloor] \\ c < 0 & \rightarrow [\lceil \frac{-b}{-c} \rceil, \lfloor \frac{-a}{-c} \rfloor] \\ c = 0 \wedge a \leq 0 \wedge b \geq 0 & \rightarrow \ ]-\infty, +\infty[\\ c = \bot \wedge a \leq 0 \wedge b \geq 0 & \rightarrow [0, 0] \\ \text{default} & \rightarrow \emptyset \end{vmatrix}$$

In other words, $I' \stackrel{\text{def}}{=} \text{reduce}(I, c)$ is the maximum interval such that $cI' \subseteq I$. The reduce operation allows to compute K_{ij} in just four simple steps:

- $I_o^- \stackrel{\text{def}}{=} [o_j - o_i - b + 1, o_j - o_i - w]$
  (I_o^- contains all the $k\delta$ such that $o_j - o_i - k\delta \in]w - 1, b - 1]$)
- $I_o^+ \stackrel{\text{def}}{=} [o_j - o_i + w, o_j - o_i + b - 1]$
  (I_o^+ contains all the $k\delta$ such that $o_j - o_i - k\delta \in [-b+1, -w+1[$)
- $I_d \stackrel{\text{def}}{=} [t_{ij}^- - m + 1, t_{ij}^+ + m - 1]$
  (I_d contains all the $k\lambda$ such that $t_j - t_i - k\lambda \in [-m + 1, m - 1]$)
- $K_{ij} \stackrel{\text{def}}{=} (\text{reduce}(I_o^-, \delta) \cup \text{reduce}(I_o^+, \delta)) \cap \text{reduce}(I_d, \lambda)$

It is easy to check that K_{ij} computed this way is tight, that is, it does not contain values of $k \overset{\text{def}}{=} k' - k''$ which do not satisfy conditions (a), (b), and (c).

An important property is that we are able derive non-empty K_{ij} even if the induction step δ is undefined ($\bot$). In that case, only memory reference pairs from the same iteration may merge together, a condition which is good enough for many of the loops unrolled by the high-level optimizer. The main point of handling undefined induction steps however is that the technique now applies to block scheduling as well. All that is required in this case is to carry the K_{ij} computations with a suitably large value of λ.

2.2 Modulo Scheduling Extensions

According to the description of modulo scheduling given in section 1.2, the integration of memory reference merging involves the following extensions:

- Introduce a single "Cache Bandwidth" (CB) resource in the processor modelization. Extend the reservation tables so that all mergeable memory references use the CB resource for some time. Only two mergeable memory references that are scheduled within one of the associated merge intervals may use the CB resource at the same time. This CB resource modelizes the bandwidth limit between the two levels of the memory hierarchy where read buffers and write buffers operate.

  First, we considered introducing resources to represent individual read buffer and write buffer entries. However, the primary purpose of these buffers is to supply a continuous flow of read or write requests to the lower level of the memory hierarchy (the Scache on the DEC Alpha 21164). As long as these buffers do not overflow, the single CB resource accurately represents the run-time behavior of the memory system. In our implementation, a mergeable memory reference reserves CB for 2 cycles.

- When computing *resMII*, take into account the fact that some memory references will be merged. Compared to modulo scheduling without memory reference merging, the only difference is the need to introduce the minimum possible use of the CB resource as a lower bound for *resMII*.

  The minimum possible use of the CB resource is computed by constructing the *merge sets*, defined as all the subsets of the equivalence classes of the "merge intervals are not empty" binary relation. These sets are weighted by their minimum collective use of the CB resource, and the total minimum use of the CB resource is obtained as the solution of the so-called "Weighted Vertex Cover" problem [1]

  An exact computation of the minimum possible use of the CB resource could be expensive, but is not required. Indeed this value only impacts the computation of *resMII*. Assuming zero as the minimum possible use of the CB resource when computing *resMII* only enables the modulo scheduler to attempt modulo scheduling at values of the *II* that are too low to succeed.

- In case of a heuristic modulo scheduler, when selecting a mergeable memory reference as the current instruction to schedule, we first try the schedule dates that intersect the maximum number of merge intervals from the pairs whose first member is the current instruction, and whose second member is an already scheduled memory reference instruction.

Indeed heuristic modulo schedulers make decisions at two levels: what is the next instruction to schedule, and what are the schedule dates to try first. In our implementation, memory reference merging only impacts the first decision in an indirect way: our scheduling priority function weights the not yet scheduled instructions by adding their use of the loop critical resource, and by subtracting their scheduling slack [13]. Trying the schedule dates where merging will occur first is a very light modification of the scheduling engine that produces very satisfactory results.

3   Experimental Results

The experimental results presented in this section are performance numbers obtained in dedicated mode[3] on a Cray T3E-600. On this first-generation Cray T3E, the microprocessor clock frequency is 300 MHz, leading to a theoretical peak performance of 600 MFLOPS per processing node. The more recent Cray T3E-900 presents several improvements over the Cray T3E-600, including versions of the DEC Alpha 21164 microprocessor with the redesigned DEC EV-56 logic core, and a microprocessor clock frequency increased to 450 MHz.

In order to better appreciate our performance numbers, let us first provide some quantitative data about the memory bandwidth problem on machines powered by a DEC Alpha 21164 such as the Cray T3E. Typical scientific applications are known to require a balance of about two LOADs and one STORE per floating-point multiplication-addition. By tabulating the floating-point operations (FLO) per cycle scaled from the bandwidth by 2/3, we obtain a realistic upper bound on the floating-point performance of a typical scientific application:

Level	Words / Cycle	Scaled FLO / Cycle	Restrictions
Dcache	2	1.33	Direct-Mapped
Scache	2	1.33	32-byte Block
Streams	.53	.35	6 Streams
E-registers	.33	.22	Distribution
DRAM Page Hit	.31	.20	1-Entry Buffer
DRAM Page Miss	.21	.14	Local Memory

For more details about the various levels of the Cray T3E memory hierarchy, please refer to [25]. Although the DEC Alpha 21164 of a Cray T3E-600 is rated at 600 MFLOPS peak, a 2/3 ratio between floating-point operations and memory accesses imply that the performance upper bound is more in the range of 450 MFLOPS under the best cases of Scache bandwidth exploitation. For applications that need to access memory off-chip, an upper bound of 84 MFLOPS is expected in cases the accesses hit the DRAM in non-paged mode.

---

[3] Special thanks to Sean Palmer, Tuyet-Anh Tran, and Anand Singh, from Cray Research, for preparing and running these experiments.

When running the experiments, the Cray f90 Fortran compiler was used with options -Ounroll2 -Opipeline2. The -Ounroll2 option enables automatic unrolling by a compiler-selected amount, typically 4. Unrolling by 4 is a good overall tradeoff, as it creates groups of 4 memory references which could theoretically merge in a single MAF or WB entry, in the case of dense 64-bit access streams. Higher levels of unrolling can be specified at the source code level by inserting compiler directives. Unrolling by 8 potentially yields higher performance, but significantly increases the chance that the software pipeliner runs out of registers. When this happens, the loop is not software pipelined.

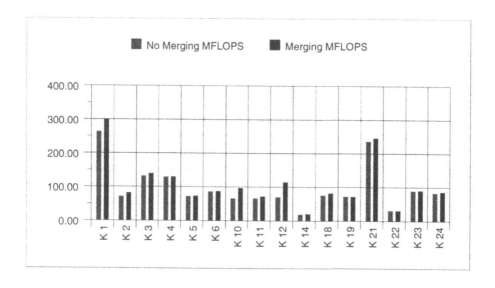

Fig. 1. Livermore loops.

The first set of results, displayed in figure 1, was obtained by running the livkern.f program (9/OCT/91 version mf523), also known as the Livermore loops. Although performance numbers are collected by this program for 24 kernels, we only include results for the loops that were successfully software pipelined. In particular kernels 7, 8, 9, 13, are not software pipelined under -Ounroll2, due to high register pressure. The other reason some of the kernels are not software pipelined is the lack of IF-conversion in the Cray T3E compiler. In figure 1, memory reference merging is effective on loops K1, K10, and K12.

The second set of results, displayed in figure 2, comes from the "Linpack" benchmark by Dongarra. Among the 19 loops in this program that do not contain subroutines calls nor conditionals, 17 were software pipelined. A geometric mean performance improvement of 1.41 was obtained, and is explained by the fact that all data referenced is in Scache, while all the pipelined loops are parallel or vector

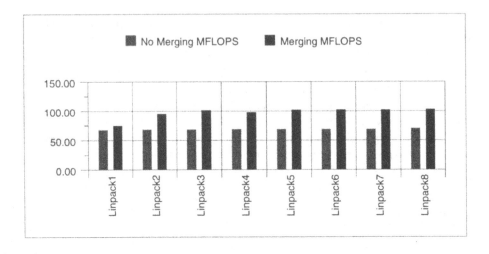

Fig. 2. Linpack benchmark.

with dense access streams. Under these conditions, memory reference merging is able to exploit most of the Scache bandwidth available.

The third set of of results appears in figure 3, which displays the percentages of relative performance improvement of memory reference merging over the non-merging case for different applications from the Applied Parallel Research suite. Here again some improvements are significant, in particular for programs X42 (351 lines, 21.75% increase), and APPSP (4634 lines, 9.5% increase). In some cases such as SCALGAM and SHALLOW77, performance is degraded by as much as 2%. We could trace these degradations to MAF entry full conditions, which are triggered because memory reference merging only manages *bandwidth* between Dcache and Scache, and not the number of read or write buffer entries.

4   Related Work

The principle of memory reference merging is to compute and associate "merge intervals" to "mergeable" memory reference pairs, and to introduce a single "Cache Bandwidth" (CB) resource in the processor modelization. The modulo scheduler is then extended to assume pairwise conflicts on the CB resource for all mergeable memory references, except for those that are scheduled within one of the merge intervals associated to the mergeable memory reference pair.

Computing the merge intervals bears similarities with *reuse analysis*, that is, identifying the number of distinct cache blocks referenced in a loop, in order to guide locality-enhancing loop restructuring [19], or to insert a minimum number of prefetch instructions [20]. Although we only perform reuse analysis at the innermost loop level, we are able to handle compile-time unknown induction steps, whereas traditional techniques require compile-constant induction steps. Work reported in [4] applies reuse analysis to the static prediction of hit / miss

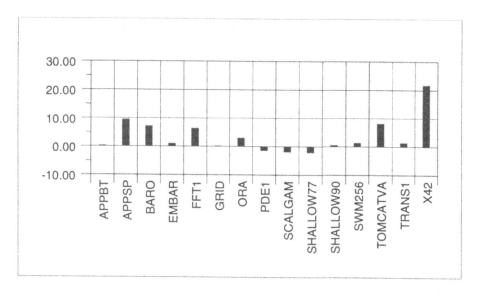

Fig. 3. Applied Parallel Research suite % relative improvements.

behavior. It can be seen as a preliminary step for memory reference merging, as we do not consider LOAD hits as mergeable (they do not use the CB resource).

Following an innovative line of research, López, Valero, Llosa, and Ayguadé [18, 17] develop a compilation technique where loop bodies are unrolled, and the memory accesses are packed in case the target architecture supports "widened" data and memory paths. The resulting scheduling graph is then scheduled using a traditional modulo scheduler. The primary difference between "compaction of memory accesses" [18] and memory reference merging, is that the technique of López et al. operates before modulo scheduling, and requires a specific architectural support: packed versions of arithmetic and memory instructions.

More related to our work is the "memory bank pairing" optimization formulated by Stoutchinin [27]. This technique avoids level-2 cache bank conflicts on the MIPS R8000 by preventing two loads that may access the same cache bank from issuing at the same cycle. This optimization appears as a form of memory reference merging with single-cycle merge intervals ($m = 1$), once the constant offsets of the effective addresses are reduced modulo 16. This work is significant to us, as it demonstrates that a simpler variant of the memory reference merging problem can be formulated and solved in the framework of optimal modulo scheduling using integer linear programming.

Conclusion

This paper describes the design, implementation, and experimental results, of the memory reference merging extension of the Cray T3E modulo scheduler. This technique takes advantage of the read and write buffers present at the higher levels of a memory hierarchy, specifically the MAF and the WB of the DEC

Alpha 21164 microprocessor. Experiments demonstrate that memory reference merging is quite effective: on the Cray T3E-600 production compiler, it improves the geometric mean performance of the Linpack benchmark by as much as 41%.

More generally, memory reference merging improves block scheduling and modulo scheduling on processors whose memory hierarchy favors a regular form of coupling between spatial (effective addresses) and temporal (schedule dates) locality of memory references: read and write buffers (DEC Alpha 21164, DEC Alpha 21264), and multi-banked interleaved caches (MIPS R8000). Memory reference merging also provides the proper foundations for automatic packing of memory references (IBM POWER 2, "widened" [18] processors).

References

1. R. BAR-YEHUDA, S. EVEN: *A Linear-Time Approximation for the Weighted Set Cover Problem* Journal of Algorithms, Vol. 2, 1981.
2. S. CARR, Y. GUAN: *Unroll-and-Jam Using Uniformly Generated Sets* Micro-30 – Proceedings of the 30th International Symposium on Microarchitecture, Dec. 1997.
3. J. C. DEHNERT, R. A. TOWLE: *Compiling for Cydra 5* Journal of Supercomputing, vol. 7, pp. 181–227, May 1993.
4. C. DING, S. CARR, P. SWEANY: *Modulo Scheduling with Cache-Reuse Information* Proceedings of EuroPar'97, LNCS #1300, Aug. 1997.
5. B. DUPONT DE DINECHIN: *Insertion Scheduling: An Alternative to List Scheduling for Modulo Schedulers* LCPC'96 – 8th International Workshop on Languages and Compilers for Parallel Computing, LNCS #1033, Colombus, Ohio, Aug. 1995.
6. B. DUPONT DE DINECHIN: *Parametric Computation of Margins and of Minimum Cumulative Register Lifetime Dates* LCPC'97 – 9th International Workshop on Languages and Compilers for Parallel Computing, LNCS #1239, San Jose, California, Aug. 1996.
7. B. DUPONT DE DINECHIN: *A Unified Software Pipeline Construction Scheme for Modulo Scheduled Loops* PaCT'97 – 4th International Conference on Parallel Computing Technologies, LNCS #1277, Yaroslavl, Russia, Sep. 1997.
8. *Internal Organization of the Alpha 21164, a 300-MHz 64-bit Quad-issue CMOS RISC Microprocessor* Digital Technical Journal, Vol. 7, No. 1, Jan. 1995.
9. KEITH I. FARKAS, NORMAN P. JOUPPI: *Complexity/Performance Tradeoffs with Non-Blocking Loads* WRL Research Report 94/3, Western Research Laboratory, Mar. 1994.
10. A. GUPTA, J. HENNESSY, K. GHARACHORLOO, T. MOWRY, W.-D. WEBER: *Comparative Evaluation of Latency Reducing and Tolerating Techniques* ISCA'91 – 18th International Symposium on Computer Architecture, May 1991.
11. *Alpha 21164 Microprocessor Hardware Reference Manual*, Document EC-QAEQB-TE, Digital Equipment Corporation.
12. P. Y.-T. HSU: *Design of the R8000 Microprocessor* IEEE Micro, 1993.
13. R. A. HUFF: *Lifetime-Sensitive Modulo Scheduling* PLDI'93 – Conference on Programming Language Design and Implementation, June 1993.
14. R. E. KESSLER: *Livermore Loops Single-Node Code Optimization for the CRAY T3E* Technical Report, System Performance Group, Cray Research Inc., 1995.
15. D. KROFT: *Lockup-Free Fetch/Prefetch Cache Organization* ISCA'81 – 8th International Symposium on Computer Architecture, May 1981.

16. M. LAM: *Software Pipelining: An Effective Scheduling Technique for VLIW Machines* PLDI'88 – Conference on Programming Language Design and Implementation, 1988.

17. D. LÓPEZ, J. LLOSA, M. VALERO, E. AYGUADÉ: *Resource Widening Versus Replication: Limits and Performance-Cost Trade-off* ICS-12 – 12th International Conference on Supercomputing, Melbourne, Australia, July 1998.

18. D. LÓPEZ, M. VALERO, J. LLOSA, E. AYGUADÉ: *Increasing Memory Bandwidth with Wide Buses: Compiler, Hardware and Performance Trade-offs* ICS-11 – 11th International Conference on Supercomputing, Vienna, Austria, July 1997.

19. K. MCKINLEY, S. CARR, C.-W. TSENG: *Improving Data Locality with Loop Transformations* ACM Transactions on Programming Languages and Systems, Vol. 18, No. 4, Jul. 1996.

20. T. C. MOWRY, M. S. LAM, A. GUPTA: *Design and Evaluation of a Compiler Algorithm for Prefetching* ASPLOS-V – Proceedings of the Fifth International Conference on Architectural Support for Programming Languages and Operating Systems, Boston, MA, 1992.

21. B. R. RAU, C. D. GLAESER: *Some Scheduling Techniques and an Easily Schedulable Horizontal Architecture for High Performance Scientific Computing* 14th Annual Workshop on Microprogramming, Oct. 1981.

22. B. R. RAU: *Iterative Modulo Scheduling: An Algorithm for Software Pipelining Loops* MICRO-27 – 27th Annual International Symposium on Microarchitecture, San Jose, California, Nov. 1994.

23. B. R. RAU, M. S. SCHLANSKER, P. P. TIRUMALAI: *Code Generation Schemas for Modulo Scheduled Loops* MICRO-25 – 25th Annual International Symposium on Microarchitecture, Portland, Dec. 1992.

24. J. C. RUTTENBERG, G. R. GAO, A. STOUTCHININ, W. LICHTENSTEIN: *Software Pipelining Showdown: Optimal vs. Heuristic Methods in a Production Compiler* PLDI'96 – Conference on Programming Language Design and Implementation, Philadelphia, PA, May 1996.

25. S. L. SCOTT: *Synchronization and Communication in the T3E Multiprocessor* ASPLOS-VII – Proceedings of the Seventh International Conference on Architectural Support for Programming Languages and Operating Systems, Cambridge, MA, Oct. 1996.

26. K. SKADRON, D. W. CLARK: *Design Issues and Tradeoffs for Write Buffers* HPCA'97 – Proceedings of the 3rd International Symposium on Computer Architecture, San Antonio, TX, Feb. 1997.

27. A. STOUTCHININ: *An Integer Linear Programming Model of Software Pipelining for the MIPS R8000 Processor* PaCT'97 – 4th International Conference on Parallel Computing Technologies, Yaroslavl, Russia, Sep. 1997.

*TRAP*ping Modelica with Python

Thilo Ernst

GMD FIRST Research Institute for Computer Architecture
and Software Technology
Rudower Chaussee 5
D-12489 Berlin, Germany
Thilo.Ernst@gmd.de

Abstract. This short paper[1] introduces *TRAP*, a small but powerful compiler development system based on the object-oriented, dynamic language Python. Employing a very high level language as a compiler tool's base language reduces the need for additional tool support and importing library functionality to a minimum. Python in particular has the additional advantage of being a powerful and already quite popular general-purpose component integration framework, which can be utilized both for incorporating subcomponents and for embedding the compiler developed into a larger system. Exploiting these strengths, *TRAP* enables rapid prototyping and development of compilers - in particular, translators for medium-complexity special purpose languages - on a very high level of abstraction.

1 Starting point: Modelica, SMILE, and Python

Modelica[1] is a unified, object-oriented description language for dynamic models of complex physical systems being developed in an international effort. GMD is developing an experimental Modelica compiler for integration into the SMILE dynamic simulation environment[2] which in its latest revision heavily builds on the object-oriented dynamic language Python[3] as an open component integration platform. For that reason the Modelica compiler, too, was to be integrated using a Python interface. This situation triggered a closer investigation of the idea of implementing the compiler directly in Python. The language turned out to be very suitable for the purpose; in addition basic compiler construction tool components in Python were already available. As the extra effort needed was limited, the approach taken was to integrate these components and fill the remaining gaps to obtain a Python-based compiler construction system called *TRAP*, based on which the Modelica compiler is implemented.

2 Python as a compiler implementation language

Python has many features using which common compiler problem patterns can be approached effectively. These problems would require considerable coding, debugging and maintenance efforts using standard implementation languages, whereas compiler tool support is often insufficient, overspecialized, or handicapped by unrelated tool limitations. The following Python features are most relevant:

---

[1] A long version is available from the author on request

Lists and tuples, i.e. (mutable and immutable) *sequence types* with their built-in operations are useful to express simple, incremental set-manipulation based algorithms which are ubiquitous in compilers.

Dictionaries represent *mappings* between sets of Python objects, and perfectly model compiler concepts like "symbol table" or "name space".

Python's Object model is well-suited for modeling abstract syntax tree- or graph-shaped *internal representations* (IRs) , i.e., *node types* ordered into a hierarchy. The language's dynamic type system can be easily exploited to enforce local IR wellformedness constraints. Generally, the language enables the application of modern, object-oriented compiler implementation techniques.

Functional *and* imperative programming. Python's object-reference passing semantics together with the sequence types already mentioned allows the user to mix functional and imperative programming as appropriate for the task at hand.

Automatic memory management saves the developer much trouble as extensive manipulation of recursive data structures is central in compilers.

Of course there are other very high level languages offering comparably well-suited, or even richer feature sets. However, compilers (in particular those for special-purpose languages, like in the SMILE/Modelica case) often need to be embedded into larger software systems, at which point aspects like ease of integration, portability, ease of reuse, readability, ease of learning, popularity, availability of library modules and development tools, and development productivity become at least equally important as the language's internal qualities. Being admittedly prepossessed, we still find Python to represent a pretty unique balance among this interdependent (and partly conflicting) set of goals.

3 Designing *TRAP*

Compiler construction tools offer a set of more or less compiler-specific programming abstractions in the form of dedicated *compiler description language* constructs. From the description, the tool generates the actual compiler in some *implementation* or *base language*. As each tool's functionality has its limits, escape mechanisms to the base language are usually offered (and tend to be heavily used in nontrivial compilers). Unfortunately, this language often turns out to be inadequate, i.e., too low-level, for the problem that required the escape; C is employed frequently in this role. Each concrete instance of this problem can be "solved" by putting in additional coding effort, integrating suitable libraries, etc. However apart from the immediate cost, this can increase the complexity of the compiler as a software system to an extent not justified by the purpose and severely damage its readability and maintainability.

To generally avoid this problem while at the same time reduce the functionality to be added by the compiler tool to a necessary minimum, we propose to use a very high level language in the role of the base language. As motivated in the previous section, we found Python to be an excellent candidate.

The main (technical) problem areas in compiler development, which should be well supported by any compiler tool or set thereof, are: construction of the front-end (scanner and parser), definition of the internal IR data structure, and description of the transformation algorithms working on the IR.

With Python as the implementation language, we found that a new generative tool would only be needed to support the definition of IR data structures: Front-end generation tools are available and can be reused easily. W.r.t. transformation algorithms, we found Python's own expressiveness (enhanced by a set of generated IR manipulation methods) sufficient.

Based on these observations, a compiler description language consisting of a grammar description part and an IR description part was designed, and a Python-based compiler tool *TRAP* (Translator RApid Prototyping) was developed, processing it as follows: From the grammar description part, a scanner and parser module is generated using an LR parser generator[2]. From the IR description part, an IR module is generated. The resulting compiler consists of these generated Python modules and an arbitrary number of transformation and auxilliary modules directly written in or interfaced with Python. In more detail, *TRAP* has the following main characteristics:

Integrated syntax/semantics description. An EBNF-like grammar description language is offered which tightly integrates concrete syntax (including lexics), the construction of initial semantics values., and the specification of type constraints to the latter. The computation of a semantics value is expressed as Python code right in the corresponding grammar rule. Where no semantics action is specified, an appropriate default semantics takes effect. EBNF-style repetition constructs are supported, with an automatic semantics constructing Python sequences. Semantically insignificant separators and terminators can be specified here, too. A sample nonterminal definition with one rule (including an explicit semantics action):

```
nterm print_stmt::STMT     # type constraint: node type
   <- "print" ["," expr *]=eList:   # comma-sep. list
      Print_stmt(eList)      # invoke node constructor
```

Hierarchical IR description language. The IR description allows to concisely describe IR data structure patterns (i.e., node sorts with typed fields) ordered into a type hierarchy, very similar to *ast*[7]. From this description, a set of Python class definitions to be used in the compiler being developed is generated. These classes also contain generated methods for constructing, typechecking, printing, traversing, and matching IR subgraphs, to be used in initial semantics actions as well as in transformation modules.

"No" transformation language. Transformations and other IR processing algorithms are expressed directly in Python, relying on generated methods in the IR module as needed. Python is flexible enough to express important compiler-specific concepts without syntactic extensions; for example, Pythons '^' operator was overloaded to represent pattern matching when applied to IR objects, with patterns expressed by nested node constructors, and '_' acting as a wildcard. Thus, for transformations, there is no separate

---

[2] currently, A.Watters' kwParsing package (`http://www.chordate.com/kwParsing`)

description level, no interfacing problems between both levels, and no generation step in each (transformation) development cycle (only IR definition changes require re-generation).

Rapid prototyping/development (RP/RAD). Python's power as a component integration framework and its efficient development methodology are applicable to the domain of compiler construction. It is easy to replace a compiler component developed in Python by an "extension", i.e., an optimized low-level implementation. For instance, a graph algorithm is prototyped as a Python class and later on substituted by a bitset-based C implementation equipped with the same Python class interface, without a need for modifying its "client code".

The design of *TRAP*'s compiler description language was inspired heavily by concepts from and/or experience with the following tools: Gentle[4], CoSy[5], Smart[6], Cocktail[7], Depot[8], PCCTS[9], and JAMOOS[10]. Its "look and feel" attempts to stay close to the base language.

4 Conclusions

TRAP, a Python-based compiler construction tool was presented. *TRAP* largely integrates successful concepts from other compiler tools. Its main contribution is their combination with a very high level , object-oriented implementation language. *TRAP* was succesfully applied for generating compilers for two nontrivial languages: *TRAP*'s own compiler description language, and Modelica, the latter being already a medium-sized example. The RP/RAD methodology was proven feasible by integrating a fast, handwritten Modelica lexer subcomponent.

Its characteristics should make the *TRAP* system well-suited for a broad range of compiler prototyping and development tasks, in particular for special-purpose languages of small-to-medium complexity. Its high level of abstraction and its platform-independent availability could make it attractive also for educational purposes.

References

1. The Modelica Design Group: *Modelica - A Unified Object-Oriented Language for Physical Systems Modeling*. http://www.dynasim.se/Modelica, 1997
2. Ernst, T.; Jähnichen, S; Klose, M.: *The Architecture of the SMILE/M Simulation Environment*. Proc. 15th IMACS World Congress on Sci. Comp., Berlin, 1997
3. van Rossum, G.: *Python Reference Manuals*. http://www/python.org/doc
4. Schröer, F.W.: *The Gentle Compiler Construction System*. GMD Bericht 290, 1997
5. Alt, M.; Assmann, U.; van Someren, H.: *CoSy Compiler Phase Embedding with the CoSy Compiler Model*. LNCS 786, Springer 1994
6. Schröer, F.W.: *Smart Reference Manual (Draft)*. Internal report, GMD, 1993.
7. Grosch, J.: *A Tool Box for Compiler Construction*. LNCS 477, pp.106-116, Springer 1990
8. Lampe, J: *An Extensible Translator-Generator for Use in Branch Software Construction*. J. Comp. Inf. 2(1996)1, pp.1057-1067
9. Parr, T.J.: *Language Translation Using PCCTS and C++*. Automata, 1997.
10. Gil, J.: JAMOOS Page. http://oop.cs.technion.ac.il/236704-5/JAMOOS/, 1997

A Programmable ANSI C Transformation Engine

Maarten Boekhold, Ireneusz Karkowski, Henk Corporaal and Andrea Cilio

Delft University of Technology
Mekelweg 4, P.O. Box 5031, 2600 GA Delft, The Netherlands
{maartenb,irek,heco,smallpox}@cardit.et.tudelft.nl

Abstract. Source code transformations are a very effective method of parallelizing and improving the efficiency of programs. Unfortunately most compiler systems require implementing separate (sub-)programs for each transformation. This paper describes a different approach. We designed and implemented a fully programmable C code transformation engine, which can be programmed by means of a powerful and easy to use transformation language. Its possible applications range from coarse-grain parallelism exploitation to optimizers for multimedia instruction sets.

1 Introduction

Due to advances in IC technology, multiprocessor systems are becoming ever more affordable these days. While most of these systems are used in either the server market or in scientific research, it can be expected that multiprocessor systems will also show up in embedded systems. Especially, because of the feasibility of single-chip multi-processor implementations.

To be able to use the full computing power that is available in such systems, it is necessary to execute the embedded applications in a parallel mode. Unfortunately most of the existing embedded codes are written in a sequential programming languages. Also the programmers usually feel more at ease in writing sequential programs. (Semi-) automatically transforming sequential programs to their parallel equivalents represents therefore an attractive alternative. Direct parallelization however often does not lead to an efficient implementation. A series of code transformations [6] are necessary to enable efficient parallelization. Since the number of standard transformations (and combinations of them) is large, writing separate (sub-)programs for each of them represents a long-term and tedious task. Even if finished, any new transformation requires each time a substantial effort, due to the very low code reuse. Tools that make writing such programs easier ([3,5]), represent only a partial solution. They make programming faster, but still the transformations have to be coded separately. An alternative is to design a programmable transformation engine, which could be easily configured for most useful code transformations.

This paper presents one such source-to-source code transformation tool itself (called `ctt`, Code Transformation Tool), targeted at translation of ANSI C programs. It can be configured with new transformations by means of a dedicated *transformation language*. The language has been carefully designed to enable efficient specification of most common code transformations. Its syntax has been derived from ANSI C. Thanks to that the language is easy to learn and powerful to use. Note that the tool does not decide *if* a possible transformation should be applied. This decision is currently left to the user. The design of the program allows its use in any ANSI C translation context. Potential applications include coarse-grain parallelism exploitation [4], ILP enhancement, and optimizations for multi-media instruction sets.

This work has been inspired by a system called MT1 [1], developed at the University of Utrecht and the University of Leiden, both in the Netherlands. MT1 is a system that performs a translation from Fortran77 to Fortran90. Unfortunately it has some drawbacks making it useless in our context. First of all, the research within our laboratory is mainly concerned with embedded applications (which are most often written in C). Secondly, with MT1 it is impossible to apply a number of interesting types of transformations (for example *inter-procedural*). It has no explicit control over variables and it is impossible to create *new* variables in a transformation. Finally, it can only operate in an interactive way, and it is therefore not possible to use MT1 from within other applications. Our work aims not only at being an ANSI C version of MT1, but also at adding the above capabilities.

The remainder of this paper is organized as follows. Section 2 introduces the basics of the transformation language that is used to specify transformations (the interested reader is referred to [2] for more details). Section 3 demonstrates the use of the language for specification of a simple loop transformation, giving feeling about its power and flexibility. The implementation details of the transformation program are briefly discussed in section 4. Finally, section 5 concludes the paper.

2   Transformation language

Writing separate programs for different transformations can be avoided if we properly organize the process of applying a transformation. Our transformation engine uses such an organization. Its translation process is divided into 3 distinct stages:

- **Code selection stage:** In this stage the engine searches for code that has a strictly specified structure (that matches a specified *pattern*). Each fragment that matches this *pattern* is a candidate for the transformation.
- **Conditions checking stage:** Transformations can pose other (non-structural) restrictions on a matched code fragment. These include, but are not limited to, conditions on data dependencies and properties of loop index variables.
- **Transformation stage:** Code fragments that matched the specified structure and additional conditions are replaced by new code, with the same semantics.

The structure of the transformation language closely resembles these steps, and contains three subsections called PATTERN, CONDITIONS and RESULT (see **Figure 1**). As can be deduced, there is a one to one mapping between blocks in the transformation definition and the translation stages.

While a large fraction of the embedded systems are still programmed in assembly language, the ANSI C has become a widely accepted language of choice for this domain. Therefore, we decided to derive our transformation language from the ANSI C. As result, all C language constructs can be used to describe a transformation. Using only them would however be too limiting. The patterns specified in the code selection stage would be too specific, and it would be impossible to use one pattern block to match a wide variety of input codes. Therefore we extended our transformation language with a number of *meta-elements*. Among others the following meta-elements were added and can be used to specify *generic* patterns, i.e. patterns that represent more than one element in the input C sources:

- *Statements:* keyword STMT represents any statement.
- *Statement lists:* keyword STMTLIST represents a list of statements.
- *Expressions:* keyword EXPR represents any expression.
- *Variables:* keyword VAR represents any variable (of any type).
- *Procedure calls:* keyword PROCCALL represents any procedure, which satisfies specific requirements.

The decision of including meta-elements for the variables was motivated by the desire of avoiding direct relationship between variable names in the transformation definition and the variable names in the input C sources. Meta-element must be assigned a number (except for variables), which should be included in braces behind their keyword (STMT(1) and STMT(2) represent then different C statements). Some meta-elements take also additional arguments (for example BOUND and STEP_EXPR take also as argument the name of the loop index variable). In the following section we will present a simple example of using the language constructs in each sub-block of the transformation definition.

3 Example

Loop interchange transformation, when applied to 2 tightly nested loops, exchanges the inner and outer loops. A pattern block that describes the code selection stage of *the loop interchange* transformation is shown on the top left of Figure 1. This pattern has the following meaning: "Look for 2 tightly nested loops, of which the inner loop can contain any statement list". The expression 1 has been used twice (in both loops) and therefore the lower bounds in both loops must be the same. Before the transformation however may be applied, the program should check if there exist no $(<, >)$ dependencies [6] within the loop body. In addition, the loop-body should not contain break or continue statements. Only if these conditions are met, the inner and outer loop may be exchanged. They may be specified as shown on the bottom of Figure 1. The '*' in the second statement denotes any dependence. The result block is shown on the right. This description says: "Replace the matched code with 2 tightly nested loops, where the body of the new inner loop is the same as the body of the inner loop of the original code".

```
PATTERN {                                      RESULT {
  VAR x, y;                                       VAR x, y;

  for(x=EXPR(1);BOUND(1,x);STEP_EXPR(2,x)){       for(y=EXPR(1);BOUND(2,y);STEP_EXPR(3,y)){
    for(y=EXPR(1);BOUND(2,y);STEP_EXPR(3,y)){       for(x=EXPR(1);BOUND(1,x);STEP_EXPR(2,x)){
      STMTLIST(1);                                    STMTLIST(1);
    }                                               }
  }                                             }
}

CONDITIONS {
  stmtlist_has_no_unsafe_jumps(1);
  not(dep("* direction=(<,>)
      between stmtlist 1 and stmtlist 1"));
}
```

Figure 1 Specification of the loop interchange transformation.

4 Implementation

The transformation program has been written in C++, using the SUIF compiler toolkit. The decision of using SUIF was dictated mainly by the existence of a good ANSI C front end, a convenient internal representation (IR) with C++ interface, and by the existence of an IR to ANSI C conversion utility (s2c). Thanks to that we could concentrate more on the design of the transformation engine itself, which works entirely on the IR level only. The whole transformation trajectory is presented in Figure 2. Both input source and transformation definitions are compiled to the IR by the front-end. After linking them the translation process takes place. In current implementation, statements of the program are visited in the *depth first search* order, and at each of them all transformations are sequentially tried. The user decides which possible transformations are applied. Once the transformations have been applied, the s2c program is used to convert the IR back to ANSI C. All functionality needed to perform a transformation (i.e. code selection, conditions checking and transforming) has been implemented as a collection of C++ classes, which can be accessed through a single C++ class interface. This makes it easy to embed the full functionality within other C++ programs.

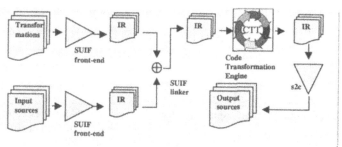

Figure 2 The transformation trajectory.

We provide a GUI, which allows users to experiment with different sets of transformations and provides an easy interface to each of the 3 transformation stages. While the translation process may proceed completely automatically, an interactive mode allows the user to *override* the decision made in the conditions checking stage (e.g. it is possible to apply a transformation even though the conditions checking stage says that this would be illegal).

5 Conclusions

In this paper we presented a programmable engine for code transformations on ANSI C programs. The knowledge about the transformations is added by means of a convenient and efficient *transformation language*. Using this language to specify new transformations is much easier and faster than having to write separate (sub-) programs for each of them. A very large subset of possible transformations is supported, including the inter-procedural ones. All of them (and their combinations) have been successfully specified using the transformation language, thereby proving the viability of its concept.

References

1. Aart J.C. Bik. *A Prototype Restructuring Compiler*. Technical Report INF/SCR-92-11, Utrecht University, Utrecht, the Netherlands, November 1994.
2. Maarten Boekhold, Ireneusz Karkowski and Henk Corporaal. *A Programmable ANSI C Code Transformation Engine*. Technical Report no. 1-68340-44(1998)-08, Delft University of Technology, Delft, The Netherlands, August 1998.
3. Dennis Gannon et al. *Sage*. http://www.extreme.indiana.edu/sage/, 1995.
4. Ireneusz Karkowski and Henk Corporaal. *Design Space Exploration Algorithm for Heterogeneous Multi-processor Embedded System Design*. In 35th Design Automation Conference Proceedings, June 1998, San Francisco, USA.
5. Robert Wilson, Robert Franch, Christopher Wilson, Saman Amarasinghe, Jennifer Anderson, Steve Tjiang, Shin-Wei Liao, Chau-Wen Tseng, Mary Hall, Monica Lam, and John Hennessy. *An Overview of the SUIF Compiler System* http://suif.stanford.edu/suif/suif.html, 1995.
6. Michael Wolfe. *High Performance Compilers for Parallel Computing*. Addison-Wesley Publishing Company, 1996.

Tool Support for Language Design and Prototyping with Montages

Matthias Anlauff[1], Philipp W. Kutter[2], and Alfonso Pierantonio[2]

[1] GMD FIRST, Berlin, Germany
[2] Institute TIK, ETH Zürich, Switzerland

Abstract. In this paper, we describe the tool Gem-Mex, supporting Montages, a visual formalism for the specification of (imperative/object oriented) programming languages.

Introduction Montages [KP97] form a graphical notation for expressing the syntax and semantics of imperative and object oriented languages. Every syntactic construct has its meaning specified by a Montage, which consist of a diagram defining graphically the control and data flow, and textually the semantic actions of the construct. The control-flow edges show how behavior of the construct is composed from the behavior of its components, and data-flow edges enable semantic actions to access the attributes of the construct's components.

The Montages formalism is tuned towards ease of writability, readability, maintenance, and reuse of specifications. The hope is that, like Wirth's 'syntax diagrams', a graphical notation may help in making formal language descriptions more accessible to the everyday user. It does not compete with existing compiler construction techniques which are designed for the flexible specification of efficient translations.

The notation is supported by the Gem-Mex (**G**raphical **E**ditor for **M**ontages and **M**ontages **EX**ecutable generator) tool[1] which guides the user through the process of designing and specifying a language. In other words, Gem-Mex forms a (meta) environment to enter and maintain the description of a language. In addition, it generates a specialized (programming) environment which allows to analyze, execute, and animate programs of the specified language. The language designer can use the generated environment as a semantics inspection tool to test and validate design decisions. Later the programmer can use the same environment for debugging programs. Further, in some situations the generated interpreter may be directly used as implementation of the language. Since language-documentation is based on the Montages descriptions, and the language-environment is deduced from this descriptions, it is guaranteed that design, documentation, debugging-support and implementation of the language are always consistent. Typically, in a realistic scenario many versions of a language will evolve over time and a tool like Gem-Mex is useful to maintain them in a

---

[1] The tool runs on Unix platforms and Windows NT; it is freely available at http://www.tik.ee.ethz.ch/~montages

consistent way. The tool is currently used by different groups for both the specification of general purpose programming languages (Pascal, Java, Smalltalk) and the design of domain specific languages [KST98].

The Montages Formalism consist of three parts

1. A canonical definition of abstract syntax trees (ASTs) from EBNF rules.
2. A simple attribution mechanism for these ASTs:
   - decoration of ASTs with guarded control-flow edges,
   - decoration the ASTs with data access-arrows (reversed data-flow arrows),
   - decoration the ASTs with dynamic-semantics-actions.

   The attribution rules are given by means of a formal visual language. The visual language relies heavily on the common intuition existing for the graphical notations control/data flow graphs, finite state machines, and flow charts.
3. A computational model based on the control/data flow graphs which result from the attribution process.

The attribution mechanism is based on standard techniques like attribute grammars [WG84] and graph grammars [REK97].

The dynamic semantic actions are given with Abstract State Machine (ASM) rules [Gur95]. ASMs are a state-based formalism in which a state is updated in discrete time steps. Unlike most state-based system, the state is given by an algebra, that is, a collection of functions and a set of objects. Both functions and sets may change their definitions by means of state transitions which are fired repeatedly.

ASMs have been already used to give the dynamic semantics of full-scaled programming languages (e.g. C, Occam, Java; see [BH98] for a commented bibliography) as well as for the systematic development of provably correct compilers [ZG97].

The computational model based on the control/data flow graphs is formalized with an ASM. In this model control flows through the graph, enabling the semantic actions attributed to the nodes. These actions use the data arrows to access attributes of other nodes, and redefine local attributes.

To summarize, a language specification consists of a collection of Montages, each specifying the meaning of one syntactic construct in the language. Such a Montage consists of subparts, containing the EBNF rule, the control and data flow attributions, the static semantics condition, and the dynamic semantics action. We show the Relation and the While Montage in Fig. 1. The dotted arrows define the control flow, the symbol I denotes the point where control enters from outside, and the T denotes the point where control exits. As expected the Relation Montage has a control flow, that first goes through the two subexpressions, which are depicted with boxes. Then the control flow enters the oval, denoting a semantic action, which is given in the last subpart of the Montage. Finally the control leaves through the T, without any branches.

In contrast, the control flow of the While Montage contains a cycle. Whether to cycle or to leave the construct is dependent on the guard which is given as the

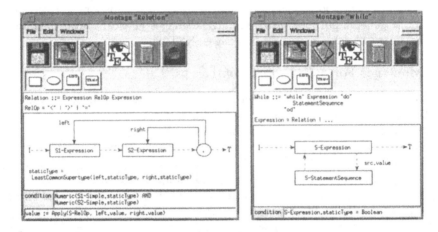

Fig. 1. Montages examples

label of the control arrow from the Expression to the StatementSequence. The *condition* part contains the context sensitive constrains formulated as a first-order logic predicate, e.g. in the Relation Montage the condition states that the types of the Expressions must be compatible. The *staticType* attribute holds the type of the expression evaluated during the static analysis.

Tool Architecture In the introduction we sketched how the user is guided by Gem-Mex through the process of designing and specifying a language using Montages. Fig. 1 shows part of the user interface. The buttons in the first line are used to: save, open a Montage, generate html and tex output, delete, and exit. The buttons in the second line allow to choose specific graphical elements during the editing process of a Montage: boxes for simple components, ovals for semantic actions, special list boxes, additional textual attribution rules. As an example of the generated environment we see in Fig. 2 the user interface of the debugger. On the left side an example program of the specified language is

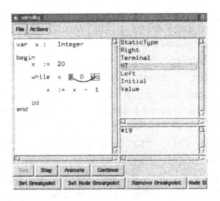

Fig. 2. The generated animation tool

shown. The arrow animates the flow of control through the program text. On the right side, attributes of the construct currently under execution are listed, and by clicking on them their value can inspected. Fig. 3 illustrates the architecture of the tool.

The implementation of Gem-Mex is based on Lex/Yacc, C, and Tcl/Tk. The core is a specifically developed ASM to C compiler called Aslan [Anl98] (ASM Language). Aslan provides support for structuring ASMs in an object oriented way. Gem-Mex generates for each Montage the ASM semantic in form of an Aslan class. Then this classes are compiled and executed.

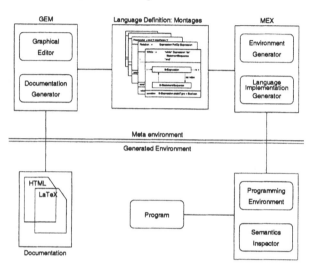

Fig. 3. Tool architecture

References

[Anl98]   M. Anlauff. The aslan reference manual. Technical report, GMD FIRST, Berlin, Germany, 1998.

[BH98]   E. Börger and J. Huggins. Commented asm bibliography. In *EATCS Bulletin*, number 64, pages 105 – 127. 1998. http://www.eecs.umich.edu/gasm.

[Gur95]   Y. Gurevich. Evolving Algebras 1993: Lipari Guide. In E. Börger, editor, *Specification and Validation Methods*. Oxford University Press, 1995.

[KP97]   P.W. Kutter and A. Pierantonio. Montages: Specification of Realistic Programming Languages. *J.UCS, Springer*, 3(5):416 – 442, 1997.

[KST98]   P.W. Kutter, D. Schweizer, and L. Thiele. Integrating formal domain specific language design in the software life cycle. In *Current Trends in Applied Formal Methods, Boppard, Germany*, LNCS. Springer, 1998.

[REK97]   G. Rozenberg, G. Engels, and H.J. Kreowski. *Handbook of Graph Grammars and Computing by Graph Transformations*. World Scientific, 1997.

[WG84]   W.M. Waite and G. Goos. *Compiler Construction*. Springer, 1984.

[ZG97]   W. Zimmermann and T. Gaul. On the construction of correct compiler backends: An asm approach. *J.UCS, Springer*, 3(5):504 – 567, 1997.

Author Index

Anlauff, M.	296		Martin, F.	63
Aycock, J.	32		Melski, D.	47
Bernstein, D.	259		De Meuter, W.	244
Bodík, R.	107		Muth, R.	76
Boekhold, M.	292		Nicolau, A.	214
van den Brand, M.	198		Olivier, P.	198
Carroll, S.	214		Patel, D.	183
Cilio, A.	229,292		Pierantonio, A.	296
Corporaal, H.	229,292		Polychronopoulos, C.	214
Debray, S.	76		Rauchwerger, L.	183
Dupont de Dinechin, B.	274		Reps, T.	47
Ernst, T.	288		Rivera, G.	168
Farach-Colton, M.	137		Rodeh, M.	259
Gao, G.R.	153		Rubin, S.	259
Govindarajan, R.	153		Rüthing, O.	91
Gupta, R.	107		Ryan, S.	153
Horspool, N.	32		Saito, H.	214
Kaestner, D.	122		Saraiva, J.	1
Karkowski, I.	292		Sloane, A.M.	17
Klint, P.	198		Stavrakos, N.	214
Knoop, J.	91		Steffen, B.	91
Kremer, U.	137		Swierstra, D.	1
Kutter, P.W.	296		Tourwé, T.	244
Langenbach, M.	122		Tseng, C.-W.	168
Liberatore, V.	137		Watterson, S.	76
			Zhang, C.	153

Springer
and the
environment

At Springer we firmly believe that an international science publisher has a special obligation to the environment, and our corporate policies consistently reflect this conviction.

We also expect our business partners – paper mills, printers, packaging manufacturers, etc. – to commit themselves to using materials and production processes that do not harm the environment. The paper in this book is made from low- or no-chlorine pulp and is acid free, in conformance with international standards for paper permanency.

 Springer

Lecture Notes in Computer Science

For information about Vols. 1–1484
please contact your bookseller or Springer-Verlag

Vol. 1485: J.-J. Quisquater, Y. Deswarte, C. Meadows, D. Gollmann (Eds.), Computer Security – ESORICS 98. Proceedings, 1998. X, 377 pages. 1998.

Vol. 1486: A.P. Ravn, H. Rischel (Eds.), Formal Techniques in Real-Time and Fault-Tolerant Systems. Proceedings, 1998. VIII, 339 pages. 1998.

Vol. 1487: V. Gruhn (Ed.), Software Process Technology. Proceedings, 1998. VIII, 157 pages. 1998.

Vol. 1488: B. Smyth, P. Cunningham (Eds.), Advances in Case-Based Reasoning. Proceedings, 1998. XI, 482 pages. 1998. (Subseries LNAI).

Vol. 1489: J. Dix, L. Fariñas del Cerro, U. Furbach (Eds.), Logics in Artificial Intelligence. Proceedings, 1998. X, 391 pages. 1998. (Subseries LNAI).

Vol. 1490: C. Palamidessi, H. Glaser, K. Meinke (Eds.), Principles of Declarative Programming. Proceedings, 1998. XI, 497 pages. 1998.

Vol. 1491: W. Reisig, G. Rozenberg (Eds.), Lectures on Petri Nets I: Basic Models. XII, 683 pages. 1998.

Vol. 1492: W. Reisig, G. Rozenberg (Eds.), Lectures on Petri Nets II: Applications. XII, 479 pages. 1998.

Vol. 1493: J.P. Bowen, A. Fett, M.G. Hinchey (Eds.), ZUM '98: The Z Formal Specification Notation. Proceedings, 1998. XV, 417 pages. 1998.

Vol. 1494: G. Rozenberg, F. Vaandrager (Eds.), Lectures on Embedded Systems. Proceedings, 1996. VIII, 423 pages. 1998.

Vol. 1495: T. Andreasen, H. Christiansen, H.L. Larsen (Eds.), Flexible Query Answering Systems. IX, 393 pages. 1998. (Subseries LNAI).

Vol. 1496: W.M. Wells, A. Colchester, S. Delp (Eds.), Medical Image Computing and Computer-Assisted Intervention – MICCAI'98. Proceedings, 1998. XXII, 1256 pages. 1998.

Vol. 1497: V. Alexandrov, J. Dongarra (Eds.), Recent Advances in Parallel Virtual Machine and Message Passing Interface. Proceedings, 1998. XII, 412 pages. 1998.

Vol. 1498: A.E. Eiben, T. Bäck, M. Schoenauer, H.-P. Schwefel (Eds.), Parallel Problem Solving from Nature – PPSN V. Proceedings, 1998. XXIII, 1041 pages. 1998.

Vol. 1499: S. Kutten (Ed.), Distributed Computing. Proceedings, 1998. XII, 419 pages. 1998.

Vol. 1500: J.-C. Derniame, B.A. Kaba, D. Wastell (Eds.), Software Process: Principles, Methodology, and Technology. XIII, 307 pages. 1999.

Vol. 1501: M.M. Richter, C.H. Smith, R. Wiehagen, T. Zeugmann (Eds.), Algorithmic Learning Theory. Proceedings, 1998. XI, 439 pages. 1998. (Subseries LNAI).

Vol. 1502: G. Antoniou, J. Slaney (Eds.), Advanced Topics in Artificial Intelligence. Proceedings, 1998. XI, 333 pages. 1998. (Subseries LNAI).

Vol. 1503: G. Levi (Ed.), Static Analysis. Proceedings, 1998. IX, 383 pages. 1998.

Vol. 1504: O. Herzog, A. Günter (Eds.), KI-98: Advances in Artificial Intelligence. Proceedings, 1998. XI, 355 pages. 1998. (Subseries LNAI).

Vol. 1505: D. Caromel, R.R. Oldehoeft, M. Tholburn (Eds.), Computing in Object-Oriented Parallel Environments. Proceedings, 1998. XI, 243 pages. 1998.

Vol. 1506: R. Koch, L. Van Gool (Eds.), 3D Structure from Multiple Images of Large-Scale Environments. Proceedings, 1998. VIII, 347 pages. 1998.

Vol. 1507: T.W. Ling, S. Ram, M.L. Lee (Eds.), Conceptual Modeling – ER '98. Proceedings, 1998. XVI, 482 pages. 1998.

Vol. 1508: S. Jajodia, M.T. Özsu, A. Dogac (Eds.), Advances in Multimedia Information Systems. Proceedings, 1998. VIII, 207 pages. 1998.

Vol. 1510: J.M. Zytkow, M. Quafafou (Eds.), Principles of Data Mining and Knowledge Discovery. Proceedings, 1998. XI, 482 pages. 1998. (Subseries LNAI).

Vol. 1511: D. O'Hallaron (Ed.), Languages, Compilers, and Run-Time Systems for Scalable Computers. Proceedings, 1998. IX, 412 pages. 1998.

Vol. 1512: E. Giménez, C. Paulin-Mohring (Eds.), Types for Proofs and Programs. Proceedings, 1996. VIII, 373 pages. 1998.

Vol. 1513: C. Nikolaou, C. Stephanidis (Eds.), Research and Advanced Technology for Digital Libraries. Proceedings, 1998. XV, 912 pages. 1998.

Vol. 1514: K. Ohta, D. Pei (Eds.), Advances in Cryptology – ASIACRYPT'98. Proceedings, 1998. XII, 436 pages. 1998.

Vol. 1515: F. Moreira de Oliveira (Ed.), Advances in Artificial Intelligence. Proceedings, 1998. X, 259 pages. 1998. (Subseries LNAI).

Vol. 1516: W. Ehrenberger (Ed.), Computer Safety, Reliability and Security. Proceedings, 1998. XVI, 392 pages. 1998.

Vol. 1517: J. Hromkovič, O. Sýkora (Eds.), Graph-Theoretic Concepts in Computer Science. Proceedings, 1998. X, 385 pages. 1998.

Vol. 1518: M. Luby, J. Rolim, M. Serna (Eds.), Randomization and Approximation Techniques in Computer Science. Proceedings, 1998. IX, 385 pages. 1998.

1519: T. Ishida (Ed.), Community Computing and Support Systems. VIII, 393 pages. 1998.

Vol. 1520: M. Maher, J.-F. Puget (Eds.), Principles and Practice of Constraint Programming - CP98. Proceedings, 1998. XI, 482 pages. 1998.

Vol. 1521: B. Rovan (Ed.), SOFSEM'98: Theory and Practice of Informatics. Proceedings, 1998. XI, 453 pages. 1998.

Vol. 1522: G. Gopalakrishnan, P. Windley (Eds.), Formal Methods in Computer-Aided Design. Proceedings, 1998. IX, 529 pages. 1998.

Vol. 1524: G.B. Orr, K.-R. Müller (Eds.), Neural Networks: Tricks of the Trade. VI, 432 pages. 1998.

Vol. 1525: D. Aucsmith (Ed.), Information Hiding. Proceedings, 1998. IX, 369 pages. 1998.

Vol. 1526: M. Broy, B. Rumpe (Eds.), Requirements Targeting Software and Systems Engineering. Proceedings, 1997. VIII, 357 pages. 1998.

Vol. 1527: P. Baumgartner, Theory Reasoning in Connection Calculi. IX, 283. 1999. (Subseries LNAI).

Vol. 1528: B. Preneel, V. Rijmen (Eds.), State of the Art in Applied Cryptography. Revised Lectures, 1997. VIII, 395 pages. 1998.

Vol. 1529: D. Farwell, L. Gerber, E. Hovy (Eds.), Machine Translation and the Information Soup. Proceedings, 1998. XIX, 532 pages. 1998. (Subseries LNAI).

Vol. 1530: V. Arvind, R. Ramanujam (Eds.), Foundations of Software Technology and Theoretical Computer Science. XII, 369 pages. 1998.

Vol. 1531: H.-Y. Lee, H. Motoda (Eds.), PRICAI'98: Topics in Artificial Intelligence. XIX, 646 pages. 1998. (Subseries LNAI).

Vol. 1096: T. Schael, Workflow Management Systems for Process Organisations. Second Edition. XII, 229 pages. 1998.

Vol. 1532: S. Arikawa, H. Motoda (Eds.), Discovery Science. Proceedings, 1998. XI, 456 pages. 1998. (Subseries LNAI).

Vol. 1533: K.-Y. Chwa, O.H. Ibarra (Eds.), Algorithms and Computation. Proceedings, 1998. XIII, 478 pages. 1998.

Vol. 1534: J.S. Sichman, R. Conte, N. Gilbert (Eds.), Multi-Agent Systems and Agent-Based Simulation. Proceedings, 1998. VIII, 237 pages. 1998. (Subseries LNAI).

Vol. 1535: S. Ossowski, Co-ordination in Artificial Agent Societies. XV; 221 pages. 1999. (Subseries LNAI).

Vol. 1536: W.-P. de Roever, H. Langmaack, A. Pnueli (Eds.), Compositionality: The Significant Difference. Proceedings, 1997. VIII, 647 pages. 1998.

Vol. 1537: N. Magnenat-Thalmann, D. Thalmann (Eds.), Modelling and Motion Capture Techniques for Virtual Environments. Proceedings, 1998. IX, 273 pages. 1998. (Subseries LNAI).

Vol. 1538: J. Hsiang, A. Ohori (Eds.), Advances in Computing Science – ASIAN'98. Proceedings, 1998. X, 305 pages. 1998.

Vol. 1539: O. Rüthing, Interacting Code Motion Transformations: Their Impact and Their Complexity. XXI,225 pages. 1998.

Vol. 1540: C. Beeri, P. Buneman (Eds.), Database Theory – ICDT'99. Proceedings, 1999. XI, 489 pages. 1999.

Vol. 1541: B. Kågström, J. Dongarra, E. Elmroth, J. Waśniewski (Eds.), Applied Parallel Computing. Proceedings, 1998. XIV, 586 pages. 1998.

Vol. 1542: H.I. Christensen (Ed.), Computer Vision Systems. Proceedings, 1999. XI, 554 pages. 1999.

Vol. 1543: S. Demeyer, J. Bosch (Eds.), Object-Oriented Technology ECOOP'98 Workshop Reader. 1998. XXII, 573 pages. 1998.

Vol. 1544: C. Zhang, D. Lukose (Eds.), Multi-Agent Systems. Proceedings, 1998. VII, 195 pages. 1998. (Subseries LNAI).

Vol. 1545: A. Birk, J. Demiris (Eds.), Learning Robots. Proceedings, 1996. IX, 188 pages. 1998. (Subseries LNAI).

Vol. 1546: B. Möller, J.V. Tucker (Eds.), Prospects for Hardware Foundations. Survey Chapters, 1998. X, 468 pages. 1998.

Vol. 1547: S.H. Whitesides (Ed.), Graph Drawing. Proceedings 1998. XII, 468 pages. 1998.

Vol. 1548: A.M. Haeberer (Ed.), Algebraic Methodology and Software Technology. Proceedings, 1999. XI, 531 pages. 1999.

Vol. 1550: B. Christianson, B. Crispo, W.S. Harbison, M. Roe (Eds.), Security Protocols. Proceedings, 1998. VIII, 241 pages. 1999.

Vol. 1551: G. Gupta (Ed.), Practical Aspects of Declarative Languages. Proceedings, 1999. VIII, 367 pgages. 1999.

Vol. 1552: Y. Kambayashi, D.L. Lee, E.-P. Lim, M.K. Mohania, Y. Masunaga (Eds.), Advances in Database Technologies. Proceedings, 1998. XIX, 592 pages. 1999.

Vol. 1553: S.F. Andler, J. Hansson (Eds.), Active, Real-Time, and Temporal Database Systems. Proceedings, 1997. VIII, 245 pages. 1998.

Vol. 1557: P. Zinterhof, M. Vajteršic, A. Uhl (Eds.), Parallel Computation. Proceedings, 1999. XV, 604 pages. 1999.

Vol. 1560: K. Imai, Y. Zheng (Eds.), Public Key Cryptography. Proceedings, 1999. IX, 327 pages. 1999.

Vol. 1563: Ch. Meinel, S. Tison (Eds.), STACS 99. Proceedings, 1999. XIV, 582 pages. 1999.

Vol. 1567: P. Antsaklis, W. Kohn, M. Lemmon, A. Nerode, S. Sastry (Eds.), Hybrid Systems V. X, 445 pages. 1999.

Vol. 1569: F.W. Vaandrager, J.H. van Schuppen (Eds.), Hybrid Systems: Computation and Control. Proceedings, 1999. X, 271 pages. 1999.

Vol. 1570: F. Puppe (Ed.), XPS-99: Knowledge-Based Systems. VIII, 227 pages. 1999. (Subseries LNAI).

Vol. 1572: P. Fischer, H.U. Simon (Eds.), Computational Learning Theory. Proceedings, 1999. X, 301 pages. 1999. (Subseries LNAI).

Vol. 1575: S. Jähnichen (Ed.), Compiler Construction. Proceedings, 1999. X, 301 pages. 1999.

Vol. 1577: J.-P. Finance (Ed.), Fundamental Approaches to Software Engineering. Proceedings, 1999. X, 245 pages. 1999.

Vol. 1578: W. Thomas (Ed.), Foundations of Software Science and Computation Structures. Proceedings, 1999. X, 323 pages. 1999.